Treating Traumatic St
in Military Personnel

Treating Traumatic Stress Injuries in Military Personnel: An EMDR Practitioner's Guide offers a comprehensive treatment manual for mental health professionals treating traumatic stress injuries in both male and female veterans. It is the first book to combine the most recent knowledge about new paradigms of combat-related traumatic stress injuries (Figley & Nash, 2007) and offers a practical guide for treating the spectrum of traumatic stress injuries with EMDR, which has been recognized by the Department of Veterans Affairs and Department of Defense clinical practice guidelines as one of the most studied, efficient, and particularly well-suited evidence-based treatments for military-related stress injuries.

Russell and Figley introduce an array of treatment innovations designed especially for use with military populations, and readers will find pages filled with practical information, including appendices that feature a glossary of military terminology, breakdowns of rank and pay grades, and various clinical forms.

Mark C. Russell, PhD, is a retired U.S. Navy commander and board-certified clinical psychologist with 26 years of military experience. He is the author of multiple publications on war stress injuries and recipient of the 2006 Distinguished Psychologist Award by Washington State Psychological Association. Currently, he serves as chair of the PsyD program and founding director of the Institute of War Stress Injuries and Social Justice at Antioch University in Seattle.

Charles R. Figley, PhD, is the Paul Henry Kurzweg Distinguished Chair in Disaster Mental Health at Tulane University. A former Marine sergeant who served early in the Vietnam War, he went on to help pioneer the modern study and treatment of trauma and many innovations in helping the traumatized, including practitioners themselves, in his more than 200 scholarly articles, chapters, and books.

ROUTLEDGE PSYCHOSOCIAL STRESS SERIES
Charles R. Figley, Ph.D., Series Editor

1. *Stress Disorders Among Vietnam Veterans*, Edited by Charles R. Figley, Ph.D.
2. *Stress and the Family Vol. 1: Coping with Normative Transitions*, Edited by Hamilton I. McCubbin, Ph.D., and Charles R. Figley, Ph.D.
3. *Stress and the Family Vol. 2: Coping with Catastrophe*, Edited by Charles R. Figley, Ph.D., and Hamilton I. McCubbin, Ph.D.
4. *Trauma and Its Wake: The Study and Treatment of Post-Traumatic Stress Disorder*, Edited by Charles R. Figley, Ph.D.
5. *Post-Traumatic Stress Disorder and the War Veteran Patient*, Edited by William E. Kelly, M.D.
6. *The Crime Victim's Book, Second Edition*, By Morton Bard, Ph.D., and Dawn Sangrey.
7. *Stress and Coping in Time of War: Generalizations from the Israeli Experience*, Edited by Norman A. Milgram, Ph.D.
8. *Trauma and Its Wake Vol. 2: Traumatic Stress Theory, Research, and Intervention*, Edited by Charles R. Figley, Ph.D.
9. *Stress and Addiction*, Edited by Edward Gottheil, M.D., Ph.D., Keith A. Druley, Ph.D., Steven Pashko, Ph.D., and Stephen P. Weinsteinn, Ph.D.
10. *Vietnam: A Casebook*, by Jacob D. Lindy, M.D., in collaboration with Bonnie L. Green, Ph.D., Mary C. Grace, M.Ed., M.S., John A. MacLeod, M.D., and Louis Spitz, M.D.
11. *Post-Traumatic Therapy and Victims of Violence*, Edited by Frank M. Ochberg, M.D.
12. *Mental Health Response to Mass Emergencies: Theory and Practice*, Edited by Mary Lystad, Ph.D.
13. *Treating Stress in Families*, Edited by Charles R. Figley, Ph.D.
14. *Trauma, Transformation, and Healing: An Integrative Approach to Theory, Research, and Post-Traumatic Therapy*, By John P. Wilson, Ph.D.
15. *Systemic Treatment of Incest: A Therapeutic Handbook*, By Terry Trepper, Ph.D., and Mary Jo Barrett, M.S.W.
16. *The Crisis of Competence: Transitional Stress and the Displaced Worker*, Edited by Carl A. Maida, Ph.D., Norma S. Gordon, M.A., and Norman L. Farberow, Ph.D.
17. *Stress Management: An Integrated Approach to Therapy*, by Dorothy H. G. Cotton, Ph.D.
18. *Trauma and the Vietnam War Generation: Report of the Findings from the National Vietnam Veterans Readjustment Study*, By Richard A. Kulka, Ph.D., William E. Schlenger, Ph.D., John A. Fairbank, Ph.D., Richard L. Hough, Ph.D., Kathleen Jordan, Ph.D., Charles R. Marmar, M.D., Daniel S. Weiss, Ph.D., and David A. Grady, Psy.D.
19. *Strangers at Home: Vietnam Veterans Since the War*, Edited by Charles R. Figley, Ph.D., and Seymour Leventman, Ph.D.
20. *The National Vietnam Veterans Readjustment Study: Tables of Findings and Technical Appendices*, By Richard A. Kulka, Ph.D., Kathleen Jordan, Ph.D., Charles R. Marmar, M.D., and Daniel S. Weiss, Ph.D.
21. *Psychological Trauma and the Adult Survivor: Theory, Therapy, and Transformation*, By I. Lisa McCann, Ph.D., and Laurie Anne Pearlman, Ph.D.
22. *Coping with Infant or Fetal Loss: The Couple's Healing Process*, By Kathleen R. Gilbert, Ph.D., and Laura S. Smart, Ph.D.
23. *Compassion Fatigue: Coping with Secondary Traumatic Stress Disorder in Those Who Treat the Traumatized*, Edited by Charles R. Figley, Ph.D.
24. *Treating Compassion Fatigue*, Edited by Charles R. Figley, Ph.D.
25. *Handbook of Stress, Trauma and the Family*, Edited by Don R. Catherall, Ph.D.
26. *The Pain of Helping: Psychological Injury of Helping Professionals*, by Patrick J. Morrissette, Ph.D., RMFT, NCC, CCC.
27. *Disaster Mental Health Services: A Primer for Practitioners*, by Diane Myers, R.N., M.S.N., and David Wee, M.S.S.W.
28. *Empathy in the Treatment of Trauma and PTSD*, by John P. Wilson, Ph.D. and Rhiannon B. Thomas, Ph.D.
29. *Family Stressors: Interventions for Stress and Trauma*, Edited by Don. R. Catherall, Ph. D.
30. *Handbook of Women, Stress and Trauma*, Edited by Kathleen Kendall-Tackett, Ph.D.
31. *Mapping Trauma and Its Wake*, Edited by Charles R. Figley, Ph.D.
32. *The Posttraumatic Self: Restoring Meaning and Wholeness to Personality*, Edited by John P. Wilson, Ph.D.
33. *Violent Death: Resilience and Intervention Beyond the Crisis*, Edited by Edward K. Rynearson, M.D.
34. *Combat Stress Injury: Theory, Research, and Management*, Edited by Charles R. Figley, Ph.D. and William P. Nash, M.D.
35. *MindBody Medicine: Foundations and Practical Applications*, by Leo W. Rotan, Ph.D. and Veronika Ospina-Kammerer, Ph.D.
36. *Understanding and Assessing Trauma in Children and Adolescents: Measures, Methods, and Youth in Context*, by Kathleen Nader, D.S.W
37. *When the Past Is Always Present: Emotional Traumatization, Causes, and Cures*, by Ronald A. Ruden, M.D., Ph.D.

38. *Families Under Fire: Systemic Therapy with Military Families,* Edited by R. Blaine Everson, Ph.D. and Charles R. Figley, Ph.D.
39. *Dissociation in Traumatized Children and Adolescents: Theory and Clinical Interventions,* Edited by Sandra Wieland, Ph.D.
40. *Transcending Trauma: Survival, Resilience and Clinical Implications in Survivor Families,* by Bea Hollander-Goldfein, Ph.D., Nancy Isserman, Ph.D., and Jennifer Goldenberg, Ph.D., L.C.S.W
41. *School Rampage Shootings and Other Youth Disturbances: Early Preventative Interventions,* by Kathleen Nader, D.S.W.
42. *The Compassion Fatigue Workbook: Creative Tools for Transforming Compassion Fatigue and Vicarious Traumatization,* by Françoise Mathieu, M.Ed.
43. *War Trauma and Its Wake: Expanding the Circle of Healing,* by Raymond Monsour Scurfield, D.S.W., and Katherine Theresa Platoni, Psy.D.
44. *Healing War Trauma: A Handbook of Creative Approaches,* by Raymond Monsour Scurfield, D.S.W., and Katherine Theresa Platoni, Psy.D.
45. *Helping Traumatized Families,* by Charles R. Figley, Ph.D., and Laurel Kiser, Ph.D.
46. *Treating Traumatic Stress Injuries in Military Personnel: An EMDR Practitioner's Guide,* by Mark C. Russell, Ph.D., and Charles R. Figley, Ph.D.

Editorial Board

Treating Traumatic Stress Injuries in Military Personnel

An EMDR Practitioner's Guide

Mark C. Russell and Charles R. Figley

Routledge
Taylor & Francis Group

NEW YORK AND LONDON

This book is part of the Psychosocial Stress Series, edited by Charles R. Figley.

First published 2013
by Routledge
711 Third Avenue, New York, NY 10017

Simultaneously published in the UK
by Routledge
27 Church Road, Hove, East Sussex BN3 2FA

Routledge is an imprint of the Taylor & Francis Group, an informa business

Library of Congress Cataloging in Publication Data
Russell, Mark C. (Mark Charles), 1960–
    Treating traumatic stress injuries in military personnel : an EMDR practitioner's guide / Mark C. Russell and Charles R. Figley.
    p. cm. — (Psychosocial stress series)
    Includes bibliographical references and index.
    1. Post-traumatic stress disorder—Treatment—United States. 2. Veterans—Mental health—United States. I. Figley, Charles R., 1944– II. Title.
    RC552.P67R87 2013
    616.85'21—dc23
    2012025060

ISBN: 978-0-415-88977-3 (hbk)
ISBN: 978-0-415-64533-1 (pbk)
ISBN: 978-0-203-82972-1 (ebk)

Typeset in Minion
by EvS Communication Networx, Inc.

Printed and bound in the United States of America by Edwards Brothers, Inc.

Mark C. Russell wishes to dedicate this book to past, present, and future healers of the warrior class, yours is the noblest of callings in keeping faith with the societal pledge to leave no person behind.

Charles R. Figley wishes to dedicate this book to Dave Cabrera who taught me the most about today's US Army, especially military social work, and who died as an EMDR practitioner in combat, 29 October 2011, Kabul, Afghanistan.

Contents

Series Editor's Foreword   xi
Foreword   xv
Acknowledgments   xvii
Introduction   xix

SECTION I
EMDR Treatment of Military Populations   1

1   Warriors, War, and Resilience: The Warrior Class   3

2   Overview of EMDR Therapy   11

3   Research on EMDR and War Stress Injury   21

4   Why Use EMDR Therapy in the Armed Services?   38

SECTION II
The EMDR Protocol for Military Populations   51

5   Phase One: Client History, Rapport, and Treatment Planning   53

6   Phase Two: Client Preparation and Informed Consent   94

7   Phase Three: EMDR Assessment   131

8   Phase Four: Basic and Specialized Reprocessing Protocols   147

9   Phases Five–Six: Standard Reprocessing Protocols   162

10   EMDR Treatment for Acute War/Traumatic Stress Injury   169

SECTION III
EMDR Treatment for Chronic War/Traumatic Stress Injury   179

11 EMDR Therapy of Pre-Military and Military Trauma and
Medically Unexplained Symptoms   181

12 EMDR Treatment of Traumatic Grief and Interpersonal
Violence   198

13 Other Military Stress Injury and EMDR Treatment
Considerations   216

14 Phases Seven–Eight: Closure and Reevaluation   227

SECTION IV
Special Considerations   235

15 Ethical and Medico-Legal Issues   237

16 Enhancing Resilience/Performance and Preventing
Compassion Stress Injury   245

Appendix A: Military Mental Health Referral Resources   255

Appendix B: EMDR Reprocessing Troubleshooting Guide   259

Appendix C: References   267

Index   277

Series Editor's Foreword

EMDR means "Eye Movement Desensitization and Reprocessing" and was named by Francine Shapiro (1989) because she believed that stimulating eye movement in a back and forth motion, together with exposure to a representative scene of the worst aspects of the trauma can only lead to "desensitization." By linking one's cognitive and emotional state with those of the past, this change is like the game of Tetris. The EMDR approach literally takes the emotional sting out of trauma memories. It also leads to reprocessing of the memories linked to other trauma.

I first became acquainted with EMDR in 1988 when, as editor of the *Journal of Traumatic Stress*, I received Shapiro's paper submission describing her initial dissertation study as was later published (Shapiro, 1989). "This is garbage," wrote one reviewer and refused to read beyond the first few pages. "Does she really think she can treat combat veterans?" another reviewer scoffed in a phone call. There were many critics of both the treatment method and the science that supports it, others like myself were skeptical of the motives of those who complained most hardily; their own treatment approaches—most often CBT and ET (exposure therapy)—were experiencing a significant drift by clients and practitioners toward this new approach that eventually proved to be their equal in terms of outcome research.

Along the way, EMDR was banned by some treatment centers in the military and within the DVA. However, the mood of acceptance and admiration is emerging within these and other programs. What is immediately useful to both clients and practitioners are EMDR's concrete strategies for making quick progress in accessing traumatic memories and working through them guided by the client. The dual attention focuses on the representative scene (the worst aspect of the trauma) and a rhythmic motion, not necessarily eye movement, which serves as a monitor of client emotion and attention.

This volume is a comprehensive treatment manual for mental health professionals working with clients who are coping with traumatic stress injuries. The book focuses on how clients can be treated within a structure of operational settings and medically-focused treatment centers such as the U.S. Department of Defense and the U.S. Department of Veterans Affairs medical systems. Dr. Mark Russell, retired Navy Commander and military psychologist currently on the faculty at the School of Applied Psychology Counseling and Family Therapy, Doctoral Program at Antioch University in Seattle and director of the recently established Institute of War Stress Injuries and Social Justice, is dual Board Certified in Clinical Psychology and Child and Adolescent Clinical Psychology by the American Board of Professional Psychology. He has worked as the Head, Neuropsychiatric Services at a Navy field hospital during the 2003 Iraq invasion, and last served as the sole staff adult and child clinical psychologist for the 5,500 residents of the Marine Corps Air Station in Iwakuni, Japan before ending a 26-year military career. Most notably, Dr. Russell has received national attention as a military whistleblower whose tireless efforts led to public recognition of a military mental health crisis and greatly improved military access to top PTSD treatments. Charles Figley is series editor and has the first book of the series, *Stress Disorders Among Vietnam Veterans*, which contributes to the conceptualization of the diagnosis of PTSD.

This book builds upon the contributions of another series book (Figley & Nash, 2008), *Combat Stress Injury*, co-edited by William Nash, a Navy psychiatrist and Bronze Star winner from his service in Iraq, and Charles Figley. Nash (US Marine psychiatrist) and fellow Navy Captains Richard Westphal (nursing research) and Robert Koffman (combat psychiatry) developed Navy Medicine's approach to more effectively preventing and managing PTSD: Focus on the injury and the window of opportunity to rehabilitate an injury and thereby prevent a mental disorder.

The volume also recognizes the notion of psychological trauma spectrum (Scaer, 2005; van der Kolk, 1988) and offers a practical guide for treating the spectrum of traumatic stress injuries with EMDR. Today, EMDR is recognized in the clinical practice guidelines of both the Department of Veterans Affairs and Department of Defense. The acceptance comes as a result of being one of the most studied, efficient, and particularly well-suited evidence-based treatments for military-related stress injuries available.

Readers will find that the book is organized in a way that facilitates the development of a treatment plan and guides the practitioner through the various presenting problems, traumatic events, and their various connections. Like the attitude of flexibility and adaptability toward assessing and treating traumatic stress injuries, the book helps explain that the approach is more rehabilitation than simply therapy.

As do most guides, Russell and Figley's book provides a comprehensive orientation to the culture of military veterans and their care. They introduce the reader to an array of treatment innovations designed especially for use with military populations, and readers will find pages filled with practical information, including appendices that feature a glossary of military terminology, breakdowns of rank and pay grades, and various clinical forms. This should be a good companion resource for those who have read a recent addition to the Series: *Families Under Fire: Systemic Therapy with Military Families* (Everson & Figley, 2010).

Charles R. Figley

References

Everson, R. B., & Figley, C. R. (Eds.). (2010). *Families under fire: Systemic therapy with military families*. New York, NY: Routledge.

Figley, C. R., & Nash, W. P. (Eds.). (2007). *Combat stress injury: Theory research, and management*. New York, NY: Routledge.

Shapiro, F. (1989). Efficacy of the eye movement desensitization procedure in the treatment of traumatic memories. *Journal of Traumatic Stress, 2,* 199–223.

van der Kolk, B. A. (1988). The trauma spectrum: The interaction of biological and social events in the genesis of the trauma response. *Journal of Traumatic Stress, 1*(3), 273–290.

Foreword

Mark Russell and Charles Figley have written a book ostensibly about "military EMDR," which it is but it is more than that, and I am hopeful that clinicians who use EMDR with people and situations outside the military will take a long, careful look at it.

I probably should admit to bias. After all, all three of us are Marine veterans and that alone would lead me to take what they write as golden. I contacted Charles back in the early 1970s when I was in Ohio working in a crisis intervention agency and encountering Vietnam War veterans who called in to our hotline. Completing a major study with that combat population at Purdue University, he readily shared his ideas and insights, and we have maintained contact ever since. In fact, he was the editor of the *Journal of Traumatic Stress* and I was on its editorial board when Francine Shapiro published her first article on EMDR. Mark Russell, having joined the Navy and serving as a psychologist during the invasion of Iraq, identified the looming "perfect storm" in military mental health and organized a major EMDR training—one of the first—for the military. I had a small hand in his becoming an EMDR trainer and have worked on several issues with him since.

My bias aside, I am delighted to see a new book on EMDR and the military. When Susan Rogers and I brought out *Light in the Heart of Darkness: EMDR and the Treatment of War and Terrorism Survivors* over a decade ago, I expected to see a number of similar volumes, not only from EMDR, but other effective therapies. After all, the published books on the use of EMDR with children already number half a dozen and growing almost every year. Particularly, given all the research on EMDR since then as well as the ongoing war on terror, it was a reasonable expectation. Unfortunately, there has been nothing. *Treating Traumatic Stress Injuries in Military Personnel: An EMDR Practitioner's Guide* is, from that perspective, overdue.

There are several points that I found interesting in the volume that I would draw to your attention.

First, and painfully, we get a brief history of the resistance to EMDR by people in authority positions. Instead of looking for therapies that work for their military personnel and their families, they have been content with the status quo. This incredible state of affairs is a situation that members of the EMDR community have been aware of but have not spoken out about—Mark and Charles are exceptions—for fear of retaliation that might make getting EMDR tools to those in need even more difficult. And that has happened, as I can unfortunately attest.

Second, while confirming much of what Susan and I wrote in regard to EMDR's application to combat reactions, Mark and Charles have pushed the boundaries back by addressing more of the totality of the military experience.

Third, Shapiro's empirically-driven protocol still stands as the foundation for work with the military, and I would urge interested clinicians to avail themselves of training opportunities.

Fourth, despite the above point, variations on the basic protocol are showing themselves to be of value and are well described not only in terms of "how to," but "when to."

Fifth, for the first time in book form we have a discussion of medically unexplained symptoms and how EMDR might be applied to their resolution. Mark has been investigating this particular issue for years, and I believe this to be one of the most important parts of the book with application well outside the area of the military.

The tide may or may not be turning. As I write this, and for several years, I have been a consultant to a U.S. Army-sponsored trauma treatment training program that includes EMDR as well as other empirically-validated therapies for PTSD. Currently, almost 500 military clinicians have completed training in EMDR. I think one of the reasons this program exists has been through the efforts of a number of people, some EMDR clinicians, some not, who, like Mark and Charles, care about those who go into harm's way on our behalf and continue to push what is too often the "unpushable."

There is much else worthy of note here and perhaps *Treating Traumatic Stress Injuries in Military Personnel: An EMDR Practitioner's Guide*'s greatest contribution ultimately may be to encourage more people to investigate the subject. The role of EMDR in the military is a rich field and a dynamic one as more and more clinical experience and research is accomplished. This book is a contribution to that richness.

Steven M. Silver

Steven M. Silver, Ph.D., is an Army National Guard clinical psychologist and a former Marine Corps Vietnam War combat veteran. Dr. Silver recently retired as Director of PTSD Inpatient Specialty Programs at the Veterans Administration Medical Center, Coatesville, Pennsylvania, after 35 years of treating war veterans. He is a Senior Trainer for the EMDR Institute who has conducted numerous EMDR trainings in the Veteran's Affairs Department and the Department of Defense and published over 50 peer-referred articles, as well as co-author of the book, *In Light in the Heart of Darkness: EMDR and the Treatment of War and Terrorism Survivors* (Silver & Rogers, 2002). Dr. Silver received the Outstanding and Sustained Service Award awarded by the EMDR International Association. Currently, he is the primary EMDR consultant to the U.S. Army Empirically Validated Trauma Treatment Training Program where he has provided consultation to over 400 clinicians who work with military clients and their families.

Acknowledgments

To Francine Shapiro, Steven Silver, and Susan Rogers a heartfelt "Thank You" for steadfast support to me, personally, and the lives of hundreds of thousands of warriors that you have, and continue to touch. To all the volunteer EMDR trainers and facilitators who have assisted training the warrior healers and/or provided direct services—a nation is grateful for your service including Richard B. Smith, Rosalie Thomas, E.C. Hurley, Barbara Parrett, James Stokes, Beverly Dexter, Robert Gelbach, and countless others. And to Howard Lipke, whose idea and urgings led to the writing of this book, I owe you a lifetime of gratitude, partner, and thank you for all you have done on behalf of war veterans. To my colleagues at Antioch University Seattle, thank you for affording me the time to write this book. To our Routledge editor, Anna Moore, we are grateful for your compassion and support in addressing issues impacting the warrior class.

To my beloved wife, and best friend Mika, without your enduring and unwavering support and self-sacrifice this warrior may not have survived, and the book project would never have been completed—thank you! To my children who have had to sacrifice so much during their military father's 26-year career—especially my two sons, both current war veterans, Navy Corpsman HM2 Alexander N. Russell, USN, and Corporal Nicholas I. Russell, USMC; and my two daughters, Meg and Natalie Russell, you all make me so extremely proud! To my deceased parents, veteran of Korean and Vietnam Wars, MGYSGT Charles M. Russell, USMC, (Ret) and my beloved mother, the rock of our family, Yvonne M. Russell, your flames burn ever so brightly in all of our hearts.

To my brothers and sisters all warrior class members whether in uniform or not, MSGT David Russell, USAF (Ret) and his wife MSGT Peggy Russell, USAF (Ret) and family; TSGT James Russell, USAF, his wife Theresa, sons Trevor (USAF) and Devon (USMC) and family; my brother CMSGT Brian Russell, USAF (Ret), his wife Penny and family; brother Robert and my sister Vivian, and her late husband Ron, and family—Semper Fi! And last, but not least, to my distinguished co-author, Charles R. Figley, who has labored tirelessly on behalf of the warrior class, I, and generations of warriors, are forever in your debt.

Mark C. Russell

I would like to acknowledge Kathy Regan Figley for support and encouragement as my wife, friend, collaborator, and my Dean, Ron Marks and their
Provost, Michael Bernstein who have provided the institutional support and
leadership at Tulane University that made this book possible.

Charles R. Figley

Introduction

The principle reason for writing this clinical guide is to offer a comprehensive, practical, reference for mental health practitioners treating, or contemplating treating, military personnel with Eye Movement Desensitization and Reprocessing (EMDR), across the full-spectrum of stress and trauma-related injuries. The term "military personnel," as used in this book, refers to members of the Armed Services in Active-duty, Reserve, and National Guard Components, as well as discharged military personnel commonly referred to as "veterans," that include military retirees. Additionally, content of this book is applicable for treating other members of the military population including military spouses, military civilian employees and contractors, embedded journalists, as well as the "healers" of the warrior class. Where possible, we have taken a cross-cultural perspective by including military research and clinical findings of EMDR from a variety of countries including Germany, Iran, Japan, Sri Lanka, Taiwan, the United Kingdom, and the United States.

Scope of Treatment Issues

It is our belief that clinicians most likely to be effective with treating members of the military population generally have a good working knowledge and appreciation of military culture, organization, lifestyle, and stressors, as well as firm grounding in the science on the effects of exposure to chronic, combat and operational stress, and other traumatic stressors. We provide a fair amount of detail, particularly in relation to stress injuries, that could prove helpful in educating and preparing military clients for treatment. As a military psychologist, it has been Dr. Russell's experience that one can most influence members of the highly educated and professional military population by speaking in terms of facts versus anecdotes and flowery prose. Therefore this volume takes a broad lens covering general topics relevant to understanding the worldview and experiences of the warrior class that can impact clinical practice, and a narrower focus on applications of EMDR within military circles. In addition, throughout the guide we post clinical notes to convey clinical implications, lessons learned, or pertinent reminders.

Recommended Resources

Despite our best attempts to be as comprehensive as possible, it is impossible to cover every salient detail pertaining to EMDR and treating military populations. Therefore, we highly recommend the following resources be used as reference companions to this handbook.

Recommended EMDR References

Leeds, A. M. (2009). *A guide to the standard EMDR protocols for clinicians, supervisors, and consultants.* New York, NY: Springer Publishing.

Lipke, H. (1999). *EMDR and psychotherapy integration: Theoretical and clinical suggestions with focus on traumatic stress.* Boca Raton, FL: CRC Press.

Shapiro, F. (2001). *Eye movement and reprocessing: Basic principles, protocols, and procedures-second edition.* New York, NY: Guilford Press.

An exhaustive, detailed, step-by-step procedural reference on EMDR therapy, covering material used in conducting both basic and advance level EMDR trainings worldwide, by the innovator of EMDR.

Silver, S. M., & Rogers, S. (2002). *Light in the heart of darkness: EMDR and the treatment of war and terrorism survivors.* New York, NY: Norton.

An invaluable inside perspective of adapting EMDR with war veterans in the Department of Veteran's Affairs, by a combat veteran, and two nationally renowned EMDR trainers in the DVA and Department of Defense.

Recommended Military References

Figley, C. R., & Nash, W. P. (2007). *Combat stress injury: Theory, research, and management.* New York, NY: Routledge.

Grossman, LTCOL D. (1996). *On killing: The psychological cost of learning to kill in war and society.* New York, NY: Back Bay Books.

Department of Veteran's Affairs (VA) and Department of Defense (2010). *VA/DoD clinical practice guideline for the management of post-traumatic stress.* Veterans Health Administration, Department of Veterans Affairs and Health Affairs, Department of Defense. Office of Quality and Performance publication 10Q-CPG/PTSD-10. Washington, DC: Author.

Importance of a Book on EMDR Therapy in the Military

This is the first resource that combines the most recent knowledge about the new paradigm of combat-related traumatic stress injuries (Figley & Nash, 2007) and offers a practical guide for treating the spectrum of war/traumatic stress injuries in military personnel with EMDR. EMDR has been recognized as an evidence-based trauma-focused treatment by the Department of Veterans Affairs (DVA), Department of Defense (DoD), and American Psychiatric Association since 2004. This book introduces an array of treatment strategies, especially designed to be effective with military populations. Although several books have been written by Department of Veterans Affairs clinicians on EMDR treatment of Vietnam War veterans diagnosed with combat-PTSD (Lipke, 1999; Silvers & Rogers, 2002;), this is the first to address the wide-range of issues and EMDR treatment in the active-duty military population including resiliency building and early intervention strategies used to possibly prevent long-term disability due to war stress injuries. In short, this book provides the first-ever comprehensive examination of the full spectrum of acute and chronic war and traumatic stress injuries, beyond combat-PTSD such as medically unexplained symptoms or "war syndromes," phantom limb-pain from traumatic amputation, traumatic grief, sexual assault, substance abuse, and compassion fatigue.

Furthermore, previous books on EMDR treatment with war veterans are written almost exclusively for clinicians in traditional brick and mortar outpatient and/or inpatient settings. However, treatment of military personnel frequently occurs in a variety of operational and clinical settings including the frontlines of war, on board warships, field hospitals, and other remote areas, which our book alone covers. Moreover, unlike treatment of non-active-duty veterans, clinicians treating military personnel must be cognizant of dealing with a host of unique ethical and cultural variables, including the very real possibility of treating clientele who will be returning to high risk occupations that regularly expose them to traumatic stressors, including war. Such nuances of working with military personnel are not addressed by other authors.

Organization of the Book

The "Introduction" includes a discussion of the purpose, structure, and intended utility of the book for practitioners. Section I, "EMDR Treatment of Military Populations," includes the first four chapters that, together, will prepare the practitioner for working within a military context. Chapter 1, "Warriors, War, and Resilience," describes common stressors in the military and provides an overview of the spectrum of war stress injuries. Chapter 2, "Overview of EMDR Therapy," provides a brief description of the standard eight-phased EMDR protocol and the Adaptive Information Processing theoretical model. Chapter 3, "Research on EMDR and War Stress Injury," provides a summary of the evidence for EMDR effectiveness and efficiency in treating military populations. Chapter 4, "Why Use EMDR Therapy in the Armed Services?," gives a comparative analysis of unique potential benefits of EMDR in contrast to traditional psychotherapy, within the context of military culture, time, and environmental constraints including mental health stigma and barriers to care.

Section II, "The EMDR Protocol for Military Populations," focuses on step-by-step procedures organized along the eight phases of EMDR protocol for various referral questions, diagnoses, treatment goals, and operational issues. Chapter 5, "Phase One: Client History, Rapport, and Treatment Planning," guides the practitioner through preparing to work with military clients, discussing possible limitations of confidentiality, cultural barriers, establishing trust and rapport, and collecting essential background information on military clientele including comprehensive screening of potential war stress injury including acute stress reaction, traumatic stress injuries, substance use disorders, anger and interpersonal violence, traumatic grief reaction, depression and suicide, medically unexplained symptoms and pain, military sexual trauma, dissociation, and sleep disturbance across the deployment cycle. An integrated, pragmatic treatment plan algorithm is utilized that matches EMDR standard or specialized protocols by considering the reason for referral, time/operational constraints, clinical presentation, client goals, and clinical judgment in order to accomplish one of five treatment goals: (a) client stabilization, (b) primary complaint/symptom reduction, (c) comprehensive standard EMDR therapy, (d) enhancement of performance or resilience building, and (e) prevention or treatment of compassion-stress injury. Chapter 6, "Phase Two: Client Preparation and Informed Consent," details providing military clientele diagnostic feedback and informed consent regarding treatment options, including EMDR. The chapter includes a thorough description of how to introduce EMDR and its theoretical rationale, establishing a credible therapeutic frame, by summarizing the most recent neuroscience of EMDR, and dealing with common military client fears, resistance, and other potential stumbling blocks. Case formulation pertaining to client stabilization is reviewed. Special operational considerations and issues of secondary gain and malingering are also discussed. Chapter 7, "Phase Three: EMDR Assessment," demonstrates conducting an assessment of traumatic memories with actual military clients for acute and chronic war/traumatic stress injuries in accordance to the EMDR treatment plan. Chapter 8, "Phase Four: Basic and Specialized Reprocessing Protocols," reviews EMDR protocols in relation to the treatment goals of either (a) primary complaint/symptom reduction or (b) comprehensive EMDR therapy for chronic war/traumatic stress-injuries along with examples of actual treatment narratives of acute combat-related PTSD. Chapter 9, "Phases Five–Six: Standard Reprocessing Protocols," reviews the last two reprocessing phases along with examples of actual treatment narratives of installation with a military member diagnosed with PTSD and severe phantom-limb pain after traumatic leg amputation. Chapter 10, "EMDR Treatment for Acute War/Traumatic Stress Injury," details implementing modified EMDR protocols for the treatment of acute stress reactions on the frontlines and combat-related acute stress disorder in operational settings.

Section III, "EMDR Treatment for Chronic War/Traumatic Stress Injury" contains Chapters 11–14 that involve the use of standard EMDR therapy for treatment of a variety of chronic stress-injuries across military environments. Chapter 11, "EMDR Therapy of Pre-Military and Military Trauma and Medically Unexplained Symptoms," provides an overview of EMDR applicability to successfully treat pre-military trauma that often increase risk for war stress injury as well as high military attrition and replacement costs associated with early discharge and separation for personality disorder diagnosis. This chapter also discusses the prevalence and treatment of war-related MUS. Chapter 12, "EMDR Treatment of Traumatic Grief and Interpersonal Violence," examines both clinical issues along with actual treatment narratives scenarios. Chapter 13, "Other Military Stress Injury and EMDR Treatment Considerations," offers the reader expert DVA/DoD guidance on clinical issues pertaining to the treatment of military sexual trauma, co-morbid substance use disorders, guilt and grief reactions related to killing, anger, and sleep disturbance. Chapter 14, "Phases Seven–Eight: Closure and Reevaluation," discusses the steps and clinical issues that arise in the final two EMDR treatment phases.

Section IV: "Special Considerations," contains the last two chapters: Chapter 15, "Ethical and Medico-Legal Issues," includes topics such as return to duty dispositions, eye witness testimony, war atrocities, false memory, and record keeping. Chapter 16, "Enhancing Resilience/Performance and Preventing Compassion Stress Injury," provides information on use of EMDR for building resilience and performance enhancement as well as self-care for the healers of warriors to prevent and treat compassion fatigue.

There are also three appendices: Appendix A: "Military Mental Healthcare Referral Resources"; Appendix B: "EMDR Reprocessing Troubleshooting Guide"; and Appendix C: "References."

Section I

EMDR Treatment of Military Populations

1 Warriors, War, and Resilience
The Warrior Class

Since the earliest recording of human warfare in 3,000 B.C.E., humankind has been at war with itself, punctuated by intermittent periods of relative peace. History textbooks of the United States and the world are often narratives of great human accomplishment and travesty, anchored to the chronology of war. On average, in any given year, there are 40 armed conflicts throughout the world. To survive in a realm where issues of human diversity, competition, and conflict are predominantly settled by violence, civilizations across time, national origin, and culture have always entrusted a special subgroup of its members, the *warrior class*, to protect and preserve that which is held most sacred and valued—even if it means forfeiting their health and life. In return, society forges a pact with its warrior class to honor its sacrifice and care for the visible and less visible wounds of the warrior and their family. To keep the hallowed promise requires a unique cadre of compassionate healers with specialized knowledge, skill, and the intrinsic desire to immerse themselves in the culture of the warrior. The inherent stress, danger, and sacrifice of the warrior life have required many societies to resort to conscription, compulsory service, or involuntary "drafts" in order to fill the rank and file. However, since 1973, the warrior class of the United States Armed Forces has been voluntary, along with most other countries in the modern world, though all have contingency plans for "selective service."

MILITARY STRESS INJURY

The concept of *stress injury* is not unique to the military—or to war. However, an important paradigm shift is gaining increasing recognition, scientific credibility, and relevancy in the 21st century for institutions of military medicine, the warrior class, and their healers. Emerging is a contemporary understanding of the interdependent mind–brain–body connection and the neurodevelopmental, accumulative effects of chronic, inescapable stress and potentially traumatic stress on physical and mental health (e.g., Bremner, 2005; Figley & Nash, 2007). Whereas ancient healers like Hippocrates relied upon observations of how life experiences impact human physiology and health, today's healers have the cumulative weight of decades-long investigations from the diverse fields of biology, immunology, lifespan development, neuroscience, epidemiology, medicine, mental health, military, history, comparative experimentation, and cultural anthropology.

PURPOSE OF THE BOOK

The aim of this book is to cover the full range of possible military stress injuries, including stress injuries from trauma other than combat or war. Occupational hazards of military service regularly involve exposure to a plethora of chronic, inescapable, and uncontrollable stressors (e.g., deployments and frequent geographical relocations), as well as a host of potential traumatic events, such as combat, sexual violence, disaster relief, training accidents, and peacekeeping missions, that can have profound short- and long-term effects on military members' health and their families. Historically, research and treatment for the military population have narrowly focused on a select number of traumatic stress injuries such as combat-related post-traumatic stress disorder (PTSD) and depression, overlooking the full spectrum of other predictable stress injuries that men and women in uniform may experience, especially medically unexplained symptoms (e.g., Russell, 2008c). Despite stringent efforts to prevent and treat conditions like PTSD, the graded dose of length, intensity, and frequency of exposure to chronic, inescapable, and/or traumatic stressors has progressively led to escalations of behavioral health challenges. Research has succeeded in identifying a host of markers—biological, psychological, interpersonal, and environmental—that predict when combatants are likely to develop war stress injuries that, like any progressive disease, when left unattended, can metastasize into severe, debilitating, and sometimes fatal health problems for veterans and their families.

THE SPECTRUM OF WAR/TRAUMATIC STRESS INJURIES

Nearly all written accounts of war or combat stress, regardless of place in time, culture, or national origin, describe a wide range of stress-related injuries that can best be divided (albeit artificially) into two major classifications: neuropsychiatric and medically unexplained symptoms (MUS), often called "war syndromes," "psychosomatic illness," or "hysteria" and currently lumped into the Veterans' Health Administration (VHA) category of Symptoms, Signs, and Ill-Defined Conditions (SSID). Historically, military, medical, and psychiatric professionals have classified war stress injuries based upon a particular constellation or pattern of physical and psychological symptoms that comprise the ubiquitous human reaction to unrelenting and/or traumatic stress emphasized at a given time and cultural understanding (e.g., Russell, 2008c). Consequently, a plethora of labels, diagnostic (e.g., nostalgia, war hysteria, shellshock, PTSD) and socio-political (e.g., lacking moral fiber, battle fatigue, pension-neurosis), have emerged during each war generation, each describing ways in which human beings adapt to the inherently toxic stress of war.

Neuropsychiatric Conditions

Neuropsychiatric terms used during the world wars and Vietnam included traditional psychiatric diagnoses of the times, such as "traumatic neurosis," "shellshock," "nervous shock," "neurasthenia," "melancholia," "combat neurosis," "alcoholism," "transient situational disturbance," "psychopathic personality," or "insanity" (Jones & Wessely, 2005). In the 21st century, neuropsychiatric diagnoses include major depression disorder, generalized anxiety disorder, substance-use disorders, traumatic brain injury, acute stress disorder, personality disorder, and PTSD, and these are the psychiatric conditions that receive the predominant focus by the military and public sector in terms of assessing the psychological toll of war (e.g., Russell, 2008c). However, what actually is identified, diagnosed, and counted as a neuropsychiatric casualty has never been consistent within or across military institutions from one war to the next, especially before the First World War (1914–1918). This has led to the false perception that dramatic escalations in war stress-injuries like PTSD are unique to the modern warrior class due to the weakening influence of 20th-century psychiatry and a "culture of trauma" (Shepard, 2001), as opposed to efficiencies of modern industrialized warfare.

Medically Unexplained Symptoms/Conditions

Modern estimates of the prevalence of war stress injury are generally limited to a handful of neuropsychiatric diagnoses (e.g., PTSD, TBI, depression, etc.) and completely exclude the other half of the equation—medically unexplained symptoms (MUS). As a consequence, all or nearly all of institutional military medicine's research, training, and treatment resources, as well as clinical books and manuals written on war trauma, ignore MUS. To our knowledge, this is the first treatment-oriented book to address the full spectrum of war stress injury. It is critical for mental health practitioners to understand, identify, and treat the whole person, which includes MUS. Therefore in order to make up ground in the knowledge deficit of MUS, we offer an overview.

War Stress and Medically Unexplained Symptoms

A progressively strong association between the prevalence rates of medically unexplained symptoms with technological advances in killing, stress, and terror is well chronicled by military medical historians since the Napoleonic era (e.g., Jones & Wessely, 2005). Similarly, changes in tactics have evolved to inflict psychological and social wounds as much as physical casualties in order to demoralize and defeat one's enemy (e.g., chemical-biological-nuclear weaponry, mass bombing of civilian populations, guerilla tactics, terrorism). The accumulative toxic psychosomatic effects of modern industrialized warfare gradually emerged as various war syndromes were identified during 1854–1895 Victorian-era campaigns (e.g., "wind contusion," "palpitation"); 1860–1865 American Civil War (e.g., "irritable heart," "mental aches"); and 1899–1902 Boer War (e.g., "disordered actions of the heart"; Jones & Wessely, 2005). However, the full psychophysical assault from modern war was not fully realized until the First World War (1914–1918), resulting in unprecedented, epidemic numbers of medically unexplained casualties—spurring cyclical, impassioned, and unresolved debates regarding etiology, treatment, and compensation of war stress injuries that continue today (e.g., Russell, 2008c).

Historically, military medical institutions have not clearly differentiated between neuropsychiatric and medically unexplained symptoms, and they avoid using terms like "war syndromes" that insinuate causal effects of war. Common inexplicable psychophysical symptoms include chronic fatigue, muscle weakness, sleep disturbance, headache, back pain, pseudo-seizures, diarrhea, muscle aches, joint pain, memory problems, concentration difficulties, gait disturbance, pseudo-paralyses, constipation, erectile dysfunction, nausea, gastrointestinal distress, lump in the throat, shortness of breath, pelvic pain, abdominal pain, dysmenorrheal, paraesthesias, fainting, sensory loss, dizziness, irritability, rapid or irregular heartbeat, skin rashes, persistent cough and tremors, and shaking or trembling (e.g., Jones & Wessely, 2005).

The understanding, diagnosis, treatment, and reporting of MUS in civilian, veteran, and military populations are greatly complicated by the inherently diverse and vague diagnostic labels that suggest a known pathological cause where none may exist. Examples of contemporary diagnoses of medically unexplained conditions include: chronic fatigue syndrome; fibromyalgia; irritable bowel syndrome; chronic pelvic pain; idiopathic epilepsy; multiple chemical sensitivity; myofacial pain syndromes; functional dyspepsia; somatoform disorders; hyperventilation syndrome; globus syndrome; and non-cardiac chest pain (NCCP; e.g., Russell, 2008c). However, all such labels describe a portion or subset of the human stress response spectrum and do not preclude actual physical etiology. How prevalent are MUS in military clientele?

War Psychiatric Lessons Unlearned: Prevalence of MUS During World War II

War and traumatic stress injuries may manifest and/or be diagnosed as only a neuropsychiatric syndrome(s) such as PTSD, major depression, and so on; as medically unexplained symptom(s) such as chronic fatigue, non-ulcer dyspepsia, and so on; or as a combination of both (e.g., generalized anxiety disorder and pseudo- [atypical] seizure disorder). The latter represents the norm; however, it is exceedingly common for military personnel to seek out and

Table 1.1   Incidence of Psychosomatic Complaints (Menninger, 1948, p. 156)

Complaint	Total Group	Combat Veterans	Noncombat Troops
Gastrointestinal	29.7%	85.4%	14.6%
Orthopedic	23.5%	88.5%	11.5%
Multiple symptoms	17.3%	84.3%	15.7%
Cardiovascular	15.9%	88.1%	11.9%
Headache	8.1%	86.6%	13.4%
Genitourinary	5.4%	80.0%	20.0%

receive medical treatment for multiple unexplained somatic complaints for years, without any consideration of connecting the mind and body.

As observed by WWII Chief Consultant in Neuropsychiatry to the Surgeon General of the U.S. Army, Brigadier General William C. Menninger (1948), and his distant predecessor Union Army Surgeon General William A. Hammond (1883), "psychosomatic" or MUS are by far the most predictably prevalent, least understood, and most under-treated manifestation of stress injury during war. In his post-war memoir, General Menninger (1948) writes: "By some people 'psychosomatic medicine' is used to refer to a limited number of diseases. By others, including the author, it is regarded as a guiding principle of medical practice which applies to all illness" (p. 153). The Army General based his conclusions on sobering War Department statistics revealing the toxicity of war stress on health, such as those listed in Table 1.1.

Institutional Military Medicine and MUS

Menninger's (1948) observations were shared by previous enlightened military medical leaders, Army Surgeon General William A. Hammond and Army Surgeon S. Weir Mitchell, who were convinced that "nerve injuries" and nervous disorders, as they were broadly categorized, were both real and treatable (Lande, 2003). Hammond and Mitchell rejected not only the prevailing explanation that afflicted soldiers were all either cowards, deserters, or malingerers, but they also abandoned dualism itself and proposed instead a "mind–body unitary theory" by describing emotional and physical symptoms as inseparably intertwined, thereby removing critical barriers to understand, study, and treat war stress injuries (Hammond, 1883). More recently, the short-lived Gulf War (1990–1991) resulted in over 100,000 of 700,000 U.S. personnel deployed to the Persian Gulf theater reporting medically unexplained symptoms (e.g., chronic fatigue, pain, insomnia, etc.), leading to another controversial syndrome "Gulf War Illness" (Ozakinci, Hallman, & Kipen, 2006). To be clear, we are not suggesting that all or most cases of Gulf War Illness were not caused or exacerbated by medical or environmental pathogens. Stability of Gulf War Syndrome in 390 Gulf War veterans revealed no significant alteration in symptom number or severity over a 5-year period (Ozakinci et al., 2006)—requiring better understanding, early identification, and treatment of war syndromes while on Active duty to prevent long-term disability (e.g., Russell, 2008c).

MILITARY DEFINITIONS OF STRESS-RELATED DISORDERS AND SYNDROMES

To enhance accurate communication between mental health providers, military clientele, and military organizations, the following definitions are adapted from the Department of Veteran's Affairs (VA) and Department of Defense (DoD) *October, 2010 VA/DoD Clinical Practice Guideline for the Management of Post-Traumatic Stress.* Veterans Health Administration, Department of Veterans Affairs and Health Affairs, Department of Defense. Office of Quality and Performance publication 10Q-CPG/PTSD-10: Washington, DC:

Acute Stress Reaction (ASR)

Acute stress reaction is a transient condition that develops in response to a traumatic event. Onset of at least some signs and symptoms may be simultaneous with the trauma itself or within minutes of the traumatic event and may follow the trauma after an interval of hours or days. In most cases, symptoms will disappear within days (even hours). Symptoms include a varying mixture of the following.

Combat and Operational Stress Reaction (COSR)

Technically, the DoD-approved term for official medical reports is "Combat Operational Stress Reaction" and it is applied to any stress reaction in the military environment. COSR refers to the adverse reactions military personnel may experience when exposed to combat, deployment-related stress, or other operational stressors. COSR replaces earlier terminology like "battle fatigue" or "combat exhaustion" used to normalize "acute stress responses" (ASR) related to deployment and war-zone stressors and acute "combat stress reactions" (CSR) associated with exposure to combat.

"*Post-Traumatic Stress.*" Recently, military leaders have increasingly embraced the term "Post-Traumatic Stress" or "PTS," which mainly refers to what is sometimes called "sub-clinical PTSD" in medical settings. The preference within the military is to omit reference to "disorder" by dropping the "D" in PTSD; however, most military personnel do not make the distinction between ASR, CSR, COSR, or PTS. Military members may disclose, "I've been diagnosed with PTS," which may mean a clinical condition (PTSD) or a sub-clinical, transient reaction.

Table 1.2

Physical	Cognitive/Mental	Emotional	Behavioral
• Chills	• Blaming someone	• Agitation	• Increased alcohol
• Difficulty	• Change in	• Anxiety	consumption
breathing	alertness	• Apprehension	• Antisocial acts
• Dizziness	• Confusion	• Denial	• Change in
• Elevated blood	• Hyper-vigilance	• Depression	activity
pressure	• Increased or	• Emotional shock	• Change in
• Fainting	decreased	• Fear	communication
• Fatigue	awareness of	• Feeling	• Change in sexual
• Grinding teeth	surroundings	overwhelmed	functioning
• Headaches	• Intrusive images	• Grief	• Change in speech
• Muscle tremors	• Memory	• Guilt	pattern
• Nausea	problems	• Inappropriate	• Emotional
• Pain	• Nightmares	emotional	outbursts
• Profuse sweating	• Poor abstract	response	• Inability to rest
• Rapid heart rate	thinking	• Irritability	• Change in
• Twitches	• Poor attention	• Loss of emotional	appetite
• Weakness	• Poor	control	• Pacing
	concentration		• Startle reflex
	• Poor		intensified
	decision-making		• Suspiciousness
	• Poor problem		• Social withdrawal
	solving		

Common COSR Symptoms

The onset of at least some signs and symptoms may be simultaneous with the acute stressor or trauma itself or may follow the event after an interval of hours or days. Symptoms of COSR may include depression, fatigue, anxiety, decreased concentration/memory, irritability, agitation, and exaggerated startle response. See Table 1.2 for a partial list of signs and symptoms following exposure to COSR including potentially traumatic events (VA/DoD, 2010).

Spiritual or Moral Symptoms

Service members may also experience acute or chronic spiritual symptoms such as:

- Feelings of despair
- Questioning of old religious or spiritual beliefs
- Withdrawal from spiritual practice and spiritual community
- Sense of the doom about the world and the future

Resilience, Adaptive Stress Reactions, and Post-Traumatic Growth

Discussions on military- and war-related stressors are often unfairly slanted toward the negative, aversive, and horrific aspects of going to war or a disaster zone and hopelessly fail to recognize many positive or adaptive outcomes. The term "adaptive stress reactions" refers to positive responses to COSRs that enhance individual and unit performance. Post-traumatic growth refers to positive changes that occur as a result of exposure to stressful and traumatic experiences. Many service personnel, especially combat veterans, often regard their war-time experiences with mixed appreciation as being one of their "best," "hardest," and "worst" life events. The following is a sample of potential adaptive outcomes from combat and operational stressors:

- Forming of close, loyal social ties or camaraderie never likely repeated in life (e.g., band of brothers and band of sisters);
- Improved appreciation of life;
- Deep sense of pride (e.g., taking part of history making);
- Enhanced sense of unit cohesion, morale, and *esprit de corps*; and
- Sense of eliteness.

Misconduct Stress Behaviors

Misconduct stress behaviors describe a range of maladaptive stress reactions from minor to serious violations of military or civilian law and the Law of Land Warfare, most often occurring in poorly trained personnel, but "good and heroic [Soldiers], under extreme stress may also engage in misconduct" (Department of the Army, 2006, pp. 1–6). Examples include mutilating enemy dead, not taking prisoners, looting, rape, brutality, killing animals, self-inflicted wounds, "fragging," desertion, torture, and intentionally killing non-combatants.

2   Overview of EMDR Therapy

Eye Movement Desensitization and Processing (EMDR) burst onto the psychotherapy scene with more impact than any new treatment approach. Introduced by Francine Shapiro in 1987, "eye movement desensitization" (EMD) was presented primarily as a counter-conditioning technique, informed by behavioral theory, that utilized patient eye movements from tracking the therapist's rapid, back-and-forth hand gestures to elicit desensitization. Shapiro's (1989) inaugural study with 22 trauma survivors, including several Vietnam War veterans, revealed the potential for significant reduction of PTSD symptoms after a single EMD session, maintained at 3-month follow-up. However, in 1990, Shapiro added "reprocessing" to EMD to better account for broad, and often rapid information processing changes believed to exceed mainstream cognitive behavior therapy (CBT) theoretical explanations (Shapiro, 2001). By rejecting an established paradigm for an untested, "accelerated" information processing theory, coupled with restrictive training requirements, a decade-long "controversy" has ensued with profound implications for military populations (see Russell, 2008a).

EMDR Theory: The Adaptive Information Processing Model

The "Adaptive Information Processing" (AIP) model of EMDR is an integrative, neuropsychological approach, positing that associative memory or "neural" networks form the physiological basis of perception, cognition, emotion, and behavior in health and pathology (Shapiro, 2001). According to the AIP model, the brain's information processing systems, like other bodily systems, are physiologically geared to move toward healthy adaptation to aid in survival. For example, the body reflexively heals a physical wound or cut, unless something is inhibiting the natural process and an infection ensues. Similarly, our digestive system is designed to extract adaptive elements we need to survive and to eliminate the rest. Shapiro (2001) reasoned that it made sense that our neurological system, with the mind–brain–body's information processing or "learning" capacities, is likewise designed to extract needed or adaptive information from our life experiences and disregard the rest.

Psychopathology

In the AIP model, most types of psychopathology are viewed as reflecting dysfunctionally stored and/or unprocessed information in neural networks often "derived from earlier life experiences that set in motion a continued pattern of affect, behavior, cognitions, and consequent identity structures" (Shapiro, 2001, p. 16) that both influence and are triggered by present experience and anticipated future events (e.g., repeatedly envisioning worst-case scenarios). The particular brain circuits involved and consequent pattern or combination of physical and psychological symptoms presented give rise to different diagnostic classifications (e.g., PTSD, depression, substance abuse, somatization, etc.). However, it is believed that the etiology, maintenance, and/or exacerbation of most pathological states are a reflection of the underlying, unprocessed components of disturbing or traumatic experience(s) (e.g., images, thoughts, sounds, emotions, physical sensations). Shapiro (2001) refers to an early pivotal incident that establishes dysfunctional affect, beliefs, and behaviors as a "touchstone event," and these are regularly targeted in EMDR therapy, along with other memories associatively linked in a dysfunctional memory or schematic network. Like cognitive information processing models (e.g., Beck's cognitive therapy; Beck, Rush, Shaw, & Emery, 1979), AIP asserts that the more expansive or active a dysfunctional network, the greater propensity for selective attention and distorted interpretations and reactions to current and future stimuli, which maintain maladaptive behavior.

Pathologic or maladaptive patterns of behavior signify that the brain's natural self-healing or processing mechanism is blocked. Unlike the majority of life experiences that often include adversity, certain highly distressful, emotionally charged, or traumatic events are not readily assimilated or accommodated and thus are not properly processed and stored in an adaptive memory network. Therefore, identifying and targeting past, present, and future (anticipated) pathogenic experiential contributors, whether conventional *Diagnostic and Statistical Manual of Mental Disorders* (*DSM*) "criterion A" or "big T" traumatic events (e.g., combat) or less conventional, yet equally disturbing ("small t") traumatic experiences (e.g., unwanted divorce), is essential for adaptive processing or healing to occur (Shapiro, 2001). EMDR is used to address the underlying experiences that contribute to clinical problems and health by utilizing the three-pronged approach of giving attention to the past, present, and future.

Hypothesized Mechanism of Action

According to the AIP model, EMDR treatment effects are the result of two essential components, "dual-focused attention" and "bilateral stimulation," in the context of a safe, secure, therapeutic alliance (Shapiro, 2001). Dual-focused attention occurs when clients are asked to focus their attention on internal stimuli (e.g., distressing image, thought, emotion, or sensation), while also attending to rapidly alternating (left–right), rhythmic external stimuli (e.g., eye movements, auditory tones, kinesthetic vibrations). The dual focus strikes a balance with the often problematic extremes of excessive self-focused attention or "self-absorption," whereby individuals are prone to exclude external information, and the equally dysfunctional state of extreme hypervigilance or externally focused attention for anticipated threats and/or avoidance of internal stimuli (e.g., emotions).

"Bilateral stimulation" (BLS) refers to the fact that our sensori-motor pathways are lateralized. For example, most of the optic and motor nerve pathway from the right eye crosses over and is processed by the left visual cortex and vice versa. Lateralization also refers to the fact that each cerebral hemisphere is "lateralized" or specializes in the processing of certain kinds of information. For instance, it has been shown that negatively valenced emotions (e.g., fear, anxiety, anger) tend to be processed more by the right hemisphere and positive emotions (i.e., joy, contentment) in the left hemisphere. Interestingly, functional brain imaging studies of clients successfully treated for PTSD with EMDR reveal significant pre-post changes in brain function and lateralization effects, whereby previously overactive right hemispheric circuits (e.g., amygdala) and hypoactive, typically left prefrontal circuits are reversed and correspond with clinically significant self-reported changes of PTSD symptoms (e.g., Lansing, Amen, Hanks, & Rudy, 2005).

The "stimulation" in bilateral stimulation occurs when clients are directed to divide their attention and track either an external visual stimulus of the back-and-forth movements of the therapist's hand, listening to alternating sounds from a headset, or attending to the rhythmic vibrating kinesthetic sensations in the palms of their hands when holding a pair of vibrating pads. Putting it together, in EMDR therapy, clients are asked to consciously "think about" a distressing memory and its representative image, thought, feeling, etc. and simultaneously concentrate their attention externally by tracking the back-and-forth movement of lights on a light bar or some other alternating stimuli. Theoretically, if not indeed factually, we have elicited dual-focus attention while fully activating or "stimulating" the information processing capabilities of both (bilateral) hemispheres.

It is believed that the combination of dual-focused attention and bilateral stimulation activates at least one of the brain–body's intrinsic information processing mechanisms that assimilates or accommodates information into adaptive memory networks (e.g., Shapiro, 2001). Moreover, EMDR cannot desensitize rational fears, nor does it induce amnesia or distort history—consistent with the adaptive function of the brain–body's hypothesized natural information-processing system (Shapiro, 2001). Initially, however, the emphasis was on the role of eye movements per se due to the critical role of REM "rapid eye movement" sleep for emotional processing and learning consolidation. However, subsequent anecdotal clinical reports and research revealed that alternating sounds, rhythmic tapping of the fingers, and experiencing alternate tapping all seemed to produce an effect (Shapiro, 2001). Studies designed to "dismantle" EMDR have primarily focused on isolating eye movements, with inconclusive findings, thereby feeding a long controversy (see Russell, 2008a).

Forging Adaptive Associations of Neural Networks

Re-processing or "learning" is viewed as the forging or strengthening of adaptive associations between the maladaptive neural networks related to psychopathological states and adaptive neural networks that contain memories related to secure attachment, coping, mastery, self-efficacy, "lessons learned," and other "positive" or adaptive experiences stored in the brain. EMDR incorporates an associative memory process whereby perceptions of present stimuli or events are interpreted and responded to by linkage with neural networks containing similar experiences such as emotions, physical sensations, and thoughts/beliefs. Accessing the experience, by directing self-focused attention to a memory, creates a link between consciousness and where the information is stored. Byproducts of reprocessing include desensitization (decrease in disturbance) but also adaptive restructuring of the client's narrative, self-initiated insights, and perspectives, as well as changes in physical and emotional responses. Conceptually, this tendency of humans to process information to adaptive resolution is also consistent with basic assumptions of humanistic psychology (e.g., Shapiro, 2001).

Clinical note.   In teaching and using EMDR, the author (Mark Russell) often finds it helpful to use a short video snippet that depicts neurons of the developing brain visibly reaching out with their growth cones to find other neurons to physically link up with a neural network. This provides clients as well as students learning about EMDR a means to give an abstract concept of linking memory networks a concrete, factual image of what we aim to accomplish with EMDR. When the two neural networks eventually link up, those new synaptic connections are what happens in learning or reprocessing. This is especially helpful in visualizing the "installation phase" as new synapses, or connections, are made between neural networks. The opportunity to "see" what is happening in the brain, what real neural or memory networks look like, has helped in our opinion to increase the credibility of the explanations that we give clients. With many military members, seeing truly can be believing.

Why Theory Matters

It is our most fervent belief and collective experience that, to use EMDR effectively, the clinician must achieve a good understanding of the theoretical model as it informs most treatment choice points (e.g., when to return to the target memory), which can be the critical variable between a successful or unsuccessful outcome. In short, the clinician should remember that the

EMDR therapist's function is to: (a) **Access** the necessary memory networks by eliciting appropriate dual-focused attention in the context of a secure, therapeutic alliance; (b) **Stimulate** the information processing system by maintaining dual-focus attention and bilateral stimulation in the presence of an attuned therapist; (c) **Move** the information along the associative links of neural networks until adaptive resolution is achieved for past, present, and future experiential contributors; and (d) **Re-assess** the adaptive resolution of targeted memory networks (Shapiro, 2001).

Comparative Theoretical Approaches

EMDR can be described as an "integrative" psychotherapy for several reasons (Shapiro, 2001). First—and perhaps foremost—clinicians using EMDR will quickly recognize many aspects from a diverse range of theoretical orientations that will spontaneously emerge during the course of therapy (e.g., recall of early non-conscious memories, adaptive insights, client-generated solutions, cognitive restructuring, desensitization, somatic expression of pathology and health).

Adaptive Information Processing model: (a) Memory networks are the basis of perception, attitude, and behavior; problems are the result of incompletely processed experiences. (b) Change is the result of the forging of associations between networks of information stored in the brain.

Cognitive model: (a) Cognitive distortion and faulty beliefs are the basis of maladaptive schemas or pathology. (b) Cognitions are changed through reframing, self-monitoring, and homework exercises.

Behavioral model: (a) Maladaptive behavior occurs as the result of faulty learning in the environment. (b) Behavior is changed through conditioning, exposure, modeling, and altering reinforcement patterns.

Cognitive Behavioral model: (a) Psychological dysfunction is understood in terms of mechanisms of learning and information processing. (b) Change is effected through a combination of behavioral and cognitive strategies.

Psychodynamic model: (a) Pathology results from unresolved, often early childhood experiences. (b) Change results from achieving insight into previously unconscious dynamics.

Humanistic model: (a) Pathology is viewed as a false, incongruous self, stunting personal growth. (b) Facilitating conditions for client-centered change in self and growth are necessary.

Gestalt model: (a) Pathology is often represented by repressed, unfinished conflicts that are stored in the body. (b) Change occurs by releasing physiological expression of unfinished business.

Neurobiological model: (a) Pathology caused by alterations in neuroendocrine and hormonal dysregulation (e.g., HPA-axis) alters brain structure and functioning of memory, emotional, and executive control circuits. (b) Change is effected by resetting physiological and cerebral regulatory and information-processing systems.

Eight Phases of the Standard EMDR Trauma-Focused Protocol

The standard EMDR protocol reflects an integrative psychotherapy consisting of eight stages that we will review below and describe in more detail in Section II when applied to military populations. It is important to remember that the standard or basic EMDR protocol is the only evidence-based protocol, as distinguished from the myriad variations of EMDR or specialized protocols published. That said, it is a fair assessment that there is no clear empirical evidence supporting the sequencing of EMDR therapy (e.g., body scan phase must follow installation phase), the necessity of including various EMDR phases (e.g., installation, body scan), or adherence to other components of the standard EMDR protocol (e.g., using safe/calm place exercise, completing the three-pronged protocol, etc.). Perhaps a more streamlined and effective type of EMDR may be possible; however, researchers remain stuck proving or disproving EMDR efficacy and theory (e.g., Russell, 2008a).

EMDR therapy is referred to as "integrative," in part due to a holistic framework that emphasizes working with imagery and other sensory input (e.g., auditory, olfactory, gustatory), cognitions, emotions, somatic or physiological sensations, and behavior, as well as attending to past-, present- (here and now), and future-oriented experiential contributors (Shapiro, 2001). A key aspect of the eight phases of EMDR can be likened to a series of "checks and balances," whereby the extent of adaptive reprocessing is sequentially re-assessed by inclusion of disparate elements and time dimensions of human experience. The following is an overview of the main goals and procedural objectives of the eight phases of EMDR therapy adapted from material copyrighted by Francine Shapiro, Ph.D., and the EMDR Institute (used with permission):

Phase One: Client History.   Goal: Assess client appropriateness for EMDR therapy and initiate treatment planning. Objectives: After standard psychiatric history taking, mental status exam, safety screening, and informed consent, the main objectives are to develop therapeutic alliance, assess client appropriateness for EMDR therapy, and identify potential past, present, and future experiential contributors to dysfunction and health that need to be reprocessed.

Phase Two: Client Preparation.   Goal: Determine client readiness for EMDR therapy. Objectives: Enhance client trust and rapport, educate the client about EMDR, explain the theory, test the use of eye movements or another type of "bilateral stimulation" (BLS), teach coping skills (e.g., safe/calm place) or other methods for building affect tolerance and stability as necessary, address client fears, and agree upon the client's ideographic "stop signal."

Phase Theee: Assessment.   Goal: Structure accessing and measurement of target memories. Objectives: Identify target memories and components by asking clients to bring the trauma to conscious awareness and select an image or other sensory stimuli, negative cognition (NC), emotion(s), physical sensation(s), and location. Obtain baseline measures, including "Subjective Units of Disturbance Scale" (SUDS) Likert rating from 0—no distress—to 10—worst ever, then solicit positive cognition (PC)—an adaptive self-statement associated with the target baseline memory and baseline rating on "Validity of Cognition" (VOC) with 1—completely untrue—and 7—completely true. Components of each target memory are assessed, and memories can be arranged in chronological or hierarchical order. Next, "current triggers" are identified (e.g., being in crowds) along with their components. Finally, the "future template" or imaginal anticipations that cause distress are solicited (e.g., going on an airplane), along with future desired behavior. Assessing for the "three-pronged protocol" (past, present, and future experiential contributors) is optimal; however, it may not be practical in all situations (e.g., operational settings—see Chapter 9, this volume).

Example Script

Presenting Issue (Target Memory): Image: Most disturbing: *"What picture represents the worst part of the incident?"* If no picture: *"When you think of the incident, what do you get?"* **Negative Cognition:** *"What words go best with that picture that expresses your negative belief about yourself now?"* **Positive Cognition:** *"When you bring up that picture, what would you like to believe about yourself now?"* **Validity of Cognition (VOC):** *"When you think of that picture, how true do those words (repeat the positive cognition above) feel to you now on a scale of 1 to 7, where 1 feels completely false and 7 feels completely true?"*

Emotions: *"When you bring up that picture and those words (negative cognition above), what emotion(s) do you feel now?"*

SUDS: *"On a scale of 0 to 10, where 0 is no disturbance or neutral and 10 is the highest disturbance you can imagine, how disturbing does the incident feel to you now?"*

Location of Body Sensation(s): *"Where do you feel it in your body?"*

Phase Four: Desensitization. Goal: Reprocessing the targeted dysfunctional memory network to decrease disturbance. Objectives: Clients are instructed to dually focus their attention on a target memory image, NC, emotions, and body sensations, while simultaneously concentrating their attention on tracking the BLS (e.g., therapist's hand movements) for approximately 24 back-and-forth movements (10 seconds). Afterwards, the clinician asks open-ended questions (e.g., *"What are you aware of now?"*); if the client's response reflects change or movement, the therapist will typically initiate further BLS sets with the client's subsequent free associations until no further change in self-report of negative elements or desensitization occurs or until the client's self-report shifts and remains at a positive or adaptive direction.

Example script: *"Often we will be doing a simple check on what you are experiencing. I need to know from you exactly what is going on with as clear feedback as possible. Sometimes things will change, and sometimes they won't. There are no 'supposed to's' in this process. So just give as accurate feedback as you can as to what is happening without judging whether it should be happening or not. Just let whatever happens happen."* (Remember to remind the client about the STOP signal.)

Next, the therapist instructs the client, *"I'd like you to bring up that picture (of the target memory), those negative words (repeat the negative cognition), and notice where you are feeling it in your body—and follow my fingers (or other type of BLS)."*

Add a set of BLS, stop, and say, *"Okay, blank it out, and take a breath"*; then ask, *"What comes up?"*, *"What do you notice?"*, *"What are you aware of?"*, *"What's going on in your mind?"*, or *"What do you get?"* If the client's self-report indicates change (e.g., shifts in memory, image, thought, feeling, somatic sensations, etc.), repeat with more BLS sets. If the client reports or demonstrates frustration over being unable to maintain dual focus of the image or other memory element while tracking the BLS, advise the client: *"That's all right; just know that you are thinking about it and allow your mind to notice whatever comes up."*

Returning to the Target Memory

If reprocessing gets interrupted (e.g., phone call, lengthy self-disclosure) and appears to be an endless string of associations ("looping"), the therapist and client lose track of direction, nearing the end of a session, and the therapist wants to check progress, or the client's self-report indicates neutral or positive changes after several BLS sets, ask, *"When you go back to the original memory that we started with (or the agreed upon title for the target memory such as "the mess tent bombing"), what do you get now?"* When the client reports a SUDS of "0," do one more set of BLS; if still "0," proceed to Installation phase. If unable to reach "0," ask *"What keeps it from being a 0?"* and continue reprocessing with BLS sets until attaining SUDS of "0" or "1" if mutually determined to be ecologically valid (e.g., client adamantly believes it's morally disrespectful to report a SUDS of "0" after the recent death of a combat buddy).

Phase Five: Installation.   Goal: Reprocessing and strengthening associations to adaptive neural networks. Objectives: After desensitization, hold the initial baseline target memory together with PC and assess if new adaptive cognitions (PC) have emerged. Pair the preferred PC with target memory and incorporate shortened BLS sets until VOC reaches "7."

Example script: Linking the desired positive cognition with the original memory/incident or picture:

1. *Do the words (repeat the PC) still fit, or is there another positive statement you feel would be more suitable?*
2. *Think about the original incident and those words (repeat the selected PC). From 1 (completely false) to 7 (completely true), how true do they feel? Hold them together.*

Do a set of BLS and ask again: *"On a scale of 1 to 7, how true do those words (PC) feel to you now when you think of the original incident?"* When the client reports a VOC of "7," do one more BLS set; if still "7," proceed to the Body Scan phase. If unable to reach "7," ask *"What keeps it from being a 7?"* and continue with BLS sets until attaining a VOC of "7" or "6" if mutually determined to be ecologically valid (e.g., client feels safe now, but is pending another deployment in three months).

Phase Six: Body Scan. Goal: Reprocessing any residual physical/somatic manifestations of the target memory. Objectives: The client focuses on the target memory and the PC and then scans their body from head to toe for any negative somatic sensations that, if present, are reprocessed with shortened BLS sets until cleared.

Example script: *"Close your eyes and keep in mind the original memory and the (repeat the selected positive cognition). Then bring your attention to the different parts of your body, starting with your head and working downward. Any place you find any tension, tightness, or unusual sensation, please tell me."* If any physical sensation is reported, do a shortened set of BLS. If a positive/comfortable sensation is reported, do additional BLS sets to strengthen the positive somatic sensations until no further change is reported. If a somatic sensation of discomfort is reported, reprocess until discomfort subsides. Phase is complete with a "clear" body scan characterized as the absence of negative somatic associations or the continued presence of neutral or positive physical sensations without adverse somatic manifestations.

Phase Seven: Closure. Goal: Stabilize the client after an incomplete treatment session. Objectives: Prior to the end of the session, and when a phase is not completed, the therapist debriefs the client. Making sure that the client distress level is the lowest possible, therapists may utilize relaxation or other self-regulation techniques (e.g., safe place) and prepare the client for possible continued processing after the session by advocating the use of a daily log for memories, dreams, thoughts, or other experiences that may arise.

Example script: Closure for a COMPLETE session (SUDS = 0, VOC = 7, clear Body Scan):

1. Tell the client it is time to stop.
2. Give encouragement: *"You have done some good work today. How are you feeling?"*

3. Read the closure statement: *"Processing may continue after our session. You may or may not notice new insights, thoughts, memories, physical sensations, or dreams. Please make a note of whatever you notice. We will talk about that at our next session. Also remember to use one of the self-control techniques once a day and after each time that you write something in your log."*

Closure for an INCOMPLETE session:

1. Tell the client it is time to stop and explain the reason. *"We are almost out of time, and we will need to stop soon."*
2. Give encouragement and support for the effort made. *"You have done some very good work, and I appreciate the effort you have made. How are you feeling?"*
3. Do relaxation or other affect-regulation exercise as needed.
4. Read the closure statement: *"Processing may continue after our session. You may or may not notice new insights, thoughts, memories, physical sensations, or dreams. Please make a note of whatever you notice. We will talk about that at our next session. Also remember to use one of the self-control techniques once a day and after each time you write something in your log."*

Note. Eliminate the Installation of Positive Cognition and the Body Scan if it is evident that there is still material to be reprocessed.

Phase Eight: Reevaluation.   Goal: Reassess treatment gains by re-accessing and reprocessing target memory in accordance with the treatment plan. Objective: Encourage the client to give a general report on time since the last session and review the log if applicable. The clinician reevaluates the status of target memory at the beginning of the next session and follow-up. If all past memories are reprocessed, then go on to present triggers and then future template (if practical).

   Three-Pronged Protocol: To complete the standard EMDR protocol, clinicians must reprocess the target memories identified and assessed during phases one and three, consisting of the past, experiential big or small "t" traumatic events, current triggers or antecedents of disturbance, and the future "template," which may include anticipatory anxiety, imagined behavioral rehearsal of future coping or mastery experiences, and/or other desired feeling, beliefs, and behavior needed in the future.

3   Research on EMDR and War Stress Injury

Psychotherapy research is concerned with essentially three broad questions: (1) determining whether a therapy works in strictly controlled settings (*efficacy*)—especially in comparison with other viable treatments and control groups; (2) determining whether rigidly controlled treatment effects from the laboratory generalize to actual clinical practice (*effectiveness*); and (3) determining whether a therapy works for the hypothesized reasons (*proving theoretical mechanism of action*).

1993–1999: EMDR RESEARCH IN THE DEPARTMENT OF VETERANS AFFAIRS

Until as late as 2005, there were no known randomized clinical trials (RCT), either funded or conducted by the Department of Defense (DoD) on psychotherapies for Acute Stress Disorder (ASD) or PTSD with active-duty military personnel (e.g., Creamer & Forbes, 2004). All clinical research on military-related PTSD treatment had been done primarily through the Department of Veterans Affairs (DVA) and almost exclusively with Vietnam War veterans, decades after their military careers had ended. From 1993 to 1999, the DVA conducted a total of four RCT on EMDR treatment for Vietnam Veterans with combat-PTSD. A number of critical reviews and meta-analyses have been conducted on the handful of controlled and semi-controlled research with EMDR treatment of war veterans (e.g., Maxfield & Hyer, 2002). As noted earlier, Shapiro's (1989) inaugural EMD(R) study included several Vietnam War veterans who reported marked PTSD symptom reduction after a single session. Shortly afterwards, in 1991, the esteemed behaviorist Joseph Wolpe, innovator of exposure-based therapies like systematic desensitization, published his own single-case study of EMD treatment of sexual assault trauma (Wolpe, & Abrams, 1991). Then, in 1992 there was a multiple-case study from DVA clinician-researchers Howard Lipke and Al Botkin reporting significant symptom reduction using EMDR with several clients in a DVA PTSD program (Lipke & Botkin, 1992).

In regards to DVA-sponsored uncontrolled and controlled EMDR research, varying levels of improvement were reported ranging from *little to none* (Boudweyns, Stwertka, Hyer, Albrecht, & Sperre, 1993) *to significant* (Carlson, Chemtob, Rusnack, Hedlund, & Muraoka, 1998; cited in Russell & Friedberg, 2009). It should be noted that similar patterns of mixed outcomes were reported by DVA researchers for other PTSD therapies, including heavily favored cognitive-behavioral and exposure-based therapies (e.g., Creamer & Forbes, 2004). Moreover, concerns over treatment fidelity and the manner in which EMDR was tested by DVA researchers were raised (e.g., Shapiro, 2001) that surely did not sit well with DVA experts—especially coming from a person without professional standing. But Shapiro and other advocates of EMDR appear to have a point. For example, RCT with Vietnam War veterans receiving only two EMDR sessions (Boudewyns et al., 1993; Jensen, 1994, cited in Russell, Lipke, & Figley, 2011) or treatment of a single memory (Boudewyns & Hyer, 1996; Pitman et al., 1996, cited in Russell et al., 2011) reduced subjective distress in relation to the memory but achieved no significant or sustained difference between control groups or at 15-month follow-up (e.g., Macklin, Metzger, Lasko, Berry, Orr, & Pitman, 2000, cited in Russell et al., 2011).

A subsequent meta-analysis of all RCT conducted with EMDR, in and outside of the DVA, revealed that the degree of positive EMDR treatment effects obtained was significantly correlated to the number of EMDR sessions and level of treatment fidelity and adherence to the basic EMDR trauma-focused protocol (e.g., Maxfield & Hyer, 2002). The importance of treatment fidelity was perhaps evident when DVA clinician-researchers outside of the National Center for PTSD found significantly more robust findings when adequate treatment fidelity was demonstrated, using a more realistic, 12-session format for treating chronic combat-PTSD. That research team was led by Dr. Steven Silver at VAMC Coatesville, Pennsylvania. Silver, Rogers, Knipe, and Colelli's (1995) large, non-randomized investigation of EMDR treatment with multiple memories from 83 Vietnam War veterans diagnosed with combat-PTSD was found to be superior in comparison to biofeedback and relaxation training on seven of eight dependent measures; impressive, but not scientifically rigorous enough for DVA executives to take notice.

Besides, by 1996, institutional military medicine's leaders had already made up their minds about EMDR. Once it was obvious that EMDR was not the single-session wonder that the media and some overzealous EMDR therapists were making it out to be, it was time to pull the plug (Russell, 2008a). It would be understandable, though, if even the harshest skeptics might have secretly hoped for the breakthrough that could possibly help thousands of broken war veterans who spend years or decades drifting in and out of the DVA's wards— but it didn't happen. It was 1996, and the results from three clinical trials by the DVA were generally mixed and unspectacular. However, not everyone in the DVA was willing to quit on something that might yet prove helpful to veterans. Seasoned clinicians like Howard Lipke who ran DVA's PTSD programs at North Chicago VA and Steven M. Silver and Susan Rogers, the Director and co-Director for PTSD Program, VAMC Coatesville—who, despite the nay-saying by DVA leadership, were still obtaining positive clinical results on the ground floor with EMDR that were not achieved with the existing cognitive-behavioral tools.

1998: DVA EMDR RCT ON COMBAT-PTSD WITH TREATMENT FIDELITY

Then, in 1998, Dr. John Carlson and his research group at the DVA Medical Center, Honolulu, Hawaii, entered the fray. Carlson noted that the main purpose of his team's study was to address the contradictory findings from the DVA's previous RCT on EMDR (Boudewyns et al., 1993; Pitman et al., 1993; Jensen, 1994, cited in Russell et al., 2011), as compared to highly supportive reports from the civilian sector. Specifically at issue were concerns over treatment fidelity of the DVA studies and an unrealistic design to study a treatment for chronic combat-PTSD, whereby EMDR was being tested after 2–3 sessions, as compared to 9–28 sessions from DVA RCT on exposure therapy (Carlson et al., 1998). Carlson and his team cited a 1995 civilian EMDR RCT within a managed care setting, not unlike the DVA or DoD, that found significant EMDR treatment effects after 12 sessions and by achieving high treatment fidelity (Wilson, Becker, & Tinker, 1995). Given the prevailing controversy and current institutional military medicine resistance toward EMDR research, a more in-depth look at this pivotal DVA study is warranted.

Carlson et al. (1998) carefully designed a research using the "gold standards" for RCT of the time in order to satisfy DVA skeptics and EMDR advocates. His team used a multimodal assessment approach including Clinician Administered PTSD Structured interview (CAPS-1); a host of established standardized psychometric measures: MMPI-2, Impact of Events Scale (IES), Beck Depression Inventory (BDI), Mississippi Scale for Combat Related PTSD (MSCRP), PTSD Symptom Scale (PSS), and the Spielberger State-Trait Anxiety Inventory (STAI); and psychophysiological measures (skin conductance, heart rate, EMG, and temperature). Blind raters were used to assess at pre, post, 3-month, and 9-month follow-up. There were three DVA therapists: one with extensive experience with biofeedback and behavioral therapies, the other a psychodynamic orientation, and the third with extensive experience with biofeedback. All three clinicians received EMDR training and implemented EMDR per the treatment manual (e.g., allowing free association to multiple memories versus 1–2), and treatment fidelity was assessed by an outside consultant (Carlson et al., 1998).

A total of 35 Vietnam War veterans diagnosed with combat-PTSD were randomly assigned to one of three groups: EMDR, a control group receiving routine DVA clinical care for PTSD, and biofeedback-assisted relaxation training. Carlson et al. (1998) explained that their choice of biofeedback was based on (a) the fact that it was active treatment modality in the DVA and could control for attentional effects; (b) the fact that it served as viable treatment for veterans; (c) the implications of physiological arousal in PTSD; and (d) previous biofeedback treatment research of chronic anxiety. There were no meaningful differences across treatment groups. All three groups had overall average combat-PTSD scores (M = 118.3), significantly above the 107 cut-off. After random assignment, there were no drop-outs in the EMDR or control group and one drop-out in biofeedback (Carlson et al., 1998).

Results. Carlson et al.'s (1998) more pragmatic approach to researching EMDR on Vietnam War veterans with chronic, combat-related PTSD revealed that, after 12 EMDR sessions, targeting multiple memories, 77% of combat veterans no longer met criteria for PTSD with results maintained at 3- and 9-month follow-up. Specifically, "very substantial" EMDR treatment effects were found on the majority of psychometrics, with statistically significant differences of EMDR treatment compared to veterans receiving routine clinical care or biofeedback-assisted relaxation therapy as measured by the BDI, MSCRP, PSS, CAPS, and significantly greater improvement and treatment satisfaction as rated by the military patients. Overall, there were lower but not significant decreases on IES and STAI with EMDR, and all groups had significant decreases in physiological arousal (Carlson et al., 1998). So what happened next? Where would the National Center for PTSD go with these results, since it came from one of their component research centers? Scientists adhering to the vaulted scientific method as means to uncover "truths" almost reflexively would opt for replication before deciding whether to accept or reject the findings.

Unfortunately, the Carlson et al. (1998) study has been the last word in the Department of Veterans Affairs National Center for PTSD's abbreviated flirt with EMDR in fulfillment of its stated mission of "searching for highest quality PTSD care." Then, on October 1, 2001, the Global War on Terror began, and so, too, the longest war in American history. All eyes went to institutional military medicine to see if, in this war, finally, the Nation would do right by its warrior class.

WHY NO EMDR RESEARCH AND TRAINING IN THE DEPARTMENT OF VETERANS AFFAIRS?

The public explanations provided by the DVA and the National Center for PTSD as for why it does not offer EMDR training or research are multifold: (a) that, while there is evidence of EMDR's efficacy for treating traumatic stress injuries, there is insufficient RCT with military and veteran's populations; (b) that dismantling studies have proven that the use of eye movements is superfluous; (c) if the eye movements are not needed for EMDR, then the theory of mechanism of action has been disproven, and therefore the treatment itself is invalid and should not be researched; and (d) there is nothing "new" about EMDR that is not already found in established cognitive and exposure therapies (see Russell, 2008a).

EMDR FUNDED RESEARCH IN THE DEPARTMENT OF DEFENSE

As noted earlier, the extent of EMDR research by military medicine can be summarized in a single word—zero. To be crystal clear, the paucity of EMDR RCT with war veterans in the DVA and the total absence of any EMDR RCT with military personnel in the DoD are an indictment of institutional military medicine for neglecting its responsibilities to the welfare of the warrior class, not the lack of efficacy of EMDR treatment per se. In fact, as we will see shortly, there is already considerable evidence that EMDR is not only an "*efficacious*" therapy, but, perhaps even more importantly, it is an "*effective*" treatment for war or traumatic stress injuries in actual real-life military settings.

FUNDED RESEARCH ON WAR STRESS INJURY IN THE DEPARTMENT OF DEFENSE

The reason for the above qualifier "funded" is that, simply put, people (and organizations) tend to invest resources, such as money, into those things they most value and are committed to. The over $400 million spent by the Department of Defense (DoD) since 2005 on researching PTSD treatments has been invested predominantly on those treatments developed and researched by the lead agency of institutional military medicine, the Department of Veterans Affairs, National Center for PTSD: Prolonged Exposure (PE), Cognitive Processing Therapy (CPT), and Virtual Reality Therapy (VRT). To be certain, PE, CPT, and VRT should and must be researched by military medicine within military settings, as they have a proven track record for reducing human suffering from traumatic stress injuries. However, as the war on terror slogged on, it was painfully clear that the hand-selected evidence-based treatments of choice were not sufficient in meeting the mental health needs of returning warriors.

Panicked, military medicine embarked on an "anything but EMDR" shotgun excursion to find any possible effective intervention for war stress injury, funding randomized controlled trials with a broad array of alternative non-evidence-based methods such as yoga, acupuncture, bioenergy (Reiki) massage, journaling, art, horses, fishing, dogs, and a host of other unconventional, yet still possibly valuable adjunctive therapies. When this too did not pan out and the prevalence of war stress injury, suicide, and incidents of misconduct stress behavior continued to escalate, military medicine appeared to have reached the conclusion that the effort to discover reliable, effective treatments to stem the tide of chronic anguish, military attrition, and disability had largely failed. Scrambling for an alternative strategy, military medicine elected to devote its scarce resources in a "new" direction—that of "positive psychology" and prevention. In January 2011, the U.S. Army desperately announced a $125 million commitment to civilian academic researchers, uncharacteristically doubling down on the broad implementation of a relatively untested Comprehensive Soldier Fitness (CSF) program—or stress inoculation on steroids—with the glimmer of hope that it might prevent or reduce war stress injury (Casey, 2011).

However since 2008, the Army had already incorporated a well-designed and cost-effective *Battlemind* resiliency training program for military personnel and family members, for use throughout the deployment cycle. On top of that, the military continues to revise its *Combat (Operational) Stress Control (CSC/COSC)* protocols employed since 1918. The CSC/COSC mission is *"to conserve the fighting force,"* which it does by normalizing, stabilizing, and returning military personnel with transient signs of acute stress reactions back to their frontline units—with 90% efficiency (Department of the Army, 2009). While perhaps effective for some military members, none of the military's previous preventative measures to date have demonstrably reshaped the problem of war stress injury; in fact, the evidence tells the opposite.

No matter how fighting-fit physically, psychologically, spiritually, or socially, there is a limit to human endurance on the modern battlefield. Exponential increase in war-related stressors associated to around the clock, air-land-sea unpredictable, and uncontrollable and inescapable threats of destruction, combined with cumulative effects of stressors related to deployment and combat, provides an abundantly toxic environmental context for acute and chronic psychophysical breakdown. The only certain preventative measure is to not expose human beings to war. Human history dictates that this will never happen; therefore, institutional military medicine is honor bound to fulfill its mission by exhausting all avenues. In sum, the Department of Defense's current commitment to researching an assortment of treatment and prevention possibilities is not only laudable—it's the "right thing to do!" There are no panaceas, as the DVA reinforced with its cursory fling with EMDR 14 years ago. Thinking outside of the box is especially critical at this time, because, until 2005, military research on preventing and treating war stress injuries has been shortsightedly "MIA" (missing-in-action). Therefore everyone is desperately playing catch-up during a "hot" war and throwing everything at the problem of war stress injury, including the kitchen sink—except that's not entirely true. Since the 2004 publication of post-traumatic stress clinical practice guidelines by institutional military medicine and the American Psychiatric Association, the only evidence-based treatment or non-evidence-based alternative not researched by the DVA or DoD is conspicuously EMDR.

Relevant EMDR Efficacy Research on Treating
Non-War-Related Trauma

This book covers EMDR treatment for the spectrum of war and traumatic stress injuries, not limited to combat trauma alone. It is similarly for practitioners treating the warrior class to not just focus on assessing for stress injuries related to war. As demonstrated in earlier chapters, inherent to the military occupation is regular exposure to a wide range of potentially traumatic stressors outside of war (e.g., military sexual trauma, training accidents, etc.). In addition, many service members enter the military with a history of adverse childhood experiences, but their difficulties in adjustment to the military environment may or may not be clearly associated with an identifiable trauma-related diagnosis like PTSD (e.g., depression, interpersonal violence). The scientific basis for EMDR's recognition as evidence-based for treating post-traumatic stress injuries has been well-summarized by any and all of the various domestic (U.S.) and international clinical practice guidelines that have reviewed the meta-analyses and RCT of EMDR (e.g., APA, 2004; Bisson & Andrew, 2007; DVA/DoD, 2010). Therefore, even clinicians wary about using EMDR because of the concerns over the sheer amount of controlled studies with military and veterans should be reassured by the extensive scientific reviews of EMDR's efficacy on other types of traumatic stress exposure.

Adverse Childhood Experiences: Treating Child-Onset and Adult-Onset Trauma

The second of two NIMH-sponsored studies on EMDR was by Bessel van der Kolk et al. (2007), who conducted a blind-rater, RCT comparison of a placebo-pill control group, EMDR, and medication (Prozac) for the treatment of adults with either childhood-onset PTSD or adult-onset PTSD. After a total of eight sessions (six EMDR treatment sessions), the researchers found that EMDR was superior to Prozac in reducing both PTSD and depression symptoms in adult-onset PTSD. For the majority of adults with child-onset PTSD, most did not achieve complete remission of their PTSD or depression symptoms in either treatment group. However, at the six-month follow-up, 75% of the adult-onset and 33% of the child-onset PTSD cases were asymptomatic after only six EMDR treatment sessions—none were asymptomatic who received Prozac or the placebo control (van der Kolk et al., 2007).

Sexual Trauma

Another pertinent study on EMDR efficacy is Rothbaum, Astin, and Marsteller's (2005) research on treating female adults with a history of single incident sexual trauma either in childhood or adulthood. The research was funded by the National Institute of Mental Health. This was a randomized, well-controlled study involving 74 female rape victims comparing EMDR, prolonged exposure (PE), and a wait-list control. Structured clinical interviews were conducted (e.g., CAPS, SCID), and a variety of well-established psycho-metrics used including for depression (BDI), dissociation (DES-II), and PTSD (e.g., IES-R). All participants received nine treatment sessions, and treatment fidelity for PE and EMDR was conducted by experts selected by Edna Foa and Francine Shapiro, respectively (Rothbaum et al., 2005). Results indicated that both EMDR and prolonged exposure produced significant treatment effects with 95% of PE subjects and 75% of EMDR no longer meeting PTSD diagnostic criteria at post-treatment. Symptom improvement was sustained at six months, although more of the PE vs. EMDR group remained completely asymptomatic. This methodologically rigorous, head-to-head comparison met all seven of the RCT "gold standards." The significant EMDR treatment effects in this well-controlled study were reported to be contrary to other, less rigorous controlled trials that compared EMDR to cognitive-behavioral treatments (e.g., Devilly & Spence, 1999; Taylor et al., 2003, cited in Rothbaum et al., 2005). In conclusion, Rothbaum states, "An interesting potential clinical implication is that EMDR seemed to do equally well in the main despite less exposure and no homework. It will be important for future research to explore these issues" (Rothbaum et al., 2005, p. 614).

Clinical note. Both studies provide evidence of EMDR's utility with treating military sexual trauma and adverse childhood experiences that are frequent within the military population, as well as other causes of PTSD-related injuries outside of war and combat. The van der Kolk et al. (2007) study is particularly relevant in the military. Many military specialities prohibit military personnel from using psychotropic medications (e.g., pilots, submariners), as well as those with top-secret or higher security clearances, and thus require temporary reassignment until they have been off medication for a specified time or members are discharged from the military. Being temporarily deemed as "unfit for full duty" can result in lower annual performance evaluation marks that may hinder one's career progression and ultimately end his or her military career. Consequently, there is considerable reluctance for military members to self-disclose stress injuries, usually until a crisis, and, at that point, the career repercussions may be unavoidable. Therefore, van der Kolk et al.'s (2007) study provides support for recommending EMDR to service members in either sensitive jobs, or who are intrinsically against taking psychotropics (and many are). Or, for those deemed temporarily unfit, EMDR may provide clinical benefit in relatively few sessions for some or many individuals—resulting in less "job loss" time and possibly lesser career impact.

Attrition and Treating Military Clients with Child-Onset

The van der Kolk et al. (2007) study and others (e.g., Shapiro, 2001) provide rationale for using EMDR to treat military clients with adverse chilhood experiences that have higher risk for war stress injury and early military separation.

For example, 46% of 204 Soldiers surveyed reported a history of childhood physical abuse, and 25% reported both childhood physical and sexual abuse. It bears mentioning that, despite a high prevalence of adverse childhood experiences in the military, most military personnel report functioning as well as those soldiers without such experiences (Seifert, Polusny, & Murdoch, 2011). Nevertheless, during the period 1997–2002, psychiatric conditions were the most common cause of early military discharges reported for Navy (47%) and Marine (36%) enlisted members and the second leading cause of discharge in the Army (15%; National Research Council, 2006). Depending on length in service and military schools attended, on average it costs the government an estimated $52,800 to separate and replace military personnel (e.g., Government Accountability Office, 2011). It is commonplace in the military to inform service members suspected of having a "personality disorder," but who want to continue their military career, to be administratively separated by saying, "I'm sorry, the military does not provide long-term therapy"—which it doesn't. If EMDR can get results in as few sessions as in the van der Kolk et al. study (2007), the benefits to service members, military units, the armed services, and greater society when these individuals transition out of the military are substantial.

Terrorism: EMDR for Acute and Chronic Trauma

As noted earlier, military personnel have been targeted, wounded, and killed in acts of terrorism. Early identification and intervention is recommended by the DVA/DoD (2010) clinical practice guidelines to prevent chronic stress-injuries like PTSD. Silver et al. (2005) reported on EMDR treatment provided to 62 direct witnesses to the 9-11 World Trade Center attack. Clients were treated from 2 to 48 weeks (mean was 20 weeks) after the terrorist attack and had either lost a loved one or coworker, were eyewitnesses to the attacks, or were involved in rescue, body recovery, or clean-up efforts at the World Trade Center. Ages ranged from 6 to 65 years. There were no statistically significant differences between women and men on pre- or post-treatment variables. The 62 participants received 1 to 8 EMDR sessions (4.2 sessions on average), by 29 different EMDR therapists. Analysis examined early versus late treatment after the attack. The late group had a statistically significantly higher level of pre-treatment disturbance as measured by the SUD, and lower VOC than the early group. At post-treatment, the early group showed greater positive changes on SUD and VOC than the late group suggesting the passage of time contributed to a worsening of reactions among those requesting treatment (Silver et al., 2005).

Neuro-Scientific Research on EMDR Treatment

The other non-military-related research we want to briefly mention is the neuroimaging and neurobiological studies that can be helpful in phase two of

EMDR (client preparation), as well as in educating reluctant military providers and agencies about the neuroscientific data on EMDR. Several EMDR neuro-imaging case studies have been published in peer-reviewed journals, describing significant pre-post changes in brain function corresponding to patient self-report on PTSD and other symptom measures. For example, multiple separate case studies utilizing neuroimaging scans before and after EMDR treatment for PTSD have found significant alterations in brain physiology corresponding to reduction in symptom measures. Neuro-physical treatment changes with EMDR have also been found with event-related brain potentials on EEG recordings (e.g., Lamprecht et al., 2004). An exhaustive review was not undertaken, but below is a sampling of relevant studies.

Harper et al. (2009) published the results of qEEG (quantifiable EEG) after EMDR treatment of six subjects with PTSD. After one EMDR session, all participants reported significant reduction of PTSD symptoms. Analysis of qEEG suggests that the neural basis for EMDR is depotentiation of fear memory synapses in the amygdalae during evoked brain state similar to that of slow wave sleep. Results appear consistent with three other reports of brain stimulation during EMDR increasing naturally occurring low-frequency rhythm in memory centers of the brain. Levin et al. (1999) used a within-subject design on a 36-year-old male with complex PTSD from childhood abuse and witnessing severe domestic violence. Standardized symptom measures included CAPS, Hamilton-D, IES, Rorschach, and Single Photon Emission Computed Tomography (SPECT). After three EMDR sessions, significant reduction in self-report of PTSD and depression symptoms coincided with changes during post-treatment recall of the traumatic memory that were now associated with increased activation (as opposed to pre-treatment hypo-activation) of the anterior cingulate gyrus and left frontal lobe. Authors hypothesize the post-treatment hyper-activation in the cingulate and frontal cortex may enhance the ability to differentiate real from imagined threat.

Nardo et al. (2010) used Magnetic Resonance Imaging (MRI) comparisons of 21 subjects exposed to occupational trauma who developed PTSD and 22 subjects exposed to train-accident trauma but did not develop PTSD. In addition, a subset of 15 of the PTSD subjects received five EMDR treatment sessions, resulting in 10 treatment "responders" resulting in significant PTSD symptom reduction and 5 "non-responders" that evidenced little to no PTSD symptom change. Prior to EMDR, the PTSD subjects, compared to no-PTSD, exhibited significantly lower grey matter density in the left posterior cingulate and posterior parahippocampal cortex—which is functionally related to the hippocampus for consolidation and retrieval of declarative memory. After EMDR, the non-responders showed a significantly lower gray matter density as compared to positive EMDR responders, in bilateral posterior cingulate, as well as right amygdala, anterior insula, and anterior parahippocampal gyrus. Nardo et al. concluded that lower gray matter density in limbic and paralimbic cortices were found to be associated with PTSD diagnosis, trauma load, and EMDR treatment outcome, suggesting a view of PTSD as characterized by memory and dissociative disturbances. Lansing et al. (2005) reported using EMDR with six police officers involved with on-duty shootings and diagnosed with delayed-onset PTSD. Pre-and-post treatment changes were measured by standardized psychometric measures (e.g., PTSD Scale Score) and high-resolution SPECT (Single Photon Emission Computed Tomography) imaging. All six police officers self-reported significant symptom reduction that coincided with significant changes in brain functioning. For example, after successful EMDR treatment, SPECT scans revealed significant decreases in the left and right occipital lobe, left parietal lobe, and right precental frontal lobe as well as significant increased activation in the left inferior frontal gyrus. Authors concluded that EMDR appears to be an effective treatment for PTSD in police officers, showing both clinical and brain imaging changes.

Clinical note. The existing neuroimaging studies are promising and reveal visible, measurable neurological changes from EMDR treatment. However, consistent and accurate findings from neuroimaging research on PTSD and psychotherapy are still on the horizon. Case studies do not prove that any specific brain region is implicated in PTSD and after treatment like EMDR. That said, there is mounting evidence, from diverse sources, indicating that successful completion of EMDR therapy is resulting in functional and possibly structural changes in the brain that appear to signify a reversal, if not a "healing," of the dysfunctional brain changes that occur in PTSD. The ends may not be unique to EMDR therapy, but the means are (e.g., no intense repetitive exposure, cognitive disputation, coping-skill building homework, etc.). Also of particular relevance is Lansing et al.'s (2005) neuroimaging case study with six police officers diagnosed with PTSD after a shooting incident. Although no neuroimaging studies have been conducted yet with EMDR in military populations, there is obviously considerable overlap between paramilitary organizations like police departments and the occasional need to use deadly force.

Unfunded Research on EMDR Effectiveness in the Military

As alluded to in the previous chapter, military medicine has elected to *follow* versus lead when it comes to the matter of investigating every possible treatment option, including all identifiable "evidence-based" psychotherapies highly recommended by its own clinical practice guidelines since 2004. Moreover, ample small-and-large clinical case studies utilizing EMDR treatment with military personnel have been widely circulated within military medicine and published in peer-reviewed scientific journals, depicting clinically significant treatment effects along a spectrum of war stress injury (e.g., PTSD, depression, phantom limb, medically unexplained conditions) and across a range of actual operational (e.g., military field hospital) and military environments (e.g., military treatment facility). Simultaneously, numerous news media accounts of military practitioners using EMDR successfully in the field add further credence to EMDR's *effectiveness* within the United States military, as well as the armed forces of staunch allies like the United Kingdom and Germany.

Of critical importance is a National Institute of Mental Health (NIMH)-funded EMDR study, in which a blind, RCT-compared EMDR to placebo control and Prozac groups in treating adults with childhood-onset PTSD and adult-onset PTSD found EMDR superior to both conditions (van der Kolk et al., 2007). These findings have profound implications for military personnel averse to taking medication, or whose jobs are incompatible with the use of psychotropic medications (e.g., submariners, aviators, special forces, top-secret clearances, etc.), as well as service members experiencing adjustment difficulties upon entering the military due to a history of unresolved child abuse or other early traumatic experiences finding is informative. Other notable non-military-related EMDR research of relevance to the military includes at least five neuroimaging EMDR treatment case studies revealing functional pre-post brain changes, coinciding with self-reported symptom improvement. Consequently, arguments about the efficacy of EMDR therapy with non-combat-related trauma (e.g., sexual assault, accidents, terrorism, adverse childhood events, natural disasters, etc.) have been largely settled, leading to its wide-spread recognition as evidence-based treatment for non-combat-related trauma (e.g., DVA/DoD, 2010). This is of critical importance for clinicians working with military clientele, many of whom may either enter military duty with a personal history of traumatic experiences (e.g., childhood abuse) and/or encounter traumatic events during non-combat-related military service (e.g., training accidents, sexual assault, witnessing atrocities during peace-keeping missions, post-disaster relief). Getting back to EMDR efficacy research, any lingering controversy has now shifted away from disputes over efficacy to a debate over proving its hypothesized mechanism of action (e.g., role of lateral eye movements; see Russell, 2008a).

Bradley et al.'s (2005) meta-analysis on PTSD treatments reaffirmed EMDR's evidence-based status, but questioned the external validity of all so-called evidence-based treatments for deficient field testing of the *effectiveness* of these therapies in actuarial contexts, versus artificially controlled laboratory settings that regularly exclude clients with co-morbidity. This is a critical observation in light of PTSD research that routinely identifies high levels of co-morbidity (50–80%) with depression, substance abuse, and medically unexplained condition, to name just a few (e.g., DVA/DoD, 2010). As will be evident in the case-study research below, nearly every therapist is dealing with co-morbidity in their military clientele.

EMDR Treatment of Acute Stress and Trauma in the Military

Elan Shapiro (2009) reviewed civilian research on EMDR as an early intervention following terrorist attacks and natural disasters, revealing its potential efficacy within the military. We will examine evidence of EMDR's potential effectiveness as an early intervention for acute stress or acute traumatic stress within military populations across national lines.

United States Military

EMDR's potential effectiveness has been demonstrated at an U.S. Navy field hospital where four American service members were medically evacuated from the Iraq battlefield at the outset of the Iraqi invasion. Each of the military clients was referred to the author (Mark Russell) by medical staff, due to a high level of disturbance and medical instability, to be transported to a stateside treatment facility. Two military clients were diagnosed with combat-related Acute Stress Disorder (ASD), and two with acute combat PTSD. The first client was a 23-year-old, Marine Lance Corporal whose armored vehicle was hit by an IED, resulting in his witnessing the grotesque death of a close friend. The second client was a 22-year-old Marine Corporal with shrapnel wounds following an Iraqi ambush, the third client was a 25-year-old Army Specialist reporting traumatic grief and over the intentional killing of non-combatants who did not heed warnings to stop their vehicle at a military checkpoint, and the fourth client was a 32-year-old Army Staff Sergeant evacuated for shrapnel wounds reporting a traumatic memory of unearthing a mass gravesite. All four service members received a single session of modified EMDR that will be discussed in Chapter 10. Each military member reported significant pre-post symptom reduction on ASD/PTSD and depressive symptoms that was corroborated by ward staff and, at next-day follow-up before medical evacuation transport to Walter Reed Army Hospital. Due to high OPTEMPO, tracking of military clients was not possible. Therefore, it is unknown whether the intervention possibly prevented chronic war stress injury (Russell, 2006).

Anecdotal reports. Even closer to the battlefield has been the work of Navy Commander Beverly Dexter, who reported using EMDR with front-line troops suffering from combat-related stress reaction, while she was assigned to a Combat Stress Control unit in Iraq. Using three EMDR sessions on consecutive days, Dexter reported that military patients were able to return to their platoons and function normally. She found that EMDR provided immediate positive results (B. Dexter, personal communication, 2007).

United Kingdom Military

Wesson and Gould (2009) successfully treated a 27-year-old U.K. soldier at a frontline, combat stress control unit experiencing a debilitating acute stress reaction after assisting in a land mine casualty 2 weeks prior to being evaluated at the medical facility. After four EMDR sessions on 4 consecutive days, the soldier's acute stress reaction resolved and he was able to immediately return to full-duty status with his military unit. Significant pre- and post-treatment changes were reported, and sustained improvement at 18 months signifies EMDR's potential utility in the trenches.

Anecdotal reports. Head of Defence Clinical Psychology, Ministry of Defence, and former Vice Chair of the NATO Task Group on Stress and Psychological Support in Modern Military Operations J. Hacker-Hughes and Wesson (2008) presented a case study of a British Soldier who was suffering significant post-trauma symptoms while serving in Afghanistan. Two weeks after combat trauma, the military therapist used EMDR in the warzone that successfully resolved the incident. The soldier was returned to full duty and avoided the negative consequences often associated with separation from the military unit and medical evaluation back to the U.K.

Summary of Early Intervention Research with EMDR

Unfortunately, institutional military medicine's ban on EMDR research has prohibited funding of critically needed follow-on research to these case studies. As reviewed earlier, Silver et al.'s (2005) EMDR case study of 62 New York City victims of the terrorist attacks included an early intervention group that reported clinically significant improvement after four sessions on average. The author (Mark Russell) is also aware of further anecdotal reports of EMDR use in forward deployed settings, from various military clinicians trained in EMDR; however, none are documented. Nevertheless, although the total sample size of five military clients is not impressive, other published civilian studies on early intervention with EMDR as reviewed by Elan Shapiro (2009), along with EMDR's status as an established evidence-based treatment for post-traumatic stress, provides more than sufficient justification for EMDR utilization and research as treatment for acute stress injuries.

Treating Chronic War and Traumatic Stress Injuries in Military Settings

United States Military

The author (Mark Russell) received a referral from the hospital case manager for a 22-year-old Marine Corporal pending medical discharge, who was diagnosed with PTSD, depression, and severe phantom-limb pain and sensations following a traumatic leg amputation from a motor vehicle accident about four months previous. After five EMDR treatment sessions, there was clinically significant reduction of PTSD and depression symptom surveys, along with significant elimination of phantom-limb pain sensations with only mild, nonintrusive "tingling" sensations reported. At a 1-month follow-up, the client reported that PTSD and depression conditions had completely resolved with sustained phantom-limb symptom improvement (Russell, 2008b). Several other case studies on using EMDR with phantom-limb pain in the civilian sector have been published (e.g., de Roos & van Rood, 2009; Schneider, Hofmann, Rost, & Shapiro, 2007).

Using EMDR to treat co-morbid combat-related medically unexplained symptoms with military personnel has been reported. The first case involved a 40-year-old Marine Master Gunnery Sergeant in Explosive Ordnance Disposal (EOD), recently returned from a second combat tour in Iraq. Diagnosed with multiple medically unexplained symptoms (e.g., chronic fatigue, headaches, insomnia, constipation, back pain, etc.) and prominent "non-cardiac chest pain," the client was referred by the primary care physician for evaluation and treatment. Assessment revealed co-morbid PTSD with severity in the "severe" range and "moderate" depression. Multiple combat-related traumatic memories were identified, including traumatic grief over the death of a close friend. The client received five EMDR treatment sessions resulting in clinically significant pre-post changes on PTSD, depression, pain, and health ratings with symptom improvement maintained at 1-, 3-, and 6-months follow-up. The client's primary care physician corroborated the significant change in physical condition (Russell, 2008c).

The second case is that of a 73-year-old Vietnam War combat veteran who was seeking EMDR treatment at a military mental health outpatient clinic. He was diagnosed with PTSD, depression, and alcohol dependence after discharge from the Army in 1968, but the principle reason for discharge was due to severe, chronic medically unexplained "myoclonic" jerks that began during close hostilities during the TET Offensive. The client and family members reported excessive neck and upper-torso "shakes" at least 20 times daily at home and 50–60 times if out in social situations. The client has been treated in the DVA since his military discharge with a variety of medication and psychotherapy. Assessment identified PTSD in the "severe" range and depression at "moderate" levels. The client "jerked" constantly during interview of Vietnam experiences and immediate post-deployment adjustment. After two EMDR treatment sessions, the client's PTSD, depression, and myoclonic jerks revealed clinically significantly pre-post improvement on all symptom measures. The client's myoclonic jerks were reported to be resolved, even when the family tested the improvement by going into crowded social situations. Sustained symptom improvement was reported and corroborated at 6 months (Silver, Rogers, & Russell, 2008).

War Stress Injury in Wounded-in-Action Personnel and EMDR

A non-randomized retrospective medical record review was conducted resulting in 72 military clients treated with EMDR in military outpatient mental health clinics at different military installations. Eight separate military therapists participated in the review. Of the 72 cases reviewed, 48 service members were diagnosed with combat-related acute stress disorder (ASD) or combat-PTSD. Other clients were treated for non-combat-related PTSD or related diagnoses. Military client rank ranged from Private (E-1) to Marine Captain (0-3). Time since trauma ranged from 14 to 24 months. Number of

EMDR treatment sessions ranged from 1 to 14. Eight of the clients had been wounded-in-action. A total of 63 cases had both Impact of Events Scale (PTSD) and Beck Depression Inventory (depression), along with SUDS and VOC ratings. Results indicated statistically significant pre-post symptom improvement on average of four EMDR treatment sessions, if not wounded-in-action, and on average of eight EMDR sessions, if wounded-in-action. Limitations of the study were discussed, including lack of control group, follow-up data, and controls for other interventions (Russell, Silver, & Rogers, 2007). Another published case study was a 22-year-old soldier who served two combat tours in Iraq, recently discharged from the military following repeated hospitalizations after several suicide attempts. The client was transitioned to VA residential care. The precipitant stressor was a break-up with his fiancé. Traumatic combat memories were identified, including severe guilt over killing an Iraqi combatant. The client was diagnosed with moderate-to-severe PTSD and was administered four EMDR treatment sessions. Clinically significant pre-post PTSD symptom improvement was reported that was sustained at 3-month follow-up (Silver et al., 2008).

Iranian Military

Iranian clinicians reported that 51 military personnel were admitted to a hospital with the diagnosis of acute combat-related PTSD. Clients were randomly assigned to three groups, EMDR, and CBT, or a control group, to assess effectiveness as an early intervention to prevent chronic disability. Both EMDR and CBT were reported to be effective in reducing symptoms associated with disturbing memories, anxiety, depression, and anger; however, treatment changes from EMDR were reported to be superior then CBT. The Iranian doctors concluded by recommending EMDR and CBT be used to prevent and reduce symptoms of PTSD in war veterans (Narimani, Ahari, & Rajabi, 2010). In a second study, 45 Iranian war veterans diagnosed with combat-related PTSD were randomly assigned to EMDR, CBT, or a control group. Both EMDR and CBT treatment groups had statistically significant pre-post changes on the PTSD Checklist-Military and the Symptom Checklist 90-Revised, as compared to the control group (Ahmadizadeh, Eskandari, Falsafinejad, & Borjali, 2010).

Sri Lankan Military

A Sri Lankan military mental health clinician, using EMDR for treatment of 18 Sri Lankan military personnel diagnosed with combat-related PTSD, reported clinically significant pre-post changes were reported on symptom measures (Jayatunge, 2006). A second case study indicated that large hostile military operations were conducted in Sri Lanka, resulting in a significant number of Sri Lankan soldiers diagnosed with war stress injuries manifested as PTSD, depression, somatization, and other adjustment reactions. Jayatunge

(2011) stated that he and other Sri Lankan mental health clinicians received EMDR training in 2005. EMDR treatment of six Sri Lankan soldiers was described. Four of the soldiers were diagnosed with combat-PTSD, and two soldiers diagnosed with a depressive disorder. After 5 to 8 EMDR sessions, Jayatunge (2011) reported positive treatment effects for PTSD and depression symptoms, with most soldiers becoming symptom free.

Republic of Germany Military

At a military hospital inpatient setting, 40 German soldiers receiving EMDR therapy for non-combat-related PTSD were compared with 49 German soldiers diagnosed with non-combat-related PTSD and received group counseling and relaxation training, with greater improvement in the EMDR group. A total of 20 soldiers who received EMDR and 14 who received group and relaxation training were reevaluated after an average of 29 months. Results indicated that those treated with EMDR were significantly improved over the supportive treatment group even after 29 months (Zimmerman, Biesold, Barre, & Lanczik, 2007).

4 Why Use EMDR Therapy in the Armed Services?

An imminently more compelling and appropriate question is "Why *not* use EMDR in the Armed Services?" In this chapter we will examine the many unique advantages of EMDR within the warrior class, especially as compared to traditional talk therapy and medication approaches. Getting back to our opening question—"Why use EMDR?"—justification of EMDR training, research, and utilization with military personnel is readily available from the DVA and the DoD's own *Clinical Practice Guideline for the Management of Post-Traumatic Stress* (2004), which concluded that

- *Overall, argument can reasonably be made that there are sufficient controlled studies that have sufficient methodological integrity to judge EMDR as effective treatment for PTSD (p. 5);*
- *Foa et al. (1995) note that exposure therapy may not be appropriate for use with clients whose primary symptoms include guilt, anger, or shame (p. 4);*
- *EMDR may be more easily tolerated for patients who have difficulties engaging in prolonged exposure therapy (p. 2);*
- *EMDR processing is internal to the patient, who does not have to reveal the traumatic event (p. 1).*

In 2010, the VA/DoD updated *Clinical Practice Guideline* after another thorough review of PTSD treatment by its clinical experts from the Veterans Health Affairs (VHA) and DoD, and it was again concluded that

the evidence-based psychotherapeutic interventions for PTSD that are most strongly supported by RCTs can be considered broadly within the trauma-focused psychotherapy category or stress inoculation training. Trauma-focused psychotherapies for PTSD refer to a broad range of psychological interventions based on learning theory, cognitive theory, emotional processing theory, fear-conditioning models, and other theories. They include a variety of techniques most commonly involving exposure and/or cognitive restructuring (e.g., Prolonged Exposure, Cognitive Processing Therapy and Eye Movement Desensitization and Reprocessing). (p. 115)

As for the lingering controversy that EMDR does *not* work, the 2010 VA/ DoD guidelines state:

> EMDR possesses efficacy for treating patients with PTSD: this conclusion is based upon a thorough review of the literature in the treatment guidelines generated by a task force for the International Society for Traumatic Stress Studies (Spates et al., 2009) as well as by Division 12 of the American Psychological Association (APA) and a Cochrane review (Bisson, 2007). The United Kingdom's NICE Guidelines for PTSD (2005) also recommend EMDR as a treatment, supported by multiple efficacy studies. (p. 129)

What about nagging reservations about EMDR propagated by the Institute of Medicine's 2008 finding that EMDR is inferior to Cognitive Behavioral Therapy and Exposure Therapy? Well, the answer again is found within institutional military medicine's *Clinical Practice Guideline* (2010): "When compared to other treatment modalities, most studies reviewed indicated that EMDR possessed comparable efficacy to other well-accepted cognitive behavioral treatments to include stress inoculation training (SIT) and exposure therapies" (p. 129). Similarly, the American Psychiatric Association (APA) designated EMDR as an "evidence-based" treatment in its recently revised guideline (APA, 2009). Therefore any question about the efficacy of EMDR is really old news. Eight war years ago, back when the United States was in its third year of an ongoing 11-year Afghanistan/Iraq War, the domestic and international scientific community had long settled queries of EMDR's efficacy in treating traumatic stress injuries. For the record, here is a list of scientific expert PTSD panels investigating whether EMDR is an evidence-based treatment:

Clinical Practice Guidelines for PTSD: EMDR is Not Evidence-Based

1. Institute of Medicine. (2008). *Treatment of Posttraumatic Stress Disorder: An Assessment of the Evidence.* Washington, DC: National Academies Press.

Domestic PTSD Clinical Practice Guidelines: EMDR is Evidence-Based

1. American Psychiatric Association. (2004/2009). *Practice Guideline for the Treatment of Patients with Acute Stress Disorder and Post-Traumatic Stress Disorder.* Arlington, VA: American Psychiatric Associatios.
2. American Psychological Association (Division 12), Chambless, D. L., et al. (1998). Update of empirically validated therapies, II. *The Clinical Psychologist, 51,* 3–16.

3. VA/DoD. (2004/2010). *Clinical Practice Guideline for the Management of Post-Traumatic Stress.* Washington, DC: Veterans Health Administration, Department of Veterans Affairs and Health Affairs, Department of Defense. Office of Quality and Performance publication 10Q-CPG/PTSD-04/10.
4. International Society for Traumatic Stress Studies, Foa, E. B., Keane, T. M., Friedman, M. J., & Cohen, J. A. (2009). *Effective Treatments for PTSD: Practice Guidelines of the International Society for Traumatic Stress Studies.* New York: Guilford.
5. Substance Abuse and Mental Health Services Administration (SAMHSA). (2010). *Eye movement Desensitization and Reprocessing.* National Registry of Evidence-Based Programs and Practices, U.S. Department of Health and Human Services.
6. *Therapy Advisor.* (2004–2007). National Institute of Mental Health—sponsored website listing empirically supported methods: http://www.therapyadvisor.com

International PTSD Clinical Practice Guidelines: EMDR is Evidence-Based

1. Cochrane Database of Systematic Reviews, Bisson, J., & Andrew, M. (2007). Psychological treatment of post-traumatic stress disorder (PTSD). *Cochrane Database of Systematic Reviews, 3,* Art. No.: CD003388. doi:10.1002/14651858.CD003388.pub3
2. National Council for Mental Health, Bleich, A., Kotler, M., Kutz, L., & Shaley, A. (2002). *National Council for Mental Health: Guidelines for the Assessment and Professional Intervention with Terror Victims in the Hospital and in the Community.* Jerusalem, Israel: Author.
3. CREST. (2003). *The Management of Post-Traumatic Stress Disorder in Adults.* Clinical Resource Efficiency Support Team, Northern Ireland, Department of Health, Social Services, and Public Safety. Belfast, Ireland: Author.
4. Dutch National Steering Committee Guidelines Mental Health Care. (2003). *Multidisciplinary Guideline Anxiety Disorders. Quality Institute Health Care.* Utrecht, Netherlands: CBO/Trimbos Institute.
5. INSERM. (2004). *Psychotherapy: An Evaluation of Three Approaches.* Paris, France: French National Institute of Health and Medical Research.
6. National Institute for Clinical Excellence. (2005). *Post-Traumatic Stress Disorder (PTSD): The Management of Adults and Children in Primary and Secondary Care.* London: NICE Guidelines.
7. Stockholm: Medical Program Committee/Stockholm City Council, Sjöblom, P. O., Andréewitch, S., Bejerot, S., Mörtberg, E., Brinck, U., Ruck, C., & Körlin, D. (2003). *Regional Treatment Recommendation for Anxiety Disorders.* Stockholm: Author.

8. United Kingdom Department of Health. (2001). *Treatment Choice in Psychological Therapies and Counseling Evidence Based Clinical Practice Guideline.* London, England: Author.

POTENTIAL ADVANTAGES OF EMDR THERAPY WITH MILITARY PERSONNEL

The proceeding segment was adapted from our chapter on EMDR therapy with military personnel in Russell, Lipke, and Figley (2011). In regards to psychotherapies with military personnel, a premium is placed on practicality, flexibility, efficiency, rapidity, and effectiveness within a believable therapeutic framework that is respectful of warrior culture and ethos. To that end, EMDR therapy appears uniquely suited.

EMDR Is Practical for Military Populations

The first major distinction and clear advantage of EMDR, over other cognitive and behavioral approaches, is that EMDR does not require clients to comply with 40–60 hours of daily or weekly homework assignments (e.g., relaxation practice, listening to exposure sessions) to be effective. Teachers have a hard time getting students to comply with homework or practice assignments; whatever the name used, it's still an external demand that will regularly be resisted by military personnel, who have an awful lot on their plates. Re-listening to their taped trauma scripts or exposure-sessions can be highly problematic in military barracks, aboard ships, in tents, or other closed quarters where privacy is a luxury many don't have—particularly junior personnel.

EMDR Significantly Reduces Time Demands on Military Clients

The other impractical aspect of skill-based approaches that require high amounts of after-session practice is that military members are very often not the keepers of their time—again, especially in the lower ranks. Long work hours tend to be the norm; "chow" or "mess" hours (where members eat) have restrictive times; exercise ("PT") is common for many members; and most military personnel have collateral or extra duties to perform as well as after-hour security watches (e.g., barracks), or preparation for upcoming inspections, military class, etc. If married, the military member must also split time with his or her spouse and/or kids. So, the luxury of time in a fast-paced, intense environment like the military often places therapy-related homework on a back-burner. EMDR gets around this issue because there is no homework or assignment requirement. If therapists do elect to have the client complete or practice skill-building etc., that is not EMDR. Therapists are free to incorporate other methods as they see fit, but standard EMDR protocol has *no* homework requirement, and that is a major advantage over most CBT approaches.

Drop-Out Rates for Prolonged Exposure and Cognitive Processing Therapy

A pair of DVA studies examined treatment adherence (Erbes, Curry, & Leskela, 2009) and premature drop-out rates (Garcia, Kelly, Rentz, & Lee, 2011) of OEF/OIF veterans in outpatient treatment of PTSD with the two predominantly favored CBT in the DoD and DVA, Cognitive Processing Therapy (CPT) and Prolonged Exposure (PE). The researchers reported 68% of OEF/OIF veterans had prematurely terminated treatment (Garcia et al., 2011), and there were significantly lower rates of session attendance and twice the drop-out rate as compared to Vietnam veterans (Erbes et al., 2009). Similarly high drop-out rates (72%) for trauma-focused CBT that includes exposure therapy have been reported in naturalistic versus laboratory clinical settings (Zayfers et al., 2005). Researchers did not specify reasons for the high drop-out and premature termination rates and speculated over cohort effects when compared with Vietnam-era veterans. There is a high probability that the homework demands might have been a factor due to the inherent time and environmental constraints that military personnel routinely deal with on a daily basis.

EMDR Reduces Demand Characteristics

This is a different use of the term that normally refers to clients over-complying with the authority figure of the researcher/clinician and feeling pressure to conform to the therapist's expressed or unexpressed desire to see lower symptom scores after treatment. What we mean by demand characteristics is similar in terms of the client feeling pressure to please the therapist and comply with expectations such as homework. However, in military culture there is nothing implicit about compliance with authority; it's "you better do it, or pay the piper." Military personnel on a daily basis are exposed to chronic, inescapable stressors related to demands for compliance by authority figures, with the "or else" always hanging over their heads. So, when military members leave their work centers and enter into the sanctity of the therapist's office, the last thing most of these folks want to hear is another set of demands from an authority figure, no matter how Socratic, collaborative, and reasonable the requests are, and it is understandable that, rather than get into an awkward, or stressful confrontation with the therapist over their non-compliance, they will bolt. Deciding to attend psychotherapy or not is one of those few aspects in military life in which some of members can exert control—especially junior ranking personnel. Again, EMDR completely skirts around this issue. The only work required is in the therapists' office, and the rest of the time is "theirs." And those readers who have worn the uniform know just how precious that feeling is to have any time that is your time.

Cost-Effectiveness: Virtual Reality Therapy and EMDR

Virtual Reality Therapy (VRT) is simply very cool and intriguing. It utilizes a head-mounted display (over the eyes video glasses) where the client either rides or drives in a simulated convoy with a dummy M-4 rifle and a mounted game controller. The therapist or operator can manipulate the multisensory connection by programming different scenarios including changing weather patterns, terrain, types of attacks, and every imaginable sight, sound, and vibration in a 360-degree interactive computer-generated environment that can be matched to the client's particular traumatic experience. Pretty amazing! According to Dr. Greg Reger, the DoD's Chief, T2 Innovative Technology Applications Division, "This treatment is repeated by the patient over and over again, until the stress is reduced, and is more effective than 'imaginal' exposure (used in PE and CPT) which is less effective for combat trauma than other types of trauma" (Smith, 2010).

Here is the rub. A single virtual reality helmet costs $20,000, software $12,000, and each detail added to the software costs $5,000 (Marshall, 2003). The helmet is as sophisticated as a flight simulator, extremely cool and possibly quite effective for warriors with PTSD, if they can tolerate the multisensory exposure. However, the cost alone is steep, even for the DoD. Clinical trials are underway in the military at select sites that have the infrastructure to support it. From a practical standpoint, recruiting and retaining reliable IT personnel trained to maintain and repair software and hardware glitches will keep this technology in major training hospitals, but roll-out beyond that is extremely unlikely. In comparison with EMDR, one can get the same desensitization effects and the added bonus of intentionally accessing and strengthening the client's associations to their own reality-based adaptive neural networks—all for no additional cost. No IT support required. No backlog of clients waiting their turn in the chair. No disruption in therapy "when" there's a glitch. All that's required is a therapist with one good hand. Or, if opting for high-tech EMDR, the therapist can use the Neurotek lights, sounds, and/or vibrations for less cost than the addition of a single detail into the VRT software. Moreover, EMDR can be transported in any "real" environment including operational settings like Combat Stress Control units or Field hospitals whereas VRT is pretty much limited to amazing those who can travel to wherever the local VRT is. Additionally:

- EMDR requires no mass reproduction or purchase of CBT workbooks, homework sheets, and daily self-rating forms; and its
- Potential for rapid therapeutic gains in fewer sessions can reduce down-time.

EMDR OFFERS FLEXIBILITY FOR MILITARY POPULATIONS

EMDR has been shown to be extremely transportable across operational and routine military treatment settings per clinical reports published in peer-reviewed journals including: combat stress control units, aboard naval vessels, field or evacuation hospitals, military outpatient clinics, and military treatment facility inpatient wards.

Flexibility in the Amount of Exposure and Self-Disclosure

One oft-cited drawback of exposure-based therapies is requiring the client to repetitively revisit traumatic experiences without escape, and many clients have difficulty tolerating the intensity of the exposure and therefore are more likely to drop-out or prematurely terminate. EMDR, on the other hand, requires a fleeting amount of exposure (<1 minute), and from there the therapist is following the client's lead in terms of adding BLS to free associations. This gives clients a greater sense of control and flexibility as opposed to a therapist redirecting the client repetitively back to the traumatic scene. Clients also have the greatest amount of flexibility in terms of the amount of self-disclosure in EMDR, more than any other psychotherapy.

Potential to Decrease Compassion Stress and Fatigue

The therapist needs only minimal information from the client about whether some aspect of the memory is changing, or shifting to another memory. The extent of detail shared is entirely up to the client, thus avoiding the compulsory vivid retelling of the client's trauma narrative that will potentially decrease exposure to compassion stress and possible fatigue or burnout.

Flexibility in Treatment Options

To be effective, nearly all evidence-based psychotherapies require the therapist to implement treatment manuals that provide a structured therapy agenda for each session, list required content for practice sessions, and other ins-and-outs of session activities. The EMDR treatment plan identifies a few "target memories" and incorporates dual focused attention and bilateral stimulation (BLS) and then follows the client's free associations. Each session essentially consists of the same or similar activities by the therapist and client. At the end of certain phases, there is a protocol that the therapist follows (e.g., Phase Six: Body Scan) when the previous phase has been completed; however, the sequencing and content remain remarkably consistent from the therapist's perspective. In other words, therapists have considerable flexibility with EMDR and are not wedded to following an explicit agenda each session as with other treatments.

In addition, EMDR can be adapted to a range of referral questions including symptom or client stabilization, primary symptom reduction, comprehensive treatment, resilience and performance enhancement, and intervention for preventing accumulation of compassion stress (see Chapter 5). Furthermore, EMDR has the flexibility to be adapted to match time and environment constraints. For example, clients on the frontlines or wanting only symptom reduction due to time limitations may receive EMD or a modified EMDR that does not utilize free associations to earlier life events (e.g., pre-military trauma). Other evidence-based protocols would have greater difficulty adapting for uses outside parameters of routine clinic schedules and completion of certain proportions of the manualized treatment content. Not so with EMDR. Again, the only manualized content in EMDR is the protocol itself.

EMDR OFFERS GREATER EFFICIENCY FOR TREATING COMORBIDITY

According to the DVA/DoD (2010) *Clinical Practice Guideline,* "PTSD and co-morbid mental health conditions should be treated concurrently for all conditions through an integrated treatment approach, which considers patient preferences, provider experience, severity of the conditions, and the availability of resources" (p. 86). Clients with PTSD have been found to frequently report physical symptoms, cognitive health concerns, and utilize high levels of medical care services. Providers should expect that 50–80% of patients with PTSD will have one or more coexisting mental health disorders; 10–20% TBI; and 40–50% substance use. PTSD is strongly associated, among veterans from recent deployment (OEF/OIF), with generalized physical and cognitive health symptoms attributed to concussion/mild traumatic brain injury (mTBI). Comprehensive treatment of war/traumatic stress injuries extends well beyond ASD/ PTSD diagnoses, including diverse *DSM* diagnosis (e.g., depression), and medically unexplained symptoms (e.g., chronic pain). In addition, high rates of PTSD and co-morbidity (e.g., mood disorder) are prevalent in wounded service members (e.g., Russell, Shoquist, & Chambers, 2005).

Efficiency and Cost Effectiveness of a Single Treatment Protocol

The traditional approach to treating co-morbidity is to add treatment types or protocols for each neuropsychiatric diagnosis or medically unexplained condition or particular symptom. For example, in PTSD treatment with Prolonged Exposure, a referral or additional sessions would be required with the therapist for treating the client's traumatic grief reaction, another to a chronic pain clinic for a pain-related syndrome, etc. This piecemeal approach adds significant treatment time, costs, and downtime for the client, and it is highly inefficient. Although no panacea for any and all conditions, there is a vast amount of treatment literature with EMDR being successfully applied to treat a wide range of co-morbidities simultaneously. The rationale that is the EMDR targets the experiential contributors for disturbance and pathology. The information in maladaptive neural networks can manifest along the spectrum of stress and traumatic stress injuries. So, while EMDR is not directly treating pain, it is attempting to help the reprocess of the past events that are maintaining or exacerbating the pain, depression, grief, etc. That said, reports of using EMDR to "simultaneously" treat military patients— including those wounded-in-action and diagnosed with ASD/PTSD and depression (e.g., Russell et al., 2007); a Marine with PTSD, depression, and phantom-limb pain (Russell, 2008b); a solider with PTSD, depression; suicidal ideation (Silver et al., 2008); and a Marine with PTSD and atypical cardiac pain (Russell, 2008c)—illustrate its comprehensive capacity. Moreover, published accounts of EMDR's effectiveness as an acute trauma intervention both within (e.g., Wesson & Gould, 2009) and outside (e.g., Shapiro, 2009) military circles suggest therapeutic efficiency.

Pre-military history of childhood trauma. Lastly, a high prevalence of childhood traumatic events and military sexual trauma has been reported within the military population with 28% childhood physical abuse, 10% sexual abuse, and 19% victims of physical assault prior to entering military service. For example, Howard and Cox (2005) reported successfully treating a Navy recruit during boot camp for a "water phobia" associated with pre-military trauma. In addition, veteran's PTSD research has implicated early trauma exposure as risk factors for adult-onset PTSD. In terms of efficiency, EMDR has been identified as evidence-based PTSD treatment for childhood trauma and sexual assault as reaffirmed by a blind, randomized controlled trial (RCT) with placebo comparison of EMDR and Prozac (van der Kolk et al., 2007), the psychopharmacological "treatment of choice" that many service members are reluctant to take for career-related concerns. As opposed to already over-stretched clinicians having to learn multiple CBT or alternative protocols to effectively treat common co-morbidities found in traumatized patients, whether acute or chronic, early childhood- or adult-onset, EMDR presents a single, modifiable platform delivering comprehensive treatment.

EMDR OFFERS A POTENTIALLY RAPID TREATMENT COURSE

While the literature is mixed on the comparative rapidity in change found with EMDR and other evidence-based approaches, there is ample evidence that, for some clients, even those with significant disturbance and co-morbidity (e.g., phantom limb, PTSD, depression), the EMDR treatment effect can be exceptionally quick and pronounced. For instance, each of the case studies we have presented in this book was conducted in less than eight sessions. In one large, non-randomized study, a total of 63 military clients, 48 with combat-related ASD/PTSD, revealed clinically and statistically significant treatment changes on an average of 4 EMDR reprocessing sessions and 8 sessions if they had been wounded-in-action (Russell et al., 2007). In a highly mobile, time-sensitive, and often restrictive treatment environment like the military, there is an inherent need for brief interventions that produce rapid, enduring outcomes (Russell et al., 2011). As noted in the DVA/DoD *Clinical Practice Guidelines* (2004, p. 127), "the possibility of obtaining significant clinical improvements in PTSD in a few sessions presents this treatment (EMDR) method as an attractive modality worthy of consideration." Although the VA/DoD (2010) traumatic stress guidelines have backed away from their previous claim, the prospect of short treatment duration is still very much in the range of possibility. For instance, the author (Mark Russell) has used EMDR extensively in the military but can think of only a handful of cases that required 12 sessions, which is the standard treatment duration for evidenced-based trauma-focused approaches—including standard EMDR protocol. Shapiro (2001) adopted the 12-session limit for multiple-trauma PTSD because of Carlson et al.'s (1998) study with Vietnam War veterans with combat-PTSD. However, there is a major difference between treating military and veteran populations, many of whom have chronic war stress injuries lasting decades.

Benefit to the Military Client and Armed Services

It is certainly possible to get rapid treatment effects with other evidence-based therapies like prolonged exposure and cognitive processing therapy, or other approaches. However, with EMDR in the military, it tends to be the norm (e.g., Russell et al., 2007), and the outlier would be the 12-session standard in manualized treatments. That said, what are the potential advantages for military clients? Significant—both in terms of reduced suffering and less "down-time" that could impact their "military readiness" and "fitness for duty." Moreover, if EMDR can deliver significant reduction in symptoms in a brief period of time, without requiring extensive self-disclosure like standard talk therapies, or compliance with extra time demands outside of session, a barrier for seeking mental health care may be penetrated for the Armed Services. We won't know, of course, until research can be conducted, but the potential for a shorter treatment course can serve to increase unit readiness, reduce attrition and replacement costs, and possible reduce unnecessary military separation and discharges due to untreated war stress injury. So, the potential gain for the military can be enormous and, for the individual military client and their family, may short-circuit problems from escalating.

Consecutive Sessions

Lastly, published clinical reports from military clinicians indicate significant symptom improvement after a single EMDR session (e.g., Russell, 2006), four consecutive sessions (Wesson & Gould, 2009), and anecdotal reports of 14 consecutive EMDR sessions at the Soldier Center (Elisha C. Hurly, personal communication, February 4, 2012) reduced suffering and loss-time.

Potential to Reduce Drop-Out and Premature Termination

It stands to reason that clients who see positive changes early or quickly, are more likely to stay and complete treatment than those that do not. Therefore, the potential advantages to the service member, their command, and the Armed Forces would logically be apparent if personnel get their stress injuries healed and avoid allowing wounds to fester and eventually debilitate.

Integration into Primary Care and EMDR

Military medicine, as is civilian medicine, is moving in the direction of integrating mental health services into primary care to provide a more timely, cost-effective, and less stigmatizing treatment experience. EMDR offers an effective treatment option for rapid, brief interventions in the primary care setting focusing not only of reduction of primary symptoms, but it can be adopted to enhances the client's access to adaptive resources and resilience (see Chapter 16, this volume). The "neuropsychological" frame and limited need for self-disclosure of EMDR therapy as "this is not your grandmother's talk therapy" has appeal to military clientele.

EMDR IS HIGHLY COST EFFECTIVE

In an age of budget deficits, cut-backs, and "do more with less" mentality, the Armed Forces can ill-afford to allow high attrition and replacement costs associated with untreated or undertreated war stress injuries. Similarly, new dazzling technologies like Virtual Reality Therapy, while truly impressive, will not be available for the majority of military personnel spread across the globe. A long treatment course for clients with multiple conditions or comorbidity negative impacts the military client and their unit's "military readiness" as well as drives up the cost of health care associated with multiple referrals to specialists.

Reduce Attrition, Replacement, and Disability Compensation Costs

Cost savings from decreasing time spent in limited or non-full-duty status is apparent, but so is the propensity to prevent attrition due to administrative separation for untreated pre-military or military-related trauma under the diagnostic label of "personality disorder." The possibility of effectively treating war stress injuries like PTSD while members are still on active-duty might reduce the need for medical discharge and long-term disability compensation, as well as replacement costs (see Howard & Cox, 2005).

CREDIBILITY OF EMDR'S NEUROPSYCHOLOGICAL THERAPEUTIC FRAME

EMDR's theory lends itself to neuro-scientifically framed, credible explanations including the role of attention, hemispheric lateralization, neural associative networks, REM sleep, and emotional processing in PTSD, along with tacit support of seven EMDR neuroimaging case studies revealing pre-post functional lateralized brain changes coinciding with significant changes in patient PTSD symptom self-report (Russell et al., 2011). As opposed to other evidence-based treatments and standard talk therapy, EMDR therapy involves the client tracking alternating lights, sounds, and/or kinesthetic vibrating sensations that, on one hand, are "weird" but mostly in a positive and intriguing way. Military clients, especially senior enlisted and officer leaders, often express a strong displeasure for standard "talk therapy." Conversely, they are curious and intrigued by this EMDR, its limited demands for client self-disclosure, and emphasis that the client remains in control as reinforced by the DVA/DoD (2004) guidelines that "EMDR processing is internal to the patient, who does not have to reveal the traumatic event" (p. 1). The presence of a Neurotek device that generates the visual stimulus, sounds, and/or vibrations is unique to EMDR, and adds a neuroscience frame, as does showing clients some of the neuroimaging before and after treatment pictures that are available on the web (i.e., Lansing et al., 2005). In sum, the unique features of EMDR (e.g., bilateral stimulation), while "odd" or "weird" to many, nevertheless have definite appear among military populations in comparison to mainstream talk therapy.

EMDR Credibility among Practitioners

Clinician knowledge and belief of treatment model and efficacy, regardless of theory, can influence client expectations and outcome (Russell et al., 2011). Survey of EMDR-trained DVA clinicians revealed that 74% reported EMDR as having more beneficial treatment effects than other methods, whereas only 4% indicated less (e.g., Lipke, 1995, cited in Russell et al., 2011). A randomized controlled trial regarding 225 trauma experts and their preference to use a particular trauma-focused treatment showed that clinicians rated EMDR as significantly more credible than supportive counseling or exposure therapy (van Minnen, Hendriks, & Olff, 2010). Additionally, the researchers reported that exposure therapy was rarely used in actual clinical settings, especially in cases that involved either multiple traumas or childhood traumatic events.

EMDR OFFERS COMPATIBILITY WITH MILITARY CULTURE

Perhaps the most important aspect of EMDR is that it comports or aligns very well with military culture and time demands for many of the reasons previously stated—it is practical, flexible, cost-effective; provides potentially rapid symptom relief, resulting in shorter down times; requires no added time demands (e.g., 40–60 hours of homework as in CBT); the emphasis is on client control over the amount of exposure to traumatic events; there is limited need for self-disclosure; the non-intrusive therapist uses a neuroscientific frame versus standard talk therapy; increases the potential to reduce dropout and premature termination; increases the potential to reduce attrition and replacement costs; offers the ability to treat co-morbidity during a single treatment course; has the potential to avoid the need for psychotropic medications, etc.—all represent legitimate issues in military culture that maintain mental health stigma and barriers to care. Again, not a panacea, but EMDR is squarely more in line with military culture and its realities than any other available psychotherapy. Other compatibility factors with military culture include:

- Explicitly assigning locus of control to military clients that can enhance a sense of safety, trust, and rapport;
- Reduce common fears associated with mental health care, which are prevalent in military culture, and run counter to warrior ethos, including coercion to self-reveal, display weakness, or admit vulnerability;
- Respecting client autonomy versus therapist control over the therapeutic process to the degree seen in EMDR.

Other Potential Benefits of EMDR Therapy in the Military

- Early intervention and possible prevention of misconduct stress behaviors (see Introduction, this volume);
- May promote resiliency and post-traumatic growth by reprocessing dysfunctional schema;
- Increase military readiness by increasing cognitive capacity in service members to reprocess dysfunctional COSR;
- Reduce military separation/discharge rates, attrition, and replacement costs;
- Prevent medical evacuations and increase return to duty rates.

The EMDR Protocol for Military Populations

5 Phase One: Client History, Rapport, and Treatment Planning

The first of eight phases in EMDR therapy is by far the most critical. In working with military clients, there are many prominent considerations that the provider must remain cognizant of that we will describe below. In many respects, the successful negotiation of Phase One will make or break treatment. Phase One involves establishing trust and rapport while obtaining a comprehensive client history that is comprised of the standard clinical intake and discussing the all-too-important limits of confidentiality, which is especially meaningful for military populations, as well as screening for suitability of EMDR and developing a treatment plan by identifying past, present, and future experiential contributors of the client's current symptoms. However, before focusing on EMDR suitability and case formulation, practitioners will likely want to prepare themselves for working with military clients.

THERAPIST PREPARATION FOR WORKING WITH MILITARY CLIENTELE

Stepping into the therapeutic setting is likely to be experienced by a majority of military personnel as part of a deployment to a threat-rich foreign land. Here are some ways that practitioners can build some credibility and trust in preparation for working with military clients:

- Develop an understanding of issues related to the entire deployment cycle, as well as experiences and exposures that America's most recent combat veterans have undergone in an effort to recognize the connection between certain health effects and military service;
- Become familiar with and anticipate common military stressors and occupational hazards associated with the warrior class other than war and combat;
- Become familiar with military culture, including military ranks and the difference between Active, National Guard, and Reserve components (see http://www.defenselink.mil/specials/insignias/);

- Understand ethical and legal considerations specific to military personnel, particularly around limits of confidentiality and mandated reporting;
- Be acquainted with the nuances of military culture and values, including norms of high standards of self-discipline, the warrior ethos of loyalty and self-sacrifice, military customs and etiquette, the emphasis on group cohesion and esprit de corps that connects service members to each other, and mental health mistrust, stigma, and barriers to care;
- Compile a resource listing with contact information for crisis management options with uniformed personnel in particular, as well as referral information for base or clinic hospital emergency department, pastoral care, substance abuse treatment, family counseling and support centers, sexual assault prevention and program coordinator, family advocacy programs, and warrior transition services offered at nearby military installations;
- Review treatment resources that are available in the DoD, including eligibility criteria to join the TRICARE provider network (see www.tricare.mil);
- Develop partnerships with medical, mental health, and other support staff at nearby military installations, especially Family Readiness Groups and Warrior Transition programs (see www.nationalresource-directory.org);
- Learn about the spectrum of war stress injuries, including TBI;
- Become knowledgeable of the Accelerated Informational Processing (AIP) model underlying EMDR therapy and how it relates to the full spectrum of war stress injuries (see Shapiro, 2001), including medically unexplained conditions (see Chapter 9, this volume);
- Obtain copies of free brochures and fact sheets available on the websites of VA National Center for PTSD (see www.ncptsd.gov), Center for Deployment Psychology (www.cdp.mil), and the DoD's Centers of Excellence for Psychological Health and Traumatic Brain Injury (see www.dcoe.health.mil), which provide critical updates and resources for both the healer and warrior classes;
- Complete the No-Cost, National Center of PTSD "PTSD 101" Web-Based Course. This DVA course is also open to any non-VA or DoD practitioners and awards 10 CE (see www.ncptsd.va.gov).

Establishing a Client-Centered Therapeutic Alliance in Military Culture

It is paramount that the therapist's initial focus is squarely on building rapport and a trusting relationship with the military member. In doing so, the practitioner should adopt a client-centered perspective—the natural therapeutic stance in EMDR—by taking time to learn what the client's concerns, needs, and goals are and by offering practical solutions when appropriate. **Clinical Skills that Enhance Therapeutic Alliance**: (a) accurate empathy; (b) demonstrating that (c) the therapist cares about the client; (d) genuine, honest, and respectful demeanor; (e) communicating a clear case conceptualization that makes sense to the client; (f) pacing of interventions to client readiness; (g) cultural sensitivity and appropriateness; (h) willingness and ability to repair client experience of mis-attunement; and (i) at a minimum, the need to assure sufficient alliance to be confident of current and accurate reporting of client symptoms and treatment response.

THE FIRST MEETING AND CLINICAL INTAKE

The first meeting with military clients typically involves a number of standard clinical practices, some of which should be universal, and others determined by the therapist's background and reason for referral. Such issues as client–therapist introductions, reviewing the reason for referral, informed consent of the limits of confidentiality, completion of standard clinical intake forms, and clinical interviewing and mental status exams are fairly routine across mental health care settings.

Client–Therapist Introduction

Generally speaking, it would be an accurate assumption and worth anticipating that many but not all military clients will present to a mental health appointment as quite anxious, ambivalent, tense, skeptical, frustrated, mistrustful, defensive, and, at times, even antagonistic. They may also be quite respectful, pleasant, at-ease, soft-spoken, and enthusiastic, but still with a level of mistrust. The military client's comfort level and degree of openness to the clinical interview will be influenced by the reason for referral, as well as the possible ramifications of evaluation and treatment services in the context of critical issues like confidentiality and career implications. Needless to say, the clinician should strive to reassure the client of confidentiality and begin to establish trust as early as possible. The clinician will want to inquire whether or not this is the service member's first-ever contact with a mental health provider, as in many cases it will be, and the client's knowledge of therapy may be limited to popular stereotypes. For example, in some military circles, mental health providers are called "wizards," not so much due to their magical curative abilities but to the notion that they can make service members "disappear" from military service by virtue of their diagnostic conclusions. This is an unnerving proposition for any career-minded service member.

REFERRAL QUESTION AND INITIAL TIMING CONSIDERATIONS FOR EMDR

The most clinically salient and important issues to clarify for treatment planning purposes are the reason for referral, limits of confidentiality, therapist role expectations, and desired outcomes. The reason for referral provides the therapist critical information regarding who is concerned about the client's behavior, ethical implications in regards to confidentiality and potential ramifications for the client, and what is the expected outcome of the referral. In addition, the referral question offers essential information in regards to identifying potential timing issues related to determining the suitability for EMDR treatment in general, or the need to incorporate modifications of the standard EMDR protocol in the treatment plan. For instance, if the client and therapist are forward-deployed and the referral is for symptom reduction or stabilization, or the client is about to deploy or PCS transfer in three weeks, or the client is asking for performance enhancing strategies to perform well on an upcoming deployment, or the JAG officer informs you the client will be testifying about a military sexual trauma they experienced—all of these scenarios depict common timing considerations for developing a treatment plan that we will get back to later.

Informed Consent and Limits of Confidentiality

Immediately after introductions, the practitioner should next inform all military clientele, including their family members, of the limits of confidentiality and solicit the client's understanding for the reason and expected outcome of the referral, if it originated outside of the client(s). To establish trust and avoid the appearance of collusion, the therapist should openly acknowledge receiving the referral and/or speaking to specific referral sources about the client. In the military, limitations of client privacy and confidentiality of therapy records are very much similar in the civilian sector. For example, adherence to HIPAA and legal mandates for disclosure to prevent imminent harm to self, others, or gross incapacitation apply with military populations; however, for military personnel there are other unique ethical and legal quandaries that often emerge. Regardless, the practitioner must provide military clients full disclosure of the limitations of confidential in regards to any assessment or treatment services.

Earning the Trust of Military Clients

It cannot be stressed enough how critically important it is for therapists to be knowledgeable and able to accurately communicate to military clientele issues around the referral question, limits of confidentiality, and access to evaluation and treatment records. An unprepared therapist who cannot adequately articulate confidentiality limitations and how external requests for information will be handled, will almost certainly be perceived as a threat by military personnel, and should not be trusted. Many service members with war-stress injury have experienced relationship difficulties after exposure to trauma. They often report that they have problems trusting, are suspicious of authority, dislike even minor annoyances, and generally want to be left alone. They also usually have not slept well, are fatigued, and generally do not feel healthy or that they have any control of their mind and body. Since the therapist–client alliance depends on the establishment of trust, respect, and openness, and since subsequently the relationship often is developed in a hectic clinical setting, the therapist might encounter a client to be withholding, negativistic, irritable, or even hostile at the initial meeting. The client may seem to have "an attitude," or "Axis II" co-morbidity. As a result, many combat veterans feel misunderstood or misdiagnosed by otherwise competent professionals. The following is adapted from the DVA/DoD (2010) guidelines regarding establishing therapeutic alliance with military clientele:

- Adopt a stance of caring and concerned involvement that takes what the client says at face value and doesn't judge or label this type of behavior;
- Try to avoid withdrawing into an "objective," "professional" role;
- Relate honestly and openly is more likely to have a client who is willing to relate to him/her as a fellow human being and an effective partner in treatment;
- Develop a general understanding of what has happened to the veteran is critical in this process of developing a therapeutic relationship;
- Read some basic material on the experience of combat and watch documentaries of the same;
- Develop an understanding that wartime and military service involves some of the most intense human experiences and that those feelings of profound rage, fear, and grief can be an expected part of these experiences;
- These feelings will be present in the interview setting and must be met with respect and compassion;
- Be careful not to assume an understanding of the military experience if they have not themselves served in the military;
- Do not hesitate to ask questions when not understanding something about the military that the client is referring to.

Importance of Confidentiality in the Military Population

It is imperative that the therapist understand the stark differences in terms of how confidentiality is managed with military personnel, their family members, and civilian DoD personnel. Moreover, clinicians should be well grounded as to how military client confidentiality concerns relate to mental health stigma and barriers of care. In short, there are many instances where military commands have a "need to know" and therefore have access to military personnel medical records to fulfill their responsibility and duty to protect the welfare of their unit members and the military mission. In addition, many military specialties require medical (psychiatric) certification of "fitness for duty" to carry out their assigned duties, and it again falls on the back of the individual's CO or Commander to ensure that their personnel of "fit for full duty." Consequently, there is tremendous pressure on military members and leaders to ensure "military readiness," another way of saying "fitness for duty." Having a major psychological diagnosis other than maybe an Adjustment Disorder or non-clinical problems of living or *DSM* "V-code" (e.g., occupational problem, partner-relational problem) is in many cases considered outright disqualifying for certain military duties regardless of degree of severity (e.g., mild), such as: (a) carrying a firearm (deployed personnel, military police, security personnel, etc.); (b) piloting an aircraft (helicopter or fixed-wing); and (c) maintaining top-secret and above security clearance.

Being diagnosed and/or treated for any major psychological condition, especially if there is evidence of modest to severe functional impairment and/or strong likelihood of relapse or exacerbation of symptoms in an operational environment, can result in "unfitness" and ineligibility for: (a) deployment to warzone; (b) deployment to patrol zones; (c) military training exercises; (d) operation of military motor or armored vehicles; (e) handling ordnance; (f) permanent change of station transfer, particularly overseas duty stations; (g) accessibility to sensitive or classified information; (h) independent military assignments; and (i) military recruiter, drill instructor, or embassy guard assignments.

Military Career Ramifications, Stigma, and Barriers to Seeking Mental Health

Therapists should understand that when military members are found "unfit" for full duty and restricted from performing either one's basic assigned duties (e.g., an EOD specialist who cannot be around ordnance) to deploy, train, or accept orders to future prohibitive assignments, for any reason (medical/mental health), the concern is that their "down-time" will translate to lower annual job performance evaluations (or Fitness Reports) when compared to peers without such limitations. Every year military personnel are ranked by their Commanding Officer/Commander (Army) along various desirable traits (e.g., leadership, mission accomplishment, military bearing, etc.). These evaluations also include the relative of ranking of the service member in terms of promotion recommendations. Being found "unfit for duty" typically will mean lower performance marks compared to their peers that can have a dramatic impact on career promotions and possibly prevent military retirement. This feeds the realistic fear of stigma and presents a barrier to seeking care that may or may not be justified. Military members can be determined unfit for duty for short periods to receive treatment (called "Limited Duty Board"), which may not have any impact on the annual evaluations as long as they are performing well at their jobs and not missing deployment.

Moreover, most service members diagnosed and treated for a mental health condition are not formally placed on a Limited Duty Status, and, as long as they don't have a sensitive job as described above (e.g., pilot), their mental health treatment will not likely impact them in any manner. Still the fears will be there, and the therapist should discuss them with the client. We will give an example later.

Therapist Considerations of Managing Confidentiality within Military Populations

The following are some considerations on managing confidentiality with military clients: (a) Conduct informed consent and limits of confidentiality before starting the clinical interview or other data gathering. (b) Clarify referral questions and disposition—Who will have access to the evaluation and/or treatment records? (c) Will the client's Commanding Officer or Commander (Army) have access to the treatment records? Discuss "need to know." (d) In most cases, non-DoD civilians are not obligated to disclose information to the client's Commander or senior enlisted personnel—if in doubt, contact the therapist's civilian legal consultant, or the base Legal Services Office before divulging client information. (e) How will the therapist handle a request for records from members of the client's command? (f) How should the therapist get in touch with the client? Will the therapist be calling the client's work center? If so, how will the therapist introduce themselves when asked by military personnel other than the client? (g) Military etiquette requires the answerer to ask the phone caller their name, agency, call-back number, and purpose of call. (h) Be careful *not* to introduce yourself as "Dr." when calling the client's work center or give other information that imply a mental health provider is calling the client's military work center.

A Leap of Faith

By addressing the confidentiality issues honestly, straightforward, and knowledgeably with all military clients, many will feel reassured and proceed, but nearly all will do so as a "leap of faith" knowing that there is always a real possibility that their mental health condition and psychological "fitness of duty" may become future issues that threatened their military career and livelihood. It is a testament to the degree of "trustworthiness" that a therapist has earned, along with their perceived credibility and competence, that allow most military personnel to risk so much, and take a leap of faith.

GENERAL STRATEGIES FOR INTERVIEWING MILITARY PERSONNEL

The following are some general strategies for interviewing military clients: (a) Try to "pluck" key words or phrases from the client's narrative. Key words may be metaphors, or words reflecting feelings. Repeat back to the client with same affective tone (Meichenbaum, 1994). (b) Don't ask in the first meeting if they have killed. (c) Don't ask for a lot of detail about traumatic stressors during the initial history taking. (d) Normalize the client's experience by reframing symptoms as signs of adaptive coping and self-protection in a warzone (e.g., hypervigilance as being on heightened alert to protect others). (e) Do not hesitate to ask military clients to define the many acronyms they use. (f) Be specific and clear and limit the number of words per sentence. Use down-to-earth, non-technical language, without jargon. (g) Be careful about the timing of information and try to avoid overloading. (h) When possible, explain to clients the rationale for the treatment regimen, the specific client behaviors required, and possible expected outcomes. (i) Avoid embellishing the client's traumatic experience by using their words. (j) Repeat important information when feasible. (k) Use concrete examples and illustrations that heighten personal relevance of the material.

Imparting a Sense of Control for Military Clients

We have spoken at length about the important need for control or self-agency within military populations and, conversely, how seeking mental healthcare can engender the opposite effect on service members. To reduce the threat load some military personnel may be experiencing, the therapist should aim to give the client a measure of control. However, there should be a balance. Therapists who give up too much control, too soon, will often generate greater threat and anxiety, rather than reduce. For example, it would not be prudent for therapists to adopt a classic Rogerian style with most military members whereby few prompts or questions are initiated by the therapist in the hope that client's will self-direct their search for truths. During the course of the interview, be sure to give clients choices and convey a sense of control to the client. Here are some ways that therapists might strike the right balance of control in the initial sessions (Meichenbaum, 1994):

• Is this a good time to talk with you about ...?
• Do you mind if I ask you some questions about your deployment experiences?
• Please do not share anything you wish to keep private at this time.

Essential Elements of EMDR History Taking and Treatment Planning

EMDR-related client history taking includes presenting complaints, identifying treatment goals, screening for medical, social, financial, legal, and psychiatric contraindications, assessing for client strengths or resources, and obtaining sufficient client history to develop a comprehensive treatment plan. Scope of screening and history taking will depend on many factors including premorbid level of functioning before the identified trauma, complexity of clinical presentations (comorbidity, quality of childhood experiences, attachments, and extent of trauma history), and stability of current environment.

Understanding the AIP Model, Client History Taking, and Treatment Planning

Therapist knowledge of the AIP model is a pivotal factor in obtaining an appropriate client history and treatment formulation. We will briefly review the relevant aspects of the AIP model as it pertains to Phase One. According to Shapiro (2001), underlying health and psychopathology are neural (memory) networks comprised of past experiences physical stored as multiple components encoded at the time, involving sensory stimuli (e.g., images, sounds, pain, smell, etc.), emotions, thoughts or beliefs, physiological sensations, and/ or behavioral reactions. Our earliest memories of attachment and other life events during the formative years serve as foundational experiences for interpreting and making meaning of our current experiences. External and internal stimuli and trigger reactions that we may or may not be conscious of, but are evidence of activation of memory networks. The brain has evolved the intrinsic capacity for learning or processing of our experiences that will help us adapt and survive. Adaptive neural networks register our positive attachments, resilience, coping resources, and sense of efficacy, while maladaptive networks emerge with repeated experiences of adverse life experiences, negative attachment, vulnerability, inescapable fear, pain, loss, and personal failures. Traumatic or other highly emotionally charged events can overwhelm the brain's capacity to assimilate or accommodate information that became associated as unprocessed experiences in maladaptive memory networks. Psychopathological symptoms and conditions therefore represent the activation of these maladaptive neural networks, resulting in selective attention and conditional responses to negative current stimuli and experiences, as well as anticipating future threats, loss, and pain. Therefore, the main goal of EMDR history taking and treatment planning is to identify the most salient past, current, and future experiential contributors of psychopathology—what Shapiro (2001) refers to as the "three-pronged protocol." There are several procedures used to help identify appropriate "target" memories for EMDR processing.

Military Client Intake Assessment

The extent of comprehensiveness of the clinical assessment is greatly dependent upon the referral question and setting. Acute or crisis presentations will naturally be significantly shorter and more germane to making a rapid clinical determination regarding safety, stabilization, and disposition. In Chapter 10, we provide an overview of EMDR-related assessment and treatment of acute stress reactions and acute stress disorder. What follows will pertain to non-acute scenarios. Most mental health agencies and clinicians have a standard protocol for gathering clinical information and background information of clients. In regards to military clientele, it's often helpful to distinguish between pre-military, military, and post-military history in order to help identify "premorbid" level of functioning along with potential experiential contributors to pathology, as well as determining health trajectory to possibly motivate for change. As for EMDR, the information gathered during the routine clinical interview can indicate areas that the therapist may want to explore further in terms of selecting possible targets for EMDR reprocessing. Current history would be if the client is or is no longer in an Active-Duty, Reserve, or National Guard component. Furthermore, the therapist can use his or her knowledge of the deployment cycle to ask the client questions that may solicit potential targets for EMDR reprocessing. Typically, clinical interview and history taking will start out by asking the client about the presenting complaint and symptoms that led to the referral or the client's self-referral.

General Tips for Assessing EMDR Reprocessing Targets

The following are some general strategies for identifying potential EMDR reprocessing targets: (a) Develop a stressor list, but understand that it may change once you start reprocessing. (b) As some issues are resolved, others may show up that hadn't been reported initially. (c) Don't ask for a lot of detail about stressors during your first pass through the history. (d) Let clients know that you want an overview of their deployment and will want details later. (e) Try to get a sense of the chronological order of events and which are most intrusive/disturbing now. (f) Ask about the social environment of their unit—was leadership good, were they adequately supplied, did they feel adequately trained, and who were they close to? (g) Don't forget to ask about non-combat trauma before and after their deployment. (h) Assess the client's reaction during discussion of the traumas. Pay attention to affect tolerance and dissociation. (i) Assess for co-morbid substance abuse, depression, suicidality, self-injury, and family relations. (j) Pay attention to a pattern of risk-taking (driving too fast, getting into fights), suggesting that they are looking for an "adrenaline rush." You may need to educate the client about this as well as reprocess. (k) Pay attention to the context of treatment—*why are they seeking treatment now*? Consider secondary gain—disability compensation, avoidance of redeployment, legal problems, and family pressures. (l) Assess the client's resources—the times when he or she felt at their best and calming practices used when upset. (m) Ask the client if there are any experiences that are distressing but that he or she isn't ready to discuss.

Primer of EMDR Treatment Planning

The reader is referred to Leeds (2009) and Shapiro (2001) for detailed descriptions and examples of EMDR treatment planning. In short, the referral question, presenting complaint, client history, perceived client suitability, and client treatment goals will usually drive treatment planning—particularly in acute, time-sensitive situations. For instance, is there a time sensitive element to the referral question, or issues of client instability, that is contra-indicative for EMDR reprocessing beyond the current traumatic stressor? Other circumstances like the treatment setting might dictate the treatment plan such as operational or forward-deployed environments that usually can be prohibitive for EMDR reprocessing of pre-military or adverse childhood experiences. In addition, sufficient therapeutic alliance, degree of client suitability, and the client's treatment goals all need to be entered into the equation when developing the EMDR treatment plan.

EMDR Treatment Planning and the Three-Pronged Protocol

The essential treatment plan for the evidence-based, standard trauma-focused EMDR protocol has always consisted of what Shapiro (2001) refers to as the "Three-Pronged Protocol":

- *Past* traumatic events or other foundational emotionally charged experiential contributors, or *small t,* as Shapiro puts it (2001), that are etiologic to the presenting complaints or psychopathological condition.
- *Current* internal or external triggers or antecedents that activate the maladaptive neural (memory) network.
- *Future* template of the client's anticipatory anxiety, worries, concerns, and/or needed coping skills or mastery achieved through imaginal or behavioral rehearsal, to prevent relapse or reactivation of the maladaptive schema.

EMDR Treatment Flow

Treatment or reprocessing priorities follow the AIP model whereby the past formative events are all reprocessed before moving onto reprocessing current triggering stimuli. If any of the previously identified current triggers remain active, they are targeted for reprocessing, as well as any new present triggers that may have emerged during the course of treatment (e.g., self-monitoring log). Once all identified current precursors are reprocessed, the therapist moves onto reprocessing the anticipatory anxieties, or other future-oriented stimuli related to future client coping and self-efficacy.

IDENTIFYING PAST CONTRIBUTORS

Presenting Complaint and Symptom History

At the outset of the clinical interview, clients are routinely asked to describe their current symptoms or complaints. Therapists should take careful notes of the language that clients used to describe their symptoms and problems and should repeat that language back in future inquiries. Additionally, it is fairly routine for practitioners to "dimensionalize" the client's self-report of symptoms in terms of who, what, when, how long, why, etc., which is important for differential diagnoses, triaging of crises, and treatment planning. Below is an example of using the client's presenting complaint to help identify possible past contributors for EMDR reprocessing along with dimensionalizing the symptom history:

- **Current onset**: "When did you first notice that you were not sleeping well, had no energy, and were being snappy?"
  - ○ Antecedents: "Do you know what might have caused this kind of reaction?" If not, "What was going on in your life when this started?"
- **Earliest onset**: "When was the very first time that you remember when you felt this way?"
  - ○ Antecedents: "What was going on in your life back then when you had these same kinds of reactions?"
- **Worst incident**: "Is this the worst it's ever been for you?"
  - ○ Antecedents: "What do you remember happening in your life that made this the worst time?"
- **Intensity:** "How often do you feel that way … every day, every week, once a month?"
- **Exacerbating factors:** "What do you notice will make it worse?"
- **Symptom relief:** "What are some things you have tried that make it a little better or more tolerable?"
- **Frequency:** "How many times in your life have you experienced something like this?"
- **Duration:** "On average, how long do these episodes usually last?"
- **Attempted solutions:** "What all have you tried to resolve (fix) this problem?"
- **Causal attributions:** "What do you think is causing it?"
- **Chronicity:** "What is the longest symptom free period you have had?"
- **Help-seeking antecedent:** "This has obviously been going for a while; what led to your coming to get help today?"

Earliest-Worst-Recent Reprocessing Sequence of Cluster Memories

According to the AIP model, earlier traumata or adverse childhood experiences establish the foundation for reactions to subsequent life events. Therefore, in regards to treatment planning, theoretically the first target memory to reprocess is the earliest event, followed by the next earliest memory, and so on.

Memory Clusters

It is typical in high-stress occupations like the military, particularly during times of war, that military personnel are repeatedly exposed to a variety of potentially traumatic stressors. Experiences that are similar in some way such as person, place, thing, event, emotion, physical sensation, behavioral response, and so on become physiologically linked in the brain in the associative nature of memory networks. Shapiro (2001) calls these *clusters* and posits that, by targeting the *earliest* memory in the cluster, the *worst* incident in the cluster, and the most *recent* memory in the cluster, it is sufficient to process the remaining associated memories. Whether a combat veteran, or a chronically abused child, therapy would be a life-long proposition if every single traumatic incident needed to be identified and reprocessed separately. Fortunately, it appears that EMDR produces a *generalization effect* that allows reprocessing to proceed more rapidly and efficiently, by targeting the earliest, the "worst," and most recent memories. Clients that have difficulty identifying the "worst" memory of a cluster can be asked to identify one that best represents the others. The earliest-worst-recent sequence makes sense intuitively as these are the events most likely to have the greatest emotional, somatosensory, and cognitive impact. The main point is to identify a few, not all, of the most disturbing and therefore activating of memories in the maladaptive memory network. Anecdotally, EMDR clinicians frequently report that other traumatic memories in the network have been reprocessed altogether, or markedly reduced by focusing on the earliest-worst-recent sequence, but the therapist should check his or her work, by instructing the client to check if there are any other related memories that are distressing, and reprocess those accordingly.

Participant Cluster

Clusters of memories associated to particular person(s) that have etiological significance can be selected such as the perpetrator of sexual molestation, physically abusive family members, or a harsh unit leader. Clients can be asked to picture the face of the perpetrator and identify within the cluster of memories the earliest-worst-recent disturbing event.

Other EMDR-Related Considerations for Selecting Past Contributors

Starting with the Worst Memory First

Therapists may want to start reprocessing the "worst" or most distressing presenting symptom first, as opposed to the conceptual preference for targeting the earliest. In most cases, the "worst" experience underlying their symptoms is usually what brought the client into treatment in the first place. By reprocessing past memories associated with the most disturbing symptom, there is a better than even chance that symptom reduction or relief will be easily recognized by the client and possibly motivate them to continue. This is particularly essential in the military culture, with its warrior ethos, performance orientation, high OPTEMPO, and inherent mistrust of mental health. A noticeable improvement in symptom relief and/or functioning is often vital to prevent premature termination. After the most debilitating symptom has been reprocessed, the therapist and client then go onto the next most disturbing symptom, and so on. The author (Mark Russell) routinely starts with the "worst" presenting symptom for the reasons stated above, and, 80–90% of the time after the first reprocessing session, clients will report some measurable change in the narrative, image, cognition, feeling, etc., not a "cure," but a visibly sufficient change that instills a sense of hope and a return appointment. The author can think of no single case whereby a military client treated with EMDR had reported some quota of change the first time out and did not return for a subsequent appointment. Conversely, those few clients not reporting any alterations were notably less likely to keep their follow-up.

Following the Client's Lead: Starting with the Least versus Most Disturbing

Therapists often have a theory about their client's most salient memories of trauma and adverse experiences believed to be driving the current pathology. However, the therapist's view and client's may not match. In this case, it is usually best to allow the client to take the lead as to what *they* identify as the most debilitating or meaningful target memory for initiating reprocessing. The therapist can place trust in the AIP model that neurophysiologically whatever target memory is selected to begin processing will inevitably be associated to the other selected memories. Some clients express a preference to start EMDR reprocessing gradually, by choosing the least disturbing target memory and working their way up in a systematic desensitization format. This may be due to a fear of the unknown and whether they will be able to remain in control and not "lose it." Whatever the reason, therapists should respect the client's preference but also advise that there is no guarantee that starting with the less upsetting events might shift to the more disturbing experiences if they are physically linked in a neural network. Clients who appear nervous about this proposition can be reminded of the information that will be covered in the preparation phase.

Starting with the Current versus Past

Similarly, it is fairly common for military members to not be sold on the proposition that past adverse childhood experiences or other distant premilitary traumatic or disturbing events are directly or indirectly relevant to their current distress. For example, a Marine Staff Sergeant (E-6) presented with acute combat-related PTSD and looked at his therapist (Mark Russell) with incredulous eyes when it was remarked that his traumatic grief reaction to the incidental killing of an elderly Iraqi woman was related to his earliest memory of asking for his somewhat overbearing Somali-born grandmother to return to her homeland. She eventually did so that year—not because of her grandson's expressed wish. A year or two later, the client learned his grandmother had died from cancer, and as many young folks do, this pre-teenage boy held himself squarely responsible. As the SNCO of his unit, the Staff Sergeant was in charge of manning vital checkpoints early in the Iraq War. Rules of Engagement (ROE) were to try all means to get vehicles to stop, including use of warning fire; however, if vehicles did not heed the warnings, service members were to assume hostile intent by violators and were under orders for direct fire to stop the vehicle. The ROE was put in place after several incidents of auto-bearing civilian occupants killing coalition forces with vehicular-IED. Most drivers were not actual combatants, but carried out their tasks under hostile threats to family members. By the way, the client was not actually at the scene of the shooting incident until immediately after the fact. However, he was "the SNCO," and it was his troops that implemented the ROE from headquarters. At any rate, the Staff Sergeant scoffed at the absurd assertion that these two tragic deaths may be inextricably linked, and expressed a firm desire to "stay on-task" by focusing on the killing incident in Iraq, and that's what we did. Not unexpectedly, at some later point during the reprocessing session, the bloodied face of the dead Iraqi grandmother became superimposed with his own grandmother's face. After further reprocessing, tears of shame, guilt, and self-condemnation eventually gave way to tears of joy, as he pictured his smiling grandmother in heaven, consoling him over the resolute fact that he bore responsibility for neither death. A couple of EMDR sessions later, the client's PTSD, depression, and traumatic grief were resolved.

Lesson learned. If the therapist had insisted to follow strict EMDR protocol, the aforementioned military client may have walked, and deservedly so. The AIP model provides an invaluable guide for clinicians for case formulation and treatment planning, but there is nothing written in stone that earliest always has to be processed before worst, or most recent, etc. It's a guide. Memories in the maladaptive neural networks are linked together for a reason, and processing one will typically mean accessing the others. Additionally, although the therapist intended to follow the client's desire to avoid processing past events and stay current, that obviously did not happen. Practitioners should inform clients when using EMDR, even for non-trauma focused reasons (e.g., RDI), that it is impossible to guarantee that their brain may not link to older, disturbing material. In fact, we should expect that it may and advise clients to report it to us.

Chronological Ordering of Combat Experiences

In their 2002 book *Light in the Heart of Darkness*, Steven Silver and Susan Rogers, two highly experienced DVA and EMDR clinicians, advocate that therapists collaborate with the veteran and develop a chronological listing of the most impactful negative and positive war-related traumatic experiences, starting from the time before they entered the warzone to the postwar reintegration period. Doing so has been shown to help veterans and their therapists to organize and reprocess the war narrative in an orderly manner. This same history taking and treatment planning method can be applied to active-duty military personnel. For service members with multiple deployments or operational tours, over a lengthy military career, therapists can identify memory clusters that are related to similar events, thoughts, or emotions. For instance, clients involved in multiple firefights would have a "firefight or direct combat cluster," or those involved in running a lot of convoys where IED or ambush may have occurred during any of their multiple deployments would have a "convoy cluster." Clients would then be asked to identify the earliest memory in each cluster, the worst, and the most recent. Doing so will yield a more manageable level of target memories. The other tack is to instruct clients to scan their memories before, during, and after war and to identify the real "hot zone" areas (the "worst" of the "worst") for targeting.

The author (Mark Russell) has utilized the chronological sequencing plan with service personnel and found it to be effective. However, when the client's or therapist's availability for treatment time is constricted, as it commonly is in the military environment, then the therapist must determine about the most efficient way to solicit a sufficient number of quality targets, and trust in the AIP model that other pertinent memories not immediately identified are indeed connected in the client's maladaptive neural networks, which is fueling the presenting complaint. Consequently, experiences either not reported by the client or reported but left off of the treatment plan are most probable to emerge during reprocessing once the client has accessed the neural network. It is fairly common for recently redeployed members, who have been on multiple deployments, to state their preference to start with the most recent or most troubling deployment experience, as opposed to starting from entrance in the military or the first deployment. Therapists should respect the client's preference. Either way, works fine.

Feeder Memories

Shapiro (2001) used the term "feeder memories" to convey the idea that sometimes clients do not report and/or are not aware of earlier life experiences that may serve as "feeders" or contributors to the client's negative neural network. If identified, feeder memories should be incorporated into the treatment plan for reprocessing as early as possible.

Therapist Screening for Feeder Memory:

- **Asking**—"When is the earliest time you remember feeling this way?" or "When is the earliest time you learned to think of yourself this way?"
- **Float back**—"Bring up the picture and those words (NC). Notice what feelings are coming up for you, where you are feeling them in your body, and just let you mind float back to an earlier time in your life. Don't search for anything; just let your mind float back and tell me the earliest scene that comes to mind where you had similar thoughts, feelings, or sensations."
- **Affect scan**—Use if the client cannot identify a negative cognition. "Bring up the last time you felt upset. Hold the image in mind and the thoughts that come up about it. Where do you feel it in your body? Hold the image and the sensation, and let your mind scan back to the earliest time you remember feeling that way."

IDENTIFYING CURRENT CONTRIBUTORS

According to Shapiro (2001), triggers consist of any stimuli that elicit a response in the form of dysfunctional images, sensations, thoughts, or feelings associated with the earlier traumatic event(s). In soliciting the current triggers, therapists might ask, "Are there any things that you see, hear, think, or feel, or certain situations or other reminders, that seem to cause you to remember what happened, or feel like it's happening again?" For treatment planning purposes, each trigger or antecedent needs to be reprocessed separately due to prior conditioning effects. After all of the current triggers have been reprocessed, the therapist than proceeds to the future template. For example, in the traumatic grief case mentioned earlier, the Staff Sergeant's current triggers were: (a) looking at family pictures—especially with his grandmother, (b) his 13-year-old daughter who has his grandmother's dimple, (c) the smell of gasoline, (d) the sound of screaming, and (e) movies or television shows depicting grandparents.

IDENTIFYING FUTURE CONTRIBUTORS

The therapist identifies future behaviors necessary for appropriate future action including strengthening associations of the client's desired state in terms of how they would like to be thinking, feeling, or acting in the future, as well as reducing anticipatory anxiety, worrying, or self-handicapping behaviors related to future performance. Clients are asked, *"How do you see yourself coping with this problem in the future?"* or *"What would you like to be doing, thinking, feeling, or reacting in the future?"* or *"What new skills or ways of thinking about things will you need?"* Typically 1–2 items are identified, but however many, each is reprocessed separately. The reprocessing phase is con-cluded after the last future contributor has been reprocessed and checked. In regards to the aforementioned case study, the Staff Sergeant's future template consisted of: (a) being able to relish the positive memories with his family and grandmother, (b) being able to feel and express a father's love for this daugh-ter, and (c) feeling relaxed when he pumped gas into the family car.

Optimal Number of Target Memories?

Novice EMDR therapists and their military clients can quickly feel over-whelmed if they attempt to list all of the service member's exposure to poten-tially traumatic stressors and early adverse experiences. The EMDR textbook (Shapiro, 2001) answer to the question posed above would be however many it takes to accomplish *four* goals for comprehensive EMDR treatment:

1. Has the individual target been resolved?
2. Has associated material been activated that must be addressed?
3. Have all the necessary targets been reprocessed to allow the client to feel at peace with the past, empowered in the present, and able to make choices for the future?
4. Has an adequate assimilation been made within a healthy social system?

To accomplish the above goals clients would have reprocessed:

- *Primary events*—the earliest-worst-recent memories associated with the presenting complaint usually involving no more than 20 memories;
- *Past events*—negative memories that arise when the client is instructed to concentrate on a particular negative cognition(s);
- *Progressions*—any salient, spontaneous negative associations that emerged during reprocessing which the therapist believes may be contributory;
- *Clusters*—reprocessing of all identified clusters and re-checking clusters during reevaluation phase to see if any residual associations are present;
- *Participants*—clusters of memories associated with particular person(s) that have etiological significant such as the perpetrator of child abuse, or pertinent family members;
- *Current triggers*—each processed separately and any new triggers that have emerged, along with any negative past associations that may arise via the client's log or daily report;
- *Future template*—future associations with significant people (e.g., per-petrator chance meeting); anticipatory anxiety associated with future important situations; and integration of adaptive beliefs, mastery behaviors, and self-regulation in future events question.

Using the AIP model as our guide, by identifying several of the most hotly charged memories in the maladaptive neural network, we can reasonably expect generalization effects to other associatively linked memories. Therefore, in EMDR, we do not need, nor want to, identify and reprocess every single incident. Typically, the treatment plan we start out with is not the treatment plan we end with. New or previously undisclosed recollections (aka progressions) regularly emerge during EMDR and may become targets.

PRACTICAL CONSIDERATIONS OF TREATMENT PLANNING FOR MILITARY ENVIRONMENTS

In regards to selecting targeted past memories there is no magic number of sessions, so one strategy is to consider the well-regarded "KISS" principle: Keep It Simple Stupid. With serious time and environmental constraints, high OPTEMPO, and a very mobile military population, there is an intrinsic need in the military to work as safely, rapidly, and efficiently as one can. Long-term, week-to-week therapy in the military does not exist for most. Therefore, to maximize time, the therapist needs to establish trust and rapport early and fast, and identify a sufficient number of quality targets for reprocessing. At a minimum, we want to identify preferably "3" high value (psychophysically charged) targets (earliest-worst-most recent). Most often it will be the most disturbing events associated with the presenting complaint. On average, therapists can expect to select and reprocess between 3 to 6 past memories, the current triggers, and future template during the course of treatment with a particular military client. The modal range of mental health treatment in the military is around 3 to 4. In contrast, VA clinicians in brick-and-mortar facilities advocate identifying at least the 10 worst and 10 best memories for treatment planning purposes. Ideally, therapists can implement the full comprehensive treatment plan with however many past memories need to be reprocessed. Unfortunately, that may not be the norm in the military. A list of more than 10 past memories selected for reprocessing starts to become remotely practical in many military treatment scenarios. For example, each of the selected memories needs to be fully assessed in Phase Three, so if the therapist is working off a treatment plan that selected 10–20 past memories for targeting it would likely take nearly two 50-minute sessions. If the therapist needed two sessions earlier to complete phases one and two, we are looking at initiating reprocessing on the fifth meeting, assuming there is one. Keep in mind that, the longer the treatment duration, the greater the probability of treatment disruption and drop-out. Therapists can list as many etiologically salient past memories that arise during the history taking; however, they are encouraged to collaborate with the client to initially select *at least* the top "3–5," for treatment planning purposes, or up to "10"—if time permits.

Military Client History Taking

The information provided below is to demonstrate the wide variety of information that is often useful to gather when working with military populations, much of which is highly specific to military culture and occupational hazards. Going beyond treatment planning for using EMDR, the following template for military client history taking is essential for developing a comprehensive treatment plan that takes the whole person and contexts into consideration. For instance, exercise routines, recreational activities, spirituality, dietary factors, caffeine intake, sleep hygiene, and many other areas tapped may not be regularly assessed by mental health providers but can often have significant impact on treatment responsiveness and outcomes.

Presenting symptoms and course of illness (see above).

Client demographics: Age, gender, current marital status, race/ethnicity, military rank and pay-grade, and branch of military service.

Military service: (a) The number of years of continuous active duty. Is the client currently Active, Reserve, or National Guard component? If there is broken time, note the year he or she re-entered the military. If the client is an officer, note the years of prior enlistment and service branch and date of commissioning. (b) Reason(s) why the service member joined the military and, if over 4 years of military service, reason(s) why they stay in service? (c) If he or she is less than 4 years in service, how has adjusted been to being in the military? What does the client like the most and least about the military? (d) What is the client's current military occupation? What is the length of time in the job and level of job satisfaction? (e) If the client is active military, when is his or her EAOS or end of obligated duty? (f) Recent military promotion, change in responsibilities, change in relationships due to higher paygrade, positional authority, and/or concerns over fraternization. (g) Does the military member plan to re-enlist, make a career, and/or plan to retire after 20–30 years? (h) How long has the client been in his or her current command? How supportive is his or her chain of command? (i) Has the client ever been disciplined in the military via NJP (non-judicial punishment), what for, and when? Did he or she ever get "busted" (reduced in rank)? How long ago? Has the client ever been Courts Martialed? Are any legal charges currently pending? Finally, (j) has the command initiated any administrative separation actions for misconduct, personality disorder, or some other reason? If so, how does the client feel about it?

Marital history: (a) Past marriages/divorce, length of relationships, reasons for ending, any past or current Family Advocacy Program (FAP), or other legal involvement for domestic violence? (b) What is the level of marital satisfaction in the current relationship? (c) Is the spouse/significant other also in the military? (d) How frequently does the couple argue? Has there been any recent talk of separation or divorce? If the client is engaged, note how long, the location of the fiancé, the date of the marriage, and the quality of the relationship.

(e) Does the client have children? What ages? Gender? Who do they reside with? What is the quality of the parent–child relationship? Is there a history of FAP or Child Protective Services (CPS) involvement?

Social history: (a) Do they have any really close friends or confidants inside or outside of the military? (b) Do they currently have a boyfriend or girlfriend? (c) Has there been a recent break-up with a close friend or romantic partner? (d) Do they have friends or co-workers in the military that they hang out with? (e) If the client is single, do they live in the barracks? Does the client have a roommate? How do they get along with their roommate?

Recreational, hobbies, and relaxation activities: (a) What does the client do for "fun" or "relaxation" during off-duty hours? What about weekend or holidays? How often, when was the last time, and with whom? (b) What kind of sporting or other recreational activities (e.g., fishing, boating, hiking) does the client enjoy doing? How often, when was the last time, and with whom? (c) How regularly do they exercise? How many days a week, and how long are the workouts? What kind of exercise do they usually do (e.g., weights, running, etc.)? (d) Do they have a work-out partner? (e) Has there been any change in their work-out schedule (e.g., skipping, stopping, or increasing work-outs)? (f) Does the client enjoy working out as much as she or he used to? (g) What other kinds of hobbies or interests do they have? Does the client like videogaming, listening to or playing music, or using social media? Has the level of enjoyment changed recently? Finally, (h) how has the client performed on their recent physical readiness test (PRT)?

Religious or spiritual history: (a) Was the client raised in a particular religion? Is the client currently active in an organized religion? Is spirituality important to the client? (b) Has anything recently caused the client to change their religious or spiritual beliefs? When? Finally, (c) Does the client volunteer at events or organizations to help the less fortunate?

Family of origin history: (a) What is the parental, marital, or divorce history? If the parents are divorced, how old was the client at the time of divorce? Whom did the client live with? Did the parents remarry? If there is a single parent or the parent never married, did the client have any relationship with the biological father or mother who was absent? Was the client adopted? (b) Is there a history of childhood abuse, emotional neglect, and/or foster care placement? (c) Did the client witness domestic violence? (d) Were the parents or the caregiver incarcerated or did they have a substance-use problem or a mental illness? (e) Was there a death of a parent or sibling during the client's childhood? (f) Was a parent, sibling, or other close relative in the military before? Finally, (g) what did the client's parents or caregivers think of his or her decision to join the military?

Diet and lifestyle history: (a) What is the client's level of daily activity— aside from work, are they mostly active or sedentary? (b) How is the client's diet? Does she or he skip meals or try to eat a balance diet? (c) Does the client describe cycles of binging and purging or compulsive eating? (d) Is the client or are people closest to him or her bothered by any compulsive or addictive behaviors related to gambling, internet porn, hoarding, etc.? (e) Does the client report sleep disturbances? (f) Over-sleeping (hypersomnia) and under-sleeping (insomnia)? When did the sleeping problems start? Is there any identifiable trigger? (f) Does the client's spouse/partner report that the client has engaged in sleep talking, sleep walking, or sleep fighting behaviors? (g) What has the client attempted so far to improve his or her sleep habits? Has the client used a prescribed or over-the-counter sleep aide? Finally, (h) has the client developed a *sleep phobia*—purposely trying to stay awake to avoid stressful dreams?

Legal history: (a) Is there any past history of arrest or conviction for assault or other violent behaviors? Is there a protective order against the client? (b) Is there any other history of court conviction? Finally, (c) are there any pending civil lawsuits or legal actions?

DEPLOYMENT CYCLE HISTORY

Pre-deployment history: (a) Were there any health or other problems that prevented a deployment? (b) Did he or she have any condition that should have prevented deployment but was deployed anyways? (c) Is the client currently pending deployment? How soon, where, and estimated length? (d) How does the client feeling about the upcoming deployment? (e) If the client is Reservist or National Guard, how supportive are his or her employer and co-workers about their mobilization? (f) What does the client worry about the most? (g) How are family and friends reacting to the deployment? Finally, (h) what does the client look forward to the most during their deployment?

Identifying EMDR-Specific Pre-Deployment Past Contributors:

- *Earliest.* What was the most disturbing incident that you experienced before your deployment (if multiple deployer—*before your first*) deployment?
- *Most Recent.* What was the most difficulty thing that you had to deal with just before you deployed (if multiple deployer—*before your most recent deployment*)?
- *Worst/Hardest.* What would you say is the single hardest thing that you experienced before you deployed (if multiple deployer—*before any of your deployments*)?

Clinical note. Any of the above questions, or other queries about pre-deployment experiences, could be used to identify potential targets for EMDR therapy. Moreover, regarding pre-deployment feelings of anticipatory anxiety, fear of failure, foreboding, self-doubt, etc., the therapist can ask the client whether he or she can recall earlier times when similar cognitions, feelings, or physical sensations, including childhood were experienced, or use the "float-back" technique (Shapiro, 2001). The decision to solicit possible pre-military adverse life experiences or traumas depends on the agreed upon treatment plan (see EMDR Treatment Planning section)

Non-war-related deployment history: (a) Has the client deployed to assist in humanitarian or disaster relief operations? If so, where, when, and what duration? What was the client's role? (b) Has the client deployed to participate in peace-keeping operations? When and what was the client's role? (c) What were the highlights and worst or most difficult experiences of the deployment(s)? (d) Did the client witness the wounding or death of others, including atrocities? (e) Was the client involved in body-recovery duties they handled or transported human remains? Finally, (f) Was there a particular incident(s) that they cannot shake off?

War-related deployment history: (a) Total number of deployments to a warzone, location, and duration? (b) Did the client ever deploy as an Individual (mobilization) Augmentee (IA/IMA)? Did the client experience any problems integrating with other members of the unit, or when returned to their home unit? (c) What was the client's primary job or duties in the warzone? Did she or he ever go outside the wire on patrol? (d) Was the client involved in direct combat? How often? Was she or he ever wounded in action? Has he or she seen other unit members killed or wounded? Was any unit member the client was close to or a valued leader wounded or killed? Do not ask on first meeting: Did she or he ever fire their weapon at an enemy combatant? Did she kill or wound an enemy combatant? When was the first time the client killed? (e) Was she or he ever involved in a friendly-fire incident? (f) Was she or he ever involved in the accidental shooting of non-combatants? (g) Has the client ever had to handle or transport human remains? (h) Did the client ever experience sexual harassment or assault while deployed? (i) Had she or he experienced any harassment or discrimination along racial or ethnic lines? (j) Did the client ever develop an acute combat stress reaction in the warzone? Describe what symptoms she experienced. Did the client receive help from a Combat Stress Control unit or mental health specialists in the warzone? How many times? Was any use of psychotropic medications prescribed in the war zone? (k) What was the reception the client received from unit members and leaders about using mental health services? (l) Had the client ever contemplated suicide or attempted suicide in the warzone that nobody knew about? (m) Did she or he ever have to be medically evacuated for health or mental health reasons? (n) Has the client been a P.O.W.? For how long? Are there any lingering health effects? (o) Did the client get into trouble for any kind of misconduct in the warzone? Describe what happened. Finally, (p) Are there any particular incidents that happened while deployed, that the client can't stop thinking about, and which are especially disturbing?

Identifying EMDR-Specific Deployment-Related Past Contributors:

- *Earliest.* What was the most disturbing incident that you experienced during your (if multiple deployer—*first*) deployment? If working on traumatic grief, when was the *first* time somebody you were close to was wounded or killing (or *the first time you killed someone*)?
- *Most Recent.* What was the most disturbing incident that happened before your deployment ended (if multiple deployer—*during your latest deployment*)? If working on traumatic grief, when was the *last* time that someone you were close too was wounded or killed (or, *the last time you killed someone*)?
- *Worst/Hardest.* Of everything you have been through, what would you say is the single most disturbing event that you experienced during your deployment (if multiple deployer—*during any of your deployments*)? If working on traumatic grief, what was the worst or most troubling (*time you killed someone?*) loss of someone you were close to?

Clinical note. Any of the above questions or other queries about deployment experiences could be used to identify potential targets for EMDR therapy. When clients identify experiences related to fear, shame/guilt, pride, etc., the therapist can ask whether they can recall any earlier times they experienced the same cognitions, feelings, or physical sensations, including childhood, or use the "float-back" technique (Shapiro, 2001). The decision to solicit possible pre-military adverse life experiences or traumas depends on the treatment plan (see EMDR Treatment Planning section).

Post-deployment history: (a) If deployed, how long ago did the client return from their most recent deployment? (b) How was she or he received by family, friends, and co-workers after returning home? (c) What was the most difficult part of returning from deployment? (d) How long did it take the client to feel re-adjusted, if ever? (d) What was the overall level of support the client felt after returning from deployment? (e) How did the client get along with co-workers or supervisors who did not deploy? (f) What did the client miss the most about being deployed? (g) How much alcohol does the client drink since returning from deployment? Is the client drinking more or less than before being first deployed? (h) Has the client experienced other problems related to their anger or aggressive impulses? Finally, (i) Ceremonial rituals are ways in which returning war veterans seek to normalize their worlds and help them to ground and anchor themselves; has the client developed any ceremonial rituals?

Identifying EMDR-Specific Post-Deployment Past Contributors:

- *Earliest.* What was the most difficult experience you remember after you returned from (if multiple deployer—*your first*) deployment?

- *Most Recent.* What has been the most recent difficulty that you experienced after returning from (if multiple deployer—*your most recent*) deployment?
- *Worst/Hardest.* Overall, is there a single incident that stands out as being the "worst" or hardest thing you've experienced since returning from (if multiple deployer—*your last*) deployment?

Clinical note. Any client history-related questions or other queries about post-deployment experiences can be used to identify potential targets for EMDR therapy. Remember that next to the intensity and duration of combat exposure, the strongest predictor variable for war stress injury is a low level of perceived social support (e.g., Kulka et al., 1990). When clients identify experiences related to shame/guilt, emptiness, pride, etc., the therapist can ask whether they can recall any earlier times they experienced the same cognitions, feelings, or physical sensations, including childhood, or use the "float-back" technique (Shapiro, 2001). The decision to solicit possible pre-military adverse life experiences depends on the treatment plan (see the EMDR Treatment Planning section).

Medical history: (a) Is there a significant history of disease, illness, injury, surgery, or hospitalizations? (b) Is there a history of closed head injuries, Loss of Consciousness (LoC), diagnosis of concussion, or TBI? (c) Is there a military history of positive PDHA/RA health screenings, history of medical evacuation, wounded-in-action, traumatic amputation, or receipt of a Purple Heart? (d) Is there a history of medically unexplained symptoms? (e) What medications are currently being taken; what dosage and for what reason? (f) Is there any VA treatment history?

Substance use history: (a) Is there a history of substance use problems? What type, frequency, and length of abstinence; (b) Have there been outpatient, residential treatment periods? (c) Is there current substance use or is the client actively involved in a 12-step program? Does the client have a sponsor? (d) Does the client have past, current, DUI or other legal convictions? (e) Does the client take over-the-counter medications and supplements including dextromethorphan (common ingredient in cough syrup)? (f) What is his or her current caffeinated substance intake and size coffee, tea, soda beverages, energy drinks, no-doz, and other OTC stimulants? (g) What is his or her current amount of nicotine use (chewing, smoking, cigar, or dipping), including timing up to bedtime?

Secondary gain: (a) Is the client intentionally deceiving the therapist by simulating, faking, or grossly elaborating on their symptom presentation to create a negative impression for external reward? For example, to avoid military deployment or other duties, to receive a service-connected disability and VA pension, workers compensation, or civil suit damages? (b) Is the client currently pending a PEB/MEB-related medical discharge? (c) Are there current or pending legal proceedings against the client? (d) Has the client's attorney initiated a civil lawsuit that is related to the reason for referral (e.g., treatment for

PTSD after a motor-vehicle accident)? (e) Is the client pending VA disability determination for a related condition (e.g., PTSD)? (f) Is the client intentionally faking "good" and deceiving the therapist and other personnel involved over the extent of their war stress injury, in order to receive a *favorable* report from the therapist that will permit them to be returned to full-duty? And (g) Is the client motivated to simulate illness in order to primarily assume the patient role in keeping with Factitious Disorder?

Post-Traumatic Growth and Positive War Stress Reactions

One of the truly positive aspects of EMDR therapy is that it's a strength-based approach. During EMDR assessment (Phase Three), the therapist collaborates with the client to identify more adaptive, resilient self-statements, even if only a distant possibility in the client's current mind-set. That adaptive, positive cognition (PC) is measured (Validity of Cognitions Scale) and then deliberately paired with the disturbing target memory and enhanced with further sets of bilateral stimulation in the installation (Phase Five). Whether using EMDR or not, it's just good clinical practice to recognize and respect our client's strengths. Therefore, during client history taking, we are trying to identify the early mastery, positive attachments, and success experiences that are physiological stored in the client's adaptive neural (memory) networks. Again, the AIP model provides a rationale and guide as to what kinds of information the EMDR therapist needs to gather in order to construct with the client a workable treatment plan. We are interested in those mastery and resilient experiences before, during, and after the client's military career. It is also useful to incorporate the deployment cycle as a means to solicit adaptive coping and mastery experience before, during, and after military deployments, so we will examine both scenarios.

Clinical note. It would be prudent for therapists to not pull for client strengths and post-traumatic growth experiences too early. There is a need to first hear the client's emotional pain before focusing on potential growth experiences; otherwise the client may perceive the therapist as disconnected to their inner turmoil (Leeds, 2009). Intermingled in stories of death, destruction, and atrocities are likely reports of good times—with one's buddies—the camaraderie and feeling of prowess. Encourage vets to describe what they did to survive, and what they took away from their war experience. The following is a sample of some ways for clinicians to identify client resiliency experiences that may be utilized in EMDR treatment (see Chapter 16, this volume).

Pre-Military Adaptive Resources: (a) Can the client recall any particular memories in which she or he accomplished something to feel proud of at school, in sports, or other recreational or social activities? (b) Was the client involved in volunteer events or helping people in distress? (c) Was there a particular teacher, coach, spiritual leader, or other mentor relationship that was particularly meaningful to the client?

Military-Related Adaptive Resources: (a) Did the client complete the rigors of recruit training? Did the client complete a basic military specialty school? (b) Did the client ever think about quitting in boot camp or during their specialty school? Did the client persevere? (c) Inform the client that many military personnel fail to complete boot camp or their first military specialty school. (d) Can she or he think of anything positive, even something small that that has come out of this experience? (e) Did she or he ever feel pride over accomplishments during a deployment? (f) During deployment, did she or he experience helping a struggling unit member or civilian non-combatants? (g) Was the deployment experience as bad as it could have been, or could it have been worse? (h) Has he or she experienced helping others in distress? What was that like for the client?

Post-Military Adaptive Resources: (a) What were the most positive or meaningful things the client took away from his or her military experience? (b) Looking back, did the client surprise him/herself in a positive way with what she or he accomplished in the military? (c) Does the client feel more confident about him- or herself as a result of being in the military? (d) Has being in the military helped at all in dealing with stress?

Assessing EMDR Suitability and Readiness for Reprocessing

The clinical interview, history taking, and mental status examination will reveal possible targets for reprocessing, as well as potential indicators and contra-indicators of suitability for EMDR trauma-focused processing. Determining client suitability with EMDR is essentially no different than other trauma-focused treatments. There are no contraindications specific to EMDR, except perhaps using eye movements with someone with a history of retinal detachment or other current discomfort from the eyes. Research has demonstrated EMDR to be effective with alternative bilateral stimulation such as sounds, taps, or vibration pads held in the hands. Clients presenting with any of the following conditions, generally, would not be suitable for EMDR or other trauma-focused therapy, or if in therapy, EMDR reprocessing should be postponed when:

External crisis—if a work, personal, or family crisis or urgent matter emerges that requires the client's full attention, postpone reprocessing until crisis is resolved.

Imminent pending combat mission—personnel who will be participating in an imminent (within 12 hours) combat-related mission should postpone EMDR reprocessing until after completion of mission. Common after-effects of intense EMDR reprocessing include fatigue and possible distractibility from continued internal reprocessing that may interfere with decision-making and reaction time. Use of RDI or other performance improvement strategies may be considered (see EMDR Treatment Planning section below).

Impending client or therapist absence—short-fuse (1–2 weeks before) client or therapist absences due to pending deployment, training exercise, firearm qualifications, promotion board testing, temporary assigned duty (TAD/ TDY), Red Cross emergency leave, or annual leave should have EMDR reprocessing postponed until the client completes the tasking or returns back to their home base (see EMDR Treatment Planning section below).

Poor affect tolerance—client presenting as emotionally unstable, with protracted periods of intense crying, anger, terror, or shame, during history taking may benefit from Resource Development and Installation (RDI) or related procedures to develop affective tolerance and regulation skills before EMDR reprocessing (see EMDR Treatment Planning section below).

Medical or health concerns—therapist should get medical clearance for clients with a recent history of or treatment for: stroke, heart attack, malignant hypertension, severe bronchial asthma, brain tumor, medical surgery, detached retina, delirium, or any other acute or serious, unstable medical condition.

Seizure disorder—therapist should get medical clearance for recent onset of seizures. EMDR has been safely used without the likelihood of initiating genuine epileptic seizure (Leed, 2009). Pseudoseizures from conversion are fairly common in clients with history of complex-PTSD or other severe traumatic stress injuries. Several EMDR case studies have been published on treating pseudoseizures (e.g., de Roos & van Rood, 2009).

Traumatic brain injury (TBI)—EMDR should not be used with personnel presenting with acute TBI until medically cleared. For military clients who have been medically cleared and/or present with a history of TBI, EMDR reprocessing should be considered—*not* as a treatment for TBI (which it is not), but it may help address the past contributing traumatic events, current triggers related to the past trauma or recovery, and future-oriented client worry, concerns, or coping resources that are needed.

Pregnancy—all clients who are pregnant should be informed of the level of risk associated with increased stress from trauma-focused treatments. If there is a complicated pregnancy, and/or in the final trimester, it is recommended to postpone EMDR reprocessing.

Bipolar depression—when a greater risk of suicide is reported, the therapist may try resource development and installation to help stabilize symptoms. Inpatient reprocessing would be recommended, especially if there is consideration of misdiagnosis. Clients with genuine bipolar disorder should be discharged from the military. Military stress will exacerbate the client's condition and place them at risk (recheck the diagnosis—many times bipolar is diagnosed instead of stress-injury).

Severe debilitating depression—clients presenting with catatonia, malnourishment, psychotic features, severe melancholia and disability represent a medical emergency, even in the absence of suicidal ideation and should be not be treated with EMDR until stabilized.

Schizophrenia or other psychotic condition—acute psychosis represents a medical emergency. Clients with transient, acute psychotic reaction may be suitable for EMDR after resolution of psychotic features. However, clients with schizophrenia or other chronic or severe psychotic conditions should be discharged from the military. Military stress will exacerbate the client's conditions and place them at risk (recheck previous diagnosis for accuracy).

Severe agitation or hostility—clients exhibiting extreme agitation, restlessness, or hostility and who are unable to self-regulate or calm even with therapist interventions would not be suitable for trauma-focused therapy including EMDR reprocessing until their state stabilizes. Instead, the therapist will want to assess and, if possible, address the precipitants for the imbalanced state. Extreme psychomotor agitation such as pacing, hand wringing, muttering, an inability to stay seated for brief periods, and pressured speech should be assessed for dangerousness or incapacitation and treated as a medical emergency.

Chronic, severe sleep deprivation—can impair concentration, information processing, decision making, and emotional regulation; consider postponing EMDR until restorative sleep. If PTS-related symptoms are contributing to or causing sleep disturbance, then EMDR may be appropriate. After EMDR reprocessing, many clients report fatigue, which can exacerbate sleep deprived condition. For night sweats, nightmares, or sleep phobia, consider referral to medical for short-term sleep aide per *2010 VA/DoD Clinical Practice Guidelines for Managing Post-Traumatic Stress*. Clients should not operate heavy equipment, pilot aircraft, etc., immediately after intense reprocessing. Possible signs of severe sleep deprivation include: (a) neglecting personal hygiene, (b) blood shot eyes, (c) difficulty understanding information, (d) attention lapses, (e) decreased initiative or motivation at would, (f) poor insight of the impact of sleep deprivation, (g) falling asleep (micro-sleep) at inappropriate times, (g) excessive irritability or negativity, (h) transient psychotic symptoms, (i) excessive caffeine intake to counter fatigue, and (j) significantly falling behind on maintenance of equipment or work demands.

Active suicidal or homicidal ideation/attempts—consider hospitalization and postpone reprocessing (see Assessing Dangerousness section below).

Self-injury—serious life threatening, self-mutilation to reduce tension particularly if in crisis may not be suitable for EMDR reprocessing until client is more stabilized. In the meanwhile, the therapist might consider using RDI to help stabilized the client's tension reduction behaviors (Leeds, 2009). In doing so, it is important to understand client's motivation for self-mutilation:

- What led to your wanting to hurt yourself?
- When did you start feeling like hurting yourself—what was going on before that?
- How were you feeling beforehand?
- What other feelings did you have?
- When was the first time you remember hurting yourself like this?
- What was your immediate reaction when it happened?
- How did you expect to feel afterward?

Dissociative disorder—it is rare, but military clients with *dissociative identity disorder* (DID) or other severe forms of dissociation (e.g., psychogenic fugue) should not be in the military. In all cases, military stress will greatly destabilize clients with chronic, severe dissociative problems, and treating while on active-duty will likely exacerbate risks to those clients. Efforts should be made to assist the client to contact military medical personnel to initiate medical evaluation and possible discharge.

Screening for Dissociation Symptoms/Disorder

Shapiro (2001) advocates a "universal precautions" approach to EMDR treatment and dissociative disorders. It is recommended that all clients be screened for dissociation and given adequate preparation. Therapists are advised to not use basic EMDR skills with dissociative disordered clients, and are encouraged to attend EMDRIA-approved specialty workshops on the use of EMDR with dissociative disorders. That said, there are few, if any, circumstances that military personnel with a serious dissociative disorder (e.g., dissociative identity disorder) should be treated with EMDR while serving on active-duty given the inherent time and environmental constraints in military treatment settings as well as routine exposure to military stress and other occupational hazards. Such individuals, when identified should be referred to their military healthcare provider or the local military mental health clinic for evaluation and medical discharge. The more common scenario is for service members with war stress or other traumatic stress injuries to exhibit dissociative symptoms that in most cases can be reprocessed with the standard EMDR protocol.

Substance use disorder—clients with acute intoxication, suffering from severe withdrawal symptoms such as delirium tremens, which is a medical emergency, or diagnosed with a severe life-threatening addiction are not be suitable for EMDR reprocessing.

Medications use—anecdotal reports of certain medications that may complicate reprocessing effects have arisen. Use of certain medications will prompt medical screening for suitability of EMDR such as Lithium or Depakote for bipolar disorder, or Digitalis for cardiac patients. The general rule of thumb for psychotropic medications is reprocessing effects should be rechecked after the client tapers off medication in the case of possible medication-induced distortion effects.

Denial of diagnosis—clients who do not believe they have a treatable mental health condition should not be duped or pressured to undergo treatment. Attempts to proceed when in denial may put the client at risk.

Secondary gain—ordinarily, clients who are not being truthful with the therapist will not benefit from treatment including EMDR. There may be occasion where the client's blocking belief or motives for deception in order to deploy or remain on active duty could be targeted for EMDR reprocessing.

FUNCTIONAL ASSESSMENT

One of the main goals in treating clients with war stress injuries is to assist warriors to return to as "normal" or adaptive a level of functioning as possible. Therapists who are managing clients suffering from stress reactions or PTSD should consider a variety of factors when deciding if, and when, the client is suitable for EMDR, or ready to return to work or military duty. In making such determinations, therapists should consider the severity of the condition, level of occupational impairment, nature of the client's occupation, and the level of social support (Adapted from: *2010 VA/DoD Cinical Practice Guideline for Post-Traumatic Stress*).

Work: (a) Is the client unemployed or seeking employment? (b) If employed, is there any change in productivity? (c) Have co-workers or supervisors commented on any recent changes in appearance, quality of work, or relationships? (d) Is there any tardiness, loss of motivation, or loss of interests? (e) Has the client been more forgetful or easily distracted? (e) Does the client get low annual performance reports?

School: (a) Are there changes in relationships with friends? (b) Is there recent onset or increase in acting-out behaviors? (c) Is there recent increase in disciplinary actions? (d) Is there increased social withdrawal? (e) Does the client have difficulties with concentration and short-term memory? (f) Does the client experience frequent social conflict?

Marital and Family Relationships: (a) Are there negative changes in relationship with significant others? (b) Is the client irritable or easily angered by family members? (c) Does the client experience a withdrawal of interest in or time spent with family? (d) Has there been any violence within the family? (e) Are there any parenting difficulties? (f) Does the client experience any sexual function difficulties?

Recreation: (a) Are there changes in recreational interests? (b) Does the client experience decreased activity level or (c) poor motivation to care for self? (d) Is there a sudden decrease in physical activity or (e) Anhedonia?

Housing: (a) Does the person have adequate housing? (b) Are there appropriate utilities and services (electricity, plumbing, and other necessities of daily life)? (c) Is the housing situation stable? (d) Is there family advocacy or Department of Social Services (DSS) involvement?

Finances: (a) Does the patient have the fund for current necessities, including food, clothing, and shelter? (b) Is there a stable source of income? (c) Are there significant outstanding or past-due debts, alimony, or child support? (d) Has the patient filed for bankruptcy? (e) Does the patient have access to healthcare and/or insurance? (f) Are there letters of indebtedness?

CLIENT STABILITY CHECKLIST

Check if the client has adequate stabilization/self-control strategies in place to manage distress during or between sessions. Does the service member have adequate social support within and/or outside his or her unit? Systems issues that might endanger the client have been addressed. Does the client know about after-hours emergency resources between sessions if needed?

Special Considerations for Determining EMDR Suitability

Clients may present at intake, or later in treatment, with episodic crisis, or unstable mood or behavior including dangerousness to self or others that may postpone reprocessing.

Assessment of Dangerousness to Self or Others

Therapists need to assess for safety and dangerousness in all clients with war stress injuries and other traumatic stress injuries, including current risk to self or others, as well as historical patterns of risk. Evaluation of clients with suicidal ideation should include the determination of current intent, available means, and previous history of parasuicidal or suicidal behaviors. Clients with PTSD may be at increased risk for violence toward others. Problems with explosive anger, a past history of violent behavior, and substance use problems are all associated with heightened risk for violence. In regards to assessing client dangerousness in the DVA and DoD (2010), therapists should note that all clients with war stress injury, including subclinical PTSD, should be assessed for safety and dangerousness, including current risk to self or others, as well as historical patterns of risk.

In addition, the therapist should assess for the following: (a) suicidal or homicidal ideation, intent (plan), means (e.g., weapon, excess medications), history (e.g. violence or suicide attempts), behaviors (e.g., aggression, impulsivity), and co-morbidities (substance abuse, medical conditions); (b) family and social environment—including domestic or family violence, risks to the family; (c) witnessing a particularly gruesome or horrific loss of life, (d) home front or unit problems; (e) Suffering a combat loss, i.e., a friend or unit member wounded or killed in action; (f) ongoing health risks or risk-taking behavior; (g) anger toward or lack of support from higher command; (h) medical/psychiatric co-morbidities or unstable medical conditions; (i) potential to jeopardize mission in an operational environment; (j) history of disciplinary actions and UCMJ proceedings; (k) past history of violent behaviors; (l) pushing the ROE to the maximum extent; (m) severely agitated, aggressive, threatening, or hostile behaviors; (n) active psychotic symptom;, and (o) perpetrating war atrocity or other serious misconduct stress behavior (DVA/DoD, 2010).

Furthermore, therapists should ascertain: (a) any history of suicidal attempts—a family history, or a unit member history of a completed or attempted suicide should be taken seriously; (b) pay careful attention to patients with behaviors that may signal dangerousness (e.g., agitation, threatening, intimidation, paranoia, misconduct stress behaviors); and (c) access to weapons or other means of harm should also be taken seriously. Also assess for domestic or family violence, because these are elevated in clients with PTSD. Clinicians should keep in mind the possibility that thoughts or plans of violent acts toward others may represent thoughts of suicide, either after committing violence against another person, or by creating a situation where another person will be forced to harm the patient (e.g., "suicide by cop"). Other possible signs of at-risk behaviors include appearance and/or behavior changes such as: (a) lax military dress/bearing, (b) appearing on edge, (c) displaying angry outbursts, (d) taking excessive and/or intentional risks, (e) having minimal or no contact with others, and (f) changes in sleep patterns and appetite (DVA/DoD, 2010).

Assessing Military Unit Risk Factors

Unit risk factors are higher for unlawful behaviors and may precede violent inhuman acts or injuries to unit member when (Department of the Army, 2009): (a) there is an incidence of multiple military and civilian deaths occurring in the same area of operation and over a short period of time; (b) high OPTEMP with little respite between engagements; (c) rapid turnover of unit leaders; (d) manpower shortages; (e) overly and unreasonably restrictive or confusing Rules of Engagement (ROE); (f) perception of lack of support from higher command; and (g) an enemy that is indistinguishable from non-combatant civilians (DVA/DoD, 2010).

Assessing for Possible Dangerousness

- You sound like you've had a very difficult time recently. Has life ever seemed like it's not worth living?
- Have you ever thought about acting on those feelings? Have you thought of how you would do this?
- Sometimes, when people get really upset or angry, they feel like doing harm to other people. Have you had any thoughts recently about harming others?
- Giving everything you said that's been going on, what is it that has kept you from acting on these thoughts?

EMDR AND SUICIDAL OR HOMICIDAL IDEATION

Is it ever appropriate to use EMDR with clients endorsing suicidal or homicidal ideation? The answer is "it depends." If a therapeutic alliance has yet to be established, and a client is presenting with active suicidal or homicidal ideation, then it would be most prudent to activate the emergency response system (e.g., contact ER). However, with sufficient therapeutic rapport, and if a careful safety risk assessment of dangerousness indicates that the risk is "low," therapists can attempt to identify and reprocess the current, earliest, and worst incidents of self/other harm ideation. Afterwards, a reassessment of dangerousness should always be conducted prior to the client leaving the therapists' office.

EMDR TREATMENT PLANNING, GOALS, AND INTERVENTION CHOICE IN MILITARY SETTINGS

EMDR treatment planning involving military populations is premised on considering *six* key factors: (a) the referral question; (b) strength of the therapeutic alliance; (c) client treatment goals; (d) timing and environmental constraints; (e) clinical judgment regarding client safety, stability, and suitability for standard trauma-focused EMDR reprocessing protocol; and (f) utilization of any adjunctive intervention and referral. Synthesizing the information above will lead to choosing one, or a phased combination of *five* treatment goals: (a) stabilization, (b) primary symptom reduction, (c) comprehensive reprocessing, (d) resilience building or performance enhancement, and (e) prevention or treatment of compassion-stress injury. The recommendation for specific type of EMDR-related intervention (e.g., ERP, RDI, EMD, Mod-EMDR, EMDR, BIFP) is tailored to the treatment goal.

1. EMDR Treatment Goal: Client Stabilization

In the immediate aftermath of a traumatic event, the majority of survivors experience normal stress reactions. However, some may require immediate crisis intervention to help manage intense feelings of panic or grief. Signs of panic are trembling, agitation, rambling speech, and erratic behavior. Signs of intense grief may be loud wailing, rage, or catatonia. Clients may develop severe, debilitating Acute Stress Reactions (ASR)/Combat Operational Stress Reaction (COSR) that render them un-stable and/or unresponsive to medical or unit personnel as characterized by conscious, acute dissociation state, no or limited orientation to the present, or unresponsiveness or muteness to verbal interchange. In such cases, attempt to quickly establish therapeutic rapport, ensure the survivor's safety, acknowledge and validate the survivor's experience, and offer empathy after all basic safety needs have been taken care of and medical triage has been completed. A referral question from medical/nursing, unit medical or command, or other emergency personnel may request the therapist to assist with psychological stabilization in order to medically assess and/or transport to the next echelon of care.

Recommendations:

- **Emergency Response Procedure (ERP)**—see Chapter 6: EMDR Stabilization Intervention section for ERP description and protocol.
- *Purpose:* Stabilization by increasing orientation to present focus.
- If stabilized and deemed appropriate and consent is given, consider suitability for a higher level of EMDR intervention (symptom reduction, comprehensive reprocessing, or resilience building).

In the immediate or near-immediate aftermath of exposure to a severe, or potentially traumatic event, personnel may present with severe, debilitating Acute Stress Reactions (ASR)/Combat Operational Stress Reaction (COSR). If forward-deployed, the client has either refused, or not responded to standard medical/Combat (Operational) Stress Control, or other supportive interventions. Or, medical/clinical/unit personnel, or the client themselves, have requested intervention to stabilize neuropsychiatric symptoms in order to further assess, return to duty, or move to higher echelon of care. For instance, the client is too unstable for aeromedical or other transportation. If symptoms are severe, and include dissociative and traumatic stress symptoms, the client may meet diagnostic criteria for Acute Stress Disorder (1–30 days). All basic safety needs and medical triage, if indicated, have been completed. The referral question from medical/nursing, unit medical or command, or other emergency personnel is for the therapist to assist with reducing primary symptoms sufficient for psychological stabilization and movement to the next higher echelon of care. Treatment focus is crisis intervention limited to the precipitating event.

Recommendation:

- **Eye Movement Desensitization (EMD)**—see Chapter 6: EMDR Stabilization Intervention section for EMD protocol.
- *Purpose:* Reducing primary symptoms associated to the precipitating event only.
- If stabilized and deemed appropriate and consent is given, consider suitability for higher level of EMDR intervention (symptom-focused reduction, comprehensive reprocessing, or resilience building).

During EMDR client history taking or preparation, the client was determined to be unsuitable for EMDR reprocessing due to emotional or behavioral instability, safety, or other clinical indicators including time or environmental constraints (see Chapter 6, this volume). The referral source may be medical/clinical/unit or other involved personnel, including client self-referral requesting treatment, possibly specifically EMDR. Clinical findings revealed the client requires additional adaptive resources in order to be adequately stable and appropriate for future EMDR reprocessing. If forward deployed or in an operational environment, the principle aim is to stabilize the client's emotional or behavior state by increasing their access to adaptive, coping resources. It is appropriate for any acute or chronic neuropsychiatric and/or medically unexplained condition consistent with a war stress or other traumatic stress injury. Possible indications that the client may not be adequately stable or suitable for EMDR reprocessing include: (a) early neglect or inadequate attachment with caregiver; (b) client is alexithymic (cannot name their feelings); (c) client floods with feeling without being able to identify trigger; (d) client cannot speak when distressed; (e) standard self-care methods do not alleviate distress; (f) client can't give coherent narrative of recent distressing events; (g) client shows poor impulse control; (h) client does not trust perceptions and feelings; (i) client lacks adult perspective; and (j) client lacks skills for obtaining social support (F. Shapiro, 2005).

Recommendation:

- **Resource Development and Installation (RDI)**—see Chapter 6: EMDR Stabilization Intervention section for RDI description and protocol.
- *Purpose:* Increasing access to adaptive neural network to stabilize for reprocessing.
- If stabilized, appropriate, and consented to, consider suitability for higher level of EMDR intervention (symptom-focused reduction, comprehensive reprocessing, or resilience building).

2. EMDR Treatment Goal: Primary Symptom Reduction

A variety of contexts may arise that may preclude adherence to the standard EMDR trauma-focused protocol for otherwise stable and suitable military clientele. Such variables include: *time-sensitive constraints* (e.g., impending client or therapist absence, impending client deployment, etc.), *environmental demands* (e.g., forward-deployed, operational settings), and *client-stated preferences* (e.g., expressed desire to not address earlier foundational experiences other than such as pre-military incidents), that may lead to the joint decision to deviate from the standard EMDR protocol after full-informed consent if provided. Generally speaking, comprehensive EMDR reprocessing that includes reprocessing of pre-military memories, even on consecutive days, will usually not be appropriate if within *two weeks* the client will be deploying, PSC transfer (relocation), extended training exercise etc. Clinical judgment and full informed consent are necessary to determine if reprocessing can occur safely with a very short window. It is the author's (Mark Russell) experience that it can; however slight modifications of EMDR protocol may be needed.

In addition, depending on time, environmental constraints, and clinical judgment, primary symptom reduction may or may not include the installation or body scan phases, or reprocessing of current triggers and future template that is the standard EMDR protocol. Some clinicians (e.g., Russell, 2006) have reported successful symptom reduction in operational environments using a modified EMDR approach that was limited to the circumscribed recent or precipitating event (e.g., a current deployment) or a specific past combat or other traumatic incident and did not reprocess current or future antecedents because of time limitations. Therapists need to be familiar with the existing literature and provide informed consent to clients regarding potential advantages and limitations from deviation of an evidence-based protocol (see Chapters 7 and 9, this volume, for more information on this option). There are essentially two methods for limiting client focus to the primary presenting complaint: (a) EMD and (b) Modified or Mod-EMDR.

EMD: Essentially a behavioral exposure therapy that adds BLS and does not reinforce free associations outside of either a single-incident target memory (e.g., primary presenting complaint), or a circumscribed event (e.g., a recent deployment). Free associations reported outside the treatment parameters require the client to be returned to target memory whereby SUDS are re-accessed and BLS initiated. Clients may be returned to the target memory at any time by the therapist where SUDS are obtained to assess progress of desensitization effect. Repeat the process until the target memory has SUDS of "0" is obtained or "1" if ecologically valid. Installation, body scan, current triggers, and future template are not included.

Advantages: (a) Allows more strictly controlled reprocessing by reducing the chance for generalization to other memories, which might speed up symptom relief. (b) When free associations outside of the target occur, the client is immediately returned to target memory, which may prevent the client from in-depth exposure to other sources of emotionally intense material. (c) It may provide clients a mastery experience with EMDR that may open the door for comprehensive reprocessing with standard EMDR protocol. (d) It provides potentially more rapid relief of most intense symptoms than either modified or standard EMDR. (e) Primary symptom reduction may prevent escalation or exacerbation of stress injury and more readily improve client functioning at least in the short term. (f) It may reassure military clients concerned about culture expectations that emphasize self-control and military readiness in the context of accessing earlier life events. (g) It provides a viable option for military clients who otherwise may refuse therapy.

Disadvantages: (a) Desensitization effects may not sustain due to unprocessed other past, current, and future contributors. (b) Reduction of primary symptoms may result in client termination without addressing other contributors. (c) The increased possibility that stress injury may persist as sub-chronic is more prone to kindling and relapse in response to future acute stress. (d) The client will probably be exposed, even if fleetingly, to other negative associations in the maladaptive neural network—thorough informed consent is needed.

Mod-EMDR: Similarly, client attention is limited to single-incident target memory or a circumscribed event (e.g., specific operational mission). Negative free associations reported outside treatment parameters require the client to be returned to target memory. Installation, body scan, current triggers, and future template are selected in relation to the target memory and reprocessed according. Adaptive or position free associations may be reinforced outside of target parameters; however, if negative associations arise, the client is returned to the target memory. SUDS and VoC are measured in accordance with the standard protocol.

Advantages: (a) There is less controlled processing than EMD, but more than standard EMDR, thus lessening chance of generalization to other memories and may speed up symptom reduction. (b) It includes reprocessing of adaptive neural networks (installation, future template). (c) It provides a mastery experience with EMDR that may lead to comprehensive reprocessing down the road. (d) Probably more rapid relief from presenting symptoms is achieved than in standard EMDR. (e) It reduces the possibility of relapse more than EMD by targeting current and future antecedents, as well as strengthening adaptive resources via installation. (f) It may reassure military clients concerned about culture expectations that emphasize self-control and military readiness in the context of accessing earlier life events. (g) It provides a viable option for military clients who otherwise may refuse EMDR or other mental health treatment.

Disadvantages: (a) There is a longer treatment duration than with EMD due to inclusion of installation, body scan, current, and future antecedents. (b) Desensitization effects may not be sufficient after a single memory or cluster is processed that will allow successful installation and body scan. (c) There is a greater chance of relapse than with standard EMDR due to remaining unprocessed past memories. (d) The reduction of primary symptoms may result in client termination without addressing other past contributors. (e) There is the increased possibility that stress injury may persist as sub-chronic, thereby making the client more prone to kindling and relapse in response to acute stress.

3. EMDR Treatment Goal: Comprehensive Reprocessing

This is the only evidence-based EMDR protocol, and it follows the standard three-pronged approach involving all identifiable and/or representative past contributors, current triggers, and the future template. It is appropriate for the treatment of the full-spectrum of neuropsychiatric conditions and medically unexplained conditions that are associated with war stress injury or other traumatic stress injury. Adaptations to the standard EMDR protocol have been developed by clinicians that may enhance EMDR reprocessing with diagnoses such as substance use disorder, chronic pain, phobia, panic disorder, recent events, and dissociative disorder (see Shapiro, 2001; Leeds, 2009; Luber, 2009). However, military clients presenting with primary or secondary conditions associated with ASD, PTSD, chronic pain, anger, phantom limb, substance abuse, traumatic grief, dissociative symptoms, MUS, etc., have been successfully treated using just the standard EMDR protocol or those reviewed earlier (see Chapters 8–13, this volume).

Advantages: (a) Reprocessing is uncontrolled, as opposed to EMD or Mod-EMDR, which significantly increases generalization to other memories and may result in more comprehensive treatment effects. (b) It includes greater strengthening of adaptive neural networks (installation, future template) than Mod-EMDR by expanding the number of target memories. (c) Overall, it may shorten the treatment period versus a piecemeal approach that also potentially reduces client suffering over time. (d) It is the only evidence-based, trauma-focused EMDR protocol. (e) It reduces the possibility of relapse more than Mod-EMDR or EMD by expanding to past contributors, current, and future antecedents, as well as strengthening adaptive resources via installation. (f) Short-term worries of diminished control can be overshadowed by significantly gaining control after resolving past issues. (g) It may decrease the need for medications. (h) There is a decreased possibility that stress injury will persist as sub-chronic and be prone to kindling and relapse in response to acute stress. (i) It may prevent chronic or permanent health effects from stress injury. (j) It can be more rapid, less intrusive, less time-consuming, and more user-friendly than other non-EMDR treatment options.

Disadvantages: (a) It has a longer treatment duration than EMD or Mod-EMDR due to comprehensiveness of the treatment plan. (b) There's a potentially greater risk to military personnel in imminent, time sensitive or environment settings (e.g., operational deployment) due to accessing past material that can temporarily impact the client's stability and capacity to function in high-stress environments. (c) Irregularity in session frequency due to scheduling conflicts or other disruptive demands may interfere with continuity of care during periods of intense reprocessing. (d) It may not be appropriate in many forward-deployed or operational environments. (e) The prospect of accessing pre-military and early adverse life events, especially in a high OPTEMPO environment, can be intimidating for military personnel immersed in a culture that emphasizes maintaining self-control and military readiness at all time. (f) It has possibly greater likelihood of treatment refusal, premature termination, or drop-out than Mod-EMDR or EMD.

4. EMDR Treatment Goal: Resilience Building and Performance Enhancement

There is great interest within military populations to improve in any feasible way the resilience and performance of men and women working in high-stress environments. To that end, EMDR has considerable untapped potential. Variations of the standard EMDR protocol have been published by various clinicians demonstrating the potential for bilateral stimulation to be applied to strengthening the client's resiliency and improve their ability to perform unhindered by distractions such as performance anxiety and self-defeating beliefs, including athletes and professional entertainers. We chose to focus on *Resource Development and Installation* (RDI; Leeds & Korn, 2002) as one tool for building resilience because it has been incorporated in standard EMDR trainings and shown to have clinical effectiveness in stabilizing chronically distressed clients by increasing access to their adaptive neural networks— which is the essence of resilience.

Brief Intervention Focusing Protocol (Lendl & Foster, 2009) has instant appeal by offering a quick, simple intervention to potentially reduce internal and external distractions such as performance anxiety and fear of failure that prevent military personnel from performing to the best of their ability in high-stress operational environments. Similar to RDI, clients should be informed that, while case studies have shown that EMDR may help some clients with decreasing performance-related anxiety and increase self-mastery and possibly their performance, there are no controlled studies to support this variation of EMDR as evidence-based. However, there are no known reports of client harm, and it is conceivable that some military clients may benefit from this approach to ease a wide-range of performance-related anxiety such as leading a small unit, conducting a mission, or performing weapon qualifications, etc. (see Chapter 16, this volume).

Recommendation:
- **Resource Development and Installation (RDI)**—see Chapters 6 and 16, in this volume.
- *Purpose:* To strengthen resilience by increasing access to adaptive neural networks.
- **Brief Intervention Focusing Protocol (BIFP)**—see Chapter 16, in this volume.
- *Purpose:* To enhance task performance by reducing distractions.

5. EMDR Treatment Goal: Prevention and Treatment of Compassion Stress Injury

The healers of the warrior class are themselves vulnerable to the exposure of chronic, inescapable compassion-stress and potentially traumatic stress that can lead to acute, transient compassion-stress injury, or more severe and chronic compassion-stress injury including burnout. Therapists are strongly encouraged to monitor the balance of their protective and risk factors and develop a regular self-care program. In addition to traditional self-care plans, we outline the daily use of bilateral stimulation and compassion-stressors as a means to avert accumulation and progression into compassion fatigue, secondary or vicarious PTSD and the like. In the event the therapist does develop a compassion-stress injury, treatment would be in the form of either modified-EMDR that restricts self-focus attention to particular client(s) or one's clinical practice, or standard EMDR to potentially address other past contributors that increase occupational risk (see Chapter 16, in this volume).

Recommendation:
- **EMDR Compassion-Stress Protocol**—see Chapter 16, in this volume.
- *Purpose:* Preventing accumulation of compassion stress to avert compassion fatigue.
- **Mod-or-Standard EMDR**—see Chapter 16, in this volume.
- *Purpose:* Treatment of compassion fatigue and its underlying experiential contributors.

FINAL CHECKLIST FOR COMPLETION OF PHASE ONE

Is there sufficient or emerging trust and truth telling evident in the therapeutic alliance? Have the therapist and client jointly reviewed the referral question, informed consent, and discussed limits of confidentiality? Does the client demonstrate adequate capacity to tolerate affect and manage stress? Have client stability and suitability for EMDR been assessed? Have immediate safety issues, if present, been addressed? Have secondary gain issues been identified and appropriately addressed? Has a collaborative treatment plan has been developed appropriate for the referral question, client's treatment goals, and other clinical considerations? Have the clinician and client considered severity of issues which may be activated based on history and clinical assessment? Does the treatment plan for standard EMDR therapy include the selection of appropriate past, present, and future experiential contributors? Do the client and clinician have sufficient time to implement the treatment plan? If there was a "check" response to each of the applicable items, then we are ready to move onto Phase Two.

6 Phase Two:
Client Preparation and
Informed Consent

After completing Phase One, the therapist readies the client for EMDR therapy by strengthening the collaborative, therapeutic alliance through discussing the assessment results, treatment options, and the initial treatment plan. If the client opts for a trial of EMDR, practitioners provide the client an explanation of traumatic stress injuries, and a working hypothesis of EMDR treatment. The procedural method of EMDR is then reviewed and demonstrated, along with client and therapist expectations. The second phase may conclude with an in-session stress management practice session that typically involves introducing dual-focused attention and bilateral stimulation. Clients deemed too unstable or unsuitable for EMDR reprocessing will continue with preparatory sessions utilizing variant EMDR procedures like Resource Development and Installation (RDI).

ENHANCING THE THERAPEUTIC RELATIONSHIP

Earlier we mentioned that there are times and settings within the military (e.g., forward-deployed, operational environment), whereby the EMDR intervention maybe limited to a 1–2 sessions. Therefore a workable alliance needs to be established very quickly. The history taking and target selection will be significantly abbreviated and narrowly focused on the precipitant event. In these scenarios, client preparation moves extremely quickly. This is obviously quite different for therapists implementing the standard EMDR protocol. We will cover both scenarios in this section.

ACUTE STRESS REACTIONS/COSR IN THE MILITARY AND EMDR EARLY INTERVENTION

Acute interventions can be envisioned as the mental health correlate of physical first aid, with the goal being to "stop the psychological bleeding." The first, most important measure should be to eliminate (if possible) the source of the trauma or to remove the victim from the traumatic, stressful environment. Once the patient is in a safe situation, the provider should attempt to reassure the patient, encourage a professional healing relationship, encourage a feeling of safety, and identify existing social supports. Establishing safety and assurance may enable people to get back on track, and maintain their pre-trauma stable condition. Some want and feel a need to discuss the event, and some have no such need. Respect individual and cultural preferences in the attempt to meet their needs as much as possible. Allow for normal recovery and monitor.

Recommended Interventions for COSR

According to the DVA/DoD (2010) *Clinical Practice Guideline*, Combat Operation Stress Control (COSC) utilizes the management principles of brevity, immediacy, contact, expectancy, proximity, and simplicity (BICEPS). These principles apply to all COSC interventions or activities throughout the theater, and are followed by COSC personnel in all mental health and COSC elements. These principles may be applied differently based on a particular level of care and other factors pertaining to mission, enemy, terrain and weather, troops and support available, time available, and civil considerations. The actions used for COSC (commonly referred to as the 6 Rs) involve the following actions:

- **R**eassure of normality (normalize the reaction)
- **R**est (respite from combat or break from work)
- **R**eplenish bodily needs (such as thermal comfort, water, food, hygiene, and sleep)
- **R**estore confidence with purposeful activities and talk
- **R**etain contact with fellow Soldiers and unit
- **R**emind/**R**ecognize emotion of reaction (specifically potentially life-threatening thoughts and behaviors)

Early Treatment of Severe ASR/COSR and ASD

In regards to intervening with severe ASR/COSR and ASD, the DVA and DoD (2010) recommend the following:

- Acutely traumatized people who meet the criteria for diagnosis of ASD and those with significant levels of post-trauma symptoms after at least two weeks post-trauma, as well as those who are incapacitated by acute psychological or physical symptoms, should receive further assessment and early intervention to prevent PTSD. Trauma survivors, who present with symptoms that do not meet the diagnostic threshold for ASD, or those who have recovered from the trauma and currently show no symptoms, should be monitored and may benefit from follow-up and provision of ongoing counseling or symptomatic treatment.

- Service members with COSR who do not respond to initial supportive interventions may warrant referral or evacuation.

Prepping for EMDR

After addressing the acute needs of military members, including possible implementation of BICEPS and the COSR "6 Rs," some or many personnel may continue to be negatively impacted, and develop severe debilitating ASR/COSR or even Acute Stress Disorder (ASD). According to the DVA/DoD (2010), individuals developing ASD are at greater risk of developing PTSD and should be identified and offered treatment as soon as possible. In order to stabilize, reduce, or heal the worsening stress injury, early interventions such as EMDR or a variant may be helpful. Unfortunately, due to institutional military medicine's ban on EMDR research (see Chapter 3, this volume), only case studies and anecdotal clinical reports have been published on EMDR treatment for acute war stress injury, but controlled and uncontrolled reports on EMDR and ASR in the civilian sector have been reviewed (e.g., Shapiro, 2009). Nevertheless, the *Clinical Practice Guideline for Management of Post-Traumatic Stress* (DVA/DoD 2010) have concluded that cognitive-behavioral techniques are the current early intervention of choice. Although the military's practice guidelines do not single out EMDR as an early intervention per se, EMDR is explicitly listed by the guidelines as a trauma-focused cognitive-behavioral treatment that is evidence-based for the treatment of traumatic stress injuries. Therefore EMDR can and should be reasonably considered a viable frontline option. A variety of situations in the military may arise, whereby there is a very tight window for intervening with EMDR and the extent of client history taking and rapport building is extremely compressed.

EMDR STABILIZATION INTERVENTIONS

In Chapter 5 we provided an outline of treatment options including specific EMDR-related protocols for addressing the treatment goal. The first treatment goal is client "stabilization." Below is a description and example of the protocol for each of the EMDR-related interventions that might be used explicitly to enhance client stability either to refer to a higher echelon of care, or to prepare for EMDR reprocessing. The three stabilizations procedures were Emergency Response Procedure (ERP), Eye Movement Desensitization (EMD), and Resource Development and Installation (RDI).

Emergency Response Procedure (ERP)

Purpose: Stabilization of client by increasing orientation to present focus. Gary Quinn, an Israeli psychologist, reported utilizing a modified EMDR protocol he called Emergency Reprocessing Procedure (ERP; Quinn, 2009). Following a terrorist bombing incident in Israel, traumatized patients were brought to emergency rooms, and Dr. Quinn was on call. Clients suffering from acute stress reaction sat in "shock" and were unresponsive to verbal questions or commands by medical personnel needed to perform triage. After routine attempts to engage the blankly starring client, Dr. Quinn contemplated whether an EMDR-variant might reach the client. Speaking calmly in the client's ear, Dr. Quinn identified himself and his role in the hospital, and he reassured the client of their safety in the hospital. Afterwards, he informed clients that he was going to tap them gently on the shoulder and remind them where they are, that they had survived the bombing, and they were now at a safe place. After brief periods of the bilateral taps and therapist-directed attention to safety, clients became responsive to outside stimuli and could then be engaged verbally about their medical status and so on. To our knowledge this has not been tested or replicated in military settings. In regards to the therapeutic alliance and client preparation, even in emergency scenarios like this, the therapist conveyed a caring, respectful, and empathic approach toward acutely distressed clients, and provided a measure of control by informing the client of each step to be taken. The total intervention time would be measured in minutes (see Quinn, 2009).

Eye Movement Desensitization (EMD)

Purpose: Reducing primary symptoms associated to the precipitating event only. In the immediate or near-immediate aftermath of exposure to severe or potentially traumatic event, personnel may present with severe, debilitating ASR/COSR. If the client is conscious and medically cleared but presents as acutely dissociated and verbally unresponsive (AKA psychic shock), then the therapist should consider ERP or another grounding technique instead. If forward-deployed, the client has either refused or not responded to standard medical/Combat (Operational) Stress Control or other supportive interventions. Or medical/clinical/unit personnel—or the client his/herself—have requested intervention to stabilize neuropsychiatric symptoms in order to further assess, return to duty, or move to higher echelon of care. For instance, the client is too unstable for aeromedical or other transportation. If symptoms are severe and include dissociative and traumatic stress symptoms, the client may meet diagnostic criteria for Acute Stress Disorder (1–30 days). All basic safety needs and medical triage, if indicated, have been completed. A referral question from medical/nursing, unit medical or command, or other emergency personnel is for the therapist to assist with reducing primary symptoms sufficient for psychological stabilization and movement to next higher echelon of care. Treatment focus is crisis intervention limited to the precipitating event.

EMD Description

EMD is essentially a behavioral exposure therapy that incorporates bilateral stimulation (BLS) in a desensitization paradigm, with BLS serving as the reciprocal inhibitory response to the client's stress-response. In EMD, the therapist does not reinforce or pursue free associations outside of the single-incident precipitating event.

EMD Stabilization Protocol

Client history, preparation, and informed consent.   When possible, obtain information about the precipitating event, and the client's involvement should be obtained from the referral source (e.g., medical, nursing, or unit personnel). The therapist introduces himself, his role, and the reason for referral. The therapist should ask, "Is it okay if I talk to you?" If the client consents, ask him or her to share the narrative of the event and his or her involvement. See the case study for Acute Stress Injury below for further information related to history, preparation, consent, etc.

Selecting Target Memory: Ask the client, *"What is the most disturbing part to you about what just happened?"* or words to that effect. Remember to keep the focus on the precipitating event. Only one past memory is selected. Current trigger and future desired behavior are not targeted.

Image or sensory memory: *"Is there one image or picture in particular, that represents the worst part of that gravesite (name the incident) scene?"*

Negative Cognition: *"All right, so as you keep thinking about the gravesite (name the incident) memory, and the picture of the _____ (name the image), what words go best with that picture that expresses your negative belief about yourself now?*

Note: The Positive Cognition and VOC are not usually assessed in EMD for stabilization purposes, as the intention is symptom reduction and stabilization. Installation and Body Scan Phases are not included.

Emotion: *"When you think of this dog incident and the words 'I can't stand it anymore,' what feelings or emotion come up?"*

SUDS Rating: *Ex. "I can see you're in a lot of pain Staff Sergeant, on a 0 to 10 scale, 0 you feel no distress or other disturbance and 10 the worst disturbance you can think of, how disturbing does it feel now?"*

Physical Sensations and Location: *"And where do you feel it in your body?"*

Reprocessing: After the therapist writes down the location of the physical sensations say, *"Ok, pay attention to those (name physical sensations) in your (state body location) and that picture (name the picture) and follow my hand with your eyes"* and slowly start the eye movement (EM) and make sure they are tracking, then speed up as fast as they track. Be aware that dissociative symptoms like derealization and depersonalizing make it more difficult to concentrate on external stimuli, so the EM speed can be slower than nonacute, dissociative states. Changing direction, flickering of the fingers, and verbal prompts by the therapist may prevent the client from habituating to the stimulus.

Dual-Focused Attention: It is vitally important to maintain the client's dual-focused attention during the reprocessing by talking to the client, "That's it ... good ... just keep tracking ... you're safe now ... that's it ... just notice it ... you're safe now ... good ... it's in the past ..." etc. In Chapter 9, a treatment case study is provided with a solider presenting with a high level of dissociation, and it is apparent how verbally engaged the therapist needs to be at times to prevent self-absorption and maintain the dual-focus.

Reprocessing to Completion: If during BLS, the client reports a free association that appears unrelated to the precipitating event, gently say *"Ok, now I would like you to go back to the bombing incident (name the event), what do you notice now?"* Obtain a SUDS rating each time the client returns to the target memory. After obtaining the SUDS instruct, *"Just think of that...."* Repeat this sequence each time the client self-reports an association outside of the treatment parameter. The client may be returned to the target memory and asked for a SUDS rating any time the therapist wants to check the progress of the desensitization effect. Repeat the process until target memory has a SUDS of "0" or "1" if ecologically valid. Installation, body scan, current triggers, and future template are not included.

Reevaluation: Generally, it is a good idea to contact the client, their medical attendant, or command within a day to check on the client's condition. If appropriate, additional reprocessing (e.g., EMD, EMDR) or strengthening resilience (e.g., RDI) may be recommended.

Resource Development and Installation (RDI)

Client history taking may reveal that certain clients are too unstable or not appropriate for reprocessing due to temporary time constraints, emotional or behavioral instability, or poor self-regulation skills. Resource Development and Installation (RDI) was developed by Drs. Andrew Leeds and Debra Korn as a means to enhance or strengthen the client's access to internal "resources" associated with their adaptive neural networks (Leeds, 2009). During EMDR client history taking or preparation, the client was determined to be unsuitable for EMDR reprocessing due to emotional or behavioral instability, safety, or other clinical indicators including time or environmental constraints (see Chapter 5, this volume). The referral source may be medical/clinical/unit or other involved personnel, including client self-referral requesting treatment, possibly specifically EMDR. The potential need and use of RDI are evident by the high prevalence of pre-military history of trauma and other adverse childhood experiences in newly accessioned military personnel. Moreover, according to the DVA/DoD (2010) post-traumatic stress guidelines, individuals with severe childhood trauma (e.g., sexual abuse) may present with complex PTSD symptoms and parasuicidal behaviors (e.g., self-mutilation, medication overdoses) (Roth et al., 1997, cited in DVA/DoD, 2010). Further, limited cognitive coping styles in PTSD have been linked to a heightened suicide risk (Amir et al., 1999, cited in DVA/DoD, 2010). Fostering competence and social support may reduce this risk (Kotler et al., 2001, cited in DVA/DoD, 2010). Co-morbid substance use disorders may increase the risk of suicidality. Additionally, persons with PTSD may also be at personal risk of danger through ongoing or future victimization in relationships (e.g., domestic violence/battering, or rape).

Clinical findings revealed the client requires additional adaptive resources in order to be adequately stable and appropriate for future EMDR reprocessing. If forward-deployed or in an operational environment, the principle aim is to stabilize the client's emotional or behavior state by increasing their access to adaptive, coping resources. This is appropriate for any acute or chronic neuropsychiatric and/or medically unexplained condition consistent with a war stress or other traumatic stress injury. Possible indications that the client may not be adequately stable or suitable for EMDR reprocessing are reviewed on pages 79–82. The following are potential resources targets (from F. Shapiro, 2005; used with permission):

Types of Possible Resources

Mastery: Experience of past coping, self-care, or self-soothing stance or movement that evokes needed state.

Relationship: (a) Positive role models, (b) Memories of supportive others.

Symbolic: (a) Natural objects that represent the needed attribute, (b) Symbols from dreams, daydreams, or guided imagery, (c) Cultural, religious or spiritual symbols, (d) Metaphors, (e) Music, (f) Image of positive goal state or future self.

RDI Protocol

1. **Identifying the Resource:** "When you think about that memory (or incident) what positive resource, skill, or strength would help you to deal better with the situation?"
2. **Explore the Most Helpful Resource: (mastery experience, relational resource, or symbol/metaphor):** "Has there been a time or a situation in your life when you have successfully used that _____ (resource, skill, or strength)?" If the client answer is no, then: "Do you know anyone who has this quality? Or can you think about someone who has this quality? Or a character from a book, movie, or TV?" If

the answer is still no, then: "What image or symbol or metaphor might represent this resource?"

3. **Add Emotions and Sensations:** "When you think about this resource, is there an image that comes to mind?" "And when you think about the resource and that image, what emotions do you notice?" "And what physical sensations do you notice?"

4. **Checking the Resource:** "When you think about that challenging memory (or situation) would being able to use this resource be helpful?" "Can you rate how helpful it would be on a scale of 1 to 7 where 1 is not helpful at all and 7 is very helpful?" "And can you think about that resource and the related image, emotions, and feelings without any negative associations or feelings?" If not helpful at all, or if the client can't connect without negative associations, then return to Step 2 and identify a different resource.

5. **Resource Installation:** "Now bring up that resource, and the image, the emotions, and notice where you feel it in your body … than follow my fingers." Add short sets (6–12) of bilateral stimulations (BLS). Then, "What are you noticing now?" If positive, add another few short sets of BLS. After each set, ask what the client is noticing.

6. **Cue Word-Par With a Word or Symbol:** "Is there a word or a symbol that could represent this resource?" Pair word or symbol with resource and add short-sets of BLS. After BLS, always ask clients what they are noticing now.

7. **Future Desired Outcome:** "Now hold that resource together with the thought of that challenging memory (or situation) … and follow my fingers." Add short sets of BLS: "You can feel that resource exactly as you need to feel it." "You can experience that resource exactly as you need to experience it."

8. **Verify the usefulness of the Resource:** "Now when you think about that challenging memory (or situation) how useful would this resource be on a scale of 1 to 7, where 1 is not helpful at all and 7 is very helpful?"

9. **Practice and Reevaluation:** Ask the client to practice bringing up the resource between sessions. The therapist can access and strengthen the resource prior to trauma work. Reevaluate the strength and usefulness in future sessions.

CASE STUDY: CLIENT PREPARATION FOR ACUTE WAR STRESS INJURY

Another example of a time compressed military environment is one that the author (Mark Russell) is immanently familiar with. A 250-bed Navy field hospital served as one of two aeromedical evacuation points for Iraqi battlefield casualties at the outset of the invasion. A high OTEMPO environment, aircraft would land daily, unload medical casualties, and load and transport those stable enough to Walter Reed. We ran a neuropsychiatric service that included a reconditioning ward, and screened over 1,300 evacuees for war stress injury (Russell et al., 2005). The average length of patient stay was 2–3 days, so there was very high OPTEMPO. Four wounded military personnel were referred to the author (Mark Russell) because they were too severely debilitated by their combat stress injury, and were not stable enough for medical transport within the next few days (the following was adapted from Russell, 2006). To make a long story short, the author met with each client on the ward and utilized the following EMD protocol:

Client History (15 minutes):

Referral question.   As we discussed earlier, the referral question is pivotal for treatment planning. In this case, we knew the clients would be leaving within the next 1–3 days, but possibly as early as the next day if their war stress injury stabilized. Therefore it was evident that the standard EMDR protocol was impractical, as were possibly other procedural steps that we will discuss in order. With the AIP model as a guide, previous clinical experience with EMDR dictated that by focusing on the most emotionally charged memory related to the client's presenting complaint, we should be able to see a reduction in symptom intensity, hopefully, to the point of stabilizing the client's condition so they can be transported to the next echelon of care. Neither the referral source nor the client, were requesting a "cure" of the war stress injury, and if they had, it would be prudent to indicate that the current time and environmental constraints would make that hard at best. No, the referral question was clear, and the treatment plan was designed accordingly.

Establishing a therapeutic alliance.   Introduction, reviewed reason for referral, and informed consent was obtained to speak with a mental health staff. The therapist attempted to establish rapport and trust by communicating genuine care, concern for the client's well-being, empathy, and a desire to help, as well as respectfully informing clients of the reason and purpose of the visit, and asking permission to speak to the clients about their current difficulties.

Selecting past target memory—worst memory from deployment.   In the operational setting, client history was limited to inquiring about the client's presenting complaint, and more specifically, to the most disturbing event that was causing the debilitating acute stress reaction. This was solicited by asking clients something like: "If you had to pick one thing that stands out, what is the most disturbing event that's bothering you the most right now?" As the clients shared their combat narrative, the author (Mark Russell) jotted down details of the incidents given along with their descriptive phrases which would be used to convey empathic understanding.

Selecting current and future target memories.   The therapist did not solicit current trigger and future template. The best explanation as to why is that it has been the author's (Mark Russell) experience with EMDR that the generalization effect from reprocessing the most highly emotionally charged past memory, tends to greatly diminish and sometimes ameliorate the current trigger and future anticipatory anxiety, etc. The other reason for by-passing the three-pronged protocol was time, the referral question, and the client's goals.

Client stability. Clients were asked if they have any active suicidal or homicidal thoughts. Afterwards, clients were asked if they were up to continuing, as many became quite visibly distressed in relaying the "worst" part of their deployment experience.

Baseline symptom measures. All clients were asked to complete the Impact of Events Scale. All clients meet criteria for either acute combat-stress disorder or acute-combat PTSD.

Client Preparation (10 minutes):

Enhancing therapeutic trust and rapport. The therapist continued to build rapport by communicating in a caring, respectful, empathic manner. Emphasis was on clients having control over the consent process as well as EMDR session itself.

Informed consent about treatments. "There might be something we could do to help with some of the worst parts of your memories so that you might be able to sleep and go home without the memories bothering you as much as they are right now. However, I cannot guarantee that the treatment will work for you. I can also recommend to the psychiatrist to prescribe something to help you sleep and reduce some of your symptoms, either instead of EMDR, or after treatment if you need it. If you do choose a trial of EMDR, you will still need to follow up at your CONUS MTF (stateside hospital) to make sure that things haven't changed for the worse. EMDR stands for eye movement desensitization and reprocessing; a mouthful, I know, which is why we just say EMDR. In a nutshell this is what we will do: I'm going to ask you some questions just to get an enough of an idea of what's giving you these nightmares. If you don't want to answer a particular question, or any questions, that's entirely up to you. In normal EMDR we would let your memories shift anywhere they need to go including before you joined the military. What we're going to do in this case is keep the focus just on the immediate issue that's giving you the hardest time. Almost all of the time, you're going to know before I do if things are changing for you or not, and whether it is helping. Doing the eye movements will require you to revisit some bad experiences, but it sounds like that's already happening anyways. From time to time, I'll ask you to give me a 0–10 rating, so we both know where things are going. Any questions? Is this still something that you want to try or do you want to look at other options?"

Stop signal was established. "During EMDR you are the one in control, so anytime you want to stop, we stop, no questions asked … however just so that I am clear, if you want me to stop, in addition to saying "stop," is there a hand signal or something you can also give me … so that I know you mean for ME to stop, and not something that you are remembering?" Client chose to raise his hand and say "stop."

Brief EMDR procedural overview.   "I am going to ask you to bring up the memory of X, and, at the same time, while you are wide awake I am going to ask you to follow my fingers with your eye, like this ... (demonstrated diagonal eye movements that client's tracked with their eyes) ... that's it, just track my hand with your eyes only."

Clarifying therapist and client role expectations.   "I've been using EMDR for many years now, and each person has a slightly different experience ... sometimes they report the memory changes to another memory, or the image might change, the feeling, people's thoughts, or physical sensations might change ... sometimes people report nothing changes ... when we start EMDR, I just need you to tell me honestly what you are noticing, you don't have to tell me all the details, and you can tell me as much as you like, the main thing that I need to know, is if something is changing or not, does that make sense?"

Informed consent regarding potential pros and cons of using EMDR.   "I need to also tell you that it is common when we use EMDR that people may remember things very clearly, just like it was when it happened the first time; the thing to remember is that it has already happened and is just a memory, so you are safe here. But that can happen.... The other thing is that people report that, when they start EMDR with one memory, it might shift to other memories, including things that happened long ago, like in childhood, but are somehow maybe related to the current event ... so I want you to know that those are some of the things that 'might' happen.... Again, for some people nothing might happen ... does that seem clear to you? Do you still want to go forward with EMDR, or maybe try something else?" All clients selected to stay with EMDR.

Review of theoretical models.   There was no explanation of the theoretical model of acute stress disorder or PTSD, nor was there an explanation of EMDR theory. Time was one consideration, but mainly it seemed inappropriate because of the acute nature of their distress to lecture, however briefly, about what we think is going on in the brain, or why EMDR works; it seemed to be information overload. However, as it would turn out, clients did ask about EMDR theory after the session as they grappled with understanding what just happened.

Stress reduction methods.   No instruction on calm/safe place or any other coping skill was given. The reason was because of time consideration, and teaching calm or safe place immediately after being medically evacuated from war, struck me as problematic. Many patients I spoke to were infinitely more upset about having to be evacuated away from their unit members, than the wounds or injuries they sustained. At any rate, I chose to forgo the practice session, and move onto Phase Three.

Clinical Note. All four interventions went according to the script described above. The actual time spent on the first two phases maybe shorter for some, or slightly longer for others, but generally speaking, things moved quick and for a purpose. The author (Mark Russell) had confidence in the AIP model and the potential generalization effects of EMDR, even when there was deviation to the standard protocol. Those modifications, however, were in concert with the exigencies at the time. There was no pretense that a single session of a modified EMDR, what some have referred to as "EMD," was going to permanently resolve the client's acute war stress injury, and this was appropriately communicated to every client. Emphasis on honest, respectful, and empathic communication, along with seizing opportunities to instill a sense of client agency or control, was intentional, and served to create the therapeutic conditions for change. When clients were asked repeatedly whether they wanted to proceed further, it was with sincere readiness to shift gears. Regularly, clients are informed that EMDR is no panacea, and a change in direction can occur if EMDR does not work for them. Reducing the so-called demand characteristics in good faith seems to resonate with military clients that the only real agenda of the therapist is their health and well-being.

CASE STUDY: CLIENT PREPARATION FOR CHRONIC WAR STRESS INJURY

We have already mentioned most of what is covered in Phase Two. After elaborating upon the specific components of client preparation for EMDR, our discussion will turn to examining military-specific applications.

Psychoeducation of Traumatic Stress Injuries

Most therapists are familiar with the need to educate their clients about their diagnosis, practical ways to cope or reduce their symptoms, and items to avoid that can worsen their condition and/or response to treatment—this is especially the case with war stress/traumatic stress injuries. Education can help establish the credibility of the therapist and make treatment seem immediately helpful to the patient, and help prepare the patient for next steps in treatment should continue throughout PTSD treatment, sometimes in brief discussions. Clients should be educated of available support services and during and after their course of treatment. For clients experiencing relationship, or grief issues, education about pastoral care through the chaplain's office, or family counseling support programs can be useful to address the whole person. Military culture does not attach any stigma to speaking with a chaplain although some military members may be reluctant to seek mental health assistance. Education from military chaplains may reduce barriers to care. Similarly, there are dieticians and personal exercise trainers through the base health clinics or Morale Welfare and Recreation (MWR) including yoga and other meditative activities.

The *DVA/DoD Clinical Practice Guideline for the Management of Post-Traumatic Stress* (2010) makes the following recommendations regarding military client education: (a) Teach the client to label, recognize, and understand PTSD symptoms (and other trauma-related problems) that they are experiencing; (b) Discuss the potential consequences of further exposure to traumatic stress; (c) Discussion of the adaptive nature of many of the symptoms, which have to do with survival and the body's normal responses to threat; (d) Review practical ways of coping with traumatic stress symptoms; (e) Inform about co-morbidity with other medical health concerns; (f) Provide simple advice regarding coping (such as sleep hygiene instruction), explain what can be done to facilitate recovery, and describe treatment options; (g) Help the client identify and label the reactions they are experiencing; (h) Teach the client to recognize that emotional and physical reactions are expected after trauma, understand how the body's response to trauma includes many of the symptoms of PTSD, and understand that anxiety and distress are often "triggered" by reminders of the traumatic experience that can include sights, sounds, or smells associated with the trauma, physical sensations (e.g., heart pounding), or behaviors of other people; (i) Teach ways of coping with their PTSD symptoms in order to minimize their impact on functioning and quality of life; (j) Help the client distinguish between positive and negative coping actions. Positive coping includes actions that help to reduce anxiety, lessen other distressing reactions, and improve the situation. They include relaxation methods (e.g., Tactical/Combat breathing, yoga), physical exercise in moderation, talking to another person for support, positive distracting activities, and active participation in treatment; (k) Advise the client to avoid negative coping methods may help to perpetuate problems and can include continual avoidance of thinking about the trauma, use of alcohol or drugs, excessive caffeine and nicotine or other stimulant, social isolation, and aggressive or violent actions; (l) Examine whether clients have unrealistic or inaccurate expectations of recovery and may benefit from understanding that recovery is an ongoing daily gradual process (e.g., it doesn't happen through sudden insight or "cure") and that healing doesn't mean forgetting about the trauma or having no emotional pain when thinking about it; and (m) Explain and encourage discussion of treatment options, including evidence-based treatments.

Treatment Informed Consent

Shapiro (2001) describes several considerations for the therapist in regards to discharging the ethical duty to inform clients of the potential treatment risks and benefits associated with EMDR. However, before discussing risks related to EMDR, we need to back-up a step. After completing the clinical intake, therapists will usually provide the client feedback as to the assessment results including diagnostic impression and treatment recommendations. Included in that interchange should be an overview of all appropriate treatment options (including no treatment), so clients can truly make an "informed" choice. In the case of diagnosing a traumatic stress injury like PTSD, how does one properly inform clients about the range of treatment options, including EMDR?

Informing Clients of Treatment Options

In the case of a diagnosed war or traumatic stress injury, we advocate having copies available of the most recent (2010) DVA/DoD *Clinical Practice Guideline for the Management of Post-Traumatic Stress.* The guideline has a summary that can be photocopied and handed to clients during the feedback session. EMDR is listed among the "A-level" evidence-based treatments, meaning those with the highest level of efficacy established via randomized controlled trials. The guidelines also say that every A-level treatment is roughly equivalent to the others, and there is insufficient evidence to indicate the benefit of contraindication to combining medication and psychotherapy over only one of the two approaches (DVA/DoD, 2010). Client preferences and the particular evidence-based treatments that the therapist has the most training and expertise with usually determine the initial treatment choice. Although every session will be different, here is one way to provide clients and informed overview of treatment options.

Th: Major D, glad you could come in today sir ... as we spoke about earlier, today I'd like to go over some strategic options, so that we can try to unload some of the weight in the duffel bag you've been hauling around....

C: Damn right ... I need to get back to the fight.

Th: Right ... well ... here is a copy of the most recent VA and DoD clinical guidelines for treating PTS (post-traumatic stress) ... there are no panaceas or magical cures yet, but there are several strategies that have been identified as having significant benefit, what are often called "evidence-based" or best practice. So we'll start from there, sound good?

C: Let's do it.

Th: Ok, well, essentially there are evidence-based procedures that have consistently been identified as the best of the best ... those are: prolonged exposure therapy, cognitive processing therapy, stress inoculation training, virtual reality therapy, and EMDR or Eye Movement Desensitization and Reprocessing ... a mouthful, so we'll go with just EMDR ...

C: Sounds good to me ...

Th: Each of these strategies has some advantages and disadvantages, but all have been shown to be pretty much equally effective and are recommended by every valid clinical guideline for PTS in the U.S. and international community ... ok ... so I'll go over each briefly, and will give you some reading material that spells out more detail ...

In a nutshell, prolonged exposure involves retelling and re-experiencing the most troubling experience over and again, until essentially your nervous system rests, and becomes "desensitized," that's a very crude synopsis, but that's the gist of it. You will usually be taught some kind of stress management tool like deep breathing or relaxation training, and will be asked to listen to tapes of the "exposure" sessions and practice the stress reduction techniques on a regular basis, any questions?

C:　Nope.

Th:　Well there's more to it than that, but like I said earlier, exposure therapy has been found to be one of the best tools we have … the downside, is that some people can find it causes more stress because you are constantly going over the same material, the other downside is that some folks don't do the daily homework (listening to the tapes etc.) and they may not improve as much as those who do.

Next is cognitive processing therapy or CPT. CPT and prolonged exposure were developed thru the DVA's National Center for PTSD … CPT was originally designed to treat female victims of sexual assault, but since the war started, the DVA and DoD have been researching CPT as a treatment for combat PTS … CPT combines what I said earlier about prolonged exposure, but adds a cognitive component, which teaches people to regain control of their emotional reactions by changing how they interpret events … the basic idea is that when troops return from war, they have been conditioned to be alert, quickly recognize and respond to threats … and being back home, the brain is still interpreting events as if we were in the warzone … anyways, like prolonged exposure, there is strong scientific evidence that many people can recover from PTS with CPT.

The downside of CPT is similar to prolonged exposure, it too requires repetitive exposure to the traumatic event, and weekly homework to include the monitoring how you are interpreting events and learning to challenge that automatic reaction, so there is about 1–2 hours of homework that you will be asked to perform daily, with the idea that, the more you work on these things outside of the therapy office, the quicker you may get over the PTS … ok?

C:　I'm following ya, doc.

Th:　Ok, next is Virtual Reality Therapy or VRT … like it sounds, it has to do with computers, people sit at a computer terminal and are hooked up to the smells, sounds, vibrating sensations, and images just like in Iraq or Afghanistan … great computer graphics, it too was developed by the National Center for PTSD … just like prolonged exposure and CPT, you will be required to re-experience the most disturbing experiences until you are no longer reaction the same way … all of these strategies generally take up to 12 meetings, 12 weeks if you would … the downside of VRT, is that few places have the special computer equipment … we don't have it here either, so if you were interested, we would have to refer you to the East or West coast …

By the way Major there are also medications that have been used to treat PTS, and many can be effective to reduce some of the really bad problems like insomnia and agitation … I know you expressed reservations about going on meds, but just want to put that out there, and it's in the guidelines …

All right, the last of the top evidence-based strategies is EMDR … it's got a weird name, so it has to do with eye movements, like the other exposure treatments I mentioned earlier, EMDR requires people to think about the most upsetting events, however, unlike the other methods, people benefit from EMDR without having to repetitively repeat the same image or memory, there are also no tapes or other homework assignments that you have to do every day in order to resolve the PTS …

C: What do you do then?

Th: This is the odd part, you will be asked to think of the bad things that happened, and follow the docs fingers back and forth like this, or track lights, sounds going back and forth with … you do that for maybe a 30–60 seconds, and report what comes to you mind … typically something will change, a different memory comes up, or change in the picture or something, and you will be asked to just think about it, and track the lights again …

C: That seems pretty weird; how does it work?

Th: The million dollar question, Major; all we really know is that it does … one theory is that the eye movement are like REM (rapid eye movement) when we sleep … REM is important for processing emotionally charged memories and helps us remember what we learned during the day…when people have PTS, they often wake up at night because the experience is too emotional, too disturbing, that's why folks wake up with night sweats, anyway, the brain isn't able to process the information like it does with other things … so one idea about EMDR, is that we're using something similar as REM, but while people are wide awake … there's no trance or hypnosis …

Oh … and in EMDR … you don't have to tell the doc everything that's going through your mind. Just whether something is changing or not … so it's a lot different than most talk therapies … and that's one of the downsides … because it is different than regular psychotherapy, it doesn't require constant re-exposure, daily homework, or sharing a lot of personal details … there are some people who are very skeptic … especially high level people in the VA and DoD … the other downside with EMDR, is that you will probably remember some bad things, you would like to forget and not think about … however, in EMDR, you won't have to think about probably as much as the treatments I mentioned …

Anyway … there are other treatments including support groups, but those are the best we have right now…. How about you think this over, you can read up on the guidelines, do your own research, or ask people other people that you trust, and we can meet and see what you've decided …

Nine times out of ten, maybe ten of ten, military clients will opt for a trial of that weird sounding thing. There is an effort, maybe not fully reflected above, to be above board when discussing other treatment options, as it is the client's choice. That said, if one is being honest, then you have to bring up the requirements for repetitive exposure, daily homework, and degree of personal disclosure of mainstream cognitive-behavioral therapy, and conversely, mention that EMDR is different in that respect and more. In any event, the take-away is to make a good faith effort to inform clients of their treatment options.

Informed Consent Specific to EMDR Treatment

Here are the standard teaching points for obtaining client consent to EMDR, or, for that matter, any trauma-focused therapy, as none of the cautions is unique to EMDR: (a) Potential changes in memory and emotion related to EMDR in legal testimony, (b) High level of emotion and/or unexpected memories may occur while processing, (c) Appropriate safeguards are in place in case substance abuse history is reactivated by EMDR, and (d) Cautions about reliability of memory—meaning that not everything in our memory networks is necessarily factual. Dreams, movies, and fantasies can be merged with other memories and information is stored "as if" it happened, but it may not have. This is related to broader concerns over suggestibility and recovered child abuse or other trauma. Case in point, the author (Mark Russell) was using EMDR with a civilian client who had memories of alien abduction, once we reprocessed that trauma, and a few others, the presenting complaint involving a bridge phobia resolved. Therapists are not the memory police.

Additional items that should be covered with EMDR informed consent to protect both clients and therapists alike include: (a) Use of modified EMDR protocols are not evidence-based, and therapists should inform clients if they are modifying the standard EMDR protocol and that those variations have not been shown empirically to work; (b) Clients with active suicidal or homicidal ideation should be assessed for dangerousness and postpone EMDR until they are more stable. EMDR reprocessing or other trauma-focused therapy should not be conducted with clients with active, serious suicidal or homicidal ideation as it could exacerbate client level of distress; (c) Clients with a serious, life-threatening medical condition should inform their therapist and physician and get medical clearance for certain unstable conditions such as malignant hypertension, recent stroke, recent heart attack, etc. Clients should be informed that trauma-focused therapies including EMDR may cause a rise in blood pressure, heart-rate, and other stress-related response that could exacerbate a serious, unstable medical condition; (d) Clients who are pregnant should inform their therapist and physician before undergoing trauma-focused therapy including EMDR—this is especially true for clients experiencing complicated pregnancy, have a history of miscarriage, underweight, or premature deliveries. Clients in the final trimester should consider postponing EMDR therapy unless doing so presents greater risk. Consultation with the client's physician should occur if any questions or concerns arise; and (e) Disclosure of a crime—clients should be informed during the review of limits of confidentiality that certain client disclosures such as perpetrating child abuse, elder abuse, or committing a serious infraction against the UCMJ (Uniformed Code of Military Justice) may have to be reported by the therapist, who is a mandatory reporter. Military mental health providers are also military officers, and under some circumstances, may be obligated to breach client confidentiality. Therapists should consult an attorney or JAG.

EXPLAINING THE AIP MODEL

Explanation of the EMDR theory and method is dependent upon the age, background, experience, and sophistication of client. Preparation of clients for EMDR includes a description of the AIP model such as the following: "Often, when something traumatic happens, it seems to get locked in the nervous system with the original picture, sounds, thoughts, feelings, and so on. Since the experience is locked there, it continues to be triggered whenever a reminder comes up. It can be the basis for a lot of discomfort and sometimes a lot of negative emotions, such as fear and helplessness that we can't seem to control. These are really the emotions connected with the old experience that are being triggered. The eye movements we use in EMDR seem to unlock the nervous system and allow your brain to process the experience. That may be what is happening in REM, or dream sleep: The eye movements may be involved in processing the unconscious material. The important thing to remember is that it is your own brain that will be doing the healing and that you are the one in control" (Shapiro, 2001, pp. 123–124).

Clarifying Client and Therapist Role Expectations

The standard EMDR description of the client's expectations goes something like this:

What we will be doing is a simple check on what you are experiencing. I need to know from you what is going on with as clear feedback as possible. Sometimes things will change and sometimes they won't. I'll ask you how you feel from 0 to 10—sometimes it will change and sometimes it won't. I may ask if something else comes up—sometimes it will and sometimes it won't. There are no "supposed to's" in this process. So, just give as accurate feedback as you can as to what's happening without judging whether it should be happening or not. Just let whatever happens happen. We'll do the eye movement for a while and then we'll talk about it. (Note. Includes material copyrighted by Francine Shapiro, Ph.D., and the EMDR Institute; used with permission.)

Another way of explaining the client's role is:

All I need is for you to tell me the truth about what you are experiencing. I don't need to know all the details; that's up to you to decide how much to tell me, but, at a minimum, we need your honest feedback if things or changing or not. Please don't try to force yourself to concentrate on a certain memory, picture, or whatever; just be an observer, and notice whatever it is that comes. Just notice it. Remember you've got the controls, so if you want me to stop, you're the boss.

Demonstrating the Mechanics of EMDR

After arranging the chairs in the classic "ships passing in the night" arrangement (Shapiro, 2001), the therapist also introduces bilateral stimulation (BLS) to clients. For eye movements, the therapist collaborates with the client to determine the comfortable distance and direction of eye movement by asking *"Where does it feel most comfortable to have my hand?"* Distance from the visual stimulus to the client should not be so great (more than four feet) where the client's visual field is occupied by background distractions.

Bilateral stimulation using eye movements: (a) Using the therapist's hand or a wand; (b) Start with the therapist's hand in the center of the face; (c) Slowly move laterally, side-by-side, and remind the client to track only with his or her eyes; (d) Speed up the hand movements until the client is unable to track; (e) The therapist can test out diagonal (left to upper right) movements; (f) Vertical eye movement is anecdotally reportedly as helpful for dizziness or vertigo; and (g) When using *Neurotek devices and visual tracking* initiate slow frequency and speed up to find upper limit of client tracking. Most clients prefer and respond best to the faster BLS rate.

Bilateral stimulation using auditory sounds: (a) *Alternating snapping fingers*—although it's demonstrated in EMDR trainings that snapping fingers on alternate sides of the client's head works—it does not, especially for any length of time. Moreover, it looks really tacky; and (b) *Neurotek devices and headphones*—much better. The author (Mark Russell) has had good success with the headphones and alternating sounds. Adolescents and young adults seem to prefer the headphones for some reason. Also, combining the auditory and other stimuli can be effective.

Bilateral stimulation using kinesthetic vibrations or taps: (a) Different variations of bilateral kinesthetic stimuli have been reported; (b) *Alternating finger taps* was the first, when it was used as a control group for testing the effects of eye movements in one of the first DVA random clinical trials on EMDR. At the time, only eye movements and alternating finger snapping were taught; (c) *Alternating taping*—Priscilla Marquis on a trip to Central America was working with blind survivors of land mines. Eye movements were not feasible, so she had clients hold out their hands and she tapped alternately either the hand or knee; (d) *"Butterfly hug"* was almost not included because the image of a group of Marines being instructed to give themselves butterfly hugs just did not sit right. Still some research with children after a natural disaster reported it was effective and some hardcore GIs may have fun with it; and (e) Use of *Neurotek device and alternating vibration pads* is the preferred method. Clients hold onto pads in their hands that generating vibration sensations.

Combining bilateral stimulation. The author (Mark Russell) has on numerous occasions chosen to combine visual and auditory bilateral stimulation with generally good effects. An indicator for considering combining stimuli is when the client appears to be "looping" and/or under-responding to one or the other. Only future research will illuminate for certain, but if clients are not responding to one, rather than switch outright, the therapist might check for an additive effect. The idea of introducing a third type of stimuli (kinesthetic) is intriguing, but no experience to back it up. Preparing clients for the possibility of dual-forms of BLS is helpful.

ESTABLISHING THE THERAPEUTIC FRAME

Jerome and Julia Frank's (1991) classic *Persuasion and Healing* spoke about the history of healing rituals across human civilizations. According to Frank and Frank (1991), the healing setting is often adorned with cultural artifacts that reinforce the status of the healer in society. We have bookshelves filled with impressive sounding book titles and the walls, desktops, and file cabinets reinforce our credentials as healers, as do our professional titles, Doctor, Counselor, Therapist, and Social Worker. The Franks (1991) also describe how restricting public access to healers has always served to reinforce the value of the healer's services. The notion of a therapeutic, healing frame is particularly meaningful within the warrior class. However, cultural and institutional stigma and barriers to mental health care have left a deep-seated mistrust of traditional psychotherapy in the military.

Practitioners working with military populations may want to take an objective look at their therapeutic frame, particularly in light of the value placed on authority, credibility, and accomplishment. That said, the author (Mark Russell) always kept children's toys and crayon-drawn pictures strewn across his office that were usually met with cautious, skeptical expressions by military visitors. However, several other cultural artifacts were also within eye's grasp: a model of the human brain; blown-up pictures of neuroimaging from Lansing, Amen, Hanks, and Rudy's (2005) study of six police officers diagnosed with PTSD, demonstrating visible pre- and post-changes in brain functioning via SPECT scans; and a Neurotek device that raises everyone's curiosity. Leeds (2009) aptly entitled a section under client preparation as "Seeing is Believing"—Brain Images of PTSD Patients Before and After Treatment (p. 104). He even mentioned Lansing et al.'s (2005) study, and military personnel ears perk up when it's revealed that this psychology research was with six *police officers*, a paramilitary organization whose employees are no strangers to occupational hazards like their warrior cousins.

As kooky as EMDR might sound, when introducing it to hard-nosed, battle-tested warriors, there is an instinctual appeal, which is what may have attracted me to EMDR. Nearly a dozen neuroimaging and neurophysiological studies have been published to date, the majority being case studies, but sufficient to exclude chance findings. Framing EMDR in neuropsychological terms has instant credibility for many warriors, and the Neurotek serves to reinforce that this is a very different kind of mental healthcare—a new age form of healing. Therapists are advised to pay attention to their therapeutic frame when preparing clients for EMDR. In doing so, it may be helpful for therapists to consider that by establishing the conditions for therapeutic change, including building of a therapeutic alliance and therapeutic frame, all serve to strengthen associations on a neurobiological level between the client's maladaptive and adaptive neural networks. Increasing client access to, and activation of their adaptive neural networks, has the converse effect of reducing the predominance of pathogenic memories.

Introducing Metaphor for Expected Client Role During Reprocessing

Shapiro (2001) and Leeds (2009) both utilize a train metaphor to describe "mindful noticing" whereby clients are instructed to recall looking out of a train and watching the scenery go bye. For many of us, this is a powerful metaphor. Increasingly, however, younger generations, at least in the U.S., do not have the experience of riding in a train. They could imagine what it would be like, but it would not likely be as strong an experience then those who had. Consequently, with younger cohorts, using the metaphor of looking out of the window of a car will unquestionably be an experience they can relate to.

Why introduce treatment metaphors now? The purpose of going over metaphors at this juncture is that the therapist wants to "front-load" certain information for clients during the relatively non-stressed context of preparation to avoid unnecessary overloading clients with new information during intense reprocessing. By facilitating the development of a therapeutic alliance and discussing metaphors, stop signals, role expectations, and the like, the therapist is in essence creating an adaptive neural network relating the conditions of therapeutic change and EMDR to the maladaptive neural network. Appreciating that memory systems have evolved for the primary purpose of helping us understand, predict, and control our life experiences and behavior in an adaptive fashion informs us why such front-loading can be beneficial.

The Stop Signal and Metaphor for Reprocessing

Clients are routinely asked to identify a non-verbal way to communicate their desire that the therapist cease with the bilateral stimulation. Often, the author (Mark Russell) just advises clients to raise their hand and say "stop" if they are "wanting" (versus "needing") to stop. Where possible, it can help reduce the sense of threat from vulnerability that military clients may experience by just being in the mental health space. Be mindful of phrases like PTSD ("PTS"), therapy ("strategy"), needing ("wanting"), or patient ("client," or refer by rank) that might have negative connotations for some personnel, particular senior enlisted and officers.

The "Break and Gas Pedal" Metaphor

Since most adults of whatever cohort have had the experience of driving a vehicle, the use of the "Break and Gas Pedal" metaphor consistently serves well. After soliciting the client's "stop signal," the Break and Gas Pedal metaphor is introduced, and will assuredly be used again during reprocessing. The client is told that when we start using EMDR, they are in the driver's seat. The break is their stop signal, and the bilateral stimulation is the gas pedal. Clients are advised that by keeping their foot on the gas pedal they will get us to our destination quicker, and conversely, using the break will slow our arrival. Nevertheless, all cars have a break and gas pedal for a reason, so clients can use them as they see fit. Therapists using this metaphor will find it useful to remind clients of this frequently especially those who want to verbally process their experiences, sometimes for lengthy periods. There are conceivable reasons why clients would choose to do so, and we should respect their desire. But when stopping and talking, and more talking becomes the norm, one way to reset the norm is to remind them of the gas pedal. If the pattern continues, therapists will need to assess for a possible blocking belief (see Chapter 9, this volume).

Length and Pace of EMDR Treatment Sessions

Shapiro (2001) has recommended 90-minute EMDR sessions from the beginning, which is still taught as the preferred meeting duration in order to ensure sufficient time to complete reprocessing. However in many healthcare settings, particularly managed-care and the military, providers often do not have the liberty, nor might it be feasible if they did, to utilize the extended session format. Fortunately, a large, well-controlled study on EMDR in a managed-care setting has been conducted. For example, Marcus, Marquis, and Sakai (1997) compared 67 adult clients diagnosed with PTSD who received either 50-minute individual EMDR, psychodynamic, cognitive, or behavioral therapy or group therapy at Kaiser Permanente Hospital. The results demonstrated not only that EMDR can be implemented effectively within a standard 50-minute therapy format, but that clients receiving EMDR reported significantly lower symptoms of PTSD, depression, and anxiety than clients from the other treatment groups on average of 6.5 sessions versus 11.8 sessions. Moreover, 100% of single trauma and 77% of EMDR clients no longer met diagnostic criteria with most treatment gains maintained at six-month follow-up (Marcus, Marquis, & Sakai, 2004).

Pacing of EMDR Sessions: Weekly and Consecutive Meetings

In the ideal therapy world, treatment sessions would occur on a regularly scheduled weekly basis until concluded. That may work in strictly controlled laboratory settings to evaluate treatment efficacy and perhaps other clinical environments, however in the military environment a lot can transpire that makes weekly meetings a fantasy. For example, military personnel are often not the masters of their time, and, due to stigma and concerns over repercussions, are often reluctant to press their work center supervisors to grant time away from their military duties to attend weekly counseling sessions. Moreover, military personnel and sometimes their therapists may have high work demands and are frequently on the move, attending to mandatory trainings, annual inspections, after-hour watches, and deployment preparations, that can result in multiple cancellations and rescheduling. Specialized treatment programs for war stress injuries like The Soldier Center may receive military clients under orders to complete treatment, and thus can offer EMDR on a weekly or even consecutive day basis. Published accounts of consecutive-day treatment with EMDR in the military exist (e.g., Wesson & Gould, 2009) and should be strongly considered when military clients have "dwell" time or extended periods of relative inactivity. However, this is not the norm and reinforces the need for therapist and clients to proceed as safely and efficiently as possible. Therefore therapists and clients need to discuss the frequency of the meetings and collaborate on identifying the most opportune meeting day and times that pose the least risk for disruption. Ideally, any therapy including EMDR, appears to work best with a mutual sense of continuity that weekly sessions provide. That said, the author (Mark Russell) has had to adapt to "every other week" or even less regular EMDR sessions. We can do the best we can. Therapists need to reconcile that, in most circumstances, clinical practice in the military will usually be less than optimal. When that is the case, we look to the Marine Corps motto of "adapt and overcome."

COPING STRATEGIES FOR REPROCESSING PHASES

Shapiro (2001) added coping skills strategies like a safe/calm place exercise to be used to prepared clients for EMDR reprocessing, particularly when an incomplete sessions occurs and the therapist believes that the client needs support in making the transition from reprocessing distressing material to re-entering the outside world after the session ends. Conducting the safe/calm place exercise with clients during the preparation phase provides an opportunity for therapists to gradually introduce the idea of dual-focused attention and bilateral stimulation to clients, with hopefully a positive outcome, to reduce anticipatory anxiety. In terms of the AIP model, the therapist is attempting to access the client's adaptive neural (memory) networks where our past secure attachments, achievements, mastery, coping, and other "positive" affect-laden experiences are physiologically linked and stored. The exercise itself is a form of guided imagery that has been a staple in behavioral therapy for years. However, adding short sets of bilateral stimulation to the relaxing images and cue words is a new twist. Conceptually, the bilateral stimulation is intended to strengthen the positive and relaxing associations. It is not clear, however, that the addition of eye movements causes any greater enhancement effect than traditional guided imagery whereby the therapist induces heightened relaxation through their verbal discourse. Just as in standard relaxation training, some clients may experience a Relaxation Induced Panic (RIP), whereby the relaxed state triggers an intense sympathetic stress response, or others may experience negative versus positive associations during the exercise depending on their selected place (e.g., bedroom). In the later circumstance, clients are simply instructed to select a more neutral safe or calm place. Otherwise the therapist might switch to another form of stress management activity, or use RDI that we will cover shortly. The reader is referred to Shapiro (2001) for the safe/calm place exercise that has become standard part of EMDR trainings. Another effective and perhaps more familiar stress reduction technique in the military is what some military and police agencies refer to as "Combat" or "Tactical" Breathing, which is described below, as are "grounding techniques" that therapists may want to teach their clients who present with high levels of dissociation.

RESOURCE DEVELOPMENT AND INSTALLATION

Resource Development and Installation (RDI) was developed by Korn and Leeds (2002) as a means to enhance or strengthen the client's access to internal "resources" associated with their adaptive neural networks. Having supervised or consulted with numerous recently trained therapists in EMDR, a trend has emerged whereby RDI is the preferred, and sometimes the only intervention, for clients with stress injuries. Most of us were quite nervous about using EMDR outside of the training comfort zone, and, before RDI, the option was to jump in the water or go to the park instead. To be certain, when used appropriately and for the right reasons, RDI is an effective tool. However, most clients do not need RDI, and using RDI will not address the issue that led to clients seeking help.

EMDR Reprocessing versus RDI?

Leeds (2009), the innovator of RDI, offers sage advice that we concur with: "When patients are clearly suffering from symptoms of PTSD and meet readiness criteria, there are several *invalid* reasons to use RDI before standard EMDR reprocessing" (p. 121): (a) The therapist may have a vague or uneasy sense that the client is too frail or unstable; (b) the therapist is concerned about the client's intense emotional experience or abreaction; (c) the therapist is uncomfortable or fears they cannot handle the content of the client's memories; (d) the therapist has a preference for wanting their client to "feel good"; and (e) the therapist fears they do not have enough time to complete reprocessing. It has become somewhat EMDR lore that a certain subgroup of clients that meet criteria for a developmental traumatic stress disorder like complex PTSD or Borderline Personality Disorder will almost universally require RDI before EMDR reprocessing. Yet less than 5% of adult clients with PTSD, even with child-onset PTSD, were reported to need RDI in a large controlled study, and those who received RDI, needed only one session before EMDR reprocessing (Korn et al., 2004, cited in Leeds, 2009). Of course, there are also many clients without complex PTSD or Borderline traits that can benefit from RDI. The safest bet, of course, is to ensure that the treatment plan fits the person, not the diagnosis, or the therapist's needs.

Why might delaying EMDR reprocessing matter? On average, therapists may have a limited opportunity to work with military personnel and make a real difference, that's the reality. Service members who brave the stigma and barriers to care and risk their military careers to seek help need and deserve the best we can offer. If RDI is clinically and/or operationally indicated, then it should be offered. However, most clients will not differentiate between EMDR, RDI, and any of the other modified approaches. If RDI is all they got, and their war stress injury has not been helped, then EMDR would have failed, not RDI. Remember, the only evidence-based treatment is standard EMDR protocol. In sum, practitioners should use RDI and other EMDR variants very judiciously, and only when it is clinically and/or operationally in the best interest of the client.

COMBAT/TACTICAL BREATHING

Law enforcement and the military regularly include martial arts training and what is referred to as "Combat or Tactical Breathing," a simple, but effective controlled breathing technique that has been used by warriors for centuries to rapidly gain control over the body's acute stress response and adrenaline rush (sympathetic nervous system) even in extreme, high stress, and hostile environments. Tactical/Combat Breathing in civilian parlance is often referred to as "Deep," "Diaphragmatic," "Lamaze," or "Autogenic" breathing. LTCOL David Grossman's (2007) *On Combat* describes how he trains police officers, surgeons, and Army Green Beret to effectively use Combat/Tactical Breathing as a means to quickly calm themselves by activating the parasympathetic nervous system and de-linking the intense physiological response from the memory of the recent event. Like any skill, clients are encouraged to practice as regularly as possible and to use Combat/Tactical Breathing before, during, and after combat or other operational missions.

Combat/Tactical Breathing Steps

Four-Count Method

1. Breathe in through your nose with a slow count of four (two, three, four)
2. (Therapists may request clients place their hand on their stomach to see if they are properly filling the diaphragm with air, as evident when their stomach and hand rise)
3. Hold your breath for a slow count of four (hold, two, three, four)
4. Exhale through your mouth for a count of four until all the air is out (two, three, four)
5. (Client's hand should lower as their stomach lowers)
6. Hold empty for a count of four (hold, two, three, four)
7. Then repeat the cycle three times

Reprocessing Acute Dissociative States

Dissociation can be a common component in many war and traumatic stress injuries and is usually reprocessed like other adaptive reactions associated with the flight/fight/freeze response. EMDR reprocessing, like any trauma-focused approach, can be emotionally intense and result in either accessing or generating a dissociative response during session. In some rare cases (at least from the author's [Mark Russell] experience in the military) a client's attentional focus may significantly constrict and become excessively self-absorbed and non-responsive to the external environment. In-session, clients may stare blankly ahead or what's referred to as the "1,000 yard stare." In this detached, dissociated state, client's attentional focus is generally too self-absorbed to maintain dual-focused attention; therefore EMDR reprocessing is shut down. It is natural, and to be expected, that traumatized clients will report and/or exhibit dissociative symptoms during reprocessing, especially those with notable history of childhood trauma. These are typically transient states like other emotional conditions that therapists observe during reprocessing (e.g., fear, terror, anger, grief, rage, pain, etc.). In the majority of cases, the dissociative symptoms will spontaneously resolve through the combined effects of dual-focus attention and bilateral stimulation.

It is critical for the therapist to understand the AIP model, particularly in relation to dual-focused attention, dissociation, and reprocessing. The majority, if not all, psychopathological states arise from maladaptive neural networks that can be characterized as excessively self-focused or self-absorbed conditions, with strong emotionally negative valence (see Nasby & Russell, 1997; Russell, 1992). In common terms, depression arises out of "depressogenic schemas" (e.g., Beck et al., 1979) and anxiety disorders are said to be a reflection of "fear structures" (Foa & Kozak, 1986). The maladaptive neural networks, when activated, tend to dominate our attentional focus resulting in a highly selective, negative attention and thus interpretation of past, current, and future events. The selective negative bias reinforces the habitual cognitive, emotional, behavior, and physiological responses that maintain an imbalanced, maladaptive condition. To be effective, EMDR requires both dual focused attention and bilateral stimulation, a vital point that many seem to overlook as fascination turns to the eye movements. We generally do not ask clients to close their eyes during reprocessing because it's harder to detect whether clients are maintaining a dual-focused attention. Standard EMDR protocol asserts that when therapist observes their client stop-tracking the bilateral stimulation, they respond with a verbal and/or non-verbal prompt to maintain that dual focus (e.g., therapist wiggles their fingers and says, "ok keep tracking!"). This is also why therapists are strongly advised to maintain verbal contact with their clients, particularly during intense reprocessing. The sound of the therapist's voice serves to split-away the client's awareness from internal preoccupation to perceive stimuli of threat, pain, and terror, to a joint internal and external focus, that allows access to other neutral, positive, or more adaptive perceptions from the *here-and-now*—it's this dual-focus awareness that frees up our cognitive capacity to attend to reprocessing information in a more adaptive direction. If the therapist is adhering to the standard protocol and their clients appear "stuck" in an dissociative state that interferes with reprocessing, then therapists can shift gears and utilize one of many "grounding techniques." These techniques, in effect, are designed to restore the balance of the client's self-focus by re-engaging their attention or awareness to external sight, sounds, and physical sensations from the outer environment, including their physical body. Some authors have developed specific exercises to reduce the dissociative response (e.g., Leeds, 2009).

Grounding Activities for Dissociative States

In general, however, any instruction to re-direct the client's attention to a present-oriented focus to the outer world will have a "grounding" effect. Here are some others: (a) Therapists should use a normal, firm, audible, and matter of fact speech tone to increase the client's alertness; (b) Ask clients to rate (e.g., 0–10) their perceived degree of dissociation, or how loud they hear a certain sound, or how vivid the color of a specific object is in the office; (c) Avoid mirroring the client's low affective tone by using slow, soft, low audible speech tones that may reinforce a dissociative detachment; (d) Direct the client's attention to their hands gripping the arm of a chair, the texture of the chair or sofa, the physical sensations of their feet touching the floor; (e) Turn on a radio or music player, ask them to rate how much they like the song; (f) Direct the client's attention to environment cues such as their reporting the time on the clock or on their watch, or attend to environment sounds (e.g., cars passing bye, the fan, music, etc.); (g) Direct the client's attention to scan the environment for specific objects (e.g., can you see the statue on my desk, please describe it to me, what color is it?); (h) The therapist can hand clients a cup of water and ask them to sip, and pay attention to the sensations in the mouth and throat; (i) The therapist can try ERP discussed earlier in this chapter; and (j) The therapist should keep in mind, to not panic or sound overly fretful, or otherwise convey a sense of fear or threat to the client. The disconnected state will end—and most very rapidly. If, for whatever reason, the client remains in the dissociative state, then activate the medical emergency response system.

Summary on Stress Reduction Techniques in the Military

One final note on the use of stress reduction techniques, the author (Mark Russell) has rarely utilized any stress management or coping skill exercises with military populations in conjunction with EMDR, with the exception of one to two clients where we did deep breathing exercise (now called "combat/ tactical breathing" by the Army). During the basic EMDR trainings, participants are taught the safe/calm place exercise and RDI, and many other clinicians working with the military may have used these approaches religiously, so this is only one person's opinion. However, with a treatment sample in the hundreds, reliance upon a stress reduction technique for transitioning purposes rarely has been warranted. Therefore, the author (Mark Russell) generally leaves it out of the preparation phase, unless the client demonstrates he or she are poor at self-regulation during the history taking. On an aside, adopting common cognitive-behavioral stress reduction techniques into the standard EMDR protocol may have made sense conceptually, and has been proven clinically useful in certain cases, but the net effect has been a clouding of the distinction between EMDR and CBT.

Addressing Military Client Treatment Concerns and Fears

Ambivalence in clients consenting to mental healthcare occurs frequently, however in military populations it's the norm. Whether it's trepidation about the inherent negative bias and stigma associated with seeking mental health services in the military, fears around repercussions on promotion and career, or the service member's instinctual motivation to avoid the threat of reopening wounds of inescapable pain, there are legitimate reasons for ambivalence that the therapist must address at the outset. Some of the predictable barriers to care such as confidentiality or potential implications of the client's diagnosis and treatment on their ability to deploy, or remain on active-duty, would have been addressed at the initial clinic visit and informed consent proceedings. However, during client preparation and education specific to EMDR treatment, new concerns may arise, and merge with other lingering worries or confusion that can fuel an ambivalent state-of-mind. Not being upfront and discussing the elephant in the room, breeds an undercurrent of mistrust that will likely derail the best laid plans. The eight-phase EMDR protocol has built-in a series of checkpoints for therapist to solicit client feedback on the status of their knowledge and experience before moving onward. At the end of the preparation phase, we want to explicitly inquire about the status of the client's understanding and motivation toward EMDR therapy, and any potential barriers that may impact the trajectory of treatment. So what are the common reservations many military members may harbor, and how might a therapist work through it?—this is the final section of the preparation phase.

THE AMBIVALENT MILITARY CLIENT

Like all clients, military personnel maybe ambivalent around the process and outcome of EMDR (Shapiro, 2001). Concerns over the process may pertain to the degree of safety, trust, and rapport developed in the therapeutic relationship. A general uneasiness that may be expressed as repeated confusion of questioning about certain aspects of the protocol or timing of the treatment (e.g., may report feeling rushed, needing more time, etc.), or the confidentiality of treatment, and maybe the desire to postpone for another day. The therapist non-defensively should attempt to answer the client's questions, and give them the benefit of the doubt. Sometimes questions may be asked that are not challenges to the therapist or relationship, but reflect a knowledge gap, understandable given the context and amount of information clients are bombarded with, and the fact that they are not as familiar with EMDR or mental healthcare as the therapist. Unresolved concerns about confidentiality and informed consent to treatment need to be satisfactorily addressed before therapy can proceed.

The Coerced Mental Health Seeking Client

It is not uncommon for military personnel to show up to a mental health appointment, kicking and screaming. For a few it may be a public display to save face, for others the therapist will have no problem recognizing. When asked what brought them into the clinic today? The client will make it crystal clear for the therapist that it wasn't their idea. If not their wife or husband, the next likely culprit is the client's "Command." This may be a formal consequence of a disciplinary action, or proactive urgings by a leader in the client's chain-of-command, in either case, usually there is a threat of a break-up, marital separation or divorce, or a command suspending discipline in lieu of the client's getting help. Other scenarios are possible too, but the main point is that the client's reluctance to engage in therapy is in part because they are not here by their free will, and probably believe that they are being treated unjustly. Nevertheless, the therapist can sympathize with the client over his or her predicament, but indicate that treatment will not be effective, and in fact could make things worse, if the client is not ready, willing, and able. Some clients will say whatever it takes to appease the therapist so that treatment can proceed and they can get their family member, friend, or command off their back. Others may be interested in engaging the therapist in a discussion of the possible benefits of the time spent in the therapy office. However, if the therapist has reservations about the client's level of free will to consent without undue pressure or coercion, they should not use EMDR.

During the client history and preparation phases, the therapist should be mindful of the client's verbal and non-verbal communications suggesting either concern or confusion over the information that is being shared by the therapist. Clarifying the client's questions and concerns at the time they arise, can help avoid having to backtrack later on. It is always good practice to check the client's understanding and anticipate questions not expressed before moving forward. However, when questions, confusion, and postponements arise or persist, it can also signify client fears and concerns over treatment outcome in general and EMDR specifically. When known or identifiable, these too must be confronted and resolved before treatment can ensue.

Issues of Secondary Gain

For instance, in Phase One, we identified possible secondary gain issues and might ask, "What would be the potential downside, or negative effect you might experience if you PTS was completely over?" The therapist should anticipate and not accept the client's first response, which is almost always "There is no downside." If that indeed is the client's response, the therapist may want to say something like, "Yeah I understand that, but I also know that most people do report that while they are relieved not to have PTS anymore, they experienced some negative consequence as well." The client may ask "Like what?" and the therapist can mention a few like having to go back on deployment, separations from family, or losing a possible disability pension. Observe the client's reactions. More often than not, clients will forcefully, and sincerely express their choice to be relieved of PTS over any of the other considerations. Others may say the right things, but harbor secondary gain, and the therapist may never know the difference. If potential or actual secondary gain are disclosed by the client that signifies a reluctance to get better (e.g., want to leave the military, benefit from a legal settlement, do not want to deploy), then the therapist must exit EMDR mode, debrief or counsel the client about their options, and recommend they speak with their chaplain. A twist would be a client with war stress injury, who genuinely wants help, but is ambivalent for the secondary gain. The therapist can help the client explicitly identify all the pros and cons of treating their PTS in the military, even if it meant a return to duty finding. See Table 6.1 for a list of some potential pros and cons for treating military personnel diagnosed with a war stress injuries in the military.

Table 6.1

Pros	Cons
End their suffering from PTS	End their diagnosis of PTSD
Prevent long-term, or permanent health effects	May have to deploy again
Maintain current income and benefits	Unemployment and future uncertainty
Provide means to support family	Uncertainty how to support family
Leave door open for future reenlistment/ career	Negative impact on annual job evaluations
Leave open future careers outside military	Restricts career options
Maintain family health and stability	Family separations
Healthier impact on family members	Risk divorce/domestic violence
May prevent legal troubles	Risk of substance and legal troubles
May prevent suicide from PTSD	Higher risk of suicide
Improve quality of life	Higher risk of poor quality of life
Improve health and longevity	Risk poorer health and longevity
Maintain military friends and support	Risk of social isolation

Exiting service members with an *active* mental health diagnosis of depression, PTSD, or other significant Axis I or II diagnosis will typically lose their security clearances and may be ineligible for many civilian jobs that military personnel often transition to after leaving active duty, including law enforcement (e.g., Police, FBI, Border Patrol, CIA, Secret Service, etc.), airlines (pilots—fixed or rotor wing—air traffic control), diving, fire department, emergency medical service, and most federal, state, or city positions that require a federal background check and/or security clearance.

MILITARY CLIENT FEARS OR CONCERNS ABOUT SEEKING MENTAL HEALTH CARE

Regardless of whether it's a military member with an actual war stress injury who is ambivalent about treatment due to secondary gain (e.g., military discharge/pension), or ambivalence for seeking mental health by military personnel in general without secondary gain lurking, therapists will often need to have conversations with their clients during the client history or preparation phase regarding the pros and cons of treating their stress injuries. Fears of mental health stigma and barriers to care in the form of career repercussions are very real in the military, there is no guarantee that military members who seek and benefit from mental health treatment might suffer on their annual performance evaluations or career options. That is something that neither the therapist nor client has any control over. Today, the military has been making significant strides to change the mindset, but it is possible that unenlightened, immature leaders in the enlisted and officer ranks may hold it against the service member in some way. There is also a fairly good chance that they will not. Nevertheless, the therapist needs to acknowledge that the client's concerns are legitimate and real because they are, at least to a degree. So, what can the therapist say to an ambivalent treatment-seeking client?

Similar to informed consent procedures, the therapist discusses the potential advantages and disadvantages of treatment and no treatment. There is no guarantee that EMDR or any treatment will "fix" their problem, but there is a 100% chance that, if their PTS is not reduced or resolved and their symptoms last into the months, things will get worse—and sometimes a lot worse. This is where it helps to give warriors information on the effects of untreated PTS. Since nearly 50% of the all-volunteer military is married, the therapist is right to include the potential negative effects of chronic untreated PTS of the service member's spouse and children. This may sound heavy-handed, but military members need to be informed that chronic PTS is a medical emergency and, just like signs of a heart attack, to ignore and wait is to risk being too late.

Concerns that Treatment will Interfere with Deployment, Promotion, and Career

The vast number of ambivalent service members will be in this category. Again, the reality is that treatment "might" impact their ability to deploy, it "might" have a negative impact on their annual performance evaluations (e.g., because they did not deploy), and, thus, it "might" have a negative impact on the longevity of their career. Unfortunately, that is the sad reality. Treatment "might" get in the way, at least temporarily, if a deployment is imminent and the therapist's judgment is that the client may not be psychologically fit to enter the warzone. So, here is the other inconvenient truth, not treating PTS, especially as months pass, and it becomes more chronic, which is the norm, is going to cause more problems for the service member the longer it goes on. With a 99.9% certainty, untreated, chronic PTS "will" significantly impact their ability to perform and serve in the military. Future deployments will have an accumulative effect. They may be fine next deployment, or the one after that, but the third or fourth is where it all crashes down. They will have problems at work from chronic sleep deprivation and fatigue, they will have troubles concentrating and remembering, and they will start to make a lot of mistakes; the overall quality of their work will noticeably be slipping from where they are now, and that will reflect on their performance evaluations. Irritability, short-fused anger, fatigue will make it more difficult to remain cordial and upbeat. They will overreact to minor things that used to not bother them, and, eventually, this will lead to conflict with relationships at home and at work, including with their superiors.

Chronic stress, frustration, and tension will start to have progressively more negative effects on the physical and mental health. They will develop a wide range of health problems and likely depression, and many will develop addictions on alcohol, prescription drugs, or other things to cope with their chronic PTS. Eventually—and there's no telling if it's 6 months or 6 years— untreated chronic PTS will get them either psychiatrically retired or kicked out of military for cause. Military personnel are all aware that one can have 5 or 10 years of sterling performance of the walking-on-water variety; however, all it takes is an impulsive, momentary lapse in judgment, and someone snaps and says or does something very wrong. That could be all it takes to unwind everything they have accomplished.

That's a hard sell, and other therapists may find a lot more effective ways that work for them to confront their client's fears about military-specific ramifications. Here's the last hard news: for military personnel with PTS who do not want to skip a deployment to take care of their health issue, think twice. In the heat of combat, life and death decisions are made in fractions of a second. It is the hardest situation a human being can be in, and it's a whole lot worse if someone's judgment is clouded by their PTS. It may seem harsh, but it is warranted as a matter of "informed consent," that deploying with active PTS risks their safety, and those around them. So, the really hard question that needs to be asked is are they prepared to live with the possible burden of knowing that their PTS "may" have contributed to someone being injured or killed? Even if the PTS had nothing to do with happened, human nature being what is often means lifelong doubt and second guessing. Obviously, the list is far from complete, and appears heavily biased in favor of treating military stress injuries while in the military versus waiting until people transition out. That's because the evidence overwhelmingly indicates that once military personnel with a war stress injury leaves the military, the outcomes exponentially get worse, as the financial, medical, and social support structure is no longer there, and the longer problems persist, typically the more negative impact on the former military member and their families.

Fears of Losing "The Edge"

Some military personnel may be afraid that EMDR will cause them to lose their "edge," that quality of understanding what it takes to survive in a hostile environment. Being vigilant and on constant guard protects the warrior from unpredictable "surprise attacks" and thus keep them and their unit members alive and well. Losing the edge may also be represented by a fear of forgetting all the hard-fought, painful lessons learned. Unit leaders in combat are taught that they will all make mistakes in the heat of battle, and that tragically, lives will be lost. But the "good leader," is one who never forgets those lessons. To this end, the therapist may want to educate the concerned warrior that EMDR does not erase life experiences needed to adapt and survive; in fact if anything, it may actually strengthen those adaptive connections, and at the same time, it may help reduce the excessive baggage that can get in the way of thinking clearly and reacting properly. Shapiro's (2001) idea of "ecological validity" applies, whereby the brain's natural information processing systems have evolved like other system in our body, to absorb or digest material, extract the nutritive elements needed to maintain healthy adaptation, and eliminate the waste.

Fears of Forgetting Fallen Heroes

Deeply embedded in the psyche of most who have worn a military uniform is that cultural pledge: "We leave no person behind!" The special, intimate, social bond forged out of war between the Bands of Brothers and Sisters has been likened to that of a mother and a child. There is no greater, more profound grief than that of a parent who has lost a child. The survivors carry the burden of losing those whom they held most dear, and no power on earth will let them forget. For some military members, EMDR reprocessing may represent a threat to keeping a pledge to never forget or abandon the fallen. The therapist respectfully agrees and then might add, "There is nothing devised by man that could ever break that bond ..., if we chose to use EMDR, it would not diminish the memory of your friend in any way ... in fact, what others have reported in the same situation, is that the positive memories of the fallen had been strengthened ... of course, I cannot guarantee that will be so, but I can guarantee that there is nothing about EMDR that would ever let you forget _____."

Fears of "Losing It"

The fear of falling into the abyss of insanity—and never being able to climb back out—is not unique to military personnel, but can be high on the list of concerns when confronted with the prospect of facing a duffle bag packed loaded with pain. Therapists can reassure clients that since EMDR's introduction in 1989, there have been no reports worldwide of anyone ever succumbing to insanity as a result of EMDR. If anything, the opposite appears true. Namely, by unloading the emotional burden that Soldiers, Marines, Airmen, and Sailors carry, this will significantly more likely reduce the chances of becoming insane. By the same token, military members who never lessen the emotional baggage they accumulate, and keep adding more to their load, have a significantly greater probability of "losing it."

Fear of Losing Control

Fear of losing control can be related to a fear of becoming uncontrollably crazy, but also may be associated with a deep concern that if allowed to feel or experience hurt, rage, and pain, that neither the service member, nor the therapist, would be able to control the resulting reactions. Clients may have explicit concerns about the safety of others, particularly those closest to them, family and friends. Additionally, losing control of one's emotions and behavior might cause them to lash out at work and thereby jeopardize their standing in the eyes of their superiors, peers, and subordinates. Relatedly, clients may fear that by letting go of the tight control of their emotions, it will unleash a flood of tears that won't stop and will require the building of a second ark. To these concerns, the therapist might inform the client that it is true that, by using EMDR, they will likely feel and re-experience many of the ugly and horrific things that they and any human being would instinctively want to avoid. However, it is also true, and has been the therapist's experience (assuming that's the case), that for some people, EMDR appears to reprocess the painful material much quicker than other means available. The therapist will also want to remind the client that during EMDR reprocessing they are in control. They have the brake and gas pedal, and the therapist is the backseat navigator. Clients are also reminded that, during the EMDR reprocessing, old memories may arise that can be quite painful or distressing, but they are memories of past events; they are not happening now. Moreover, we do not want to client to get immersed into these memories, and remind them of the metaphor of observing the scenery from a car window, just mindfully noticing, observing the memories as they go bye. By just observing, we tell the clients, they can help prevent dwelling or getting stuck in a particular painful place. "Just observe what's happening, try not to force yourself to think or not think about anything, just notice who comes up, like scenery from a car ... then we'll stop, and I'll ask you what do you notice, and you can tell me as little as or much as you want, I just need to know enough whether something has changed or it hasn't ... you're in control of that."

Fear of Revealing Embarrassing, Shameful, or Unlawful Material

Another concern that some service member's may espouse is that EMDR will open them up and make them spill their guts about all of their embarrassing, shameful, and possibly unlawful behaviors, either during, and/or before the military. Many military personnel secretly worry that the military will find out that they lied, or deceived their recruiters about their past history prior to entering the military. And, if found out, they would be prosecuted or worst. Similarly, deployments can sometimes lead to unlawful behaviors, referred today as "misconduct stress behaviors." This can range from minor rule infractions, to a host of inappropriate and sometimes serious felony acts including rape and murder. Whether perpetrated or witnessed by the client, disclosure of these behaviors goes against the unwritten code amongst the Band of Brothers and Sisters, that's akin to "What happens in Vegas, stays in Vegas." Of course, commission of war atrocities is not typically included in the code of silence. Other behaviors of an embarrassing nature is the unpleasant fact that many combat veterans know, but are ashamed to admit they may have urinated or defecated during a fire fight. Understanding what are the "normal" reactions to direct combat may help alter the client's negative self-perception (see Menninger, 1948). There is also the possibility that the client may have frozen in the field of fire, and he or she feels cowardly. Or perhaps, the client committed adultery, or is afraid of crying in front of the therapist. The list can be endless. In response, the therapist would remind the clients that they are in control of what they say, or do not say, all the therapist needs from them is an indication whether what they are observing has changed or not. Any other sharing of detail is up to the them. At this point, the therapist may also want to remind clients of the limits of confidentiality if it comes to the commission of a serious crime, if that applies to the therapist. Non-uniformed practitioners may not have that obligation. The level of crime would be a felony, such as rape or murder, and some therapists may be legally required to report, and clients should be informed before the fact.

Fear of Absolution

On occasion, clients will express fears of therapeutic change that will lift their self- or deity-imposed punishments for mortal sin. This may be expressed by statements that the client does not deserve to be happy or symptom-free, just the opposite. It may be that they have killed, accidentally or intentionally, or seriously harmed enough, or that they survived, and others, perhaps more deserving did not. One case in particular comes to mind. A towering mountain of a Soldier with a pro-wrestler's build came into the office. The Staff Sergeant was a decorated combat veteran, hard as nails, but his life spirit was broken, as he revealed a horrific story of returning from deployment and working on his truck in the garage. That tragic day, while momentarily distracted, the truck slipped from its blocks, landed and crushed his 6-year-old daughter as she who went under it to retrieve her ball. The deeply tormented father wanted nothing to do with healing his pain; he felt he deserved a lot more. It is tempting to describe the perfect reframe or a soul-correcting inspiration that led to the client's change of heart about EMDR or any other "treatment"—but there isn't any. This case was a stark reminder of the limitations of mental healthcare. Perhaps, a later time, there might be more ambivalence to work with, but it was made painfully clear that this was not about seeking absolution. Clients with traumatic grief will almost invariably have some ambivalence around whether they deserve better in life, when someone dear has none. The reader is referred to Silver and Rogers (2002).

Final Comment on Identifying and Addressing Client Ambivalence

If identifiable, it behooves the therapist to address the client's ambivalence toward EMDR or treatment in general, as early as possible. However, many times the client's ambivalence will not be known or knowable until after reprocessing has started. This typically is demonstrated when reprocessing gets derailed, such as if the client frequently stops tracking in the middle of a set, or they frequently cite distractions when asked by the therapist what keeps there SUDS from reaching a "0" or VOC to a "7." In EMDR vernacular, the client's ambivalence, fears, or concerns are a form of "blocking belief." We will further discuss blocking beliefs in subsequent chapters.

FINAL CHECKLIST FOR PHASE TWO CLIENT PREPARATION

(a) Enhanced the therapeutic alliance; (b) obtained informed consent for treatment and EMDR specifically; (c) explained theory of EMDR and the treatment procedure; (d) clarified clients' and therapists' role expectations; (e) introduced treatment metaphors and developed a stop signal; (f) demonstrated bilateral stimulation; (g) implemented in-session stress reduction technique if needed; (h) re-checked client understanding and consent to EMDR treatment; and (i) addressed identifiable client fears or concerns. With a "check" on each item, we march onto Phase Three.

7   Phase Three: EMDR Assessment

The assessment in Phase Three of EMDR should not be confused with the clinical assessment that would normally occur either before or during Phase One. After the client history has been completed and the initial treatment plan developed, clients deemed stable and suitable for EMDR were properly informed and prepared for eventual reprocessing. In collaboration with the client, the therapist has selected a certain number of etiological past events, current triggers, and future-oriented goals that are believed to be the principle cause of the client's presenting complaint and suffering. However, before actual reprocessing can commence, the therapist must complete two vital tasks: (1) Identify the critical core components of each target memory and (2) Obtain baseline measures for each target memory.

IDENTIFYING CORE COMPONENTS OF THE TARGET MEMORY

Completing the EMDR assessment in an effective manner is more likely when the therapist has a firm understanding of what we are trying to achieve.

The AIP Model

Introduction to psychology students learn about three types of memory storage: sensory memory, working or short-term memory, and long-term memory. Sensory memory is the fleeting imprint in the lower brain centers that register sensations related to vision, audition, gustation (taste), olfaction (smell) and pain, pressure, and temperature, and proprioception (awareness of location of body parts). Every sensation we experience is held in sensory memory for fractions of seconds until replaced by new sensations. However, if we pay attention to what our senses register—and if the occasion is particularly meaningful, emotionally charged, or otherwise important to us in some manner—those sensory memories, along with our thoughts, emotions, and actions at the time, get stored in short-term memory. Short-term memory allows us to fill our cognitive capacity to deliberate, calculate, translate, and share our experiences, but only for seconds or a few minutes, before it too is displaced. Again, those events that we attend to, and go over in our minds, especially when emotionally significant, and possibly meaningful or useful in the future, get transferred to declarative, or explicit long-term memory by brain structures like the hippocampus. We can have explicit awareness of these types of memories. That permanent, limitless storage of life experiences contained in the billions of neurons dispersed throughout the third-of-an-inch cortex. If these trillions of memories were stored randomly, we could not function beyond a cat. However, nature has evolved an organizing system for man that is rival to none.

Networks of neurons are formed by forming associations or links between neurons with similar information. These memory networks help organize our life experience and understanding of the world. They are centrally organized by broad functions needed to adapt and survive. For example, language, knowledge, and facts (semantic memory); personal experiences (autobiographical memory); and motor skills and emotional conditioning (procedural memory). Strong emotional experiences acquired through our interaction with the environment and the somatosensory, muscle memory of early, pre-verbal life, and rote, learned skills like walking, are stored in procedural memory, also referred to as non-declarative, or implicit memory because they involve activity from mid-brain structures like the amygdala that is generally outside of our conscious awareness. Within these broad categories of memory, neural networks are organized by core, recurring experiences like emotions, beliefs, and events. Like experiences get wired together.

Because of the complexity of human social groups and the world around us, our brain has evolved neural networks that specialize in managing certain kinds of information, with particular functions lateralized to one of the two hemispheres. Hemispheric specialization allows us to parallel process significantly greater amounts and diversity of information. Research has shown quite robustly that the non-dominant hemisphere (right-side for most) is specialized in processing implicit, procedural memories, with a bias toward negative valence of emotions and the self, whereas the dominant hemisphere appears more specialized to store and process explicit or declarative memories, particularly neural networks with bias toward positive emotional valence and the self. Redundancies have evolved, so the two hemispheres overlap a good deal, but neuro-scientific research on psychopathological conditions like depression, anxiety, and PTSD have consistently demonstrated lateralized effects.

AIP Model and EMDR Assessment

What does this have to do with EMDR assessment and reprocessing? Almost everything. In Phase Three, therapists need to identify a representative sensory image (picture) or other form of sensory memory (e.g., audition, olfaction); select a negative cognition (NC) or negative core-belief; identify the associated emotions and location of physiological sensations; solicit a future oriented, adaptive core belief, or positive cognition (PC); and do this with each targeted past memory, along with baseline ratings signifying the level of disturbance from 0 to10 on a Subjective Units of Disturbance Scale (SUDS), and the level of perceived strength of the adaptive self-statement (PC) from 1 to 7 on a Validity of Cognitions (VOC) scale. A fairly simple and straightforward exercise but what are we really after? We will examine each memory component separately.

Image

The first memory component to be identified is the sensory memory of the event. For most people, this will be a visual image or picture: *"What picture represents the incident?"*

Clients will often report a litany of images associated with the disturbing memory—after all, most of our declarative memories have a beginning, middle, and end. So, we might ask: *"What picture represents the worst part of the incident?"*

We only need a single, representative sensory memory—an image in this case. Why? The KISS principle in part, having multiple images of the same memory, along with the NC, emotions, PC, etc., is ripe for confusion; that's true, but there is another, simpler explanation. One is all we need, and if we can select one from the dozen or more pictures, we ask for the "Worst" or "Most Disturbing" picture. Why? Because it is the most salient and emotionally charged sensory memory that was encoded at the time. Selecting the most distressing memory means the client will be accessing the maladaptive neural network, and the "worst" sensory memory will be one of the more active, and dominant memories in the network, activating the others. So, we select the single most disturbing picture that represents either a single incident (e.g., a specific IED attack), or when there are multiple memories of a similar nature, place, or person, we ask for the representative, worst of the worst from that memory cluster.

What if clients struggle with identifying an image? When clients are unable to identify a specific image of the incident or representative of a cluster of incidents, there is an excellent chance that the most prominent sensory memory is not an image, but maybe a smell, a sound, pain, or taste. For example, the author (Mark Russell) met with a JAG officer who returned from Iraq after investigating the Abu Ghraib debacle. The JAG recalled his months in the Green zone, sleeping with his flak jacket and Kevlar helmet on, as nightly motors and rockets whistled by and occasional sounds of explosion were heard, but he reported he was unfazed. He was amazed at how quickly he adjusted; none of the chaos around him seemed to affect him at all: "What's all this fuss about combat stress?" Shortly before redeploying back to the States, the JAG recalled an incident while standing in line at the Burger King truck with a bunch of other GIs, when the familiar whistling sound of an incoming rocket penetrated the clear blue sky, but this sound was different, he said.

Instead of fading off, it grew louder and louder, and soon people in line started hitting the dirt, even those bearded, long-haired special forces guys, he chuckled. But to his amazement, the JAG related, he stood his ground in line for that hamburger as the rocket slammed into a parked truck and exploded on impact. "Didn't even faze me," he quipped. So, why was the JAG in my office; was it just to brag what a tough guy he was? Nope. Three months after returning home from Iraq and reuniting with his wife and kids, life was good. No signs of combat stress; "slept like a baby," he said. Then one Saturday, he and his family went to Home Depot to get some house repair materials, when a heavy pallet fell and struck the ground. Instantly the JAG reported that he hit the ground, and broke into full body sweat, heart bounding, trembling hands, flushed face, gasping breaths, and eyes widened with a look of terror, as his wife and kids looked worriedly down at him. When I asked the JAG for his worst picture, nothing came up. He said, "All I notice, like right now as I think about this, is a strong taste of metal in my mouth … it was there at Home Depot, and I can taste it now—metal." The metallic taste the JAG is referring to is adrenaline. If clients cannot identify an image we might ask: *"When you think of the incident, what do you get?"* and if they struggle, we can prompt…. *"Is there a particular sound, or smell, or taste that stands out?"*

Below are other sensory memories that military personnel might experience:

Audition (Sounds): (a) Explosions; (b) gunfire, ricochets, and near misses; (c) cries of wounded; (d) whistling of incoming rounds; (e) pleas for help or mercy; (f) wailing of mourners; (g) shouts of rage and taunts; and (h) multiple commands.

Olfaction (Smells): (a) Rotting garbage; (b) burnt flesh and hair; (c) heavy chemical and industrial smoke/fuel; (d) open sewage, feces, and stale urine; (e) decaying animals; (f) gun powder; (g) burning rubber; and (h) gun grease.

Military Client Censorship

It is worth noting that some military clients may reflexively edit their responses to the therapist, particularly so with male clients with female therapists. This will be evident by the absence or apologizing for any slips of vulgarity or language that others may offend. Service members may also try to sanitize their narrative to shield the therapist from exposure to the horrors of human violence, or white wash information that may paint themselves in an unfavorable light. A therapist believing that his or her client may be filtering their responses might say, *"It's really important for me to be able to understand the world through your eyes, so don't worry about offending or upsetting me, just tell me what is your honest gut response—can you do that?"*

Negative Cognition

After identifying the sensory memory of the target, the therapist now solicits the client's negative self-statement. Clients are instructed bring up the memory, and the image or other sensory memory they reported, and say: *"What words go best with that picture that expresses your negative belief about yourself now?"* Or we can also ask: *When you think of that picture what do you believe about yourself? What does that say about you as a person?"* or *"What belief about yourself goes with that picture?"*

Ideally, the negative cognition (NC) will be a negative, self-referencing, irrational, presently held belief that accurately focuses the client's presenting issue, generalizes to related events or concerns, and resonates with client's affect. During EMDR training, participants are taught to aim for an "I" statement, ergo the "self-referencing" feature, and the negative belief should be related to what they believe about themselves in the present, "now," as they recollect what happened. And what are therapists to do should clients report five NC? We ask: *"Which one stands out for you, and really represents your belief about yourself now?"* In other words, we want one, and only one, negative cognition. Trainees are also advised what makes a poor choice of a NC, such as a description of the past, "It was awful," or a feeling statement, "I'm pissed," or wishful thinking, "I wish I had never deployed." So, what is it that we are really after?

The purpose of the negative cognition is to try to identify the most prominent, affect-laden cognition in the maladaptive neural network. By its nature, the self-referencing "I am" ... worthless, a coward, weak, etc. statement is more likely to generalize to other beliefs of the self and other adverse events. Such a core belief will be associated with affect. The stronger the belief, the stronger the affect, and this allows the client greater "access" to the existing maladaptive neural network, and more likely to be linked to other similar networks during reprocessing. So that's the idea. Therapist familiar with cognitive therapy may have less problem with "peeling the onion" to get to the negative core belief. For instance, one of my medic clients said, "There's too much blood!" This is a statement or description of the event, it's not self-referencing or present focus, so we might say, "When you see that there's a lot of blood, does it bring up a certain negative belief about yourself now?" The client replies, "I was a coward." Closer now, it appears to be self-referenced, but still a statement of the past versus a presently held core belief of himself. So, the therapist might ask: "If you think you were a coward, what does that say about you now?" or words to that effect. And the client might answer, "I am weak." We peeled the onion.

Now we will contradict ourselves. The search for the perfect NC: self-referencing, present focus, generalizable is theoretically optimal, but may not be the most relevant to the client. It has been observed on frequent occasions where therapists get wrapped up on soliciting the ideal "I" statement, they frustrate their client and themselves and delay or derail treatment. Remember the ultimate goal is to identify a single representative, powerful negative cognition that is affect-laden, prominent in the etiology of the client's condition, and therefore will help the client access the maladaptive neural network. Access to the maladaptive network generally means we have access to other memories, sensory images, cognitions, emotions, and sensations, as they are physiologically linked. That means that the cognitions from the onion we peeled above were most assuredly in the same neural net. All right, let's take the first negative statement from the medic, "There's a lot of blood!" Is there any doubt that we can access the neural network with that statement? None. But it may be worth challenging to get to something more self-focused and generalizable, so the client gives us "That I was a coward."

If the therapist and/or military clients are pressed for time and it starts to feel like water boarding to get a self-confession, we can run with any of these three negative cognitions! What isn't apparent is that this young medic was a first responder to a grotesque suicide bombing in a mess tent (where people eat). Dozens were killed instantly and three to four times that many seriously wounded. Blood and body parts were laying everywhere, the mortally wounded were pleading for help with their body cavities exposed, and this young man was among the first to go into this living hell: "There's a lot of blood!" Affect, access, likely generalization—this medic has been through hell—we need to get to the reprocessing and not get hung up on academic perfection. That's exactly what we did, and it processed without a hitch. By the way, there is absolutely no empirical basis whatsoever that any of three NCs described above would result in superior outcome. So, as a common sense rule of thumb, therapists should take one peel of the onion, challenge the first imperfect self-statement if need be, but unless the second statement is completely out in left field, we are done for now. The core self-referencing belief is still in the neural net, waiting to be reprocessed.

Positive Cognition

The positive cognition, or PC, is a self-referencing belief that addresses the same concern as the negative cognition, accurately focuses client's desired direction of change, is initially acceptable, and can generalize to related events or concerns. Ideally, the PC is 180 degrees diametrically opposite of the negative cognition. For example, a NC of "I am weak" might lead to a PC of "I am strong." We solicit the PC by saying, *"When you bring up that picture what would you like to believe about yourself now?"* Similar to the negative cognition, the PC is not an absolute or magical thought about changing events or attributes, "I will never follow orders again," and the PC should be worded positively to avoid confusion. *"I am strong"* rather than *"I am not weak."* So, what is the PC all about?

Soliciting the PC provides us a window into the realm of adaptive possibilities. It is akin of a therapist having a crystal ball. A client enters our office and we work with him or her to resolve the particular problem, irrespective of EMDR, what would be the adaptive resolution we hope that clients reach? For a client with PTSD from a motor vehicle accident 5 years ago, and no serious injuries sustained by either party, it might be something like, "It's over now, it's in the past, I survived, life goes on." So, in EMDR, we are having the client look into our crystal ball and ask what would there adaptive resolution be for their situation? There are several reasons why we might want to do this. One is to determine if the client can access the more adaptive neural networks that store the mastery, secure attachment, past success and the like. Accessing the adaptive memory network is what EMDR reprocessing is all about. When the client's maladaptive neural networks are activated, as in PTSD let's say, it dominates the client's attentional focus, cognitive capacity, emotional regulation, sleep, and so on. The adaptive neural networks cannot compete because the brain–body is in full survivor mode. So, we invite the client to access the adaptive neural networks and by doing so, we are now linking, making a neuronal synapse to be exact, between the two neural networks. The second reason why therapists solicit the PC is that it provides a measure of how demoralized the client is. If they can entertain for a few minutes an adaptive response to their war within, there is reason to hope. When a client is not able to come up with any PC, the therapist should assess for dangerousness and probably consider RDI for the time being. Why assess for dangerousness? The single strongest predictor for suicide is the absence of hope.

Sometimes clients were culpable. For example, a young Marine Lance Corporal (LCPL) suffered from depression and traumatic grief, with excessive guilt and nightmares after he returned from deployment and the dead Iraqi insurgent he killed was haunting him. The insurgent was about to open fire and a group of the LCPL's unsuspecting unit members, and the decision was made in a split-second to protect the lives of innocents. He provided a NC of "I am evil." What would be an appropriate PC? In this case, the LCPL offered: "I will never kill again." Well, he was still in the Corps and had several years left on his EAOS (obligated service), and he was a rifleman, likely to deploy again within a year. So, the therapist remarked, "That's what your gut says, and there is no doubt that you would never kill just for the sake of it, but if the same situation happened, and you have this guy in your cross-hairs, and he's taking aim at your unit members, and its him or your buddies, what would you do? And the LCPL replies, "I'd fuckin kill him sir!" Obviously not the PC we are looking for, so the therapist asks, "Well, what does that say about you Lance Corporal, as a human being, as a Marine, that you are willing to put yourself through hell like this about killing, but would do it again to protect innocent lives?" The Lance Corporal was stumped for a while, "I don't know.... I guess it means that I try to help protect people who don't deserve to die, even if that meant killing someone." Then the therapist replied, "And if you kill only to protect, what does mean about you Lance?" Client, "I don't know … that I am a protector or something." Therapist, "So how does: I am a protector sound to you?" Client, "Good I guess sir, but I still feel evil." So the PC we went with was "I am a protector." There are probably a million better options, but we do the best we can. "I am a protector" seems nearly 180° more adaptive than "I am evil." The therapist's own beliefs, values, and conscience may be challenged, when having to address the hard realities of what many of these young men and women have experienced—if it was your kid what would you say?

Validity of Cognition

Now we come to one of the two baseline measures for the target memories. The Validity of Cognition (VOC) is intended to be a measure of the client's felt confidence of their adaptive self-statement. How strongly do they feel in their gut that "I am a protector?" So, we ask: *"When you think of the incident, how true to those words ____ (PC) ___ feel to you NOW on a scale from 1 to 7 where 1 feels completely false and 7 feels completely true?"* If the initial VOC is a 1, we stop and check for a replacement. In the scenario above, the Lance Corporal said, "I don't know sir, right now I think it's maybe a 1½ or 2." We need to keep things simple, so respond by, "If you had to pick one or the other, which feels the more true about yourself now, 1 ½ or 2?" Client, "I guess 2." The VOC provides a useful baseline for the sense of hopefulness and adaptive possibilities on the horizon. More precisely, the simple 1–7 VOC rating gives the therapist and client an estimation of the relative strength in the tentative association between the maladaptive and adaptive neural networks. Looking ahead, what is the prototypical EMDR effect? It's a reduction of (hyper) activation of maladaptive neural networks (decrease in SUDS), coinciding with an increased activation of the adaptive memory networks (increase in VOC), whereas psychopathological states is the converse. This is exactly what the EMDR neuroimaging studies have shown in terms of the functional changes in the brain. Just to be clear, brain structures with names like amygdala, anterior cingulate, hippocampus, hypothalamus, orbitoprefrontal cortex, etc., are labels of neural networks.

Emotions

After accessing the adaptive neural networks and soliciting and measuring the positive cognition, the therapist redirects the client's self-focus to the maladaptive neural network—and specifically the target memory—and says, *"When you think of that incident and the words ___ (NC) __ what emotions do you feel?"* What and how many emotions the client offers we accept them and right it down. Clients who report, "I don't feel anything," "I just feel empty," or "I feel numb," are probably reporting the similar subjective experience. Numbness and emptiness are emotional states and should be recorded as such.

Common Perceptual Disturbance in Combat

When therapists are working with military populations who have been exposed to high stress environments like war and combat, the perceptions are the sensory memories likely being encoded at the time the incident, and upon retrieval might explain responses like numb, empty, no feelings, etc. Quickly, while the client's self-focused attention is accessing the negative emotions from the maladaptive neural network, we want to obtain our second baseline measure. To illustrate, these are the common perceptual experiences of soldiers involved in direct combat (Grossman, 2007): (a) 85% Diminished Sound, (b) 47% Partial Amnesia for Actions, (c) 40% Dissociation (detachment), (d) 26% Intrusive Distracting Thoughts, (e) 22% Memory Distortions, (f) 16% Fast Motion Time, (g) 16% Intensified Sounds, (h) 80% Tunnel Vision, (i) 74% Automatic Pilot (scared speechless), (j) 65% Slow Motion Time, (k) 7% Temporary Paralysis, and (l) 51% Partial Event Amnesia.

SUDS

Immediately after writing down the client's emotions, the therapist should follow with, *"From 0 or no disturbance to 10, the worst disturbance you can think of, how disturbing does it feel now?"* It's important for the therapist to not ask clients to explain their emotions in anyway during this phase, because once they have re-accessed the negative neural network, we want their self-rating. If the client gives a SUDS range of "between 8 to 10," the therapist should ask: "If you have to pick-one, which SUDS rating, 8, 9, or 10 best describes how distressed you feel about the incident right now?" The therapist should be prepared for client ratings that may not always match the content of their narrative. For example, when the client gave a SUDS rating of "2 or 3," for some really horrendous experience like the mess tent suicide bombing described earlier, the lower than expected subjective rating may be a sign of the client's previous level of exposure or habituation to such scenes (e.g., first responder), or the client may be restricting their attentional focus in order to control the amount of exposure to the scene for self-protective reasons, or they are experiencing a numb, dissociative state, along with probably a few other explanations. At this point, the therapist should not challenge the rating as along as it is above a 2, meaning that it's two clicks above zero and reflects some measure of disturbance. Therapists can anticipate that a low SUDS rating at assessment does not predict the level of disturbance during reprocessing, although it invariably increases.

Physical Sensation

Again, without delay, immediately after obtaining the SUDS, the therapist should say, *"Where do you feel it in your body?"* Even with feelings of nothing, emptiness, void, numbness, and so on, the therapist should ask, "And where in your body do you feel the numbness the most?" They may report a location or diffuse throughout their body, just record it. Like emotions, clients can report as many physical sensations as they see fit. The therapist does not need to do or say anything other than record what the client says and the location. When clients report multiple physical symptoms, it is not necessary for the therapist to map out each one. The therapist can repeat back all the physical sensations the client reported and simply ask, "and where do you feel these in your body?" Clients may describe each individual sensation and its locale, but most times they may report locations but not specify which sensation is where. In the grand scheme of the EMDR assessment, locating each specific physical sensation is not necessary.

What's the Importance of Attending to Physical Sensations?

Getting back to the AIP model, the purpose of soliciting the physical sensations and location is to enhance client access to the target memory within the maladaptive neural network. The more "hooks" or access points, the greater the activation of the neural network. Those hooks are sensory memory (image), negative cognition, emotions, and physical sensations that were present during the time of the incident, and, in most cases, also present during other similar events that constitute the maladaptive neural net. Another reason why it's critical for the therapist to be aware of the client's physiological symptoms is that along with the client's emotional responses, physical or somatosensory sensations are what is typically encoded in implicit memory. Implicit, non-declarative memories have been established years before our explicit memories and articulated life narratives. For the first 1–2 years of life, our earliest memories are pre-verbal and sensori-motor originating from the critical periods of human attachment and development. In EMDR speak, the client's emotions and physiological sensations provide our only access to our most foundational life experiences associated with interpersonal attachment, intimacy, a secure base, the emerging self-identity, and patterns of early emotional conditioning that are regularly triggered in the present, but are not within our conscious grasp. Remember, procedural, implicit memories are "non-declarative." But they do declare themselves all the time in the form of our "gut instincts," and other involuntary, automatic reactions to people and events. So by paying attention to the client's emotions and physiology, we are now accessing and intervening with both hemispheric and top-down neural networks: the explicitly, conscious memories of the client's narrative, and the implicitly, involuntary, non-conscious, and formative experiences.

There are times where the client's physical sensations are the primary, and sometimes near exclusive focus during reprocessing, which we will examine in the next chapter. Lastly, if the client reports no semblance of a physical sensation then the therapist may want to conduct a body scan (Phase Six), or utilize an alternative strategy to see if a sensation can be identify. Sometimes clients will just report emotional states when asked about physical sensation, which makes sense given that all emotions have a physiological component. In this case, the therapist can attempt to clarify or just ask the client to give the location of where they feel the emotion, and proceed. Similarly, if the client is still unable to identify a physical sensation during the assessment phase, we make a note, and move on.

Summary Statement on EMDR Assessment

The therapist should strive to get through the EMDR assessment with as minimal intrusions by the therapist as possible. By intrusions, we are referring to active-listening techniques, or cognitive disputation, psycho-education, or psychodynamic exploration in response to what the client reports during the assessment phase. In short, the therapist really should try to stick to the assessment script and not try to weave in other theoretical approaches. If the therapist adheres to the assessment protocol, he or she will achieve better assessment results, get through the assessment phase much quicker, and reduce the wear and tear on clients.

Altering the EMDR Assessment Script or Sequence

If therapists wish to alter the wording of the assessment questions to better suit themselves or their clients, that is perfectly appropriate (see Shapiro, 2001). However, keep the questions short and ensure that the adaptations address the actual intent. For instance, when we solicit the NC and PC, be sure clients are asked to describe their currently held belief. Following the script sequentially assures a rhythm that allows the client to access the appropriate neural network and assess the strength of the associations to those networks. Therapist intrusions interfere with that process. For example, when eliciting client emotions, the therapist should immediately ask for the SUDS rating while the client is accessing the appropriate neural network. If instead therapists choose to dialogue with clients about their choice of emotions, asking for clarification, repeat it back, challenge the emotions reported and so on, in effect the therapist has pulled the client's attentional focus away from the target memory to other neural networks to respond to the therapist's inquiry. If the therapist follows later with asking for a SUDS rating, the client has only a memory trace to work with. Moreover, if the treatment plan contains 5, 8, 10, or however many target memories, the therapist needs to go through each one of those.

Therapists have asked whether it's a good idea to alter the sequence of the assessment questions, such as assessing the negative-valence (emotion) components first (image-NC-emotions-sensations-SUDS), followed by the positive-valence (PC-VOC), or vice versa. Some EMDR purists may argue that therapists must strictly adhere to the assessment sequence because that is what is "evidence-based"—true, in a strict sense. Others would assuredly argue that the assessment sequence is purposefully designed to end with the client still accessing the target memory in the maladaptive neural network (body sensation), so that the therapist can more naturally and readily transition into reprocessing mode—and that indeed was the intent. Does it matter? It seems highly improbable, theoretically inexplicable, and empirically unsupported, that changing the sequence of the EMDR sequence would demonstrably alter treatment outcome. On the other hand, if it isn't broke, why fix it? Meaning the current sequence of the evidence-based protocol is working fine. We will defer the rest to clinical judgment and preference. After assessing the target memories, the therapist will need to review the current triggers and future template. To complete the EMDR assessment in as rapid, efficient, and effective manner as possible, stay to script.

Case Study: EMDR Assessment for Acute War Stress Injury

The following case material was adapted from Russell (2006). The client was a 32-year-old, Caucasian, male, Staff Sergeant (E-6), U.S. Army, who was MEDEVAC'ed to Fleet Hospital Eight for mortar shrapnel wounds inflicted three weeks earlier. He related that although the memory of his injuries was quite unpleasant, the most upsetting memory he had related to the unearthing of a mass gravesite and seeing a dog eating a corpse. The subject expressed acute anguish whenever the image of the dog at the mass grave appeared to him, which was several times a day. His score on the Impact of Events Scale (IES) was consistent with PTSD, his symptoms being in the severe range (IES = 44). In his clinical interview, he endorsed 20 items as well as three dissociative symptoms (detachment, numbing, and depersonalization), which led to a diagnosis of Acute Stress Disorder (client history and preparation have already been completed—we are picking up the session at the EMDR Assessment phase):

Th: Ok. Staff Sergeant … well it looks like you've been through hell and back … When you think of the gravesite incident, what picture or image comes up the most?

C: Probably watching the dog eat that corpse, it looked like it was a young woman's body, and the dog was eating it, you could see body parts coming off, and when I yelled at the dog, it went back and ripped off an arm or hand and ran off.…

Th: Is there one image or picture in particular, that represents the worst part of that gravesite scene?

C: Probably when the dog had the arm in its mouth.

Th: All right, so as you keep thinking about the gravesite memory, and the picture of the dog with a dead women's arm in its mouth, What words go best with that picture that expresses your negative belief about yourself now?

C: I don't know … it was just the last straw after everything else I've seen … sobbing heavily … I can't stand it anymore? [Negative Cognition: I can't stand it anymore/suicidal ideation]

Note: The positive cognition and VOC were not assessed during this inter-vention. The client was scheduled to be aeromedically evacuated to Walter Reed within the next 1–2 days. The client was having nightmares on the ward, screaming, and crying inconsolably and expressed suicidal ideation. Sedatives were not very helpful. The purpose of the intervention was to provide acute symptom reduction and stabilization so the client can be airlifted, therefore the main focus was on reprocessing the most disturbing memory, therefore the installation and body scan phase was not attempted. As a consequence there was no PC of VOC either.

Th: When you think of this dog incident and the words I can't stand it any-more, what emotions come up?

C: Just everything that's happened, and to see that on top of it…. I've never felt like this before … really depressed…. I … just want to die and make this all go away. [Emotions: depression]

Th: I can see you're in a lot of pain Staff Sergeant; on a 0 to 10 scale—0 you feel no depression or other disturbance and 10 the worst disturbance you can think of—how disturbing does it feel now?

C: A 20 … 10, I guess [SUDS = 10].

Th: And where do you feel it in your body?

C: (lifts his trembling arms).

Clinical note. It is conceivable that the therapist could have completed the full assessment and attempted the installation and body scan phase, so this was a judgment call. In any other than acute situations, the full assessment and protocol should be offered. The AIP model informs the therapist that we need to ensure the client access the maladaptive neural network, and that is the main purpose of the assessment. Baseline measures of the target memory used only SUDS, which provides an index of the strength of the association to the maladaptive neural network. Clearly the client is accessing the target memory and negative neural network with negative image, negative cognitions includ-ing suicidal ideation, depressed emotion, and physically trembling and cry-ing. Therefore, we have all we need for EMDR reprocessing. The client is on a nursing ward, under 1:1 watch, he has been informed of the potential risks and benefits, and other options. We will pick up the case next chapter.

Case Study: EMDR Assessment PTSD and Medically Unexplained Symptoms

Background. The client was a 73-year-old male, retired, U.S. Army, Korean and Vietnam War combat veteran self-referred to receive EMDR therapy after 35-year-long disability from combat-related PTSD, depression, and promi-nent, severe myoclonic jerking movements that started after his base was overrun by the North Vietnamese on the night of the 1968 TET offensive. The client's odd, upper-body "shaking" or jerking movements occurred *"at least*

20 times" a day when alone and "*over 50–60 times*" in social situations (e.g., shopping, church, etc.) and were eerily familiar to the author (Mark Russell). During another era, the client would have been diagnosed with "shell shock." VA records indicated "*longest time without shaking is 5 hours.*" A review of VA diagnoses per medical records was corroborated at time of intake reporting PTSD symptoms in the "severe" range (IES = 72), with "moderate" levels of depression (BDI = 22) and hopelessness (BHS = 12). He denied any current suicidal and/or homicidal ideation. A target memory list was solicited in chronological order following standard EMDR three-pronged protocol of past experiential contributors, present triggers and future desired behaviors (Silver, Rogers, & Russell, 2008).

Assessment: Standard EMDR Protocol

Below is a summary of the completed assessment utilizing the standard EMDR three-pronged protocol. The client was seen at a robust military mental health clinic during OEF/OIF, therefore routine appointment times were sparse for non-active-duty, especially since enrolled in the VA. The therapist asked the client to name "*The five worst memories that are bothering you the most related to the jerking starting when you arrived in Vietnam and after returning.*"

First Target. During transportation via helicopter to his Vietnam command he was told by the crew he must walk, unarmed, 1–2 miles alone to his base at night that was surrounded by jungle. The image was the darkened road leading to the base with the negative cognition (NC) of "I'm going to die," with the emotional reaction of "scared" and "nervous" physical sensations in his whole body, with SUDS at "9." Recalling the event the experienced 6–8 jerking movements. His positive cognition (PC) was "I'm alive" with VOC of "2."

Second Target. The image of a rocket round landing 20 feet from his unit's position—but the round did not detonate and was sticking out of the ground. His NC was "nowhere's safe," with the emotion of "emptiness" and physical sensations of "tightness" in his chest and shoulders. He rated the current degree of disturbance (SUDS) as "8" with PC of "somebody was looking out for me" a VOC of "5." During recall, the client had at least 4 jerking episodes.

Third Target. An image of a burntout truck rocketed within minutes after he and his buddies had disembarked with the NC of "son of a bitch," feelings of "scared" associated with a "tight" feeling in his whole body. He rated this particular memory a "9" and PC of "I survived" with VOC of "4." As the client discussed this event, he was observed to have at least 6 jerking episodes.

Fourth Target. An image of recurrent nightmare experienced at least once a week of being awakened by 4 to 6 Vietcong soldiers dressed in black who had slipped into his tent with machetes drawn. He reported a NC of "This is it!" with the emotion "panic, fear" and the associated physical sensations of "shaking, nervous" throughout his body. He ranked this image SUDS of "10," but that bewildered him because he knew it did not happen in real life. A PC of "I survived" was identified with VOC of "1." The client had at least 6 jerking episodes while describing the nightmare scenes.

Fifth Target. Recalling coming under nighttime assault during the February 1968 TET offensive with an image of being in a bunker with sounds and visions of gunfire and explosions all around, the NC was "where's the next one going to be" in reference to incoming rocket and mortar rounds. The emotion of feeling "scared" was associated with physical sensations of "tight, nervous" feelings throughout his body, particularly upper-torso and neck area with SUDS of "7" and PC of "I survived" a VOC of "3." The client experienced at least 10 jerking episodes while recalling this memory and became tearful.

Throughout the assessment phase, the client exhibited numerous jerking movements especially as material become increasingly more emotionally charged. Afterwards, he was visibly anxious and upset that was relieved with short deep-breathing relaxation exercise.

Current Triggers. The client reported social situations (sitting in church, shopping at the commissary, getting an ice cream cone) created "panicky" feelings along with jerking movement with SUDS of "8."

Future Template. The client's imagined desired behavioral state was attending church with his wife and being confident and relaxed without "jerking" rated as VOC "2."

Treatment Summary

The client completed the three-pronged protocol after a total of four sessions, two of which were EMDR reprocessing sessions. While reprocessing the fourth combat memory, he spontaneously reported the adaptive cognitions "someone was looking out over me" and "I'm lucky to be alive" as the image of his smiling granddaughter's face emerged from the ashes of Vietnam and his chest finally felt "relaxed." Three days after the second and final treatment session, the client's daughter called the author (Mark Russell) astonished that her father had experienced "no jerking movements" since the last meeting. Moreover, they had gone shopping, ate at a restaurant, and spent several hours in a small room with noisy children at the hospital that normally would have solicited an irritable grandpa along with "50 or more jerks." Four days later, I met a radiant client and his daughter at the clinic—still no jerking! The reevaluation revealed that all SUDS were 0 and VOC 7, and, most amazingly, no negative physical sensations on the body scan to boot. When asked about Vietnam, he said, "*I feel a sense of peace with myself.*" Upon reevaluation at 12-months, there was still no jerking. The client videotaped his sentiments about EMDR therapy, expressing: "*I hope that this generation does not have to wait 35 years to get help. Everyone should be aware of the treatments available and get help; don't wait 35 years like me.*" The entire transcript of this case study is available in Silver et al. (2008).

EMDR Treatment Session Flow Considerations

As mentioned earlier, the pace of EMDR sessions is dependent upon a host of factors including whether there is a single incident, or "simple-PTSD," or multiple traumas and complex presentations, the extent of trust and rapport, and so on. The main consideration, however, is the treatment goals and plan that we examined earlier. On many cases, it is feasible to complete the first two phases (client history and preparation), and possibly the third (assessment) in a single 50-minute session. Other times, it may be one meeting per phase. It is rarer, however, to be able to complete three phases and begin phase four reprocessing in the same day, except for acute scenarios using a modified approach. By and large, the assessment and first EMDR treatment phase (Desensitization) are often held on separate days in standard EMDR protocol.

FINAL CHECKLIST FOR PHASE THREE EMDR ASSESSMENT

(a) Completed full assessment of every target memory; (b) obtained baseline measures of SUDS and VOC for each target memory; and (c) if applicable, assessed the three-pronged protocol. If that was a "check" to each item, we are go-fly!

8 Phase Four: Basic and Specialized Reprocessing Protocols

In this chapter we will cover the "Desensitization" EMDR reprocessing phase. Our main purpose is to demonstrate applications of EMDR treatment along the spectrum of war stress injury. We will start by providing an overview of the reprocessing phases. Readers wanting more detailed description of the standard EMDR protocol are referred to Shapiro's (2001) textbook. After reviewing the standard EMDR protocol, we will examine implementing the EMDR treatment plan (see Chapter 5, this volume) toward addressing the treatment goals of either primary symptom reduction or comprehensive reprocessing. A series of clinical case studies will be presented to illustrate what EMDR treatment might look like in actual military settings. Case studies: (1) combat-related acute stress disorder, (2) MUS with comorbid PTSD, (3) phantom-limb pain from traumatic amputation comorbid PTSD, (4) traumatic grief, and (5) military spouse survivor of domestic violence.

PHASE FOUR: DESENSITIZATION

Phase Four marks the beginning of EMDR treatment. Although the name of the phase is "desensitization," the name of the game is "reprocessing"—a fancy label for "learning." Rather than regurgitate the procedural steps, an effort is made to explain without jargon, what we aspire to accomplish and why. Once therapists are confident in the purpose, application of EMDR to the spectrum of stress injuries will be translucent. Moreover, as revealed in the first two chapters, the controversy over EMDR has shifted entirely to its theory. Consequently, therapists utilizing EMDR with military populations should anticipate institutional and individual skepticism and be prepared to explain in clear terms *"What is EMDR?"* and *"What's different than other therapies?"*

"Desensitization" versus "Reprocessing"

The overarching goal of this certain reprocessing phase is to instigate the client's nervous system's innate information processing mechanism to adaptively metabolize unprocessed emotional experience stored in a maladaptive neural network. The impetus for learning and change resides squarely within the client. To accomplish this goal, the therapist's objective is to encourage client access to the negative associations emanating from a maladaptive neural network. When accessed, the therapist instigates corrective emotional learning by coaching the client to direct their internal self-focused attention to one of the disturbing network's board members, the "target memory," while simultaneously dividing their attentional focus externally to a bilaterally (side-to-side) alternating neutral sensory stimulus. Once the conditions of therapeutic change (therapeutic alliance and dual-focused attention) are met, the therapist's predominant role in EMDR therapy is to unobtrusively sustain client dual-awareness of the negative associative material while employing bilateral stimulation (activating both sides of the client's brain) and, most of all, to avoid interfering with the client's learning or "reprocessing" experience.

Reduction in disturbing symptoms from sympathetic arousal or "desensitization" is a consequence of reprocessing not the end goal—albeit an important byproduct for clients—but still incomplete. However, true "corrective emotional learning" (Foa & Kozak, 1986), or EMDR reprocessing, is not evident until the client's spontaneous adaptive associations of "It's over," "I survived," "I did the best I could," and "I can honor his sacrifice by living a good life." EMDR reprocessing ultimately represents a shifting in the balance of attention and processing of information through simultaneously strengthening physiological associations between disturbing memories and the adaptive neural networks, coinciding with decreasing activation or associations to the negative memory networks. We need negative neural networks (e.g., anticipating threats, remembering danger zones, etc.), but we also need access to the bigger adaptive picture.

STANDARD EMDR REPROCESSING PROTOCOL

Preparing the Client for Reprocessing—*The Final Safety Check*

Before aircraft launch, the flight-line crew on the ground collaborates with the pilot to conduct a final safety check before take-off. In EMDR, the pilot (driver, captain) is always the client, and the therapist is the support crew. The author (Mark Russell) uses an analogy like this with military personnel but tries to tailor to the client's military experience (e.g., tank crew, ship crew, etc.). Explicit effort is made to foster the client's sense of control and therapists' presence in order to mitigate over-arousal and abort.

Reviewing the Safety Checklist

"We'll start reprocessing now. As we start the BLS (or eye movements, taps, tones—but military personnel are used to speaking in acronyms), *sometimes*

things will change and sometimes they won't. You may notice other images, thoughts, emotions, or body sensations. Other memories may come up. Other times you may not be aware of anything but the BLS (or eye movements, taps, etc.).... Most people find it hard to focus on a picture or image and the BLS at the same time, that's normal, just know that you are thinking about it."

Anticipating Problems (blocked processing) from Confusion over Client Expectation

Many clients will try to follow the therapist's instructions to the "T," by attempting to maintain self-focus attention to the image, negative cognition, emotions, and body sensations, all at the same time, while dually focusing on the BLS. After all, that is what the doc said! However, it is also impossible to pull off. Therefore it's important to avoid unnecessarily frustrating the client and risk eliciting a sense of personal failure when he or she is not witnessing changes in the target memory, or capable of focusing on every memory component. Remember, when the client becomes too self-focused, or absorbed, and starts to meta-analyze the experience, it derails dual-focus and processing. The client may be tracking the BLS however internal self-focus is predominantly on the meta-cognitions, not the negative associations—resulting in reduced access and little to no learning. Therefore, it is always best to preempt problems before they arise. The therapist should advise the client that he or she need only *"know that they are thinking"* about an image, thought, memory, etc.

Clarifying Client–Therapist Role Expectation

"Remember what we discussed earlier about the metaphor of riding in the train or car. Just observe whatever comes to your attention like scenery from a window. If old memories come up, just remind yourself, like a re-run of a live T.V. show, it's in the past. There's nothing in there that you haven't already been through and survived, it's old news." Many clients avoid focusing on the past because it stimulates access to state-dependent conditions of fear, despair, loss, and pain that are often perceived by the brain as current threats warranting a fight-flight-or-freeze response. Reminding clients that there is nothing in their memory networks that they haven't already experienced and survived, might reduce the fear of the unknown or of being overwhelmed and losing control, etc. This reminder is always given during client preparation phase, but needs to be re-stated before take-off when things get more real. Clients may feel like they are being hurt or terrorized again, but it's a "re-run" of something that they already experienced and they were strong enough to survive it. EMDR is a strength-based approach. Reminding clients of their adaptive resources does more than pump-up somebody's self-esteem. Reducing the activation level of the threat-driven maladaptive neural network often serves to increase

activation and access to the client's adaptive neural networks—and that opens the possibility for reprocessing.

Instilling Client Sense of Agency and Control

"You're the pilot (driver, captain); *you've got the flight controls. Remember the gas pedal is keeping the BLS going while you're thinking about the stuff in the past, and tracking the BLS. We will stop, and have a short dwell time. If you* <u>Want</u> (avoid the word "need") *to stop at any point, remember you've got the brake pedal, just show me the stop sign. You also decide how much, or how little you* <u>want</u> (again avoid the "need" word) *to tell me about what you're experiencing."*

Restating the degree of client control is vital, particularly when working with professionals that train to perform in high-stress environments. Perceived threats of vulnerability to losing control over oneself will often derail dual-focus and motivation for reprocessing. Therapists love to talk about "needs." In military culture, individuals are trained from accession (e.g., bootcamp) to deny their personal "needs" and focus on the group and mission. *Needs* are typically negatively associated as "weakness" in alpha-male, masculine organizations like the military. Female warriors may feel they have to prove themselves to their male-counterparts as equal members of the club—so expect equal opportunity aversion for military members to admit "needing" to stop. Military leaders that are clients, will covertly bristle when therapists mistakenly suggest that *"We can stop when you* <u>need</u> *(aka have) to"*—implying frailty. Conversely, informing clients that *they* can stop reprocessing *"when you* <u>want</u> *to"* resonates very well with most male and female warriors—and more importantly—it communicates the agency of control resides within the client.

Reaffirming Therapist Presence and Alliance

"Often we will be doing a simple check on what you are experiencing. I need to know from you whether anything is changing or not…. I don't need to know all the details … just honest feedback. Again, sometimes things will change and sometimes they won't. There are no 'supposed to's' in this process. So just give as accurate feedback as you can as to what is happening without judging whether it should be happening or not. Just let whatever happens, happen" (Shapiro, 2001, p. 431). This statement serves to inform clients of their control over the content disclosed in the session. It also imparts a critical message that the therapist will be present with the client and will be coaching them through the process. *"No person is left behind!"* strongly resonates in military culture, as does *"I've got your Back!"* (Soldiers/Marines). Therapists strive to earn the client's trust by showing the client they are caring, honest, and concerned about the client's welfare. So, we review informed consent and try to anticipate and address potential harm. Therapists are reminded to maintain connection with their client during reprocessing (e.g., "that's it, good," etc.), and ramp it up a few notches when clients enter rough seas (or turbulence): *"We're in this together Shipmate!"* (Sailors) or *"I'm your Wing Man! "* (Airmen).

Accessing a Maladaptive Neural Network

The therapist coaches the client to access the negative associative contents of a maladaptive neural network by directing their internal self-focused attention to the emotionally potent features of a targeted disturbing memory by saying, *"I'd like you to bring up that memory of* (name the incident) *incident … do you got it? … good … now think of the image* (repeat the image from the assessment)*, those negative words* (repeat the negative cognition)*, and notice where you are feeling it in your body—and follow my fingers."* We are now in the client's neuronal network of disturbance.

Dual-Focused Attention

Once we have stimulated and accessed the client's maladaptive neural network, he or she is exposed to the negative associations that may arise in the form of horrific images, visceral physiology and emotions of their sympathetic and parasympathetic nervous systems, along with a voice from the negative narrator. The client experience with their maladaptive neural networks is what brought them to the therapists' office. If the therapist encouraged the client to immerse themself in the negative net, their attention span narrows, excluding more and more potentially adaptive information, as he or she soon becomes self-absorbed by the contents of the negative neural network. Clients usually find such absorption to be quite unpleasant, but their attention is often compelled because brain circuits (neural networks) detect threats; thus a vicious circle of approach-avoidance emerges. Neuroscience has demonstrably shown that hyperactive maladaptive neural networks laterally inhibit (lower activation) access to areas of the brain that function to adaptively process information. Neuroimaging and neurophysiological studies of successful psychotherapy, including EMDR, reveal a reversal effect that correlates with the degree of client report of symptom change (e.g., Levin et al., 1999). What does the EMDR therapist do next? Before a client becomes overwhelmed by their self-absorbed attention span, he or she is advised to divide their attention and focus on the therapist's moving hand, an alternating sound in their ears, or vibrating sensation in the palms. Dividing the client's attentional focus invites other possibilities, whereas before it was monopolized. This is why distracted, depressed, and anxious clients can sometimes forget their problems and experience transient relief from inner torment. There can also be no logical dispute that by having the client split their awareness between an internal negative self-focus and joint attention of an external, neutral stimulus—that is dual-focused attention.

Bilateral Stimulation (BLS)

The therapist begins the bilateral stimulation slowly and should increase the speed as fast as the client can comfortably tolerate the movement. Therapists will adjust the speed of BLS to the client's ability to attend. Length of the BLS will vary based upon clinical indicators (e.g., intense emotional processing with longer sets), however, the average is 24–30 back-and-forth "sets." The client who is experiencing severe Acute Stress Reaction from a potentially traumatic stress may exhibit the body's "freeze" response. Dissociation results and can be elicited by a constricting of the client's attentional focus that is experienced by the client as a feeling of disconnection, a surreal, dreamlike state which hypnotherapists know well. To avert client self-absorption into intense traumatic stressors and dissociation, therapists are instructed to help their clients maintain dual-focused attention at least once or twice during each set of bilateral stimulation, or when there is an apparent change. For example, comment to the client: "*That's it. Good. That's it.*" Even more therapist verbalizations are needed when clients are in intense emotional states of fear, dissociation, and pain. It is also helpful to reassure the client (especially if the client is upset): "*That's it. It's old stuff. Just notice it.*" Therapists can also use the metaphor(s) the client has chosen earlier about "*just observing the scenery from a car or train window … just notice*" as a means to convey safety, while preventing the client from becoming overwhelmed via self-absorption, and sustain dual-awareness.

The Therapist's Presence—Establishing the Conditions for Change

The therapist's presence is needed far more than to engineer the division of the client's attention and producing BLS. Trust and rapport through the therapeutic alliance serves to stimulate access to the client's adaptive neural networks, where felt, sensed, and verbal recollections reside reminding us about nurturing, care taking, soothing, mastery, security, love, and encouragement—those internalized "resources" that helped us get through rough seas and celebrate victories. Dual-focused awareness of "the other" in the room stimulates associations of safety and support that can permit clients to peek out their scary windows. Sharing the burden with another can by itself have a calming influence—emotionally and physiologically. The supportive presence of another reduces the panic experienced from a sudden fright when we are alone. The duality of the client's divided attention and the soothing influence of the therapist can both serve to lower arousal, fear, and avoidance.

Adaptive Information Processing (AIP)

Where does reprocessing come into play? The therapist has created the conditions for change, as any good therapist will do—so what's new? The AIP theory posits that bilateral stimulation within the context of change (dual-focused attention and therapeutic alliance) simulates the brain's natural information processing mechanism. The identical mechanism, by the way, that helps create the neural networks. In ways we are not remotely close to understanding, somehow elements of sensory-perceptual experiences from our life are captured and stored amongst these networks of neurons. Obviously, there is some mechanism that has evolved to help us adapt by physically storing the experiences so that we can learn from our and other's experiences. Whatever cerebral process that translates abstract principles of classical and operant learning to the physical realities of the synapse is the intrinsic processing mechanism, or at least one of them, hypothesized to be responsible for EMDR learning effects. There is no scientific dispute that classical, operant, and observational learning is valid. Neurophysiological and neuroimaging research on EMDR and BLS have shown that clients report a learning (aka reprocessing) effect via symptom change indicators that correspond to neurological measures after successful EMDR treatment (e.g., Lansing et al., 2005). Psychotherapists of any ilk would not dispute that effective therapy involves client learning or change. Yet the "mechanism" for how the brain actually learns and converts these experiences into raw material for the neural networks is a mystery not unlike the origins of the universe. But no one questions the brain has inherent learning or information processing mechanism(s)—we just don't know what it is, where it is located, and how it works in such amazingly reliable and complex ways.

Reprocessing Is Adaptive Information Processing

Francine Shapiro (2001) originally named the AIP model "accelerated information processing," referring to the relative speed of desensitization and corrective emotional learning from EMDR treatment effects. However, the more profound treatment effect was not the tempo of change, but the fundamental shifting from a state of disturbance to one of adaptive learning that spontaneously emerged from successful treatment. Reprocessing does not stop at desensitization to disturbance when sympathetic arousal is reduced to SUDS of "0" like exposure-therapy. Quite the contrary, during EMDR "desensitization" clients spontaneously generate new insights, metaphors, and affirmations—re-writing their personal narrative often with the most brilliant summations that usually come out of the mouths of master therapists or writers. Client self-initiated resolutions lend wisdom to Piaget, Rogers, and others about the inherent adaptive qualities of human information processing. That human beings acquired the ability to select, store, recall, and use information to promote survival in complex social worlds appears without question. Nor is there serious question that humans have retained that adaptive capacity. In EMDR, we experience that as "reprocessing."

Therapist Response after Stopping the Bilateral Stimulation

After a set of bilateral stimulation, the therapist instructs the client to: *"Blank it out (or let it go) and take a deep breath."* The therapist then asks open-ended, non-demanding queries of the client's reprocessing experience, *"What do you get now?" "What are you noticing now?" "What are you aware of right now?" "What comes to mind now?"* On the face of it, the therapist's open-ended prompts may seem trivial—but they're not. Avoiding demand characteristics is only a part. Therapists using other psychotherapy models begin with explicit theories about what is causing the client's psychopathology and a set of beliefs and interventions to implement their theory. In EMDR, the therapist publicly admits complete ignorance of what associations will arise from within the client's neural networks. Other than a general theory that psychopathology is caused by overactive maladaptive memory networks and reprocessing will restore a balance by strengthening client access to their adaptive neural networks, the EMDR therapist starts therapy armed with a small list of target memories solicited from the client; the therapeutic alliance, dual-focused attention, and BLS. The therapist has no actionable intelligence of the therapeutic content that will emerge after stopping the BLS.

The *Sound of Change* and Reprocessing

Therapists are taught to keep a look out for evidence of possible movement—however seemingly small, including shifts to a new memory or changes within a memory (e.g., new or altered image, sounds, smells, tastes, touch, thoughts, beliefs, feelings, physical sensations, pain, behaviors). The location, intensity, or type of physiological sensations may change. Change in participants, or the actions of participants, or the amount of detail in the memory may be reported. Therapists also learn the *language of change*: "More, less, smaller, bigger, brighter, darker, fading, closer, farther, warmer, colder, scarier, longer, happier, growing, shrinking, lighter, hotter, wetter, drier, meaner, harder, easier, clearer, stronger, weaker, worse, better, etc." Therapists are taught to listen for certain words in the client's self-report that connote change has occurred as an indicator to continue with the reprocessing.

Therapist Response after Soliciting Client Self-Report

"Go with that," or *"Just notice that."* One would be hard pressed to find any traditional psychotherapy model whereby the acceptable (and expected) level of therapist verbal discourse during trauma-focused work is *"Focus on that!"* After the client reports *change*, the therapist does nothing more than say: *"Go with that,"* or *"Notice that"* and re-initiates BLS. Therapists using EMDR are strongly encouraged to avoid using their well-honed active-listening skills in EMDR reprocessing. Common therapist behavior in mainstream talk therapies such as paraphrasing, clarification, mirroring, interpretation,

restatement, empathic listening, rationale disputation, confrontation, etc., are all believed to actual *impede* client learning or EMDR reprocessing.

One of the most difficult aspects of learning EMDR is not the treatment itself, it is for the therapist to put aside preconceived notions of psychopathology and the active ingredients of therapeutic change. In EMDR, the therapist must learn to trust a new model of human change process that takes client-centered therapy to an all-new extreme: *"Just notice that!"* The therapist should not interfere with the client's reprocessing by acting like a typical psychotherapist. Why is that? Engaging clients in discussion after a reprocessing set requires the client to remove their attentional focus from the information they were experiencing, and shift to a cognitive, self-observer mode. When clients are distracted by the therapists' queries or comments, it is impossible to recover that moment. At best the therapist can say, *"Think about what you were experiencing before I interrupted."* Or start BLS after the client answers a question ("Just think of that"), or, if too long removed from their experience, the therapist can always return the client to the target memory and start again, "Ok, let's go back to the memory we started with, the mess tent bombing ... what do you notice now?" Then, after the client's report, say, *"Just go with that"* and start another BLS set.

Case Study: EMDR Treatment of Acute Combat-Related PTSD

The client was a 24-year-old, male, Marine Lance Corporal, whose unit was ambushed in Iraq, the client was WIA, but his combat buddy (John-fictional) was a father of a newborn and tragically killed on impact by RPG. The setting is a 250-bed Navy tent hospital. The diagnosis is combat-PTSD. The target memory is the image of John's mutilated corpse (SUDS = 8) with the negative cognition, *"I'm not ever going to see my family again."* Numb feeling with no physical sensations. Positive cognition was not solicited. The referral was to stabilize acute PTS for aeromedical evacuation to the next higher echelon of care.

Th: Okay Corporal, bring up the memory of John's death and the words "I'm never going to see my family again" ... and follow my hand with your eyes ... that's it ... good ... just notice ... etc.

Th: All right blank it out and take a breath.... What do you notice now?

C: As soon as you started the hand movements ... everything got a lot more vivid ... like I can remember everything ... like when I was there ...

Th: [More vivid, more detail connotes change] Okay ... just stay with that and track my hand ... good ... keep noticing whatever comes up ... just observe it ... it's not happening now ... blank it out, take a breath, what are you aware of now?

C: Man ... I see everything ... not just John but we lost 3–4 other guys, good guys too ... and a whole bunch of dead Iraqi combatants.

Th: [More details in the memory connote change] Stay with it. Add BLS etc. What do you get now? [About 4–5 BLS sets later—repeating the above sequence]

C: There was a lot of messed up people … and John, man he just had a kid, he was so jazzed about being a dad, I never saw him happy like that before. [Sobbing—lengthier BLS set]

Th: [Softly] I know it hurts Corporal, just stay with it. [Add BLS—but slower rate and sweep was about cheek to cheek when crying] What comes up now?

C: Man … this is weird. I'm at the bridge now, another attack, there's an explosion, it knocked me down, then I noticed a wet feeling in my leg, I looked, down and I can see blood everywhere, and I'm just thinking I'm going to die!

Th: Ok … just think of it [Add BLS] and anything else that comes up … remember your safe here, these are things that already happened … etc. What do you get now?

C: I remembered an old, rag-tag Iraqi man with an AK-47 got out of a car … and I killed him. [An additional 7 BLS sets were added]

Th: What do you notice now?

C: I remember rolling into South Baghdad and there were a lot of Iraqi kids smiling and waving, and they all looked like they were starving … I gave one of them an MRE; the kid smiled and said "America OK."

Th: Stay with that…. What are you aware of now?

C: Wow. I forgot about this … but when we got to Baghdad there was a big crowd smiling and cheering for us … I felt like a hero.

Clinical note. The client ended with a SUDS of "0" that maintained over the next couple of days before medevac to Walter Reed. The client's initial SUDS of "8" shot up to "10+" shortly after starting the BLS. Based on the content of the target memory it was expected that once the "numbing" lifted, so too would the level of distress. Notice the spontaneous shift from disturbing to adaptive. Adaptive does not mean the absence of anxiety, sadness, or grieving; those emotions evolved for a reason. Maladaptive is constantly reliving experiences that dominate and color our reaction to the present and future when no longer on the battlefield.

What Causes Reprocessing in EMDR?

There are three main ingredients for reprocessing in EMDR: (a) therapeutic alliance, (b) dual-focused attention, and (c) bilateral stimulation. In EMDR, it is imperative that the therapist keep a co-foot on the *gas pedal* (dual-focused attention and bilateral stimulation), and coach their clients during reprocessing. The only time it would be appropriate for therapists to deviate from protocol, and transiently adopt a more directive stance is when reprocessing has never started or has stopped moving.

Blocked Reprocessing

If no movement is evident, therapists are to change direction of the eye movements or the speed of bilateral stimulation, or increase the length of the BLS set (see Changing BLS Mechanics below). Therapists should be capable of eliciting faster and/or longer bilateral eye movements, which is made a lot easier with a Neurotek machine (neither author has a financial stake in Neurotek). Slow eye movements with a restricted range from cheek to cheek may be all a client can track when they are crying during intense emotional release or "abreaction." Adjusting the BLS to the client should be the norm, not the other way around. Therapists that find it physically uncomfortable to generate rapid eye movements or fatigue easily and must stop to rest should purchase the tool of the trade. Conversely, if the client is unable to track the BLS because the speed may be too fast, then reprocessing will stop, so the rule of thumb is as fast as the client can track. See the EMDR Troubleshooting Guide (Appendix B) for further information and strategies to deal with blocked reprocessing.

Returning to Target

Therapists will repeat the above sequence of: BLS, pause, self-report-*change*-BLS or BLS-pause-self-report-*no-change*-change-BLS speed/direction/type until they believe the client is at the end of a channel of associations (e.g., the material reported is neutral, or stays positive). Then ask: "*When you go back to the original experience/or incident* (name the target memory to eliminate confusion), *what do you get now*?" Whatever the client reports, add a BLS set. If new material opens up, continue down that channel with further sets of bilateral stimulation.

If the therapist believes that the client is at the end of an associative channel as reflected by the client reporting the same thing twice, or two positive associations consecutively, the therapist asks, "Ok, how about we go back to the original memory we started with, the friendly fire incident ... you can keep your eyes open or closed, it's up to you ... just concentrate on remembering that memory ... you got it?" or "Go back to the incident we started with, bring it up ... what do you get now?" or "Bring up the tent memory we started with, try to remember as much as you ... what do you notice?" Add BLS after re-accessing the target memory.

Obtaining a SUDS Rating

If after going back to the target memory and reprocessing whatever the client reports the client still reports *no change*, check the SUDS by asking, "When you bring up the experience, on a scale of 0–10, where 0 is no disturbance and 10 is the highest disturbance you can imagine, how disturbing does it feel to you now?" If the SUDS is greater than "0," the therapist adds more BLS sets and returns to normal reprocessing protocols until *no change* is reported.

Once that happens, the therapist returns him or her to target memory. Ask what he or she notice, and whatever the client reports is followed by more BLS sets. If the self-report indicates change, then add BLS. If the client reports no change, then the therapist will pursue a SUDS rating. Again, therapists only obtain a SUDS rating when the client continues to report no change.

When Is a Target Memory Considered Desensitized?

When the SUDS rating for the target memory is a "0," the therapist adds another BLS set to ensure that the SUDS rating remain a "0" and that no new associations have emerged. When the client reports no change at the target memory and SUDS of "0" after two consecutive BLS, the target memory is considered to be desensitized. The therapist will then proceed to Phase Five: Installation of the Positive Cognition.

Ecological Validity of Baseline Measures

In regard to the baseline measures, SUDS and VOC ratings, Francine Shapiro (2001) believes that the "ecological validity" of a client's self-statement and circumstances should be considered by therapists. EMDR treatment goals in regards to the baseline measures are a SUDS of "0" and VOC of "7," each maintained after two BLS sets. However, as Shapiro and a legion of others have observed, there are times when clients may report a SUDS of "1" and/or a VOC of "6" and it will not budge.

SUDS that Stay Above "0"

If the client reports that the SUDS is close to, but not at "0" and change of direction or speed has not reduced it, the therapist should ask the client to focus on body sensations and do a set of BLS. *"Bring up that picture, put it together with the words (repeat the negative cognition), notice the sensation and follow my hand."* Clients who report that the SUDS is still above a zero should ask, *"What, if anything, is preventing this from going to 0?"* and whatever the client reports, initiate a BLS set. The purpose is to assess whether negative associations possibly related to different memory, or possibly earlier life events might be evidence of a "blocking belief." For example, if the client's response is "Bad things always happen to me" or "I deserved what happened," both of which may implicate another source of disturbance. The therapist can say, *"Just think of that"* and add BLS, or they may try to assess for the client's earliest recollection, *"When was the first time that you remember when you felt you deserved something bad that happened?"* and this memory and its neural network, would be added to the treatment plan. However, if the client responds with "Because my best friend died, and I don't think that would ever be a zero!" Or they were culpable in some manner, "Because I killed people, and even though I did it to protect others, it's still against God's law." Typically, after the client's rationale, even those we deemed as "ecologically valid" we add one BLS set. Just to be certain that there may be negative associative networks related to a seemingly understandable response: "Okay, just think of that" ("because I killed people," etc.); add BLS, "What do you notice now?" "I remembered when I was 15 and stupid and broke into a sporting goods store." Add BLS and see if it lead to another neural network or may reprocess along with other memories of law violations linked together.

Ecological Validity and SUDS Rating Above "1"

Should the therapist consider SUDS of "2" or "3" or VOC of "5" as ecologically valid? Generally speaking, the answer is no. Occasionally, for clients who perpetrated certain acts (e.g., misconduct stress behaviors, fatal car accident due to DUI), or the loss was so intense, or for other reasons, this may be the best it will get. In those cases where this has happened, going from a "10" or a "9" to a "2" was a meaningful change. The therapist should expect that for SUDS above "0" and VOC below "7," there may be the possibility that other problematic neural network issues lay dormant. We inform the client that should difficulties arise in the future, to come back in. *Caution.* The therapist should be careful to quickly assume ecological validity of SUDS above "0" and VOC below "7." For instance, an Army Ranger reported a SUDS of "1" because a friend of his was killed in a "friendly fire" incident; this sounds reasonable because someone close died. However, when asked what kept it from a zero, the reply was filled with self-loathing: "*It should have been me instead!*" Therapists who get in a hurry to move on, or don't take the time to check their work, may be leaving land mines for the client. Instead of moving onto Phase Five, we reprocessed the Ranger's survivor guilt. It took another session before moving onto the current triggers and the rest of the treatment plan, but at least we cleared one mine field.

Military-Related Blocking Beliefs: Sometimes a previously unidentified negative belief is lurking behind the curtains and preventing the client from reported a lower SUDS. The therapist can easily assess for a blocking belief by saying, "*What keeps it from being a 0?*" The following might be on the minds of service women and men: (a) failing to act, (b) surviving when others did not, (c) failing to save or protect others (military or civilian), (d) killing or injuring others, (e) helplessness, (f) loss of control, and (g) personal weakness for have COSR symptoms.

Managing Intense Emotional Reprocessing

Some clients (10–15%) experience an intense emotional release or "abreaction" during EMDR reprocessing. For some military clients, this could be their worst nightmare coming true. This is why client preparation has its own phase. In many cases, it's not the client who is overly distressed about emotional venting, but the therapist. Keep in mind the AIP model. As the client is accessing negative valence memories associated with the maladaptive neural network, some of these experiences were not metabolized by the brain's information processing mechanism. It may be the nature of the event, who was involved, the degree of dissociation or terror, and/or just random bad luck, but the experience was consolidated in its state-dependent form in implicit, nondeclarative memory, or at least that is what some believe. Nevertheless, this is an event from the past from which the client did survive. And moreover, they will get through this again. Therapists need to remind themselves, and the client, that the reprocessing of these experiences has a beginning, middle, and an end.

Keeping the foot on the gas pedal (BLS and dual focus attention) using longer BLS sets and allowing the brain to reprocess the memory in a more declarative, explicit manner will most likely mean they will never go through this experience again. Therapists should frequently reassure the client of their presence: "it's okay ... just old stuff ... just notice it ... you're doing fine ... just observe ... like scenery through a car/train window ... etc." The use of a tunnel metaphor can be helpful. Advise clients that when driving a car through tunnels, most of us feel a little panicky, but keeping the foot on the gas pedal, as opposed to the break, means we get out of the tunnel sooner. Therapist presence, dual-focused attention, and longer sets of bilateral stimulation will get the majority of clients through the tunnel in a few minutes. By keeping calm and reassuring, clients will be able to weather the storm. Look for non-verbal cues or pauses to stop the BLS. Often soon after the release of intense emotions, clients body posture, the facial expression, or breathing rates suggest they hit a plateau, and this is usually a good time to stop the BLS and obtain a self-report. If the client's crying is making it difficult to track eye movement, even as the therapist slows down the rate and is moving 2–3 inches side-to-side, the therapist can suggest switching to vibration, taps, or sounds. Using taps would be counter indicated in many cases of a male therapist and female client where the memory involves a male perpetrator, or vice versa. Again, when the client and therapist emerge through the tunnel, these can be breakthrough moments.

Compassion Stress and Fatigue

After intense reprocessing sessions, it is recommended that therapists implement their self-care plan (see Chapter 16, this volume). A therapist whose workload frequently exposes them to highly charged sessions need to be particularly mindful of the insidious effects of compassion stress and take proactive measures whenever possible to avoid cumulative wear-and-tear that may lead to compassion-stress injury (e.g., compassion fatigue).

Strategies for Blocked Reprocessing and Under- and Over-Responding

Shapiro (2001) categorizes client treatment response to EMDR reprocessing in three broad ways: (a) complete, continuous reprocessing utilizing only the above protocol; (b) incomplete, or blocked reprocessing due to insufficient access or activation of the negative neural networks (under-responders); and (c) incomplete or blocked reprocessing due to excessive access or activation of the negative neural networks (over-responders). In the author's (Mark Russell) experience, at least 50% or more military clients complete EMDR reprocessing using the basic EMDR reprocessing protocol without any extra-intervention by the therapist. Less than 10% of military clients demonstrate an over-responsive reaction to EMDR reprocessing characterized by acute and sustained inability to continue reprocessing by virtue of being overwhelmed by the negative associations emanating from their maladaptive neural nets. Several of the over-responders were in military psychiatric inpatient wards, where sufficient safety was afforded that allowed reprocessing to continue. Most, if not all, clients who are unable to tolerate the reprocessing effects have extensive history of early adverse childhood experiences consistent with diagnostic formulations of complex-PTSD. Therapists should consider incorporating RDI into the treatment plan before proceeding with additional reprocessing if clients demonstrate persistent inability and/or unwillingness to continue with reprocessing. See the EMDR Troubleshooting Guide (Appendix B) for details on assessing and fixing blocked reprocessing including use of "cognitive interweave" with military personnel.

9 Phases Five–Six: Standard Reprocessing Protocols

In this chapter, we will cover the last two reprocessing phases in the basic or standard EMDR protocol: Installation (Phase Five) and Body Scan (Phase Six).

PHASE FIVE: INSTALLATION

The term "installation" is an extremely unfortunate choice of words that represents a misleading description of what this critical reprocessing phase of EMDR treatment is about. The therapist does not "install" anything—but does aspire to "strengthen" the already established associations between the disturbing target memory and its maladaptive neural network and the client's adaptive neural networks. Those connections were made evident in Phase Four reprocessing as the maladaptive neural networks became deactivated coinciding with an increased activation of the adaptive neural networks, restoring the relative balance between information processing brain circuits. In Phase Four, the client had already self-generated adaptive coping statements long before the therapist "installation." In this phase of reprocessing, the overriding goal is to enhancing the associations to the adaptive neural network. The Validity of Cognitions (VOC) provides a valuable baseline measure of the client's gut-check level of confidence in their adaptive self-belief, the Positive Cognition (PC), and also indicates the relative association strength to the adaptive networks.

Phase Five Protocol

The therapist initiates this reprocessing phrase by first checking the suitability of the client's existing positive cognition that was selected back in Phase Three. Many times, the positive cognition chosen before EMDR reprocessing starts represents a slight opening of the window to the client's adaptive neural networks. As the dominance of the maladaptive networks waned during reprocessing, client access to the adaptive resources increased. The therapist therefore wants to check if there is an even more adaptive self-statement available by asking, "*When you think of the event (or incident), do the words (repeat the positive cognition) still fit, or is there another positive statement you feel would be more suitable?"*

If the client responds by offering an even more adaptive belief, then that becomes the new Positive Cognition (PC); otherwise the original PC is kept. The next step is for the therapist to ask the client to use the VOC to measure the power of the PC and its connection to the adaptive networks by saying, *"Think about the original incident and those words (repeat the selected positive cognition). From 1, completely false, to 7, completely true, how true do they feel now?"* What is remarkable is the backdrop for the client's rating of their adaptive cognition is the disturbing target memory itself. Doing so is important because it demonstrates the relative dominance between the two broad types of information processing networks. This is perfectly illustrated when comparing the pre-treatment SUDS and VOC ratings with the post-treatment ratings. As one is higher, the other is lower, and reprocessing effects shift the balance in the favor of adaptation.

Whatever VOC rating is provided, the therapist responds with, *"Think of the event (or incident) and hold it together with the words (clinician repeats the positive cognition),"* which is followed by a bilateral stimulation (BLS) set of approximately 24 back-and-forth movements. Then, the therapist reassesses the VOC: *"When you think of the event (or incident), how true do those words (clinician repeats the positive cognition) feel to you now on a scale of 1–7, where 1 feels completely false and 7 feels totally true?"* The reprocessing steps are repeated as the client is reporting change or movement in a more adaptive direction (e.g., stronger, more relaxed, better, etc.). This is replicating the reprocessing procedure during "desensitization." Therefore, if the client reports a VOC of "7," for the first time, the therapist will respond by adding a BLS set, and continue the reprocessing until the client no longer reports change and the VOC stays a "7" representing the strongest associative link possible at this time. Two consecutive BLS sets with VOC remaining at "7" is the end of the so-called installation phase. The therapist and client will then proceed to the final reprocessing phase, the Body Scan.

Case Study: Reprocessing During Phase Five for PTSD and Phantom-Limb Pain

The following excerpt is from Russell (2008b) describing implementing Phase Five. *Background.* A 22-year-old Marine was treated for PTSD, depression, and severe phantom-limb pain (PLP) and sensations (PLS) following traumatic leg amputation from a motor vehicle accident (MVA). Towards the end of Phase Four, Desensitization, the client spontaneously generated and shared his metaphor of life with a prosthetic leg, *"steel bends but does not break,"* which was strengthened or reinforced with three additional BLS sets and led to progressively more confident self-statements, positive imagery, and sensations of feeling strong that he likened to *"the pump you get when you lift weights."* This anecdote offers a powerful illustration of EMDR reprocessing effects and why EMDR reprocessing can be much more profound than desensitizing disturbance alone. The client's adaptive self-statement originated from his own adaptive neural networks during the reprocessing of the disturbing traumatic memory. The combined use of dual-focus and BLS in the context of a therapeutic alliance were used to enhance, or strengthen the existing connection that spontaneously emerged between the target memory of this young man holding his severed amputated leg and thinking *"I'm going to die!"* to the new association of *"steel bends but does not break!"* His reference to an "adaptive resource," by the way, was to a family-owned steel company's motto that he had "forgotten" a long time ago. This is also why "installation" is a terrible name—Francine Shapiro would be the first to agree. The target memory reprocessed for Phase Five was the client's "worst" image of the MVA, a scene immediately after impact and perched with his leg nearly detached and trying to stem the bleeding. The negative cognition was *"I'm going to die"* with "panicky" emotion, racing heart sensations, and phantom-limb pain (PLP) of "8/10." The initial target memory SUDS rating was "8," with a positive cognition (PC) of *"I'm alive"* and VOC rating of "4."

Th: When you think of the accident scene bleeding, and sitting with your amputated leg do the words "I'm alive" still fit [checking the PC], or is there another positive statement you feel would be more suitable?

C: Huh … I actually have an image of myself at the scene now, feeling strong, and standing tall with my prosthetic.

Th: Does "I'm alive" still fit, or is there another positive statement you feel fits better with the accident scene?

C: I am strong. [Reminder as to why we check the PC-information shifts during reprocessing]

Th: Ok … think about the accident scene, your bleeding-out and your amputated leg and those words "I am strong." From 1, completely false, to 7, completely true, how true do they feel now?"

C: 6.

Th: All right think of the accident scene and hold it together with the words I am strong and follow my hand with your eyes. [BLS set of 24 eye movement]

Th: When you think of the accident scene, how true do those words "I am strong" feel to you now on a scale of 1–7, where 1 feels completely false and 7 feels totally true?

C: Probably still a 6.

Th: What do you think keeps this from going to a 7? [Checking for a blocking belief or "feeder memory" some negative association that may be keeping the VOC below 7]

C: I don't know. I'm getting discharged soon, and I got some tingling [PLS] in my leg.

Th: Ok, think of that and concentrate on the tingling in your leg. [Negative tingling sensations keep adding BLS until reprocessed]—what do you notice?

C: Huh … the tingling is getting lighter. [Change, add BLS]

Th: Stay with that, and focus on the lighter tingling [Add BLS] what are you aware of now?

C: The tingling is kinda different, it feels more like when you get a good pump from a workout. [Change reported from a negative to a positive/adaptive sensation]

Th: Stay with that, and focus on the tingling [Add BLS] … what are you aware of now?

C: Yeah, kinda feel strong. [Still changing so add BLS]

Th: Just think of that [Add BLS] … what are you aware of now?

C: Nothing it's about the same. [No change—back to target]

Th: All right, when you think of the accident scene, how true do those words "I am strong" feel to you now on a scale of 1–7, where 1 feels completely false and 7 feels totally true?

C: Hmm, I'm going to still say a 6, the tingling is still there, but it's a good tingling.

Th: All right think of the accident scene and hold it together with the words "I am strong" and notice the good tingling in your leg and follow my hand with your eyes. [BLS set of 24 eye movement]

Th: All right, when you think of the accident scene, how true do those words "I am strong" feel to you now on a scale of 1–7, where 1 feels completely false and 7 feels totally true?

C: Still a 6 and the good tingling is still there. [Second consecutive BLS of 6 with no negative associations]

Th: What do you think keeps this from going to a 7? [Checking for a blocking belief or "feeder memory" some negative association that may be keeping the VOC below 7]

C: I don't know, same thing I guess, I've got to check out of Marine Corps and look for a job or go to school, just a lot going on … but it feels good, doc.

Th: Does this seem like a good place to stop then? [It may appear ecologically valid for the client. We want to challenge to see if the associations to the adaptive neural networks can be strengthened further, but over-persistence just frustrates people.]

C: Yeah, I'm pretty wiped-out.

Blocking Belief Screening: Should the client report a VOC of "6" or less, the therapist can try changing the BLS mechanics like in Phase Four, however, if the VOC remains below a "7," the next step is for the therapist to evaluate the possibility of a "blocking belief" as we did in the previous reprocessing phase by asking, *"What, if anything keeps this from going to a 7?"* Note the client's response, and follow with an additional BLS set (see the above case study).

Emerging Negative Associations: In the event that negative associations occur during reprocessing or when checking for a blocking belief, associations are reprocessed and the installation steps are repeated from the beginning (see the above case study).

Ecological Validity: Similar to the SUDS rating, there are a variety of possible reasons that clients may not attain a VOC of 7 (e.g., they don't believe in absolutes). After we checked for a blocking belief, the provider must rely upon their clinical judgment and their knowledge of the client's history and circumstances to determine whether a VOC of "6" is ecologically valid or reasonable (see the above case study).

Completion of Phase Five: The reprocessing phase is complete after two consecutive BLS sets of a sustained VOC rating of "7," or "6" if ecologically valid. Once completed, we can move onto the final EMDR reprocessing phase—the Body Scan.

PHASE SIX: BODY SCAN

This phase represents the final EMDR reprocessing. The primary goal of the Body Scan reprocessing is to: (a) identify and reprocess any residual negative associations in the form of physiological sensations, and (b) strengthen the client's connection to their adaptive neural networks. Preferably, the Body Scan is completed immediately following Phase Five, but, where time does not permit, Phase Six can be introduced after the reevaluation at the beginning of the subsequent session.

Body Scan Protocol

The therapist begins Phase Six by asking the client to *"Close your eyes and keep in mind the original memory and the (repeat the selected positive cognition). Then bring your attention to the different parts of your body, starting with your head and working downward. Any place you find any tension, tightness, or unusual sensation, tell me."* Whatever valence of the physical sensation(s) the client reports, positive (e.g., relaxing), or negative (e.g., tightness), the therapist follows with a BLS set of 24. If the client is reporting a change to the positive or relaxing sensations (e.g., more relaxed, calmer, warmer), the therapist will continue to add BLS sets until no further enhancement effects are reported. Conversely, if the client reports negative or discomforting sensations, these are reprocessed until the negative associations have all been reprocessed.

Case Study: Body Scan (Carry Over from Phase Five Case)

Th: Close your eyes and keep your mind focused on the accident scene and the words "I am strong." Then bring your attention to the different parts of your body, starting with your head and working downward. Any place you find any tension, tightness, or unusual sensation, tell me.

C: I feel good … I notice the tingling, but it's the good tingling, not the bad kind.

Th: Stay with the good tingling [Add BLS to see if enhancement effect occurs]—what do you get?

C: Same thing.

Th: Stay with the good tingling. [No-change reported—add BLS to make that the client sure stays positive]

C: Feels the same.

Completion of Phase Six: *The Clear Body Scan*

Clients have completed the Body Scan phase when their positive or comforting physical sensations have been strengthened the most possible (client reports no further change), and all negative associations have been processed. Therapists check the status of reprocessing by following the client instructions above on how to conduct the body scan. When the client reports no negative residual sensations, that is called a "clear" Body Scan, and the phase is complete. In some cases, particularly for clients with chronic medical or pain conditions, obtaining a "clear" Body Scan may not be ecologically valid, and that is a matter of clinical judgment and client consent. Clients who end treatment without a clear Body Scan should be advised to contact the therapist should they notice symptoms returning, as there might be an increased risk of relapse or activation of a different negative neural network that was not reprocessed earlier.

Following the Treatment Plan: Time permitting, the therapist moves onto the next targeted past memory per the treatment plan. Or, if this was the last of the past, then move onto the current triggers and then the future template to complete the three-pronged protocol. Due to generalization effects, however, once the earliest and/or worst past memory has been reprocessed, the remaining past target memories, the current, and future targets, have also been reduced significantly in terms of subjective distress measured by SUDS, therefore the completing the later part of the treatment plan almost invariable proceeds quickly. The next step, Phase Seven Closure, provides guidance on how to end a complete or incomplete reprocessing session, and Phase 8 Reevaluation, describes the procedure for therapist to check the client's reprocessing between sessions and transition back into reprocessing according to the treatment plan. Both phases are described in more detail in Chapter 14, this volume.

STANDARD EMDR PROTOCOLS AND WAR/TRAUMATIC STRESS INJURY

The basic or standard EMDR protocol that we just reviewed is the only recognized evidence-based treatment. In Chapter 5, we introduced an EMDR treatment planning algorithm premised on considering six key factors: (a) the referral question; (b) strength of the therapeutic alliance; (c) client treatment goals; (d) timing and environmental constraints; (e) clinical judgment regarding client safety, stability, and suitability for standard trauma-focused EMDR reprocessing protocol; and (f) utilization of any adjunctive intervention and referral. Five treatment goals were identified: (a) stabilization (see Chapter 6, this volume); (b) primary symptom reduction; (c) comprehensive reprocessing; (d) resilience building or performance enhancement (see Chapter 16, this volume); and (e) prevention or treatment of compassion-stress injury (see Chapter 16, this volume). We also offered recommendations of the appropriate type of EMDR protocol based on the respective treatment goal. These modified or specialty EMDR protocols were developed by clinicians for situations whereby the comprehensive, three-pronged EMDR treatment would not be feasible, or even clinically contra-indicated. For example, clients experiencing a severe, debilitating ASR/COSR or referrals for brief intervention in order to sufficiently stabilize and transport to a higher echelon of care would not be appropriate for standard EMDR treatment.

10 EMDR Treatment for Acute War/Traumatic Stress Injury

In this section we will examine the implementation of the EMDR treatment plan developed in Chapter 5 that is aligned with one of two treatment goals: (a) primary symptom reduction or (b) comprehensive reprocessing. Where possible, clinical case study material is used to demonstrate actuarial application across military treatment settings and type of war-stress or traumatic-stress injury.

EMDR Treatment Goal: Primary Symptom Reduction

A variety of contexts may arise that may preclude adherence to the standard EMDR trauma-focused protocol for otherwise stable and suitable military clientele. Such variables include: *time-sensitive constraints* (e.g., impending client or therapist absence, impending client deployment, etc.); *environmental demands* (e.g., forward-deployed, operational settings); and *client-stated preferences* (e.g., expressed desire to not address earlier foundational experiences other than such as pre-military incidents) that may lead to the joint decision to deviate from the standard EMDR protocol after full-informed consent if provided. Generally speaking, comprehensive EMDR reprocessing that includes reprocessing of pre-military memories, even on consecutive days, will usually not be appropriate if within *2 weeks* the client will be deploying, relocating (PSC transfer), or going on an extended training exercise, etc. Clinical judgment and full informed consent are necessary to determine if reprocessing can occur safely with a very short window.

In addition, depending on time and environmental constraints and clinical judgment, primary symptom reduction may, or may not, include the installation or body scan phases, or reprocessing of current triggers and future template that is the standard EMDR protocol. Some clinicians (e.g., Russell, 2006) have reported successful symptom reduction in operational environments using a modified EMDR approach that was limited to the circumscribed recent or precipitating event (e.g., a current deployment) or to a specific past combat or other traumatic incident and did not reprocess current or future antecedents because of time limitations. Therapists need to be familiar with the existing literature, and provide informed consent to clients regarding potential advantages and limitations from deviation of an evidence-based protocol. There are essentially two methods for limiting client focus to the primary presenting complaint: (a) EMD and (b) Modified or Mod-EMDR.

Eye Movement Desensitization (EMD)

The EMD protocol is essentially a behavioral exposure therapy that adds BLS and does not reinforce free associations outside of either a single-incident target memory (e.g., primary presenting complaint) or a representative "worst" memory from a cluster of memories related to a circumscribed event (e.g., a recent deployment). Free associations reported outside the treatment parameters require the client to be returned to target memory whereby SUDS are re-assessed and BLS initiated. Clients may be returned to the target memory at any time by the therapist where SUDS are obtained to assess progress of desensitization effect. Repeat the process until target memory has SUDS of 0 or 1, if ecologically valid. Installation, body scan, current triggers, and future template are not included (see Chapter 5, this volume, for a listing of potential advantages and disadvantages to using EMD).

Modified-EMDR (Mod-EMDR)

In Mod-EMDR the client's attention is limited to either a single-incident target memory (e.g., the precipitating event), or a representative "worst" memory from a cluster of memories related to a circumscribed event (e.g., specific operational mission, a certain deployment). Negative free associations reported outside the treatment parameters require the client to be returned to the target memory. Installation, Body Scan, current triggers, and future template are selected in relation to the target memory and reprocessed according. Adaptive or position-free associations may be reinforced outside of target parameters; however, if negative associations arise, client is returned to the target memory. SUDS and VOC are measured in accordance with the standard protocol (see Chapter 5 for a listing of potential advantages and disadvantages).

Recent Events Protocol

The Recent Events protocol, introduced by Francine Shapiro in 1995, has been a mainstay for basic EMDR trainings. However, no controlled studies have been forthcoming. Shapiro argues for the necessity for a special protocol and, as recent memories had insufficient time to consolidate, the traditional focus on past memories did not generalize to other disturbing memories. In terms of military application, Wesson and Gould's (2009) single-case study revealed successful early intervention using 4 consecutive days of the protocol with a United Kingdom Soldier experiencing ASR within 2 weeks of post-event. The client was returned-to-duty after the intervention, and treatment gains were maintained at 18-months (see Chapter 3, this volume, for details). Elan

Shapiro (2009) cited Foa and Riggs (1994) as also putting forth the notion of fragmented early memories that require repeated processing for each fragment (see Francine Shapiro, 2001, for further details and citations). Below is an outline of the protocol: (1) Memory may not have had time to consolidate to the point where a single scene can represent the whole event. You may have to process several mini-scenes; (2) obtain a narrative of the event; (3) identify each target scene with picture, cognitions, VOC, emotion, SUDS, sensation; (4) reprocess the most disturbing scene; (5) reprocess remaining scenes in chronological order; (6) have the client run the event like a movie with eyes closed and reprocess any distress that comes up. Repeat until he or she can run the whole event without distress; (7) have the client run the event with eyes open and install positive cognition; (8) do body scan; (9) review and reprocess (if necessary), present triggers, and (10) do future template.

CASE STUDY: EMD AND COMBAT-RELATED ACUTE STRESS DISORDER

Phase One: Client History

The client was a 25-year-old, married, African American U.S. Army Specialist (E-3) with 16 months of active-duty who was MEDEVACED to a field hospital after sustaining a broken foot during combat operations 2 weeks prior. Ward nursing staff initiated the referral because of frequent, intense nightmares, lack of appetite, staring spells, and ruminations of combat experiences. A combat stress screening was conducted at the time of admission indicated post-traumatic stress symptoms in the "severe" range (IES = 42). During the interview with the staff psychiatrist, the client endorsed 18 of 27 items related to Acute Stress Disorder including four dissociative symptoms (detachment, numbing, depersonalization, and amnesia), as well as depression symptoms in the severe range. At that time, the client expressed a desire for brief psychological intervention to reduce his presenting ASD and depression symptoms. For the full clinical write-up see (Russell, 2006).

Phase Two: Client Preparation

Th: There might be something we could do to help with some of the worst parts of your memories so that you might be able to sleep and go home without the memories bothering you as much as they are right now. However, I cannot guarantee that the treatment will work for you. I can also recommend to the psychiatrist to prescribe something to help you sleep and reduce some of your symptoms, either instead of EMDR or after treatment if you need it. If you do choose a trial of EMDR, you will still need to follow up at your CONUS MTF (stateside hospital) to make sure that things haven't changed for the worse.

In a nutshell, this is what we would do. I'm going to ask you some questions just to get an enough of an idea of what's giving you these nightmares. If you don't want to answer a particular question, or any questions, that's entirely up to you. EMDR stands for eye movement desensitization and reprocessing, a mouthful I know, that's why we just say EMDR. During EMDR, I want you to notice whatever comes to your mind, good, bad, or ugly, just observe it, and at the same time, I'm going ask you to follow my back-and-forth hand movements with your eyes. Sometimes the memory might change to a different memory, or the picture, feelings, physical sensations, or your thoughts might change; sometimes nothing will change at all. Everyone's different. When we stop the eye movements, I'm going to ask you to take a breath, and I need you to tell me what if anything is changing. We keep doing that until there is nothing to change, you or I get too tired, or we decide it's not working and we'll shift gears.

If you want me to stop, tell me stop and raise your hand, that way I know you mean for me stop. Almost all of the time you're going to know before I do if things are changing for you or not, if this is helping. Doing the eye movements might cause you to see some bad experience things again, but it sounds like that's already happening a lot. In normal EMDR we would let your memories shift anywhere it needs to go. What we're going to do in this case, is keep the focus on the immediate issue that's given you the hardest time. From time to time, I'll ask you to give me a 0–10 rating, so we both know where things are going. Any questions? Is this something that you still want to try?

Phase Three: Assessment

Th: What is the most the most disturbing memory that is bothering you right now?

C: We were coming up to a road and a bunch of insurgents jumped out of the van and started opening up on us ... bullets were flying everywhere. I could somebody behind me screaming "I'm hit"; when I looked down it was Sergeant Jones, he took one in the shoulder, a lot of blood but he seemed okay, and when I turned back around I saw an Iraqi just about 20 yards to my left, aiming right at me. [Pause—body chill/shake] [Eyes fixed ahead, blank expression]

Th: Sarge, what happened next? ... Sarge? [Reached over gently and placed my hand on his shoulder] ... Sarge ... What happened when you opened fire?

C: [Slowly re-oriented back to therapist with a dazed look—another body shake—speaking slowly] I ... just ... I shot him man.... I think I emptied on him ... but don't know how many hit him.... He just fell right to the ground. [Pause ... blank stare ... body shake]

Th: Sarge, what happened when he fell to the ground?

C: He ... he just lay there crying, screaming ... I never heard anyone scream like that before ... about that time, the Iraqis were either all killed or ran, I don't know ... it got quite ... but I can still hear the guy I shot screaming so loud ... [Body shake]

Th: Is there a particular Image of that incident that really stands out as the worst?

C: Yeah ... watching this guy on ground screaming ... he was in a lot of pain screaming ... his guts were hanging out and blood was everywhere ... I wish he would just hurry up and die!

Th: What words go best with that picture that expresses your negative belief about yourself NOW?

C: I should have shot him again. [Body shake]

[No Positive Cognition or VOC was taken: Main reason was the goal of the intervention was to reduce symptoms to stabilize for aeromedical evacuation, not full EMDR treatment]

Th: Sarge ... When you think of that incident and the words "I should have shot him again" what emotions do you feel?

C: All I feel right now man is numb and maybe guilt I guess. [Body shake]

Th: Ok ... on a scale from 0 no disturbance to 10, the worst disturbance you can think of, how bad does it feel NOW?

C: I don't know ... a 7, I guess

Th: And where do you feel it in your body?

C: I feel a chill all over my body. [Displays body chill]

Phase Four: Desensitization

Th: I want you to bring up that picture of the Iraqi you shot, laying on the ground screaming, and the words "I should have shot him," and notice that chill feeling in your body, and follow my fingers with your eye? ... Good.... That's it.... Keep tracking.... Just notice whatever comes up and know that it's in the past ... it's a memory of the past ... that's it ... just observe what comes up ... don't force it ... good ... ok ... stop ... take a deep breath ... what do you notice now?

C: I feel a tightness in my chest.

Th: Ok ... just focus on that tightness in your chest and follow my fingers with your eyes ... good ... that's it ... just let whatever comes ... come up ... and know it something that happened in the past ... just notice it ...that's ... good ... ok ... take a breath ... what are you aware of now?

C: I remembering that I walked over to where this guy was after he stopped screaming ... and his body is still shaking.

Th: Ok ... think of that ... [Add BLS] and keep focusing on whatever comes up.... Just be aware ... good ... ok ... blank it out and take a breath.... What do you get now?

C: I remember looking around and seeing other dead Iraqis.

Th: Ok ... just notice that [Add BLS] ... good, that's it's ... ok ... take a breath.... What do you notice now?

C: Shit ... know I remember looking back at my boys ... there were probably 3 or 4 of our guys on the ground ... looks like they were dead.

Th: Think of that. [Add BLS] and notice anything else that might come up, good ... ok, take a breath.... What do you get now?

C: I see dead Iraqi civilians laying around too ...

Th: Stay with that.... [Add BLS] Good.... What do you notice now?

C: I see one of the dead Iraqis was a woman ... maybe in her 30s or something she was messed up pretty bad ... I feel that chill again...." [Body shake]

Th: Ok ... stay with that.... [Add BLS] What do you notice now?

C: That's weird, I remember going to my niece's funeral ... she was only in high school or something like that ... and was killed in a car crash with her friends ... I must have been in first grade or something when that happened ...

Th: Ok ... go back to the memory of the Iraqi you shot and was on the ground.... What do you notice now? [Instead of following the free associations to a pre-military/pre-event memory—as required during standard EMDR, the clinical decision was to keep the client's attention focused on the precipitating event—the main concern being that it was uncertain how many earlier associations the reprocessing may lead us to. Time is extremely limited—the referral question and treatment goal was to reduce primary symptom distress related to the most disturbing incident during the current deployment—so we return to the target memory and re-assess SUDS.]

C: That's weird ... I'm thinking of him, but the dead Iraqi woman keeps showing up too....

Th: On that scale 0–10, 10 being the worst ever, how upset do you feel now?

C: Probably a 4 or 5, man.

Th: Ok ... just stay with that ... [Add BLS] and notice anything else that might come up.... Take a breath; what do you get now?

C: I went back to the Iraqi guy I shot, it looks like he is dead now.

Th: Just notice that.... [Add 2–3 more BLS sets] What are you aware of now?

C: That chill feeling in my chest.

Th: Focus on that.... What do you get now?

C: Nothing really ...

Th: Ok, go back to the memory of the Iraqi combatant that you shot and was on the ground, what do you get now?

C: Huh ... seems like it's not really bothering me that much right now ... kinda a like I know it happened ... but that's just war ... he was shooting at us ... that chill feelings seems gone too.

Th: How upsetting does it seem to you on that 0–10 scale?

C: Maybe a 5, I guess?

Th: Just stay with it.... [After approximately 8 BLS sets]

Th: What do you notice now?

C: I can still remember it, but it's like it's over now.... I know what happened and all ... but I'm just ready to move on with my life now.

Th Ok. Just think of that.

C: I mean I feel sorry for all those people who died, especially the civilians.

Th: Stay with it.

C: Same thing, I remember everything, but it's like it just like it's over or something.

Th: Ok, go back to the memory of the Iraqi you shot and was lying on the ground. What do you notice now?

C: It's terribly that all them people died, especially the civilians, but that's war.

Th: On that 0 to 10 scale, how upsetting is the memory to you now?

C: Wow ... I don't know, maybe a 1.

Th: Stay with it.

C: The same thing, maybe a 1, I guess.

Th: What keeps it from being a 0?

C: Everybody who died was a victim of circumstances, I don't think I will ever feel a 0 when I think about it ... but for some reason, it just doesn't bother me as bad as it used to.... That's pretty amazing!

Phase Seven: Closure. Client was advised that his brain might still be reprocessing the information we working on today, so just observe it, write it down, and, if need be, ask the ward staff to get the therapist; otherwise the therapist will check-up on him in the next morning.

Phase Eight: Reevaluation. During reevaluation the next day, the client reported that his SUDS level remained at "1" and that he was feeling "a lot better" overall. IES was "8." Ward nursing staff reported a cessation of nightmares, renewed appetite, and a more talkative, social demeanor.

Clinical note. As reported by Silver and Rogers (2002, p. 149), "Under crisis intervention circumstances, processing tends to remain very specific without a great deal of linking to other experiences." Hence, given the defined target, the need for more extensive history taking is obviated unless treatment effects become blocked. Although Francine Shapiro (2001) describes the preparation phase as including a therapeutic alliance, Silver and Rogers (2002, p. 87) note an "instant rapport" between those suffering combat trauma and veteran therapists. Such appeared to be the case by the fact that all of the present patients insisted on pursuing treatment with the author (Mark Russell). As noted by all the authorities cited above, the negative and positive cognitions used during the assessment phase are often difficult to define under circumstances of high arousal, and therefore it is permitted to proceed without it. The reader will note that no positive cognition, VOC, installation or body scan phase was used. Treatment goal is the reduction in primary symptom intensity level. This case study should be viewed as an evaluation of one-session reprocessing effects, rather than as a complete treatment. Only systematic long-term follow-up can determine if such a short regime can be considered sufficient.

It is also important to recognize how the AIP model is reflected in the case material. Specifically, during assessment we are trying to access and activate the maladaptive neural network underlying the diagnosis of ASD and depression. Once done, we use the therapeutic alliance, dual focus attention, and BLS to access and reprocess the most disturbing experience, and as the negative symptoms decrease, we simultaneously observe increased access and activation of the client's adaptive neural networks. Using additional dual focus and BLS will strengthen the adaptive connections and primary symptom reduction that have been achieved.

EMDR Treatment Considerations and Research on for Acute Stress Injuries

According to Silver and Rogers (2002), combat trauma often results in complex PTSD, and therefore war veterans will usually present with greater a number of dissociative symptoms than adult-onset "simple" PTSD. Numbing is mediated by release of endorphins. Stress-induced analgesia observed in individuals who are in dangerous environments for long periods of time. This may also manifest as present as risk-taking behavior or cutting. Numbing may be more disruptive to relationships than anger. Clients reporting they feel numb, empty, robotic. Silver and Rogers (2002) suggest the following strategies for addressing numbing: (a) Assess throughout treatment, (b) educate and normalize, (c) develop a vocabulary and discuss strategies for minimizing, and (d) target the event that preceded the numbing.

Elan Shapiro (2009) published a review of the research on EMDR as an early or acute intervention for ASR and injury, commenting that at least six different EMDR protocols for Acute Stress Reaction were identified in the literature review, all case studies included treatment of military personnel for acute stress injuries (e.g., Russell, 2006; Wesson & Gould, 2009), with the exception of one randomized trial. There has been one known randomized controlled study on EMDR treatment for acute trauma. Jarero, Artigas, and Luber (2011) reported utilizing a single session of modified EMDR to treat 18 adult Mexican earthquake victims experiencing severe ASR within 14 to 24 days after the earthquake. Subjects were randomly assigned to either the EMDR treatment group or waitlist. The researchers developed an elaborate modification of Shapiro's (2001) Recent Events Protocol that appeared to allow free associations during reprocessing. Significant improvement on symptoms of posttraumatic stress for both the immediate-treatment and waitlist/delayed treatment groups were reported, with results maintained at 12-week follow-up despite frequent aftershocks.

In regards to modified-EMDR, a team of Israeli clinicians treated 40 victims of terrorist bombings and 46 accident victims experiencing acute stress reactions in an emergency room setting, with a single session of modified EMDR within 2 days to 4 weeks of the traumatic event (Kutz, Resnick, & Dekel, 2008). Similar to Russell (2006), Kutz et al. (2008) maintained a present trauma focus by redirecting patients if they freely associated to past events during reprocessing. Results indicated 50% of patients reported immediate fading of intrusive symptoms and general alleviation of distress, 27% described partial alleviation of their symptoms and distress, while 23% reported no improvement. At 4-week and 6-month follow-up, the immediate responders in the terror victims group remained symptom free. The immediate responders were reported to have uncomplicated ASR with fewer risk factors for PTSD, in contrast to nonresponder, who reported higher exposure to former traumas and endorsed more risk factors for PTSD. These results support other anecdotal reports on the rapid effects of brief EMDR intervention on intrusive symptoms in early uncomplicated posttraumatic cases.

EMDR Treatment for Chronic War/Traumatic Stress Injury

11 EMDR Therapy of Pre-Military and Military Trauma and Medically Unexplained Symptoms

EMDR TREATMENT OF PRE-MILITARY TRAUMATIC STRESS INJURIES

In Chapters 3 and 4 we discussed the high prevalence of pre-military trauma history for new military accessions along with information regarding early separation for problems related to misconduct or personality disorder. What the military discharge data does not address is the fact that many service members with a history of adverse childhood experiences and mental health difficulties are able to adjust to military culture and to reconstruct their lives in honorable and admirable ways. Screening out over 25% of the force isn't practical either, and who would replace them? Moreover, many young military members receiving an Existed Prior to Service (EPTS) discharge for one of the disqualifying conditions listed earlier might otherwise become an excellent Airman, Marine, Sailor, or Soldier. Military mental health practitioners are assigned to military medical treatment facilities (MTF) and medical clinics that provide psychological evaluation and treatment at each of the armed forces' recruit training sites, also known as "basic training," or "boot camp." Interventions, especially during intense, time-sensitive environments such as military boot camp, must be rapid and effective, particularly when military clinicians must render a decision to discharge EPTS or retain on active-duty. EMDR appears particularly well-suited to the task as illustrated in a 2006 case study by Navy Chaplain, Michael Howard.

Case Study: EMDR Treatment of Pre-Military Trauma in Recruit Training Setting

Chaplain Howard treated a "water phobia" in 23-year-old "Alex," a Japanese American male Navy recruit who was successfully meeting all the rigors and challenges of military recruit training until hitting a brick wall with the week-7 swim requirements (Howard & Cox, 2006). At that time Alex began to experience intense fear and anxiety attacks and was unable to meet the minimal swim requirements resulting in a feeling of low self-worth and depression. Diagnosed with a "water phobia," Alex was referred to Chaplain Howard for EMDR treatment. Time was of the essence, a failure to pass the swim test in week 8 would result in EPTS discharge. On the first session, Chaplain Howard probed for Alex's earliest recollection of experiencing his phobic reaction which led to the identification of an early childhood memory. At age 5, Alex had fallen into a family pool and was near drowning when his older brother jumped in to save him and, in the course of doing so, drowned. Alex reported acute grief, survivor guilt, and depression associated with the traumatic memory. In the second session, Chaplain Howard completed the assessment phase, identifying components of the target memory (death of his brother), including a SUDS of "9" and VOC of "2," and began reprocessing with bilateral eye movements ending with a SUDS of "4." Two days later, Alex received the second and final EMDR treatment session, bringing the SUDS down to "0" and VOC of "7." On the fourth and final meeting (reevaluation phrase), Alex proudly announced that he had "passed the swim test," and the reprocessing effects held. Poignantly, Alex's last comment to his therapist was "EMDR is an amazing thing, too bad I didn't come across it earlier."

Truly, not every troubled recruit or service member can be "saved." Some will express, or harbor the desire to leave the military for any number of reasons, and express no interest in treatment. Others may be overwhelmed by anxiety, grief, or distress being triggered by environmental stressors and conscious or non-conscious reminders of prior traumatic events like Alex, and just want to escape. Education of the potential advantages and disadvantages of trying something different (e.g., EMDR) rather than repeating a self-defeating cycle (e.g., hyperarousal, intrusion, and avoidance) may be enough to help people like Alex in the military. How many of the 26,000 enlisted military members separated from the military during 2001–2006 for "personality disorder" might have been salvageable, and at what cost savings to the individual and armed services (Government Accountability Office, 1997)? Regardless of presentation or circumstance, we believe that anyone who chooses to enter the military and go through all the screening, testing, and training to alter his or her life trajectory in a positive direction, and have the privilege of serving their country, at a minimum deserves the option to meet with someone like Chaplain Howard. Early, effective interventions like EMDR, applied by skilled and caring healers, can preserve dreams of a fresh start in the military, or at least allow young adults reeling from early life adversity to enter society in a stronger place than from which they came.

TREATMENT OF MEDICALLY UNEXPLAINED SYMPTOMS (MUS)

In 1862, the first American military specialized research and treatment center, Turner Lane Hospital, was established, where Union Army physician Jacob Da Costa (1864) conducted his seminal study of treating 200 soldiers diagnosed with "irritable heart," 66% of whom were successfully returned to duty using Mitchell's "resting cure"—a precursor to frontline psychiatry—"PIE/BICEPS" programs (Da Costa, 1871). The Veteran's Health Affairs (VHA) and Department of Defense (DoD) published their first and only clinical practice guidelines for managing MUS in 2001—but specific only to chronic pain and fatigue (VHA/DoD, 2001). In doing so, the VHA and DoD admitted that "the treatment of MUS, Chronic Fatigue Syndrome (CFS) and Fibromyalgia (FM) and related syndromes is as much an art as it is a science" (VHA/DoD, 2001, p. 2). When the 2001 VHA/DoD practice guidelines were published, only three random controlled trials (RCT) were available, all involving non-combat civilian-related MUS utilizing various cognitive behavioral therapy (CBT) packages involving education, teaching self-coping skills, relaxation and cognitive retraining. Subsequently, several reviews of MUS treatments have concluded that overall psychosocial treatment effects are modest at best (e.g., Russell, 2008c)

EMDR Treatment Research on Medically Unexplained Symptoms (MUS)

In 2009, a systematic review or EMDR treatment for MUS was published that examined a total of 16 studies including one RCT, two uncontrolled studies, and seven case studies involving a total of 102 patients receiving EMDR for such diverse conditions as psychogenic non-epileptic seizures, myoclonic tics, body dysmorphic disorder, olfactory reference syndrome, stress-sensitive dermatological diseases, chronic fatigue syndrome, non-cardiac chronic pain, phantom-limb pain, and fibromyalgia (deRoos & van Rood, 2009). Conclusions of the reviewers were complicated due to the use of idiosyncratic EMDR protocols, varied symptom measures, and absence of adequate controls. In addition, drop-out rates were problematic as with other psychotherapies (e.g., CBT) apparently related to dualistic models of healthcare In terms of outcomes, deRoos & van Rood (2009) reported that, of the 46 patients that had co-morbidity data (30% of the sample), post-EMDR treatment effects indicated reductions in psychological and medically unexplained conditions sustained at follow-up. The authors urged greater uniformity and scientific rigor in researching EMDR effectiveness and efficacy in treating MUS—we strongly concur. Given the historically high prevalence of war-related MUS, and the relative absence of treatment research by institutional military medicine, we present two EMDR case studies: (a) a senior enlisted Marine with multiple medically unexplained conditions with prominent Non-cardiac chronic pain (NCCP) and co-morbid PTSD and depression, and (b) a Marine with severe phantom-limb pain/sensations from traumatic leg amputation and comorbid PTSD. It is our hope that this section will lead to rediscovering the wisdom of Generals Menninger (1998) and Hammond (1883).

Case Study: EMDR Treatment of Combat-Related Medically Unexplained Conditions

Phases One and Two: Client History and Preparation

The client is a 40-year-old male Marine, SNCO with nearly 20 years of military service with extensive combat and operational tours who has been referred by his primary care physician because of persistent multiple medically unexplained conditions including back and knee pain, insomnia, headaches, irritable bowel syndrome, unspecified noninfectious gastroenteritis, diarrhea, chronic fatigue, and most prominently NCCP (Non-cardiac chronic pain). NCCP is characterized by palpitations of unknown medical etiology that developed mid-way in his second tour. In another era, the diagnosis would have been "irritable heart," "soldier's heart," "disordered action of the heart," "effort syndrome," and "war cardiac neurosis," among others. For the complete clinical write up please see Russell (2008c). A review of his medical record revealed all post-deployment health assessments (PDHA) with no mental health concerns, and the client expressed strong desire to return to Iraq (both very common for career-oriented personnel). The interview revealed that the client's Brother-in-arms, long-time, family, and personal best friend, was killed during their second Iraq deployment together. He returned 1 year ago. PTSD and depression measures all were significant. A 0–10 rating of overall health status with a 1—"never felt unhealthier in my life." Treatment plan: the client produced three of the "worst five" target memories. The client was prepped on EMDR.

Phase Three: Assessment

First Target. Image of his mutilated dead best friend killed by IED ambush after the client sent him to investigate initial IED. He remembered listening to radio communications of the units he sent to investigate the initial IED mishap that included his best friend when the IED detonated. NC: "His body was amazingly intact." Emotions: "anger" and "guilt," and physical sensations of heart palpitations and SUDS of "8" PC: "I made it back" and VOC of "3."

Second Target. Ambushed by RPG near-misses and many WIA. Sensory memory: Smell of burnt rubber. NC: "This is it" thinking they were going to die. Emotion: "anger" at the officers leading to ambush. Physical sensations: General tightness chest area and palpitations. SUDS of "6" PC: "We made it out of there," and VOC of "4."

Third Target. Bosnia mass-grave women and children. NC: "That was f...'d up what they did" Emotion: "outrage" with sensations: chest discomfort and headache. SUDS was "6" PC: "I'm just glad I got out of that place," and VOC of "2."

Current Triggers. Cars parked on road side; objects near road; sudden loud noises, seeing small children playing, including his kids. Triggers that cause his heart to race—SUDS of "7."

Future Template. Ability to relax and enjoy being with his kids and driving the car—VOC of "3."

Clinical note. The above is a sketch and interested readers are referred to Russell (2008c) for additional details. Notice the temporal link between onset of medically unexplained—NCCP and traumatic grief from the death of a friend; also associations between the three-pronged protocol, SUDS, VOC, and cardiac symptoms. The client was coerced to come to treatment by his family and initially denied any stress/mental health issues, and that he was angry, sullen, and terse. The therapist showed respect, referring to this senior enlisted as "sir." The therapist respectfully queried about recent alcohol abuse history after the second deployment, but no history after any 10-plus deployments. The client was very choked up and revealed his Brother's death. After that, the client was more forthcoming. Important not to push. The history was one session, client prep and assessment were also one session. A total of three EMDR reprocessing sessions and three follow-up (total of 8 sessions). The therapist asked for 5 but got 3 worst past memories and the rest of the three-prong. There is so much to be said; a book in itself. Sessions are irregularly spaced from 1 week to 4 weeks due to time/environmental constraints.

Phase Four: Desensitization

Th: Which of the three memories we talked about last time do you want to work on today? [Give client control on selection]

C: Dan

Th: I'd like you to bring up that image of Dan's body, the thought "His body was amazingly intact." On a scale of 0 to 10, where 0 is no disturbance or neutral and 10 is the highest disturbance that you can imagine, how disturbing does it feel to you now? [Re-checking SUDS after previous week's session: Original SUDS was "8"]

C: [Sternly] 10.

Th: And where you are feeling it in your body?

C: [Puts his hand on chest]

Th: Okay, so think of the memory, and those feelings in your chest and just follow the lights [Neurotek machine] … good, that's it … just observe whatever comes up … catch your breath …what do you notice right now?"

C: I remember going to the scene to find Dan's body, then it changed to the afternoon when I heard on the radio that unit members were down! I knew right away it was Dan and his team that I sent in. [Grabbed chest]

Th: Just think of that and notice the pressure in your chest" [Incorporate non-verbal]. What do you get now?

C: I was remembering the events leading up to when I sent Dan's unit in; then it flashed to my debriefing the witnesses about how Dan died [stoic] … by the way doc, as soon as the lights started, I got this panicky big time. [Points to his chest]

Th: Do you want to keep going? [Give client control]

C: Why not?

Th: Focus on the panicky feelings. [Repeat sequence of therapist coaching client—maintaining dual focus—longer BLS sets—stop when client appears fatigued—catch a breath] What do you get now?

C: I was remembering conversations I had with Dan weeks and days before he was killed. I completely forgot about that [looked down at his hands]. I should have been fuckin out there myself, instead sitting at a fuckin desk!

Th: Just stay with that. [Repeat sequence]

C: I was thinking what I would tell his wife about why I sent him instead of me going … but then I thought … because I have been out on the wire more than anybody else, including Dan.

Th: Go with that and pay attention the sensations in your chest. [Repeat sequence]
[30–40 minutes of negative associations to his friend's death and to near-miss ambush incident second target memory—vivid visual descriptions of his friend's mutilated body—self-condemnation—re-experiencing heat from RPG blast-assisting wounded Marines—with increases in "panicky" sensations in chest and neck]

C: I remembered telling his wife when we got back and feeling guilty that I came back.

Th: Go with that. [Repeat sequence—but then client smiles for the first time and chuckles—stop BLS mid-set]

C: [Big smile] When the lights started again, my mind was racing to all the good times we had hanging out together [chuckles]. We both loved watching *The Simpsons* together, almost every night, damn. [Smiling].

Th: Stay with that and notice the feelings in your chest. [Further BLS-associations vacillated between negative, death memories and positive memories with Dan—last set] What do you get?

C: [Smiling again, shaking head] That's amazing, doc! I was remembering things that Dan and I did together that I had completely forgotten about—that's amazing!

[Phase Seven Closure: Incomplete Session. Client reported physically drained "like I was hit by a train." Chest symptoms: "It's gone down a lot!" Given workload constraints; next session was 3 weeks]

Phase Eight: Revaluation, Second EMDR Treatment Session (3 weeks since last session)

[The client reported feeling "wiped out" after last session and that his sleep and mood were better. His overall health rating was 2.]

Th: I'd like you to bring up that image of Dan's death, the thought "His body was amazingly intact." What do you notice?

C: I can still seem him lying there all blown-up … but it's not like it used to be, and I can feel it growing again … the panicky feelings.

Th: Just notice that and track the light with your eyes.

     [Many negative associations, especially anger at ROE that placed people are more risk—details about Dan's death—wondering "what his thoughts must have been when he knew his life was over"—and increase in panicky sensations. Within 15–20 minutes, he recalls earlier good memories of Dan, laughs hard—remembers shared deployments—Bosnia—flash to war atrocity at mass gravesite (#3 target memory)—many dead women and children—then Somalia—guilt/remorse about his being absent from his own family]

C: I feel wiped out—I'm so lucky to be alive, and I have my family—I've shut them out—they deserve better!

Reevaluation: Third Session (2 weeks)

Client reported feeling overall health rating of a "5." After last session, client made effort to spend time with his family—sleeping better—started going to gym—still feels NCCP but "gone down a lot!" Return to first target memory of Dan's death: SUDS of "3" with a "little bit" of panicky chest feelings. [Started BLS—went to second target memory—and back to Dan—more combat deaths—reports guilt—feeling responsible, which appears related to panicky chest feelings]

Th: Let's do something different; can you please put your hand on your chest where those panicky feelings are and try to remember the earliest, very first time you had those panicky feelings? [Float-back technique—see Chapter 5, this volume]

C: [long pause]

C: This is really weird doc … I was remembering in elementary school I was supposed to be watching my kid brother, and I heard him cry out, and I ran as fast as I could, and he was bleeding a lot because he hit his head on something and all I could is "It was my fault!"

Th: Think of that and those panicky feelings.

C: I remember feeling really scared and panicky, I thought my brother was going die and my parents were going blame me. [Shapiro (2001) calls this a "feeder-memory"]

Th: Stay with that and those panicky feelings.
[Client recalled running home with his brother who suffered a minor laceration on his head—but he connected the panicky feelings very clearly to that event—did a few more BLS—client smiling]

Th: What do you notice now?

C: I had forgotten all about that—after I took my brother home my mom felt bad for me I guess, so she bought my brother and I ice cream cones. I got spanked by my dad later but kept thinking that "I'm just glad my brother was still alive!"

Th: Notice that and the panicky feelings.
[This led immediately to associations of Dan, who did not survive—but, instead of feeling distressed, the client reported feeling "relaxed" as more positive associations of life with Dan emerged—BLS sets were used to strengthen those associations—no more change—returned to target memory]

Th: I'd like you to bring up that image of Dan's body, the thought "His body was amazingly intact." On a scale of 0 to 10, where 0 is no disturbance or neutral and 10 is the highest disturbance that you can imagine, how disturbing does it feel to you now?"

C: I'd say a 2 and just a little bit of the panicky now—barely noticeable.
[Two more BLS with target memory but stayed positive with SUDS of 2—probed for blocking belief]

Th: What do you think keeps it from getting to 1 or 0?

C: It will never be a 1 or 0 because my best friend died.
[Client was asked to think about that, and after two consecutive BLS sets and a SUDS check that remained a 2—judgment call for ecologically valid and move onto installation. Understanding the AIP model meant that if there was another feeder memory like his kid brother or a blocking belief that we could get to it in subsequent phases and with targets to process.]

Phase Five: Installation

Th: When you think of the scene of Dan's death now, do the words "I made it back" still fit, or is there another positive statement you feel would be more suitable?

C: It still fits.

Th: Think about the scene of Dan's death and the words I made it back, from 1, completely false, to 7, completely true, how true do they feel now?

C: I'd say a 6. [Initially VOC was "3"]

Th: Think of the event and hold it together with the words "I made it back."
[After two BLS sets—VOC stayed a 6—checked for blocking belief]

Th: What do you think keeps it from being a 7?

C: I don't know … I survived and I can be with my family and feel good about that. [Add BLS—no change—judgment call as ecologically valid—end of session]

Clinical note. At the next reevaluation session the client reported "6½" overall health rating. Checked target memory: SUDS stayed a "2" and "6" VOC. We then followed the treatment plan and went to the second past target memory and reassessed SUDS because of possible generalization effect. Recall earlier that the memory came up during reprocessing. Rechecked the new target memory: SUDS: "1"—"I still remember what happened, but it doesn't bother me like it used to … just seems like any other memory now." Added BLS sets and SUDS remained "1"—checked for blocking belief—client replied, "I could have died, and my kids would have been without a father"—Did not want to assume it was ecologically valid so add BLS—no change. VOC of "7" was installed. Same session, reassessed the third memory involving witnessing atrocities: SUDS of "2" and anticipating my questioning of what kept it from progressing lower, the client related, "Doc Russell, it will never be anything less than a "2," innocent kids died who shouldn't have which is plain wrong." Asking him to merely "think of that" with adding BLS—no change. VOC of "6" installed no blocking belief. The current triggers and future template were also reprocessed rapidly due to the generalization effects.

A reevaluation at the fifth and last treatment session (3 others were follow-up screenings), the client reported improved sleep, energy, mood, and overall health rating now "6¾" and "I haven't felt as good for years." NCCP resolved—still has knee pain and has surgery scheduled. Started watching *The Simpsons* again and is coaching little league. All targets remained reprocessed—no panicky feeling in chest. Subsequent 1-, 3-, and 6-month follow-ups sustained improvement. At 6 months, overall health status was 8 and no NCCP. At termination, the now smiling and jovial senior enlisted member expressed his thanks and confided that his initial reaction to the therapist's description of EMDR was "What kind of bullshit is this?" He then added that he was convinced that EMDR helped him gain a new perspective of life.

Closing note. The reader probably noticed that the description of the EMDR protocol used to treat this type of war stress injury (medically unexplained conditions, co-morbid with PTSD, and depression) was insignificantly different that other case studies presented. The only minor variation was an emphasis on the client's physical symptoms during the BLS. Everything else was fairly usual. There is no empirical support that instructing clients to maintain dual-focus attention on their physiological responses during the BLS has any additive effect—clinically speaking—it may increase client access and activation to the neural networks. In working with clients experiencing medically unexplained symptoms, it is essential for therapists to reassure clients that their physical suffering is absolutely real, in every sense of the word. Therapists need to understand and be able to explain that use of EMDR is intended to help reprocess negative life events and stressors that can make pain and suffering worse, and not a "cure" per se of their physical ailment. Technically, we believe that EMDR is helping the client's brain reprocess the experiential *contributors* that may be *related* to the onset, maintenance, and exacerbation of their physical state. That is quite different than asserting we are treating the "cause" of the bodily ailment. It is vital for therapists to validate the client's suffering and not come across as suggesting otherwise. Another interesting aspect of this case is the possible association from the client's "feeder-memory" related to his perceived failure to live up to his brotherly leadership responsibility both during childhood and in war. Learning the "float-back" and similar cognitive-affective-and-somatic bridges can be an effective strategy to enhance reprocessing (see Leeds, 2009). This case also very poignantly illustrates the reality of adaptive neural networks and the shifting of balance that occurs as the reduced activation or strength of the "maladaptive" reflexively corresponds to increase access and connection to the brain's inherent adaptive resources. It's striking how often clients are taken by surprise as "forgotten" adaptive memories are re-stimulated in the service of adaptation.

EMDR TREATMENT OF PHANTOM-LIMB PAIN FROM TRAUMATIC AMPUTATION

As of September 1, 2010, a total of 1,621 returnees from Operations Enduring Freedom and Iraqi Freedom (OEF/OIF) were reported to have survived traumatic combat-related amputation (see Fisher, 2010). About 16% of 425 veterans sampled suffered multiple limb loss (Potter & Scoville, 2006, cited in Russell, 2008b). Historically, many of the estimated 50,000 veterans from the American Civil War described inexplicable sensations from amputated limbs attributed to a ghost or hallucination, eventually leading to the terms "causalgia" and "phantom limb" (Mitchell, 1871, cited in Russell, 2008b). Currently, the prevalence of phantom-limb-pain (PLP) or phantom-limb sensation (PLS) is virtually universal, occurring in between 50% and 90% of amputees (Desmond & MacLachlan, 2002, cited in Russell, 2008b). Phantom limb manifests in diverse ways including tingling; itching; and feelings of warmth, cold, and heaviness; to more severe PLP, such as cramping, twisting, burning, sawing, or excruciating pain. Military combat amputees sustain devastating injuries in a violent, emotionally charged context, resulting in a wide range of psychological, emotional, and social adjustment difficulties, including loss of body integrity and competence and transient feelings of depression, grief, anxiety, anger, fear, denial, avoidance, and hopelessness that if undetected or insufficiently treated can result in chronic mental health conditions. For instance, co-occurrence rates of chronic pain and PTSD have been reported as high as 87% in a sample of Vietnam veterans (see Russell, 2008b). Furthermore, clinical depression rates have been reported in 21% to 35% of amputees (Desmond & MacLachlan, 2002, cited in Russell, 2008b).

Table 11.1

Theater	Type of Amputation	Army	Marine	Navy	Air Force	Foreign	Other	Total
OIF	Major Limb	620	158	18	8	4	8	816
	Partial (Hand/Foot, Toes/Fingers)	272	49	7	11	0	3	342
OEF	Major Limb	145	53	5	6	4	4	217
	Partial (Hand/Foot, Toes/Fingers)	24	6	0	2	0	0	32
Unaffil-iated Conflicts	Major Limb	94	12	25	31	1	26	189
	Partial (Hand/Foot, Toes/Fingers)	20	1	2	10	1	25	
Total								1,621

Source: (Fischer, 2010)

PREVALENCE OF AMPUTATIONS FOR OIF/OEF VETERANS

Table 11.1 shows the number of individuals with amputations for OIF, OEF, and unaffiliated conflicts from 2001 to September 1, 2010. The total number of military personnel returning with traumatic amputations is 1,621.

Treatment Issues Working with Military Amputee and Seriously Wounded Populations

The Walter Reed Army Medical Center Psychiatry Consultation Liaison Service (WRAMC PCLS) is the premier medical center for military clients who have suffered traumatic amputations. A multidisciplinary, biopsychosocial, and phase-oriented approach is utilized in the caring of amputee clients from admittance, medical stabilization, rehabilitation, discharge, and follow-up. The WRAMC-PCLS mental health component has implemented the Therapeutic Intervention for the Prevention of Psychiatric Stress Disorders (TIPPS) program that emphasizes normalizing psychological experiences, supporting healthy defenses, and monitoring for the development of psychiatric disorders both while in the hospital as well as upon discharge (Wain et al., 2004). According to the DoD's experts, "patients with fewer emotional problems and good social support had better outcomes in adjusting to prostheses. Therefore, treatment of the amputee's psychiatric symptoms may also help restore function" (p. 50)—so there is a definite role for EMDR. The following offers guidance on the mental health issues that therapists should be aware of when working with seriously wounded military clients.

Emotional Adjustment of Seriously Wounded and Amputee Clients: (a) Amputation or blindness results in a loss of body function and is an insult to the patient's psychological sense of body integrity and competence; (b) depression, anxiety, resentment, anger, fear, helplessness, hopelessness, and loss of body integrity; (c) may develop grief responses; (d) often must endure other injuries, as well as psychological traumas; (e) every amputee faces the task of integrating a new sense of his or her body and its whole-ness.

Medical Discharge From Military Service: (a) Some amputees successfully remain on active duty after rehabilitation but many more undergo medical discharge through the Medical Evaluation Board process; (b) medically discharged service members obtain medical retirement pay and receive disability allowances through the VA system; (c) some service members appeal medical board recommendations for military discharge and request to stay on active duty; (d) helping amputees develop realistic goals for their futures may or may not include continuation on active duty status; and (e) taking care of the amputee patient is a challenging but rewarding process (Wain et al., 2004).

Case Study: EMDR Treatment of a Military Client with Traumatic Leg Amputation

The client is a 22-year-old, single, Hispanic, male Marine Corporal with a muscular build and around 5 years of military service, previously diagnosed with PTSD and severe PLP and PLS, 4 months after experiencing a high-leg traumatic amputation in a motor vehicle accident (MVA). Referral was from the medical team for brief PTSD intervention in light of pending medical board and discharge. The complete clinical write-up of this case is available in Russell (2008b).

Phase One: Client History (Session One)

The client recalled the accident whereby he lost control of his motorcycle and his leg struck a tree, resulting in a near-complete high leg amputation. Vivid descriptions of scenes of red and the smell of blood, white color of skin, and sensations of cold, as he sat on the road and bled excessively coincided with pronounced increase in sympathetic arousal and severe phantom-limb pain and sensations. There was no prior history of trauma or psychiatric illness. *Phantom-limb pain.* Baseline pain intensity was rated with 0–10 scale from "no pain" to "worst possible." Client reported a variety of PLP including: dull aching pain (6/10); daily shooting pain (8/10); cramping (9/10); and weekly excruciating "sawing" pain (10/10). He reported PLS such as itching (3/10) and daily persistent "tingling" labeled as "*like when your leg falls asleep*" (5/10). The tingling PLS serves as trigger for PTSD symptoms related to the MVA and

PLP. He also described social isolation due to his self-perception of being "a freak." Overall PLP rating: 8/10.

Phases Two and Three (Session Two)

Client preparation and assessment were completed the following week using the standard EMDR three-pronged protocol which revealed the following:

Target One. "Worst" memory was the scene sitting on the road with his leg nearly detached and trying to stem the bleeding. Negative cognition (NC): *"I'm going to die"*; Emotion: Panic; Sensations: "Panicky" sensations, palpitations, and PLP of "8" with SUDS: "8." Positive cognition (PC): *"I'm alive"* and VOC "4."

Target Two. Second "worst" memory was image: Tree prior to impact. NC: *"I'm trapped"*; Emotion: "panic" Physical sensation: "chest pounding" and PLP "6." SUDS: "6." PC: *"It's over"* and VOC "5."

Current Triggers. Driving and riding in a car: SUDS and PLP: "6."

Future Template. Anticipatory anxiety: People judging him a "freak" and worries about future livelihood with SUDS: "6" and PLP: "5." Desired behavior: Feel confident in public—VOC: "3."

Phase Four: Desensitization (Session Three)

Th: Bring up the accident scene when you're sitting on the road, bleeding and the thoughts "I'm going to die," notice the phantom-limb pain (PLP) and tingling sensations in your leg, and follow the light [Neurotek] with your eyes only.… [Add BLS] That's it, good, etc. Take a deep breath, what are you aware of now?

C: Everything is more vivid; I can see my leg almost torn-off, and I'm trying to stop the bleeding … the pain in my leg (PLP) is getting worse, I keep thinking that I'm going to die!

Th: Just notice the scene and the leg pain [Add BLS], that's it … just be aware of what comes up … and know that it's a past memory, it's not happening now … just notice, blank it out, etc.

C: I can hear a woman's voice … [surprised expression] I forgot all about that … she's saying something, but I don't know what it is.

Th: Stay with that [Add longer BLS]—repeat verbal sequence—maintaining dual focus, etc.

C: Now I remember, she was an off-duty nurse … she's helping me put pressure on my leg to stop the bleeding.… I can hear her saying to me "You're going to be okay," "you're going to be okay." I can hear it like it's happening right now.

Th: Just notice that and the sensations in your leg and follow the light. [Add BLS—repeat]

C: I was remembering working on my bike in the garage that morning—then it shifted to the scene where I'm riding my bike looking around-it was a beautiful day—I was just enjoying the ride and the scenery—then a car gets behind me—and it wants to pass—but it's a narrow road with cars parked everywhere." [blank stare—pauses]

Th: It's okay just to think about it and follow the light with your eyes. [Add BLS and more verbal comments to keep dual focus and get through dissociative window—repeat sequence].

C: The fuckin idiot sped up to pass me—and then I don't know what happened—but one second I'm holding onto the bike and it's out of control. [Pauses]

Th: Just think about it and follow the light with your eyes [Add BLS], remember it's old stuff, just notice it ... that's it, good. [Repeat sequence]

C: When I lost control of the bike, I say a car and I knew I was going to hit it, and there was nothing I can do.

Th: Stay with that and notice the pain in your leg. [Add BLS—repeat sequence]

C: I remember being in the ambulance, the next thing I remembered was waking up in the hospital—then I remember thinking to myself that "Hey I survived!" ... but then I got a panicky feeling and noticed my leg was hurting bad ... so I went to grab it ... and that's when I noticed it, it was fuckin gone—it's really hurting like crap right now as we talk about it. [PLP]

Th: Just stay with it and notice the pain in your leg. [Add BLS—repeat sequence]

C: The next I was remembering was being discharged from the hospital— then I remembered that in high school I hurt the same leg in a football game .... bad too ... it was an open fracture ... then the memory shifted to when I went to the shopping mall ... this is after I got out of the hospital ... and people were just staring at me like I'm some kind of fuckin freak show.

Th: All right ... just think of that.
       [Several more BLS sets with frequent associations more vivid sensations at the MVA scene (i.e., bright red of blood, burning and sweet odors, cold sensations in his hands touching the asphalt). Client kept repeating that he was actually feeling the sensations during the BLS—other shifts to "what is going to happen to my parents?" "I don't want to lose my leg!"), emotions (fear, panic, despair, shame), and bodily sensations (e.g., tightness in chest, jaw, eyes)—and being discharged from the hospital early because he was determined to start walking as soon as possible— nearly always coinciding with change in PLP/PLS type and intensity] ... ok blank out, "what do you get now?"

C: I went back to the shopping mall scene again, and the look on everyone's faces, like I am some kind of a freak or fuckin loser. [Dejected expression—slouched posture—looping through negative associations]

Th: Yeah, I get that, that would piss me off too … but what would they think about you, if they knew the truth about what you've been through, and how only four months you're up and about? [Cognitive Interweave]

C: [Pauses, readjusts his posture in the chair to upright] They'd think, damn that dude is strong!

Th: All right, focus on that and the leg pain. [Add BLS—client shifts his posture again and has a more determined expression] Ok, blank it off, catch your breath, what do you notice now?

C: [Smiles] I just had an image of me walking with my prosthetic—feeling strong—powerful.

Th: Stay with that and notice your leg pain [Add BLS—shifting his posture and flexing his arm muscles]…. What do you get now?

C: [Big smile—leans forward] I just remembered an old saying from my uncle's steel company that I had completely forgotten about.

Th: What is it?

C: Jones Steel, it bends and expands, but it doesn't break! [Big cheesy grin]

Th: Jones Steel, it bends, expands, but doesn't break—yeah-think about that and the leg pain too. [Add BLS—to strengthen the association with the adaptive neural network—client has a determined look and turns to the light bar with purpose] What do you get?

C: Yeah … I feel strong.

Th: Good, think of that—Jones steel bends, expands, but doesn't break—and the leg pain. [client smiles]

C: Feels good … strong … like when you lift weights and get a good pump … [Additional 3–4 BLS sets—progressively positive associations to the end of session—recheck target]

Th: So, we're almost out of time, can you please go back to the accident scene … what do you notice now?

C: It seem less vivid now, more like a matter of fact … like it happened and its over

Th: On that 0 to 10 scale, how much does it bother you now?

C: I don't know, I'd say probably a 0 right now.

Th: What about your leg pain, on the 0–10 scale?

C: Right now … I'd give that a 0 too…. I don't feel any pain…. I still notice some tingling.

Th: How would you rate the tingling and where do you notice it?

C: It's only in my foot now … I don't know, maybe a 3.

Phases Seven and Eight [Client was informed about continuing to reprocess, keep a log, etc. He reported feeling "drained" physically—and very surprised about what happened in the session. Next session—4 days later—he reports only three short episodes of PLP at 4. Two days after the session, he asked a friend to take him back to the MVA scene and experienced anxiety with SUDS of "5"—but no PLP and PLS: "2"].

Fifth Session (Second Reprocessing Session—Two Weeks Later)

[Reassessed the target memory with a SUDS of "1" due to persistent tingling—but no PLP. He reported being surprised that the image appeared to be "black and white" versus vivid color. Add BLS. Initially, reported increase in distress and PLS that moved from his toes up to his leg and the NC: "What will happen if I can't walk right?"—two BLS sets—returned to positive image of walking confidently with his prosthetic limb with "I feel strong"—and decrease distress and PLS. SUDS went to "0" and stayed after two BLS, and PLS was "1"—described as an annoyance and a good tingling reminding him of his strength]

Phase Five: Installation (see Installation in EMDR protocol section)

Phase Six: Body Scan [Although not described in Russell, 2008b, body scans were completed after reprocessing each target memory with persistent tingling reported between "1" and "2" range that did not change with BLS or checking for negative associations].

Clinical note. Due to generalization effects, the remaining target memory was reprocessed, along with the current triggers and future template in the fifth and final session. SUDS of primary target remained "0" and PC: "I am a strong person" ended as "7" with no PLP. He reported PLS "light tingling" that was easier to ignore. He was fitted with a prosthetic. Treatment gains were sustained 3 weeks later before medical discharge. In the course of 8 weeks, we met for a total of five sessions, two of which involved EMDR reprocessing. The speed at which the client was able to access and activate the adaptive neural networks is remarkable, and not likely the norm. A single-incident trauma with a favorable pre-morbid history, no doubt aided his resilience. Nonetheless, the rapidity, scope, and depth of change in his comorbid conditions evident by the fourth week—especially in regards to phantom-limb pain—was definitely noticed and excitedly commented upon by his medical team (Russell, 2008b).

EMDR Research with Phantom Limb and Other Chronic Pain Conditions

In de Roos and van Rood's 2009 systematic review of EMDR treatment for MUS, a total of five published case studies were examined resulting in a sample size of 21 clients with PLP that received EMDR treatment with generally positive results. However, the variety of so-called EMDR protocols and diversity in baselines measures, as well as the absence of controls, all limit what legitimate conclusions can be reached. Nevertheless, with so many military personnel returning home with traumatic amputations, the majority of which will develop phantom limb in concurrence with other war stress injury (e.g., PTSD, depression, etc.), utilization of the evidence-based EMDR protocol offers significant, albeit untapped promise. In terms of chronic pain conditions in general, a total of 80 clients were reported to have received EMDR for conditions like PLP, neuropathic pain, headaches, fibromyalgia, and non-cardiac chronic pain with mixed results that again is difficult to interpret given insufficient methodological rigor and the inconsistent application of the evidence-based treatment. To reiterate an earlier point, we do not suggest that EMDR cures physiological injuries associated with chronic pain and phantom limb. We do, however, believe that Francine Shapiro's (2001) AIP model appears to have fairly robust clinical support in terms of the dual reprocessing effects of reducing disturbance from past un-integrated experiences, coinciding with increasing client access and activation of the brain's adaptive neural networks that contribute to healthier outcomes—including reduction of pain.

The Relationship Between EMDR, Traumatic Brain Injury, and Phantom-Limb Pain

From a treatment perspective, there are many similarities between traumatic brain injury (TBI) and traumatic amputation resulting in PLP. Both obviously evoke the experience of a "trauma" to the mind–brain–body. Therefore, the first commonality is the presence of precipitating or etiological events associated with TBI or phantom limb from limb amputation would be natural targets for a trauma-focused intervention like EMDR. Second, the rate and extent of recovery in both conditions will, to a certain point, be influenced by the relative presence or absence and the intensity of co-morbid stress injuries and other adverse health conditions such as PTSD, depression, and MUS. Third, the speed and magnitude of recovery will also be influenced by the degree that clients can access, activate, and strengthen their natural adaptive resources. The "promise" of the current evidence-based EMDR approach as demonstrated in the clinical case above, is its potential to address all three considerations simultaneously (precipitant event, co-morbidity, and enhance resilience) using a single protocol. The fourth common factor is that both conditions are complicated and evoke intense human suffering for the individual and their families. The last shared variable is that no panacea exists that can help all clients recovering from TBI or phantom limb—including EMDR. So researchers, particularly within institutional military medicine, please take notice.

12 EMDR Treatment of Traumatic Grief and Interpersonal Violence

In Chapter 5 we reviewed some potential indicators or signs of traumatic grief reactions including the presence of guilt. What is most critical is that the client's grief and loss be treated in addition to their PTSD and depression for a more complete recovery (e.g., Pivar, 2004). One of the truly unique advantages of EMDR treatment is that it allows the therapist to assist the client in reprocessing multiple components of their war/traumatic stress injury, nearly simultaneously—as opposed to a piecemeal approach whereby one package of interventions is for addressing guilt, another for grief, depression, PTSD, MUS, and so forth (see Chapter 4, this volume). Unfortunately, there is not sufficient research to understand why EMDR works one way for some and another for others—and is there a more efficient and effective application that has yet to be uncovered? In regards to EMDR treatment of traumatic grief reactions, there are no specialty protocols or techniques that one must learn outside of the standard EMDR evidence-based approach. Here are some general treatment considerations from experts that make their living helping war veterans, as well as several EMDR-specific tips to inform the therapist's treatment planning.

Timing of Presentation—*Why Now?*

Whether the client has been referred by a medical provider, self-referral, etc., it is always helpful to know "why now?" The client either disclosed his or her distress or others saw it, but why are the problems evident now and not many months or years since returning from the warzone or other traumatic event? For most combat veterans, particularly those who suffered traumatic losses, the full brunt of their experience doesn't begin to sink in until after the homecoming and honeymoon period ends—and the numbing and distractions stop working. For many deployed personnel, the impact of the war will not be felt nearly as much until they separate from their supportive networks via PCS transfer, military separation at EAOS, ADSEP, or MED-Board, or demobilization of National Guard and must return to their past civilian lives. Individual Augmentees (IA) are also in this at-risk group. When the protective or resiliency effect of one's social support system ends, this is when most returning war veterans or other trauma survivors can be at their most vulnerable. The inherent stressors of saying goodbye, packing up households, and resettling into new living quarters, schools, and work environments, without the familiar friendly faces, can often be the tipping point—prompting the mental health referral.

"Killing in Combat: What to Say to a Returning Veteran"

That is the title of one of the chapters in LTCOL David Grossman's (2007) book *On Combat,* as he introduces the reader to the "Three Gifts You Can Give Returning Veterans That Will Last Them a Lifetime" (p. 340): understanding, affirmation, and support.

Understanding. A sense of understanding is communicated by our attempts to comprehend and show respect for what the warrior has experienced from doing society's bidding. Namely, that warring means killing, and killing, as Grossman (2007) explains, is as traumatic a personal experience there is because it is fundamentally counter to our moral and evolutionary instinct to avoid killing one's own species, or what Grossman (1996) calls the "Universal Human Phobia." Rarely do combatants brag or boast about killing, those who do are probably fabricating or sociopaths. Psychological distance is instilled in military training to allow humans to overcome their natural resistance toward killing. So, on the firing range, or in a combat zone, we shoot "targets" not people. The greatest fears that men and women carrying a loaded weapon have is to kill an innocent, cause the death of their own, or of themselves (Grossman, 2007). Grossman (2007) recommends that people don't ask a combat veteran if they have "killed" anyone, but keep it open-ended "how did things go over there?" At least until sufficient rapport has built up, we would completely concur with that recommendation. Clients who are ready and wanting to talk about their combat experiences, and killing in particular, may do so the first session. Otherwise, establishing the alliance is what is most crucial at this time, and disrespecting someone isn't a good start.

Affirmation. Whatever the therapist's political view about the war, or the morality of killing in war, members of the warrior class don't really have a say, theirs is to do. A grateful nation, citizens, and therapist can express affirmation of the veteran by shaking the veteran's hand and sincerely telling them that they did they right thing, they did what we asked them to do, and that you are proud of them (Grossman, 2007).

Support. After the parades and reunions are over, Grossman (2007) talks about the long-term ways that society can demonstrate their support of its warrior class, including thanking them and congratulating them on doing a great job.

Clinical Considerations

In working with military clients that present with war stress injuries, of the number of potential issues, it has been recommended that the first priority be dealing with the client's guilt (see Silver & Rogers, 2002). Therapists should keep in mind, however, that military members surviving a traumatic loss in the warzone will more likely mask intense emotional feelings (e.g., sadness, pain, anger, guilt) in order to carry out the mission—especially those in leadership roles. They keep their "game face on," and stay "in the zone"—living in the moment to survive, kill first or be killed. Sympathetic arousal, fear, and other emotions are compartmentalized so the combatant can carry out the business (mission) of the day. Not until people get back to their barracks does the weight of what happen start to creep in. Therefore, by the time the client sees the therapist, he or she may or may not be ready to drop the protective guard (usually anger or numbness). Therapists should carefully and patiently assess and show respect to the service member's ability to cope and manage these feelings at any time. The client may feel a sense of relief knowing that somebody understands the grief that he or she is experiencing after losing a buddy or is not passing judgment on the guilt they felt from engaging in certain acts like killing. It is important that sufficient trust and rapport have been established prior to probing too hard for the client to express the depth of their feelings—a threatening experience for some, not unlike combat. Regardless of the interventions used, central to treating war veterans for prolonged and complicated grief is recognition of the significance of their losses (e.g., Pivar, 2004).

Guilt and Shame

Guilt is among the most frequently reported emotion during assessment of targets for processing in military personnel in general, and combat veterans in particular (e.g., Silver & Rogers, 2002). It has a strong association with co-morbid depression and substance abuse that raise the risk for suicide. In regards to clinical practice, it may be helpful to keep in mind that there are essentially two major types of guilt: (a) guilt about surviving when others died and (b) guilt about actions taken (or not taken). The level of guilt deployed personnel may experience is often heightened in high-threat environments, where people may believe that they have more control over things than they do. Not to mention the fact that from day-one in the military, the constant message in the culture is developing leaders through assigning personal responsibility and accountability for whatever happens—and no excuses are tolerated. Maybe that might have something to do with the propensity for military personnel to return from war with a heap of guilt and grief when the worst case scenario becomes someone's reality. Clients often are quite secretive about their most personal thoughts around guilt and shame and may test the therapist about their willingness to "go there" with them with throw away lines like: "I'm not ready to talk about that right now," "I don't really want to go there," "I'd rather not talk about that now," "I'm not comfortable talking about these things," "I don't like talking about things I've done," etc. (Silver & Rogers, 2002). For those who may be open to it, religion and spirituality may provide a framework by which many survivors of trauma construct a meaningful account of their experience and seek solace, and may provide a useful focus for intervention with trauma survivors.

The Psychological Impact of Killing

Grossman's (1996) *On Killing: The Psychological Cost of Learning to Kill in War and Society* is the best text available on the biopsychosocial and spiritual effects of killing. He related that when someone kills another human being and watched the "mystery of life and death flicker in front of your eyes, and a living breathing person have become a piece of meat, and you are the one that caused that, you cannot help to think 'I'm going to have to answer to my maker for what I did?' Such guilt-ridden beliefs, no matter how legitimate it was by military or moral standards in terms of lives saved, etc., can set into perpetual motion the thought every negative happenstance to the client, their friends, or family, is a sign of God's punishment for his or her mortal sin."

Thou Shalt Not Kill and Thou Shalt Not Murder

Some military clients express traumatic grief and guilt around having killed and believe their souls are condemned to the depths of hell with other murderers. Grossman (2007) cites biblical passages that draws upon the moral distinction between killing and murder that can be brought into the discussion with the client as a "cognitive interweave" if reprocessing gets derailed due to the client's negative belief of themselves as "evil," "murderer," etc. Grossman (2007) reports that the King James Version of the Bible's Sixth Commandment within the Old Testament says, "Thou Shalt Not Kill"; however, in Matthew 19:18 of the New Testament, Jesus is cited as saying, "Thou Shalt not Murder." According to Grossman (2007), "in the Bible, King David is a man after God's own heart (Act, 13:22); it says, 'Saul hath slain his thousands and David his ten thousand' (I Samuel, 18:7). David killed tens of thousands of men in combat and was honored for it, and it was not until he murdered Uriah to get Bathsheba that he got himself in trouble (II Samuel Chapter 11)" (p. 352), and concludes with the question, "can you tell the difference in killing 10,000 men in lawful combat and murdering one man to get at his wife? If you can, then maybe God can too!" (Grossman, 2007, p. 352).

Cautionary notes. Expert agreement on a few non-starters for therapists include avoiding good natured joking around killing by referring to the client as "Terminator" or other off-handed jests. Therapists should refrain from overriding the client's sense or right and wrong too quickly by rushing to absolve him or her of guilt with statements like "How could you have known?" "You didn't do anything wrong," or "You have nothing to feel guilty about!"

Possible Cognitive Interweaves on Guilt Over Killing

If the client's reprocessing appears stymied and/or a blocking belief emerges—"I'm a killer, I don't deserve to live"—the therapist can introduce the cognitive interweave that is simply new information or a perspective that the client thinks about while the therapist adds BLS. For instance, the therapist can ask, "Do you know the difference between killing and murder?" or "If you (or someone) have to kill in the lawful act of your duty, in defense of yourself or another, is that murder?" "If a policeman shoots a hostage taker about to kill innocent women and children, is that murder?" The attempt is to help draw the distinction between a warrior fulfilling his or her sworn oath to protect versus acting with malevolentintentions such as greed or personal gain. For the religious-oriented client, it can also be pointed out that the first non-Jew Christian was a Roman Centurion, a soldier named Cornelius (Grossman, 1996).

Useful Metaphors and Approaches:
Guilt as a smoke alarm. Usually both are there to protect.

Responsibility pie chart. Therapist and client can fill in the pieces to show proportionality of control and responsibility that the client may realistically own and the overwhelming proportion they do not.

Concept of atonement. Steven Silver talks eloquently about using a metaphor of how the extremely conscientious, honor-bound knights of old would be wracked by guilt and self-condemnation for relatively minor offenses, and the religious leader was searching for a more adaptive punishment to fit the crime. The answer was atonement. So, the guilt-ridden knight made up for his transgression by giving back to others. In this case, watching an unlit road every night for 6 months to protect the unarmed villagers as they returned to their homes for the evening or a similar task (see Silver & Rogers, 2002). To be effective, the atonement must come from the client themselves, but the therapist can offer guidance because proper atonements must meet three standards:

1. *Sacrifice.* It should place a demand on the client that would not ordinarily be there;
2. *Look outward.* It should be something that clearly benefits others;
3. *Make use of the client's abilities.* It should be something practical that the client can realistically do, or rapidly acquire the skills to do. Examples given are volunteer types of activities, working at a homeless shelter, giving hospice to AIDS patients, and reading books to young children. (For additional details, see Silver & Rogers, 2002.)

Sources of Guilt—Kubany's Guilt Typology:
Impossible decisions. Forced choice situations with no good options—the therapist can ask, "What other choices could you have made?" or "How could you have known their consequences?"

I should have known better. "What didn't you have that would have allowed you to make the correct decision? What kept you from getting it?" (Silver & Rogers, 2002, p. 199).

The pleasure of violence. Clients make feel guilty for the natural adrenaline surge that human beings experience in high stress events like combat and mistaken their reaction as "pleasure" or "liking" to have killed. They may harbor a self-appraisal of being a "psychopath" that enjoys the sensation of killing. Clients should be given Grossman's (2007) *On Combat* to read, which clarifies many misconceptions veterans have about what they've experienced.

I should have felt worse. As Silver and Rogers (2002) write, military clients harboring guilt because they did not feel bad or "anything" when they killed, or a close friend was killed, are describing the body's natural, involuntary numbing or dissociative response that occurs when endogenous opioids are released in the blood system to block anticipated pain from injury.

Survivor guilt. Grossman (2007) offers some pointed remarks regarding how he approaches survivor guilt with warriors such as, "When someone gave their lie to save your life, you must not waste it." "If someone buys your life at the price of their life, you do not dare waste it." "Your moral, sacred responsibility is to lead the fullest, richest, best life you can." "If you were the one to die and your partner lived, would you want him/her to have the best life possible?" (p. 362).

Suicidal ideation. "Make a conscious effort to set aside self-destructive thoughts and dedicate yourself to leading a full life." Repeat with me: "Nobody takes my life without one hell of a fight, including me!" "I will fight for my life. I will seek counseling, meds, leave no rock unturned," "Because I'm a warrior and nobody takes my life without one hell of fight—including me!"(Grossman, 2007, pp. 362–363)—If phrased properly for the client, it can send a powerful message by tapping into the warrior ethos.

Saving Private Ryan. Grossman (2007) makes poignant use of cinema that may penetrate the client suffering from survivor guilt. Most warriors have seen Steven Spielberg's movie *Saving Private Ryan*, about a true story of a unit of Army Rangers during the Normandy invasion (D-Day) that was tasked by the leading Army General to find and return Private Ryan safely home immediately after his family had already lost three brothers. Before leaving the warzone, Captain Miller, who was responsible for returning Ryan home and had lost several of his men, looks up at Ryan and says in his dying words, "Earn this, Earn it!" in reference to the lives shed—be worthy. Don't waste it. At the very end of the movie, a gray-haired Ryan and his grandchildren are visiting the graves of those who fought and gave their lives so that he could live. Ryan looks at his wife and tearfully says, "Tell me I've led a good life. Tell me I've been a good man." Grossman (2007) challenges all of us who have benefitted from the sacrifices of the warrior class—to ask our loved ones the same question.

I'm a coward! Military clients may feel shame and/or guilt about freezing, urinating, or defecating during combat—especially if a friend or unit member was injured or killed during the fire fight—providing information on normal combat reactions (e.g., Menninger, 1948) is a good start—or have them read an Army Ranger's perspective (Grossman, 2007).

Participating–witnessing atrocity. This can be the toughest of all. The saying "pain shared is pain divided" often does not apply if military personnel have committed crimes or acts of vengeance that they dare not share with another, including possibly the therapist. Traumatic grief can be exponentially compounded when acutely distraught individuals with automatic weapons are blinded by revenge. Decent people can do horrendous things. Not all war atrocities are committed as a result of traumatic grief reactions, others are decisions made under the tremendous duress of high threat environments violating ancient code of the honorable warrior. Again, Grossman (2007) gives a powerful example of this as an elderly WWII veteran approaches him: "Colonel, I'm an old man now, and I'm going to have to answer to my maker soon, I'm going to have to answer for that day it was inconvenient to take those German soldiers back. The day we shot them while they were quote 'trying to escape.' I murdered those men that day; we murdered them. We didn't have to kill them. We murdered them, and soon I will have to answer to my maker for what I did!" (pp. 359–360). This is where Silver's "atonement metaphor" (Silver & Rogers, 2002) can come into good use—some sort of constructive or meaningful penance that is not intended to absolve—but to heal a society and maybe save a soul.

TREATMENT PLAN CONSIDERATIONS FOR TRAUMATIC GRIEF

Pivar (2004), who works at the National Center for PTSD, makes the distinction between acute traumatic grief reactions (less than 3 months), and chronic traumatic grief reactions (greater than 3 months). Pivar recommends the following interventions:

Acute Traumatic Grief Reaction: (a) Communicate that "I give a damn about you, that you're okay!"(b) acknowledgement of the loss; (c) communication of understanding of the depth of feelings; (d) encouragement to recover positive memories of the deceased; (e) recognition of the good intentions of the survivor to come to the aid of the deceased; (f) education about what to expect during the course of acute grief; (g) encouragement of distraction and relaxation techniques as a temporary palliative; (h) efforts to reduce symptoms of PTSD and depression as co-morbid disorders would take precedence over grief symptoms in the initial phases of treatment, unless the loss itself is the main cause of distress.

Chronic Traumatic Grief Reaction: Assist the client by (a) creating an opportunity to talk about the deceased; (b) validating the pain and intensity of their feelings; (c) offering education about the cognitive processes of guilt; (d) restructuring of cognitive distortions of events that might lead to excessive guilt (clinical experience supports the importance of education about normal and complicated grief processes); (e) looking at the function of anger in bereavement; (f) restoring positive memories of the deceased; (g) acknowledging caring feelings towards the deceased; (h) affirming resilience and positive coping; (i) encouraging the retelling of the story of the death; (j) teaching that tolerating painful feelings or part of the grieving process; (k) encouraging participation in a support group for veterans (contact the Chaplain's office or Family Support Program for information); (l) helping to reassure clients that you will not try to whitewash their experiences.

Case Study: EMDR Treatment of Combat-Related Traumatic Grief

The following case study is presented in its entirety to provide a sense of pacing and continuity within and between sessions, especially when time and environment constraints result in irregular scheduling of therapy sessions, and how the therapist can still use EMDR effectively. The reader should understand the co-morbidity of this and other cases, and how frequently medically unexplained conditions are present. Unfortunately, in the vast majority of cases of medically unexplained conditions, without an identifiable neuropsychiatric diagnosis, it will be a war stress injury that will typically go unrecognized and untreated for years until eventually a neuropsychiatric condition emerges such as depression.

Staff Sergeant (SSGT) "W" is a 37-year-old, married, African American, male, combat-decorated Marine Corps SSGT (E-6) with over 11 years of active-duty service, referred by his military primary care physician for a mental health evaluation due to a positive post-deployment health rescreening for post-traumatic stress disorder (PTSD) and major depression disorder (MDD) symptoms.

History of Presenting Illness

SSGT W related that within 1 week after returning home from his second and most recent combat tour in Iraq 2 years ago, he began to experience progressively worsening changes in his sleep, mood, concentration, behavior, and motivation, characterized by daily intrusive recollections of combat-related events triggered by a wide-range of environmental stimuli (e.g., sight of older women, children, crowded places), initial insomnia, mid-night awakenings, anxiety-related nightmares, intermittent crying jags, irritable and dysphoric mood, irritable bowel syndrome, anhedonia, chronic fatigue, problems with concentration and memory, feeling socially disconnected, frequent headaches, periods of emotional numbing alternating with intense anger outbursts or seemingly unprovoked crying spells, hypervigilance, exaggerated startle, loss of appetite, lethargy, and profound guilt feelings in the context of multiple war-related memories.

Initial coping strategies to deal with his war-stress symptoms included social withdrawal, avoid thinking or other reminders of his war experiences, contemplating leaving the military, 1–2 beers at bedtime, use of over-the-counter sleep medications, and seeking help from the military health clinic that led to his being diagnosed with PTSD and MDD. He was prescribed Ambien for sleep and Zoloft for depression and PTSD symptoms, and taken them over the past year, but with little to no benefit. He also attended 6 individual counseling sessions at the Family Support Center but claimed that none of the above was effective. SSGT W reported that he and his wife of 8 years argued frequently since his return home and his work supervisors threatened to give him low performance marks if his motivation and behavior did not improve, prompting the present referral.

Relevant History

SSGT W is the oldest of five children from an intact family. There was no reported history of childhood abuse or other early traumatic experiences. He had a history of reading difficulties but never repeated a grade or received special education services. Medical history was unremarkable. SSGT W reported that prior to his first military deployment he was a physically healthy and fit person. However, after returning from his first combat tour in Iraq, he began to receive treatment for persistent headaches, gastroesophageal reflux disease (GERD), and constipation, along with sleep difficulties that completely resolved about 6 months later. He denied any persistent PTSD or depression symptoms after his initial deployment and expressed surprise over his current inability to "snap back" to shape. SSGT W denied any previous psychiatric history until returning from his second deployment. He also denied any active suicidal ideation, but admitted to passive suicidal thoughts related to his current lack of appetite, lethargy, feelings of hopelessness, and deficient self-care (e.g., stopped exercising, social isolation).

Psychological Testing

SSGT W was administered the Impact of Events Scale (IES) to assess the severity of his PTSD symptoms and the Beck Depression Inventory-Second Edition (BDI-II) and Beck Hopelessness Scale (BHS) to measure his depressive symptoms. Testing results indicated significant PTSD symptoms (IES = 30) along with a high level of depression (BDI–II = 33) and hopelessness (BHS = 38) symptoms.

EMDR Phases One–Three: Clinical Interview and Assessment

When queried about his war-related experiences, SSGT W evidenced no particular difficulty discussing his first deployment. He described being engaged in multiple fire-fights, including his shooting and killing several Iraqi insurgents, and having several members of his unit killed and/or wounded in action. He expressed minimal distress in recalling his experiences, except when mentioning the death of one young Marine under his command who was killed when executing a battlefield maneuver ordered by SSGT W. SSGT W admitted to feeling considerable remorse and guilt over the death of one of his Marines, often second-guessing his decision. However, other than the intense emotional hardship of writing a letter to the deceased Marine's mother, he reported no persistent guilt or other post-traumatic stress symptoms.

During the second deployment, SSGT W revealed that he actually saw less combat overall, but one incident in particular stood out. While guarding a critical bridge in Iraq, a civilian vehicle crowded with many apparent Iraqi occupants came speedily toward his checkpoint. Following protocol, SSGT W and his subordinates made numerous attempts to inform the apparently elder male, Iraqi driver that he needed to immediately stop the vehicle, but the driver did not stop. Several warning shots were made, but the vehicle maintained its speed and approached a point at which it could endanger the entire platoon. SSGT W gave the command to open fire on the oncoming vehicle. He described the effects of multiple automatic weapons striking the vehicle, the driver, and other occupants, most of whom were women and one to two adolescents, in vivid detail. The disabled, smoke-filled, bullet-riddled car rolled to a stop. A few occupants slowly attempted to open the passenger doors. Exiting the rear passage door was an elderly Iraqi woman, who was mortally wounded and bleeding profusely. She cried out in obvious anguish and pain, as SSGT W and his men watched her collapse in spasms. SSGT W related that the other vehicle occupants were all badly shot-up and lay either dead or quietly dying. However, the elderly Iraqi woman writhed on the ground and moaned loudly for what he reported seemed like hours, but lasted possibly minutes until she eventually bled-out. SSGT W's facial and emotional expression changed dramatically while retelling the horrific incident. He lowered and shook his head in his hands that were trembling, as he tearfully recollected the ordeal which he reported reliving several times a day and night. Pervasive shame and guilt led him to question why he should continue to live, although he denied active suicidal thoughts.

A brief assessment of the traumatic memory revealed the worst image was the initial sight of the elderly woman exiting the car with gaping wounds leading to her collapse. His negative cognition (NC) was "I killed her," with "tightened" sensations around his jaw and eyes, and stomach queasiness coinciding with the primary emotional response of "extreme guilt," all of which was given a SUDS rating of 10+ on the 0–10 Likert scale. In contrast, SSGT W's desired positive cognition (PC) was "It was all a tragic accident" with an initial VoC rating of −1 on the 1–7 Likert scale with 1 equating to full disbelief and 7 full belief in the self-statement. The obtained NC or PC would be considered ideal EMDR targets due to their lack of a present self-referencing belief. However, the above mentioned was the best solicited from this guilt-wracked Marine who obviously associated considerable affect with the cognitions provided.

As the only clinical psychologist a remote Marine base of 6,000, there was an extremely limited amount of time available to conduct psychotherapy. Treatment options were discussed with the client including referral to state-side therapist due to grossly insufficient mental health resources. SSGT W was informed that a brief therapy like EMDR might be beneficial given the serious restrictions and he consented to a trial of EMDR therapy. A brief description of EMDR was provided, along with a demonstration of bilateral stimulation (BLS) in the form of alternating eye movements.

Diagnostic Impression

Axis I: Post-Traumatic Stress Disorder—Combat-Related
           Major Depressive Disorder—Single Episode With
           Traumatic Grief Features
Axis II: No Diagnosis
Axis III: Headaches, IBS, GERD

Phase Four: EMDR Reprocessing Session 1

SSGT W announced no changes in his psychophysical symptoms at the outset of the next session which was 2 weeks after our initial meeting. He was asked to bring up the original target memory involving the tragic bridge incident and related no change to the image, feelings, sensations, or cognitions, given the SUDS rating of "10+." He was asked to notice these memory components while simultaneously focusing on an alternating light from a light bar device. He reported no change after the initial BLS set, mentioning that he could not hold the image while tracking the light. SSGT W was asked to notice the physical sensations of tightness in his face instead and reported a shift to a different aspect of the memory going back to the beginning of the day. Further BLS sets revealed frequent associations to different experiences within the target memory, different emotions (e.g., anger, sadness, guilt, despair), alternative cognitions vacillating from maladaptive (e.g., "I killed her") to more adaptive (e.g., "the driver was more responsible because he didn't stop"), and changes in bodily sensations and location (e.g., tense jaw, tightness around his eyes, tears, queasy stomach). After approximately 30 minutes of BLS following his numerous free associations, SSGT W's responses appeared to be moving toward a progressively more adaptive manner. A recheck of his SUDS to the target indicated that it had diminished all the way down to about a "4," which followed a couple of cathartic emotional releases. Unfortunately, time was running out, so an appointment was made for a second treatment session in 3 weeks. SSGT W complained of feeling "wiped out" physically and mentally and expressed great surprise over the nature of his responses to EMDR and the puzzling string of associations that often included previous war and childhood memories.

EMDR Reprocessing Session 2

SSGT W entered the second treatment session expressing considerable optimism over the progress made since our last meeting. He reported sleeping better, more even-tempered emotional states, and overall feeling more uplifted. When the target memory was rechecked, he reported a SUDS rating of "4," which was the same level we had left off. The image of the scene had faded some, and the tightness was mostly around his eyes along with mild queasiness in his stomach when he thought of the episode. He expressed eagerness to resume EMDR therapy, and, given the restricted session time available (50 minutes), a BLS set was initiated. Similar to the previous session, SSGT W reported many changes in his associations to the original trauma, but, after 20 minutes, a recheck of his SUDS indicated we were "looping" with a SUDS stuck at "4." He frequently made references to the elderly nature of the female victim, so I asked him whether she reminded him of anyone else he knew before. SSGT W appeared to carefully deliberate on my question. He initially answered "no," but then quickly changed his mind stating, "come to think of it, she reminded me of my grandmother" (on his mother's side). When asked how so, he replied "my grandmother was from Nigeria but lived with us for a few years when I was around 8, but she and my mom constantly argued, I mean really argue and I remember one day my grandma told me she couldn't live here anymore and was going to return to Africa." I asked him whether she did indeed return to her home and he replied, "Yeah, she left almost the next day. I remember her crying when she said goodbye to me the day she flew back ... and I never saw her again." You never saw her again? I asked. "Nope, she didn't have a phone and couldn't write and did not have email ... the last I heard about my grandma was about 2 years after she went home, my mom told me she had been diagnosed with cancer and died." SSGT W lowered and shook his head, "I should have stopped her from leaving ... if I had, she might still be alive." When asked to clarify his statement he replied, "If her cancer was diagnosed in the States, she could have gotten treatment here instead of Nigeria, which could have saved her life."

SSGT W went onto express his guilt for not intervening between his mother and grandmother and preventing the rupture in the family ties. When asked how he thought that his grandmother and the elderly Iraqi woman might be connected, he gazed ahead and said, "I never realized that before, but she was about the same age of my grandma, and in both cases I felt responsible for their deaths?" At which time a BLS set was initiated, and he made several associations to his experiences with his grandmother alternating to memories of the shooting. At the end of the session, a recheck of the target memory revealed a SUDS of "2" with considerable lightening of his facial expression and body posture including a broad smile as he recalled a positive childhood memory involving his grandmother. As time expired, a follow-up meeting was scheduled in 5 days.

EMDR Reprocessing Session 3

SSGT W came into the session looking much brighter than in previous sessions. He was smiling, and appeared more animated and upbeat in his mood and demeanor. He reported his sleep had significantly improved as had his overall physical and mental health. SSGT W expressed astonishment over how rapidly the changes in his health status have emerged and disclosed that the night after our last meeting he had dreamt for the "first time in decades" about his beloved grandmother and his dream merged his recollection of his grandmother with the elderly Iraqi woman. The recheck of the target memory revealed a very faded recollection to his surprise with a SUDS of "2," which he considered to be appropriate guilt for his involvement in the death of the Iraqi woman with "just a little tightness" around his eyes and some queasiness in his stomach. Although his self-report might be considered ecologically valid, another BLS set was initiated. SSGT W reported alternations between memories of the elderly Iraqi victim, the first deployment incident involving death of his subordinate, and his grandmother, with an apparent adaptive resolution. The SUDS remained a "2," therefore we went onto the installation phase. His initial PC was still valid for him and had increased to a "6," which did not change after several small BLS sets. We went onto the body scan phase. He closed his eyes and, while focusing on the PC and his bodily sensations from head to foot, he quickly stopped and reported "maybe just a little queasiness." This was followed by a BLS set, which appeared to do nothing. Given SSGT W's previous associations to childhood events and my residual gut feeling that something else may be keeping his SUDS at a "2," I elected to use a variation of the "float-back" technique. SSGT W was asked to concentrate on the stomach sensations and the earliest time in his life where he felt those sensations along with feeling responsible or guilty about someone getting harmed. Almost immediately he recalled an outing with his younger brother when he was around 6 years old and his brother was 4. They were walking on rocks near a pond when his brother slipped and hit his head. SSGT W's hands began to tremble as he told about being "scared" and guilty as his brother cried-out loudly, with his face covered in blood. He ran home to get his father who chastised him verbally and later physically for not watching out for his brother with the familiar queasy sensations in his stomach.

Additional BLS sets resulted in shifts in the childhood memory, along with new associations to the previous memories we had worked on. This time, when the SUDS was checked, he registered a "1" rating. When asked what kept it from being a "0," he replied, "an innocent old woman died, and it will never be a '0' … even though I know I had something to do with her death…. I also know that we had no choice … all we saw was a car speeding right toward us that did not respond to our warnings…. If we did not fire, a lot more people would have been killed … it's one of those tragedies that isn't right, but is a fact of war." The SUDS rating held with two additional BLS sets, as did the VOC of "6." This time around, the body scan revealed some "warm" sensations that led to a smile as he remembered his grandmother during a happier time with no apparent negative physical sensations. Time ran out, so another session was scheduled in 2 weeks.

Phase Eight: EMDR Reevaluation

SSGT W enthusiastically reported that he was no longer symptomatic and his overall health had significantly improved. Both his wife and co-workers had all commented on the positive changes. He stated no troubles sleeping, although the night after our last session was "a little weird" in regards to the dreams he had, there was no residual depression or PTSD symptoms. A recheck of the SUDS held at "1" with a "6" VOC. SSGT W agreed to complete the IES, BDI-II, and BHS measures for us to check if there was anything we may have missed. Results from the IES indicated PTSD symptoms in the non-clinical range (IES = 8) with similar non-clinical findings regarding his depression symptoms (BDI-II = 4) and feelings of hopelessness (BHS = 7). SSGT W announced that he has already submitted his paperwork to re-enlist in the Marine Corps. He reported stopping all psychotropic medications after the second EMDR session. When asked to imagine returning to the warzone he endorsed no particular distress and added that he believed that his experiences including what he went through with his PTSD and traumatic grief had made him a better military leader. An open-ended offer to meet and check-up on him was agreed to.

Phase Eight: EMDR Reevaluation: Four-Month Follow-Up

Due to scheduling conflicts and an intolerable pressure to meet the expanding mental health demand, it took 4 months to arrange a 15-minute follow-up session with SSGT W. He patiently completed the assessment measures in the waiting area which we reviewed. Essentially, there had been no major changes in his mental and physical health since our last session (e.g., IES = 6; BDI-II = 4; BHS = 3). Other than occasional constipation, he no longer is being treated for IBS. He reported no problems with headaches and only intermittent GERD symptoms for which he continues to take medication. SSGT W informed me that he and his family will be transferring in a couple of months to another Marine base, which will very likely mean another deployment in the near future. He expressed general enthusiasm for continuing his military career and confidence that his past experiences were more a benefit than detriment to his ability to cope with another deployment and more importantly to help those under him. SSGT W explained further by disclosing that his prior attitude toward mental health care had been predominantly, stereotypically negative. However, after experiencing his own war stress injuries and the treatment he received, he was now "a major believer." He mentioned that he has already disclosed his personal struggles with PTSD and mental health treatment with several other military peers and subordinates, leading them to seek help. However, he also reiterated frustration that I had shared with him earlier, that the critical shortage of mental health treatment in the military renders it near impossible even "for those who need and want the help, to get the help," a leadership concern that he has conveyed to his chain of command.

Reversing the Flow

Clinical note. Reversing the flow refers to when clients with traumatic grief are "looping" from one negative association to another, sometimes we have had success by asking them to recall a "good memory" when their friend, spouse, unit leader, etc., was still alive, and process that. In the MUS case study above, the therapist reversed the flow, which led to the client accessing positive memories and then follow the free associations. Use this sparingly.

EMDR TREATMENT OF SURVIVORS OF INTERPERSONAL VIOLENCE

There is evidence that some military personnel with PTSD, especially if co-morbid with substance use disorder or other neuropsychiatric condition, may be at risk of perpetrating violence toward others, including their spouse, partner, and/or children. Violent incidents are usually a response to perceived threat or cumulative frustrations. Therapists should be aware of risk for domestic violence. EMDR can be effective in treatment of the experiential contributors that may have led or maintain aggressive responding (Silver & Rogers, 2002; see Chapter 13, this volume: EMDR Treatment of Anger/Aggression). Both perpetrators and victims of interpersonal violence can benefit from using the standard EMDR protocol. At-risk warning indicators for interpersonal violence include: (a) ideation and/or intent to harm others; (b) past history of violent behaviors; (c) severe agitation, aggressiveness, threatening, or hostile behaviors; (d) actively psychotic; and (e) substance abuse.

Case Study: EMDR Treatment of Domestic Violence Survivor

The following case study involves a military spouse victim of domestic violence treated at a military community family counseling program.

First Meeting

Phase One. The client is a 40-year-old, East Indian female, spouse of an active-duty Air Force member, referred for treatment at a military mental health outpatient clinic after a domestic violence incident involving altercation with her estranged husband. The client appears fatigued, with restricted affect; her mood is calm and sad. The client has been separated from her husband for the past 3 years. She has no children. There were no immediate safety concerns. Presenting symptoms included poor sleep, bruxism (teeth grinding), social isolation, strong mistrust and avoidance of Caucasian American people given the abuse from her Caucasian husband, and notable problems with intimacy: "I don't like to be touched."

Phases Two and Three. After being informed and giving consent to her therapist for EMDR therapy, a treatment plan was developed after a total of 15 past memories were identified as past experiences currently contributing to her interpersonal and sleep difficulties including chronic physical, verbal, and emotional domestic violence by her husband, motor vehicle accident, rape during adolescence and forced abortion, incidents of overt racial discrimination, familial death, and childhood physical abuse. For brevity's sake, we will not list the assessment of all 15 target memories, but we will describe the primary target memories involving domestic violence incidents.

First Target. Approximately 4 years ago, the client experienced a miscarriage after her husband punched her in the stomach several times, causing bleeding. The worst part of this incident was "the blood." Negative cognition: "I'm stupid for staying with him." Positive cognition: "I can take care of myself." VOC: "5." Emotions: "hate" and "anger." Location of "nervous" body sensations was in the "chest." SUDS: "8." [Posttreatment SUDS: "1"]

Second Target. Being pinched, shoved, and punched by her husband consistently "in places where he knew wouldn't show anyone" the injuries. This occurred 3–4 times a week over a six-year marriage. The worst representative issue of the cluster of domestic abuse events: SUDS of "9" [Post-treatment SUDS = "2"].

Resources Identified: The therapist solicited: (a) three best events/accomplishments of her adult life, (b) three best events/accomplishments of her childhood, and (c) the client's favorite activities.

Standardized Measures: Dissociative Events Scale—revealed no dissociative disorder.

Second Meeting (First EMDR Reprocessing)

Phase Four. Rechecked first target memory—no change in SUDS: "8." The therapist reported that the client reprocessed primary domestic violence incident, husband's adultery, difficult interactions with the police, and client concerns over emerging racism. *Phase Seven:* Incomplete Session First Target SUDS: "3."

Third Meeting (Second EMDR Reprocessing)

Phase Eight: Reevaluation: Client reported no distress from previous week's session: "I didn't even think about it," which had not been the case for years. *Phase Four:* Initial recheck of target memory "The way he treated me after the miscarriage." [Add BLS]. Therapist reported that client reprocessed multiple incidents of verbal and emotional abuse to include property damage, isolation, seeing her dog mistreated and "almost killed," being blamed for their marital discord, and being strangled. The client ended the session tearfully with adaptive statements that she was able to develop friendships with people who were willing to protect her and offered that the "hate" she feels is only hurting "me." *Phase Seven:* Incomplete Session/closure.

Fourth Meeting (Third EMDR Reprocessing)

Phase Eight: Reevaluation: The client is preparing for upcoming PCS transfer and reports general improvements. Rechecked the first target memory, which revealed SUDS: "9." *Phase Four:* Therapist reported that the client reprocessed multiple events of emotional/verbal abuse, disrespect to her parents by husband, her husband leaving her isolated, feeling abandoned by the military after filing domestic violence complaint. *Phase Seven:* Incomplete Session/closure: Rechecked SUDS: remained at "9."

Fifth Meeting (Fourth EMDR Reprocessing)

Phase Eight: Reevaluation: The client reported "feeling a lot better" and cited examples of finding evidence of her husband's past adultery but reacting with "I'm glad this will soon be over" versus the characteristic anger and hurt. *Phase Four:* The therapist indicated that the client reprocessed several incidents of being strangled by her husband, adultery, and property destruction. The client was able to note that these behaviors reflected poorly on her husband and, while she still took responsibility for her role in getting married in spite of not loving him, she endorsed the fact that she took the responsibility of paying off debts (incurred by him on her credit card) instead of filing for bankruptcy, being "stronger" now, and "more confident" now—in sum, "resilient" now. *Phase Seven:* Incomplete Session/closure: Rechecked SUDS: "4."

Sixth Meeting (Fifth EMDR Reprocessing)

Phase Eight: Reevaluation: The client stated that she began taking an online college course and is pending to PCS soon. *Phase Four:* The therapist reported the client reprocessed a second miscarriage, head pain, and many incidents of controlling and abusive behavior by her husband, ending with her resolve to move on. *Phase Seven* Incomplete Session/closure: Rechecked SUDS: "3."

Seventh Meeting (Reevaluation only)

Phase Eight: Reevaluation: Due to the client's imminent PCS transfer, the meeting was around termination. No further EMDR reprocessing. Primary target memory (#1)—Rechecked SUDS: "1.5"

Eighth Meeting (Two-month Follow-up)

Phase Eight: Reevaluation: After the client had geographically relocated, the therapist called to check on her mental status. The client reported that her mood remained calm and appropriate even after the hectic relocation. Rechecked primary (#1) target memory—SUDS: "1." A reassessment of all the remaining 14 target memories indicated significant generalization effects. For example, the second target memory—SUDS: "1"; the MVA went from SUDS: "8" to "1"; the memory of adolescent sexual assault went from SUDS: "7" to "1." However, other target memories showed a decline, but not as significant. For instance, the memory of forced abortion went from SUDS: "8" to "2.5"; and grief over death of a close family member went from SUDS: "10" to "7". Overall length of treatment was 5 weeks, and a 2-month follow-up reevaluation.

Clinical note: We chose this case for several reasons. First, not every EMDR session goes like clockwork, and we did not want to leave the reader with impression that, if they did not complete all eight phases within half a dozen sessions, something is wrong. Second, the above case illustrates the time and environmental constraints that are inherent within most military treatment settings that we have been mentioning throughout the book. Third, despite not getting to phases five (installation) and six (body scan) on any of the target memories, the client's access and strengthening connections to her adaptive neural networks were clearly evident in the progress notes. This case also serves to support our recommendation that therapists need to consider those realities in their treatment plans and limit the number of past target memories to the "worst of the worst." However, this too presents a dilemma of possibly not identifying all potential target memories for comprehensive reprocessing of the maladaptive neural networks. This is true. In this case, and others we presented, the generalization effects of EMDR reprocessing are striking, but not absolute. Left open is the possibility that some of the unprocessed target memories may come back and create havoc for the client. We do the best we can—just as the therapist in this case—who is not one the authors—did, and we *salute* Smith and his clinical staff for the great work they do to support military families and personnel every day!

13 Other Military Stress Injury and EMDR Treatment Considerations

EMDR Treatment of Military Sexual Trauma

EMDR treatment of Military Sexual Trauma (MST) will normally involve the standard evidence-based EMDR protocol (e.g., Rothbaum et al., 2005), but, if there are concerns about client stability, then RDI may be most appropriate to start with, especially if clients appear too emotionally fragile to tolerate trauma-focused reprocessing. Time or environment constraints may also restrict the client's focus to the precipitating event using a modified EMDR or EMD protocol. However, whenever possible, it is best to use the evidence-based standard EMDR protocol. Randomized controlled studies of EMDR treatment for sexual assault have been conducted, including favorable comparisons to Prolonged Exposure revealing that EMDR is one of the evidence-based treatments for sexual trauma (e.g., Rothbaum et al., 2005). Many service members may express concern or fear of EMDR reprocessing linking up to earlier childhood memories of abuse or adversity. For many (not all) military clients, their experience of MST is one of others in their life, so therapists should inform their clients that, for the best possible outcome, the standard EMDR treatment is more ideal than just limiting to current disturbance.

AIP Model and MST

By definition, MST includes behaviors short of sexual assault or rape itself, namely sexual harassment, sexual bigotry, sexual politics, and other related behaviors that do not meet the *DSM* criterion A description of trauma. However, using the AIP model, sexual harassment and related experiences would certainly be considered "small t" events that contribute to problems of adjustment and are appropriate targets in EMDR. There is sparse research on the treatment of sexual harassment or on the treatment of any sexual trauma associated with military service. It is also common for MST survivors to have experienced similar betrayal or adverse experiences in childhood that can feed into the client's current response.

Treatment Considerations

Every survivor of military sexual trauma will respond differently regardless of the nature, intensity, or severity of the incident. Therapists should be aware of the following clinical issues that may arise in the work with MST survivors. As themes related to safety, responsibility, and choice are all often present to one degree or another, clients whose processing becomes blocked might benefit from cognitive interweave. During client history and preparation, the therapist should try to normalize the client ASR or PTS by providing psycho-education and resource materials. Each military installation has a Sexual Assault Victim Intervention (SAVI) program that will assign a trained advocate to meet with the client, discuss his/her grievance options, accompany the client to medical if necessary, and to any legal proceedings, etc. Most SAVI programs reside in the base family counseling and support programs (e.g., Fleet and Family Service Center–Navy; Marine Corps Community Counseling Services, etc.).

Fear and Safety. For acute MST, issues involving health and safety need to be assessed and addressed first and foremost. In many cases the MST occurs on military installations or onboard naval vessels where military personnel live, eat, pray, work, and play—resulting in frequent, if not daily contact with or fear of contact with the perpetrator. Military clients in general and those with MST, in particular, typically have little to no control about living and working arrangements. Concerns or fears over safety can be directed at the possibility of being revictimized by the perpetrator, and/or acts of retribution by the perpetrator, friends, co-workers loyal to the perpetrator who may accuse the client of false accusations and betrayal. Many times the perpetrator is a co-worker and friend with whom the client has shared the same social support. Fear of retribution or reprisal is also common when the perpetrator is in the client's chain-of-command (e.g., NCO/SNCO, Division Officer, etc.). The higher ranking and greater positional authority of the perpetrator (e.g., Commanding Officer) is extremely intimidating. The client's unit Commander or Commanding Officer can issue a "Military Protective Order" (MPO) if the alleged perpetrator is from the same command as the client. The Commander can also reassign work locations and barracks rooms to protect the client's safety. The base Legal Services Office (LSO) also can issue MPOs if warranted.

By DoD instruction, commands are required to investigate formal complaints of MST like sexual harassment, which is usually conducted by members of the same command. In criminal accusations such as MST involving sexual assault, the military forensic investigating agencies take the prime lead (e.g., NCIS). If clients report their command is not supporting them enough (which may or may not be true), they can be directed to see either their command Chaplain or a base Chaplain. Chaplains often serve to help military members experiencing problems related to morale, safety, loss, or other emergency situations. The base SAVI is another excellent resource to advocate to the client's command on the client's behalf.

Shame. Almost universally, military survivors of MST feel a deep sense of shame. As members of the warrior class, men and women are instructed on how to protect themselves during time of war. Depending on their actual military job or specialty, that training may never be repeated after boot camp. Admitting to vulnerability and weakness to protect oneself is the often unspoken burden clients carry. Military enlisted leaders (e.g., NCO, and especially SNCO) and officers' greatest fear is having their credibility as a leader questioned. Fears of retribution and shame and the humiliation of being perceived as a "victim" are what prevent most military clients from filing a claim and often fuels excessive self-blame and chastisement. They are leaders, and leaders are supposed to be responsible and capable of anticipating threat and taking concerted action. Shame can be greatest for male MST survivors.

Guilt. Guilt may arise in a number of ways with MST survivors. Guilt for being present, for not identifying the problem earlier and taking corrective actions (aka armchair quarterbacking). Wouldas and shouldas are prominent. However, the greatest sense of guilt is likely to originate with a formal complaint or legal charge against a fellow unit member. Military culture emphasizes trust and loyalty to the nth degree. It is almost universal for a service member who otherwise was completely justified filing a grievance to experience considerable guilt over betraying one of their own. The higher ranking or power of the accused may result in the greater sense of disloyalty.

Anger and Betrayal of Trust. As the phrase a Band of Brothers and Sisters signifies, the importance that military culture places on trust and cohesion within military commands serves as protective or resilient factors for military stress—particularly during war. However, that same degree of group solidarity can often play a role in the negative psychological effects associated with MST. Perpetrators are frequently the client's peers, co-workers, or supervisors responsible for making decisions about work-related evaluations and promotions. In addition, MST survivors may feel they must choose between staying with their active-duty career or filing a grievance—or even having to work with the perpetrator should there be insufficient evidence to convict—and express considerable anger toward their command leaders or the military itself. Either way, such betrayal of trust and faith in the military system may generate considerable anger and disillusionment. In many if not most scenarios, the unit Commander will take action to separate the perpetrator and alleged victim, if both are from the same command. It would be rare for the military to separate or discharge a MST survivor because they desired such.

Other Clinical Issues to Monitor: (a) Substance-use problems; (b) MUS; (c) victims of sexual trauma may report problems in their interpersonal relationships, including difficulties with trust, difficulties engaging in social activities, or sexual dysfunction; (d) male victims of sexual trauma may express concern about their sexuality or their masculinity; (e) depression of and danger to the victim.

EMDR Treatment and Substance Use Disorders

There are two main considerations in regards to EMDR treatment of substance use disorders: (a) primary trauma-focused treatment associated with a war stress injury such as PTSD or other neuropsychiatric or medically unexplained condition with co-occurring substance-use disorder viewed as a secondary feature needing to be monitored or treated adjunctively (e.g., 12-step, military substance abuse treatment program, etc.); or (b) primary trauma-focused treatment on the experiential contributors associated with the substance abuse or other addictive behavior itself.

EMDR Treatment of Primary Diagnosis Not Targeting Substance Use Disorder

When there are co-occurring substance use disorders or neuropsychiatric conditions, the therapist will need to determine the best strategy for prioritizing and treating multiple disorders. In general, these conditions should be treated concurrently, although there are exceptions, such as severe substance dependence, that require medical detoxification prior to EMDR or other forms of treatment.

Informed Consent

Before treating military clients with substance use disorder co-morbidity—particularly those currently abstinent—the therapist should properly inform them of the potential risks and benefits of trauma-focused work at this time. For instance, in terms of risks, reprocessing may increase the client's desire to use substances or other addictive behavior, at least in the short run, until the experiential contributors underlying their need to use have been reprocessed, along with triggers associated with relapse.

Treatment Planning with Comorbid Substance Use Disorder

When the therapist and client elect to start EMDR reprocessing of traumatic events related to the primary diagnosis, the therapist should closely (weekly) monitor the client for changes in alcohol and drug use. Therapists can also initiate EMDR with a behavioral contract limiting the use of substances during treatment and attendance of 12-step programs. It is highly recommended that clients with substance dependence or even abuse be encouraged to attend 12-step programs (e.g., AA) during EMDR treatment in order to minimize the possibility of relapse. Military clients with substance-use disorders could also receive EMDR treatment concurrently, if clients are participating in the local base outpatient substance abuse treatment program. Optimally, a client-signed release of information should be obtained, so the therapist and chemical dependency counselors are in communication should concerns arise.

Finally, if clients are too "high risk" for EMDR reprocessing due to relapse risk, it is recommended that non-trauma-focused treatments, such as RDI, stress-management, anger management, and other current-focused coping methods be provided to lay the groundwork for EMDR. Every military installation has family support programs that offer coping-skills classes.

EMDR Treatment of Primary Substance Use or Other Addictive Disorder

EMDR has been reported to also be used as treatment for a primary substance use or addictive behavior, not as a cure of the neurophysiology of addiction but for reprocessing the experiential contributors that may be related to the reason they began and continue to use (e.g., "self-medicating" response). Whether there is a history of Criterion A trauma per the *DSM*, or early adverse events or "small t" trauma (e.g., emotional neglect, loss of parent attachment due to divorce, etc.), the AIP model provides the rationale for using EMDR to reprocess whatever experiences that are associated with the addictive behavior.

EMDR "De-Tur" Protocol for Addictive Behaviors

A. J. Popky developed a De-Tur protocol, which was published in Robin Shapiro's (2005) *EMDR Solutions: Pathways to Healing,* and focuses on reprocessing the experiential contributors of the client's urges associated with their substance use or other addictive behavior. There have been no published accounts of using the De-Tur protocol with military populations, but it offers a positive, blameless, resource development angle that may be well received by military clients. Preaching abstinence to military members because of their inability to control their behavior in relation to their drug or compulsion of choice is tricky to say the least, especially in an organization that places such high premium on self-discipline and control. The main treatment goal in the De-Tur protocol targets the client's coping around their urges to use, and, like most substance-abuse programs, views relapses as learning opportunities versus a sign of personal failure. For those reasons, we have included a cursory description of Popky's protocol (see R. Shapiro, 2005, for a more detailed description).

Popky's De-Tur Protocol for Addictive Behavior

1. *Access Inner Resources.* "Notice what you are seeing and how it feels, breathe into it, and move around in your body. Notice how it feels and smells and take it all in." [Add BLS sets to increase access and association with adaptive neural networks.]
2. *Identify Positive Treatment Goal.* The client is assisted in identifying a treatment goal that is attractive and achievable and on which they can easily maintain focus. Guide them in creating a clear image of how they would look achieving this goal in the not-too-distant future. Use

eye movement to enhance this image. The goal should be (a) stated in positive terms, (b) achievable within a fairly close time period, (c) reasonable, (d) descriptive of successful functioning in the future, and (e) compelling.

3. ***Fully Associate With Positive State.*** "Step into your picture of your positive treatment goal, into that body posture. Notice and experience the positive feelings, breathe into those feelings, move around in them, experience being successful. Notice what you see, hear, feel, smell, and taste. Notice what it's like to function successfully." Make adjustments to the visual and auditory components as needed.

4. ***Identify the Known Triggers for the Addictive Behavior.*** These can be places, people, times, emotions, smells, tastes, events, action, or objects. Create a list for processing.

5. ***Desensitize Each Trigger.*** "Bring up the picture, along with any words, tastes, or smells that go with it. How strong is the Level of Urge right now, from 0–10, where 0 is the lowest and 10 is the strongest? Where are you feeling it in your body? Hold the picture along with the associated words, tastes, smells. Notice where you're feeling it." After each set of eye movements ask, "What are you getting now? Go with that." Repeat until level of urge drops to 0. If processing leads to a core issue, process that thoroughly with 8-Phase Protocol and then return to this step.

6. ***Install Positive Alternative Behavior.*** Bring up the triggering situation and add eye movement until client is able to imagine managing the situation without the addictive behavior.

7. ***Test and Future Check.*** Have the client bring up triggering situation and obtain level of urge on 0–10 scale.

8. ***Relapse Prevention.*** If the client's behavior is stable enough, he or she can be taught to use eye movements on urges. If this is unsuccessful, encourage the client to call for help. If relapse occurs, ask the client to make a note of what triggers are present and those are reprocessed.

9. ***Follow-Up.*** At the beginning of each sessions check on previously desensitized triggers and any possible new targets for processing.

Source: Shapiro, F. (2008). *Eye Movement Desensitization and Reprocessing (EMDR) Part 2 Training Manual Bound with Military Field Manual* (pp. 15-17). Watsonville, CA: EMDR Institute; used with permission.

EMDR Treatment and Anger/Aggression

Several excellent books have been written by pioneers and long-time EMDR trainers who have spent their professional careers working with war veterans through the Department of Veterans Affairs. Drs. Steven Silver and Susan Rogers's (2002) *Light in the Heart of Darkness* provides valuable insight into managing combat veterans in therapy and reprocessing the experiential contributors underlying combat veteran anger and aggressive behaviors utilizing

EMDR. According to Silver and Rogers (2002), therapists need to appreciate the usefulness of anger in combat as a great defense against fear. Explaining to military personnel the purpose of EMDR is to reduce or eliminate their anger will likely meet client resistance of interfering with this defense (e.g., Silver & Rogers, 2002). A better tact is to define the goal as increasing their choice and sense of control about when to get angry, to what extent, how long, and how it ends. Others might be concerned about losing their competitive edge that has helped them survive in high threat environments. In those cases, simple education may be enough. According to the AIP model, EMDR is merely mimicking or stimulating the brain's own adaptive information processing system. That system evolved to remember experiences that will aide in our survival. That is the purpose of memory. If the therapist uncovers a "blocking belief" associated with client concerns of losing his or her defense or edge, assurance can be given that the brain would not allow erasure of what is needed for survival, only the excess that has been hard for the client with "anger issues" to control, and is causing problems instead of helping.

Can EMDR Reprocessing Cause Clients to Act out Violently?

Clients and/or therapists may harbor concern that EMDR reprocessing with an anger-prone client, may trigger a flashback experience whereby the client is unable to contain their impulses—leading to violence acts. Similarly, some military clients might demonstrate reluctance to directing their self-focus on events associated with their anger in the form of blocked processing, due to a fear that they may be unable to control their rage and could endanger others including the therapist. Combat veterans or other clients undergoing EMDR therapy, just like other trauma-focused treatments, can be expected to experience intense emotions including anger, but they will not be inclined to act out in ways different than outside of the therapy office. To allay the client's concern, he or she can be handed a "stress ball" to squeeze.

Targeting Primary Anger and Aggression for Reprocessing

Past Memories. Clients who report notable aggression or violent acts can be asked to recall the earliest, worst, and most recent episodes in which they lost control of their anger and/or acted aggressively, and these can become targets for EMDR reprocessing. During the assessment phase, clients may try to edit their language so as not to offend the therapist or create a negative impression such as when soliciting a negative cognition. The therapist will want to ask the client to speak plainly, because the client's language and associated emotions will provide stronger access to the negative neural networks. Silver and Rogers (2002) also recommend not being too perfectionistic when it comes to identifying a self-referencing negative cognition for an externally focused issue like anger; the therapist can consider options like "I can't get fair treatment" or similar self-statements that contain affect.

Negative Cognitions: (a) "You can't trust anyone." (b) "If I got out of control, it would be horrible/life-threatening/intolerable." (c) "After all I've been through, I deserve to be treated better than this." (d) "Others are out to get me, or won't protect me, in some way."

Positive Cognitions: (a) "Even if I am out of control, I won't be threatened in this situation." (b) "Others do not have to be perfect in order for me to survive/be comfortable." (c) "I can learn to control my anger."

Emotions: Therapists should be aware that clients may use anger as a way to distance themselves from other emotions—fear, grief, guilt, and shame. If anger is serving as a secondary emotion, the primary emotion can become a useful target for reprocessing. How does one get to the primary emotion? These may surface spontaneously during processing, or the therapist can simply ask, "Some combat veterans have told me that they are more comfortable with feeling angry, because it helps them block out other feelings ... what about yourself? If you weren't feeling angry, what do you think you would be feeling?" or a less wordy phrase—and add BLS to the client's response regardless if they identify a primary emotion or not.

Physical Sensations: Clients should be asked about what physical sensations they notice when they start to get ticked-off, angry, frustrated, etc., and identify the location in the body. Having the client monitor and describe their physical sensations will help strengthen their awareness of their physical response as a cue they are getting irritated or annoyed and can take action to short-circuit. Lastly, therapists are advised to pay attention to the client's non-verbal behaviors during reprocessing. Compressed lips, furrowed brow, clenched jaw, bracing behavior with their hands gripping the chair, and so on can be used as self-focusing targets for reprocessing. For example during reprocessing, the therapist might say, "*Tech Sergeant ... notice your jaw tightening too and keep tracking the lights.*" Pointing out non-verbal behavior during reprocessing, just like traditional therapy, can lead to new associations that the client had been previously unaware of at the moment.

Current Triggers: Help the client identify current triggers that solicit anger. For example, "*Lieutenant, what are some situations that act like triggers for your anger—like certain situations, places, or people that say or do something that you know will get on your nerves real quick?*" For example, a combat veteran may become angry when others around him (wife, children, and co-workers) don't "follow the rules." The strength of his belief is actually related to how important it was for him to follow rules during the war in order to prevent deaths.

Future Template: Help the client identify future-oriented behaviors by imagining acting in a calm, controlled manner in the presence of previous antecedents or current trigger.

Other Treatment Recommendations: The following treatment recommendations would apply to most, if not all war/traumatic stress injuries: (a) Refer the client to anger management classes at the local base family support program to help him or her recognize signs of becoming angry, self-calm, avoid escalating conflicts, and respond to anger-eliciting situations in more positive ways. (b) Teach Tactical/Combat breathing or other tension-reduction techniques to reduce their overall sympathetic arousal levels. (c) Recommend daily or near daily vigorous physical exercise. (d) Assess for traumatic grief reaction. (e) Assess, significantly reduce, and monitor intake of stimulants (caffeine, nicotine, prescription meds, weight loss supplements, caffeine-loaded caplets, and other OTC meds). (f) Assess for sleep disturbance and refer to medical for evaluation for possible short-term sleep aide if necessary. (g) Assess for substance use disorder and refer to base treatment program if necessary. (h) Monitor for depression and dangerousness, especially if "at-risk" (see Chapter 5, this volume). (i) Encourage registering for yoga or meditation classes through the base MWR. (j) Consider use of RDI to strengthen adaptive resources if necessary. (k) Invite the client to journal.

EMDR TREATMENT AND SLEEP DYSFUNCTION

Although sleep disturbances are considered secondary symptoms of war/traumatic stress and compassion-stress injuries like PTSD, depression, and many MUS, there are increasing reports that sleep disturbance itself—particularly the regulation of rapid eye movement (REM) sleep is often a precursor to stress—injuries like PTSD (e.g., Ross et al., 1994). Since EMDR's inception, the logical leap was to associate the reprocessing or learning effects from the saccadic eye movements to REM sleep, given the central role REM has in the integration of traumatic and stressful memories. Early comparisons of polysomnagrams of healthy combat veterans and those with combat-related PTSD revealed that PTSD symptoms are often manifested during REM sleep when most of the information, learning, and memories are processed, including stress and surviving related emotional material (Ross, et al., 1994).

Recent Research on EMDR and REM Sleep

We thought it might be worth taking a quick look at some recent research findings regarding the association between EMDR and REM sleep, particularly in light of the resistance of military medicine to research EMDR because eye movements have been proven superfluous (Russell, 2008a). Diversity of cultural and scientific disciplines should be noted as investigations are shifting away from the ethnocentric realm of clinical psychology to a broader neuroscientific lens. Swedish researchers found that similarity of physiological reactivity to eye movements during EMDR and REM sleep revealed similar patterns, including activation of cholinergic and inhibit sympathetic systems (e.g., decreases in heart rate, skin conductance, and an increased finger temperature), breathing frequency and end-tidal carbon dioxide increased, and oxygen saturation decreased during eye movements (Elofsson, von Scheele, Theorell, & Sondergard, 2008).

Topographical changes of EEG (and Evoked Response Potential) and REM sleep after EMDR treatment was examined by Japanese researchers with 33 subjects assigned to three groups according to varied conditions (control, provocational, and EMDR). Pre-post EMDR effects indicated that the density of eye movement during REM sleep increased after provocation and EMDR, and the left frontal activities might indicate a treatment efficacy. The researchers concluded that the findings appear to support the hypothesis that REM sleep is intimately involved with the mechanisms of emotional and memory reprocessing (Sugawara & Suzuki, 2004). In addition, researchers from Taiwan examined the effect of EMDR eye movements (EM) in relation to the changing the strength of semantic associations for negative words after saccadic bilateral eye movements on 66 subjects. The results echoed the REM-sleep-dependent memory reprocessing model, suggesting that EM in EMDR might reflect a shift in associative memory systems by activating different strength of associations of negative semantic nodes for different semantically related words (Chang, 2005).

Another team of Japanese researchers investigated the prefrontal responses of 10 healthy subjects during an emotional memory recall with and without eye movement by measuring changes in concentration of oxygenated hemoglobin (oxy-Hb) using near-infrared spectroscopy (NIRS). The results indicated that eye movements are associated with a reduction in the hemodynamic response to emotional memory recall (Ohtani, Matsuoa, Kasai, Katob, & Katoa, 2005). Lastly, researchers investigated differential affects associated with significant loss or trauma, and found that experimentally induced saccadic eye movements decreased reaction times to unexpected stimuli among those reporting traumatic distress (characterized by hyperarousal and intrusive thoughts) and increased reaction times among those reporting separation distress (characterized by vivid reminiscences and the sense of a foreshortened future). The investigators concluded that the eye movements of both EMDR and REM sleep may impact the attentional and cognitive reorienting activity differently if individuals are experiencing an attachment loss or other trauma (Kuiken, Chudleigh, & Racher, 2010).

EMDR Treatment of Sleep Disturbance and Nightmares

According to the 2010 *Best Practices Guide for the Treatment of Nightmare Disorders in Adults*, prazosin is recommended for treatment of PTSD-related nightmares, with Image Rehearsal Therapy (IRT) recommended for treatment of nightmare disorder. EMDR was recommended as a treatment that could be considered for PTSD-associated nightmares based on a low grade or amount of available evidence (e.g., Aurora et al., 2010).

226 EMDR Treatment for Chronic War/Traumatic Stress Injury

EMDR Treatment of Sleep Disturbance

In most cases thus far, the improvements in sleep have been ancillary versus primary focus in EMDR therapy. However, in one study, researchers using EMDR treatment were primarily interested in examining what if any effects does EMDR treatment have on sleep disturbance (Raboni, Tufik, & Suchecki, 2006). Seven subjects (two male, five female) diagnosed with PTSD after a minimum of 3 years since a physical assault or kidnapping were diagnosed with PTSD via structured clinical interview (SCID) and Impact of Events (IES) scale. Well-standardized measures included (e.g., Beck Depression Inventory, State-Trait Anxiety Inventory, SF-36 inventory and polysomnogram taken before, at mid-point, and after treatment). Clients received on average *five* EMDR reprocessing sessions ranging between 30 to 90 minutes in duration. Results indicated that all subjects experienced significant increases in sleep efficiency and reduced time of waking after sleep onset that coincided with significant improvements on measures of depression, anxiety, fatigue, impact of the event, and stress symptoms scores, and an improvement of quality of life, of sleep quality, energy-level, and general well-being. Raboni et al. concluded that when the traumatic memory loses its negative emotional valence, there is a decrease in arousal and, consequently, an improvement of the harmful PTSD symptoms. The increased sleep efficiency and reduction of general, social, and emotional stress are determining factors for the patients to perceive the improvement in their quality of life and well-being.

EMDR Treatment of Nightmares or Other Disturbing Dream Content

Several case studies have been published where EMDR was applied specifically to nightmare or other distressful dream content (Shapiro, 2001). To target dream content, the therapist follows the same protocol for soliciting the most representative, or "worst" image, include a negative cognition, emotions, physical sensations, SUDS, positive cognition, and VOC, and reprocess like any other experiential event in the client's neural networks. Therapists should be on the look-out for the "universal nightmare" of combat veterans' dreams of either not being able to find or fire their weapon in the presence of imminent threat (Grossman, 2007).

14 Phases Seven–Eight: Closure and Reevaluation

PHASE SEVEN: CLOSURE

During the course of EMDR therapy, a reprocessing session might end due to time constraints after completing the reprocessing of a target memory, although there are other target memories remaining in the treatment plan, or without completing a particular phase for a specific target memory such as reprocessing, installation, or the body scan. Phase Seven provides the therapist-structured guidance on how to close both types of sessions, as well as how to safely prepare clients for transitioning from the reprocessing session back to the military environment.

Managing the Clock

Whether EMDR sessions are 50 minutes in duration, 90 minutes, or somewhere in-between, it's incumbent upon therapists to remain cognizant of where they are in the session in relation to the amount of time remaining. This split in the therapist's attention can cause considerable stress for the therapist who also wants to be attuned with the client during the reprocessing session while simultaneously using clinical judgment about the optimal time to sensitively close down the reprocessing and prepare the client for debriefing. Some therapists profess an aversion to watching the time feeling it conveys an impersonal message to the client. However, abruptly stopping reprocessing in less-than-opportune moments, or apologetically ushering the client out of the office is also clearly problematic. Therapists having trouble managing the clock will finding the closure phase to be particularly uncomfortable for themselves and their clients. Given the premium on trust and safety in the therapeutic alliance, especially in trauma-focused work, structuring the therapeutic frame is best for all.

When Should the Therapist Stop EMDR Reprocessing?

Before actually starting the meeting, the therapist should calculate what time specifically they should be shutting down EMDR reprocessing using one of the below configurations: (a) Therapists will want to finish the EMDR reprocessing within at least 10 minutes (15 minutes maximum) before the end of 50-minute appointment to allow time for a short debriefing period and a stress-reduction exercise—if warranted. (b) For 90-minute sessions, leaving the last 15-minutes is adequate for debriefing and stress-reduction exercise if needed. (c) Therapists are encouraged to write down the stop time on a note pad before starting the meeting to prevent confusion at the end.

Looking for Appropriate Times to Finish EMDR Reprocessing

As the session nears the desired stopping time, the therapist should close (a) at a natural pause or plateau after reprocessing, (b) when the client reports positive reshifting of information or insight, (c) after coming down from an abreaction, (d) upon completion of the reprocessing phase, (e) upon completion of the installation phase, (f) after a shift to a positive memory, or (g) after reevaluating the target memory.

Procedure for Closing a Complete Session

An EMDR reprocessing session is considered *complete* with a SUDS of "0" (or "1" if ecologically valid), a VOC of "7" (or "6" if ecologically valid), and a body scan clear of any residual negative physical sensations associated with a target memory. Within 10 minutes (of a 50-minute session) to the end of the meeting, the therapist should inform the client that *"We are almost out of time, is it okay to stop here?"* The therapist then offers encouragement to the client: *"You have really done some good work today. How are you feeling?"* or words to that effect. A completed EMDR reprocessing session does not mean completion of treatment, which is determined by reprocessing the three-pronged protocol consisting of all of the selected targeted memories in the past, the current triggers, and future template, as well as other disturbing memories in the maladaptive neural network.

Procedure for Closing an Incomplete Session

In an incomplete EMDR reprocessing session, the target memory has not been fully reprocessed. This is exemplified by a SUDS rating of the target memory as above a "1," an incomplete installation phase with a VOC below a "6," or of an incomplete body scan that registers on client reports of unpleasant, negative-valence physical sensations associated with the target memory. When shutting down an incomplete reprocessing session, the therapists is recommended to provide the client sufficient time to debrief with the therapist about the experience in the session, and to ensure that the client has adequate time to prepare to safely leave the office. Below is the suggested framework for therapists to use for closing down an incomplete session:

1. Respectfully explain to the client that *"We are almost out of time, is it okay to stop here?"* If on the off chance that the client does not respond or communicates an unwillingness to stop, using a sensitive but firm voice, say, *"I'm really sorry about that, but we have to end now, and we can pick things up again next week."*

2. Re-assess the target memory. *"Ok, I'd like you to please go back to the memory of the ___ incident…. What do you notice now?"* Write down the client's responses. Obtain a SUDS rating: *"As you are thinking about the___ incident now, on a scale of 0–10, how distressed do you feel now?"* Write down the client's response. The therapist should understand that by returning to and re-accessing the target memory, there is a possibility for negative associations to emerge. If that happens, respectfully say, *"Ok … well how about we pick this up again next week; does that sound all right to you?"*

Clinical note. Shapiro (2001) posits that returning the client to the target memory during an incomplete reprocessing session will reactivate the target memory. That is true. The issue is whether this will unnecessarily distress or destabilize the client. The client is not being redirected to a picture or image of the original target memory, just the memory itself. The SUDS rating taken does not include the negative cognition, emotions, or physical sensations associated with the target memory. There is no empirical support one way or the other, but clinically it has proven useful to recheck the target memory and obtain a SUDS measure at the end of every session. Here's why: (a) It provides feedback to the client and the therapist about treatment progress. (b) When progress is made, either by a decrease in SUDS, or new, sometimes adaptive information associated with the target memory—in either case it may help inspire the client and motivate him or her to continue. (c) It allows the therapist to record treatment progress in the clinical notes. (d) If little to no progress is reported, the SUDS provides input to the therapist to check for possible blocking beliefs, alter speed, direction, or type of bilateral stimulation, or other mid-course corrections. (e) It offers information on progress or lack of progress to be debriefed at the end of the session. (f) Military culture is extremely results-oriented, even small shifts in target memory, or new negative associations that may arise, but can be reinforced as evidence of shifting or changing that may motivate a return visit. (g) After having the occasional client never return to therapy, call, or answer calls to explain, it seems best to create the opportunity for upfront talk on the client's progress or lack thereof. (h) The author (Mark Russell) has never had a military client require further intervention for being re-triggered by the brief access and rating taking.

3. If the therapist believes the client is too fragile and/or needs to avoid returning to and re-accessing the target memory and the maladaptive neural network it is linked to, the therapist can just ask for a generalized

rating of the level of the client's distress without returning to the target memory: *"On a scale of 0–10, how distressed do you feel now?"*

4. Stabilization. If the therapist observes or the client discloses that he or she is still fixed to negative material, the therapist can redirect the client's attentional focus to the adaptive neural network by implementing a brief stress-reduction technique such as calm/safe place, combat/tactical breathing, or other containment exercise.

Debriefing the Experience

Francine Shapiro (2001) developed a script for therapists to use for debriefing their clients about the possible residual effects of continued reprocessing: "Processing may continue after our session. You may or may not notice new insights, thoughts, memories, physical sensations or dreams. Please make a note in your log of whatever you notice. Then do a Calm/Safe Place or [Combat/Tactical Breathing—added by Mark Russell] exercise to rid yourself of the disturbance. We will talk about that at our next session. If you feel it is necessary, call me" (p. 429). Therapists can develop their own debriefing statement that better suits them and their clients; however, they should preserve the key messages: (a) reprocessing may continue after the session; (b) new memories, feelings, insights, dreams may arise; (c) suggest clients write down any changes and bring to next session; (d) if distressed, remind clients to utilize a stress-reduction technique; and (e) review the safety plan if clients are having dangerous thoughts.

Keeping a TICES Log

Maintaining a brief TICES (Trigger, Image, Cognition, Emotion, and Sensation) log or other self-monitoring tool as events arise has been a staple recommendation in EMDR circles for years. If therapists ask clients to keep a log, they should ask about it at the beginning of a session. The therapist's failure to follow through communicates that either the task itself was not really important, or the client's time and effort to comply was inconsequential. Albeit a minor issue, it can lead the client to question the sincerity or legitimacy of other communications from the therapist. So if you ask—you check.

PHASE EIGHT: REEVALUATION

The reevaluation phase of EMDR treatment occurs at the beginning of every EMDR session after the initial meeting. The main purpose is to assess the client's condition in relation to the extent of integration of reprocessed information as well as check for the emergence of new information that may have been stimulated by the previous reprocessing session.

Transitioning from Welcoming to EMDR Reevaluation

After warmly greeting their client, therapists often start a session with a general question as to the client's welfare (e.g., "So, how have you been __?"). The client's response may or may not refer specifically to EMDR treatment or its effects. Therapists working with a 50-minute framework need to closely monitor the amount of time the client uses to bring the therapist up to speed. Obviously, if the client is reporting personally significant or meaningful events, or is in crisis, then that needs to be taken into consideration. Some clients have a lot to say, and others barely whisper. At this juncture, the therapist has not inquired about any EMDR-specific changes. Therapists will want to pay attention to their client's particular pattern during this re-capping and reevaluation phase and to make adjustments if needed to curtail. It has been estimated that, in a given 50-minute session, actual time allotted for reprocessing is around 30 minutes when sessions are well structured (e.g., Leeds, 2009). That's not a lot of time.

Conducting the EMDR Reevaluation

There are essentially four ways the therapist might reevaluate their EMDR work with clients:

1. Reevaluate Between-Session Changes:

- Consequently, therapists might want to consider altering their opening remark by combining their welcoming greeting and initiating the EMDR reevaluation: *"Hi, how are you ___?"* Immediately afterward: *"What have you noticed since our last session? Has anything changed?"* or words to that effect.
- If the client launches into a general review of events from the past week, the therapist should look for the first break or pause and redirect the client's attention to any residual effects from the previous reprocessing session, *"Wow, a lot's happened with you! By the way, speaking of happening, what have you noticed after our last EMDR sessions? Has anything changed?"*
- Therapist should take note of the client's self-report of changes within the memory, new associations, insights, thoughts, images, feelings, and dreams. If clinically salient, the client might include any new associations as past events, current triggers, or future desired behavior to be added to the treatment plan.
- Next, the therapist should ask if the client kept a log or wrote down any observations since the last session?
- If so, ask if it's all right for you to see the log (or whatever term the client uses). If they are not comfortable with the therapist having the entire log, ask if the client would please read it or a portion of it.

- If the client is embarrassed or uncomfortable with sharing the log contents, or the more likely scenario, that the client did not keep or bring a written record, simply ask *"What have you noticed since our last session? What's changed?"*
- One of the important pieces of information that can often be glossed over is to ask the client whether anyone at work, home, or friends had commented about changes in the client, or had behaved differently towards the client because of the changes that have occurred?

Adopting a systems-lens, we might anticipate that if changes are becoming evident in the client's behavior, that the client's subsystems (e.g., partner, coworkers, family members, etc.) may respond positively or negatively to support or negate those changes. Sometimes clients harbor ambivalence about their own change and the prospects of becoming healthier through therapy. Some may fear that "getting better" may have an unpleasant side-effect. Therefore, when clients report observable change in their own behavior, it's often fruitful for the therapist to inquire about how others may have responded to those positive changes. Another reason this is an important question during the reevaluation is that it provides the therapist valuable information about the client's perceived level of social support and recovery environment that we know is vital for sustaining improvement or relapse.

Transitioning to EMDR Reprocessing

Once the therapist has welcomed the client, reviewed the client's log (if applicable), and inquired about any possible changes that she or others may have noticed since the last meeting, the therapist will ask the client to re-access the target memory in preparation for continued EMDR processing.

2. Reevaluate Target Memory from Previous Sessions:

- Therapists should be comfortable with rechecking their work. If the last meeting resulted in an incomplete session, we check the target memory. And, if the previous session ended as a complete session, meaning the client's SUDS was "0," VOC was "7," and the body scan was clear of negative residual symptoms—we check the target memory.
- Because of the brain's plasticity and how information can be shifted, or re-organized, we always want to check to be certain if those adaptive changes have continued or even strengthened, or conversely, that new negative associations may have emerged.
- The therapist would say *"Bring up the incident of _____ that we worked on last session* (try to name the incident; e.g., "Mess tent bombing" to ensure client is recalling the correct target memory). *What image comes up? What thoughts about it come up? What thoughts about*

yourself? What emotions? What sensations? And, on a scale of 0–10 (SUDS), how disturbing does this memory/trigger feel to you now?

3. Reprocessing the Target Memory from an Incomplete Session

If the previous session was an incomplete session, then upon re-accessing and re-assessing (SUDS) the target memory, the therapist transitions right into reprocessing the target memory (Phase Four).

4. Reevaluating the Target Memory from a Complete Session

- When reevaluating a targeted memory for completeness of its resolution, all of the following are evaluated for any indication of dysfunction:
  a. *Resolution of primary issue*—a SUDS of "0," VOC of "7," and body scan clear of any residual negative physical sensations.
  b. *Ecological validity*—a SUDS of "1" or VOC of "6" is reported and appears valid given the client's combat buddy died and no other blocking beliefs were identified.
  c. *Has associated material been activated that must be addressed?* When re-accessing the target memory, any new negative associations need to be reprocessed until resolution.
  d. *Resistance*—if the therapist suspects the client is still ambivalent about changing their condition, he might ask, "What would happen if you were successful? And reprocess either the client's overt response or just tell the client "to think about it" and add BLS.
- Any negative associations that arise in the reevaluation will become the focus of reprocessing before moving on. Continue reprocessing and re-assess the original target memory until the target is completely resolved (SUDS = "0," VOC = "7," Body Scan = clear).
- If the client reports a new current trigger emerged between sessions and requests to reprocess the triggering event, instead of an incomplete target from the previous session, the therapist can agree but must ensure that they return to and reassess the incomplete target and reprocess accordingly.
- Reprocessing continues until completion of the session and, ultimately, of the treatment plan.
- The final reevaluation session will occur after completion of the treatment plan that includes the three-pronged protocol of the past, present, and future targets. If the last target memory reveals negative associations have emerged, those are reprocessed until the last target memory is complete upon assessment (SUDS = "0/1"; VOC = "7/6"; and Body Scan = clear), at which time client is ready to terminate EMDR treatment.

Terminating EMDR Therapy

Once the therapist and client have completed processing all the target memories on the EMDR treatment plan and the positive effects have held at reevaluation, the therapist and client are ready to discuss termination of treatment. To assist the therapist and client in making a determination about the readiness for termination, Shapiro (2001) invites therapists to review the following four treatment goals:

1. Have all the necessary targets been reprocessed to allow the client to feel at peace with the past, empowered in the present, and able to make choices in the future? Has adequate assimilation been made with a healthy social system?
2. Has associated material been activated that must be addressed?
3. Have all the necessary targets been reprocessed to allow the client to feel at peace with the past, empowered in the present, and able to make choices in the future?
4. Has adequate assimilation been made with a healthy social system?

The Follow-up Session

Whenever practicable, it would be prudent to invite the client back after 1 month or so to check if the treatment effects have sustained over time. The therapist can repeat the reevaluation steps above. In addition to the SUDS and VOC baseline measures, therapists should ask the client to complete any previously used standardized symptom measures (e.g., PCL, BDI, IES, etc.). If any new negative associations arise, the therapist can discuss with the client about targeting those for reprocessing and so on. Should the therapist want to write a case study for a professional article, he or she should discuss such intentions with the client and explain how the client's identity and other healthcare information will be protected. When possible, the therapist should obtain the client's consent. The therapist can schedule additional in-person or phone check-ups if desired. For research purposes, follow-ups of 3, 6, and 12 months are not unusual but may not be practical or desired by clients or therapists.

Section IV
Special Considerations

15 Ethical and Medico-Legal Issues

There are several unique ethical and legal considerations when treating military clientele as compared to the civilian sector and several important issues specific to EMDR. We will review both aspects along with suggestions how to broach these topics with military populations.

Applicability: General Considerations

The degree to which this information may pertain directly to the therapist is contingent upon the therapist's contractual nature or legally binding relationship with the Department of Defense (DoD). For military mental health practitioners in the Air Force, Army, and Navy, it all applies; for DoD civilians, most of it will apply; and, for civilian therapists not affiliated with the military, little to none may apply—however with one exception. Issues around ethical and legal issues in the military will probably be meaningful to all military members who happen to be mental health clients.

Confidentiality of Mental Health Services for Military Personnel

The Fifth and Fourteenth Amendments to the U. S. Constitution established the fundamental right to privacy, by protecting American citizens against unwarranted invasions of their privacy by federal or state agencies. Individuals of legal age are endowed with the legal right to their privacy and are the holders of the legal privilege as to what private information to share or not. The notion of doctor-patient confidentiality is rooted in ethics dating back to the Roman Hippocratic Oath, to which physicians swore allegiance. That notion became incorporated into English Common Law, eventually being adopted by state laws. It is different than the legal concept of a doctor-patient privilege. Legal privilege involves the right to withhold evidence from discovery and/or the right to refuse disclosing private information gained within the context of a special relationship. Special relationships include those between husbands and wives, doctors and patients, attorneys and clients, and clergy and confiders. Mental health practitioners are beholden to comply with pertinent state and federal laws governing the practice and conduct for their profession as well as adhere to the ethical standards of their particular discipline. Military and other employees of the Department of Defense fall under federal and military legal jurisdiction. Mental health practitioners in the government are licensed by the states but must adhere to federal law first.

- The privilege is subject to mandatory reporting duties under not only federal and state law but also *service regulations:*
  - For example, does the member have a disqualifying condition for submarine duty such as the presence of psychopathology including personality disorder, or the inability to function in crowded, confined quarters per the *Manual of the Medical Department* (U.S. Department of the Navy, 1996).
- The privilege can be breached when it is necessary to ensure the safety and security of military personnel, dependents, property, classified information, or the accomplishment of a military mission:
  - Military personnel that present danger to self, others, or property
  - Commission of a crime in accordance with military law (UCMJ)
  - Fitness for duty determinations—a mental health condition that may impact:
    - Ability to deploy
    - Ability to remain or return to active duty
    - Ability to carry firearms or handle ordnance
    - Ability to maintain top-secret clearance
    - Ability to serve in operational or remote billets
    - Ability to perform all assigned duties without restriction
    - Ability to perform without jeopardizing the mission
    - Ability to be assigned special duty (e.g., recruiting, drill instructor).

Multiple Relationships

For military mental health practitioners, there are multiple "clients" to whom they have a duty to protect their "interests" and "well-being": (a) the military client, (b) the military client's command readiness, and (c) the overall military mission. It seems complicated; most readers not contractually obligated in the military are probably thinking they are glad not to worry about all of this—well, sort of.

ISSUES OF CONFIDENTIALITY FOR MILITARY PERSONNEL

As indicated above, the military client–psychotherapist privilege grants and even requires that the therapist disclose considerably more confidential information without client consent than in the civilian sector—and the main reason has to do with national security and the military mission. For example, "fitness for duty" is the buzzword in the military referring to a service member's physical and mental capacity to perform assigned duties to the fullest extent including deployment and going to war. If the clinician has identified or diagnosed a mental health condition (e.g., PTSD) that may be a risk to self, others, property, or the ability to fulfill any duty required, then the therapist is required to inform that individual's Commanding Officer or Commander (Army). Theoretically, so the safety of the client and those around them, as well as the security of the mission, will not be jeopardized. We will get back to that later in terms of what information is actually disclosed. Mental health practitioners, however, are also bound to follow their state licensing laws and the ethical standards of their profession—especially pertaining to the welfare of the client. Boundaries for confidentiality are grounded from ethical principles weighing the rights and interests of the individual and the group. In the military, the complexities surrounding confidentiality are considerably more complicated by notions of "fitness for duty," "mission impact," and "need to know." As mentioned in Chapter 5, the military member's Commanding Officer/Commander has a "need-to-know" about any physical and mental health condition that may negatively impact the safety of the command personnel and/or the military unit/command's ability to complete the military mission without hindrance. The military client's Commanding Officer/Commander is responsible and held accountable for what happens to their personnel and the unit performance. They are the ones who write the letters informing families that their loved ones have died—all of which creates the "need-to-know"—extending the duty to warn and protect.

"Civilian" (Non-DoD) Therapists and Confidentiality

For non-DoD-affiliated therapists, the federal/military exceptions to psychotherapist privilege do not apply. Here is the rub: they do apply to the military client! Civilian (non-DoD) mental health records containing assessment, diagnosis, treatment, etc., are confidential and protected under state and federal (e.g., HIPAA) statues; however, the military client is obligated to notify their respective medical department or command if they have any condition that might be a disqualifying or effect their "military readiness." Annually, if not more frequently, military clients have to update their medical readiness status, which usually involves having to sign a screening form whereby they must disclose experiencing certain symptoms or conditions—such as treatment for particular medical and neuropsychiatric conditions. If they report no such symptoms or conditions and if it is later discovered they were being deceptive, then a lot of things can happen—none of them positive. Falsification of an official record (e.g., medical screening forms) is a violation of military law (Uniformed Code of Military Justice; UCMJ). The therapist should assume that military clients are unaware of the ramifications if they attempt to conceal or falsify records rather than vice versa. By simply saying to clients,

"If your job has any special requirements for you to notify medical or your command about a mental health diagnosis, it's best to be truthful rather than to conceal something that might come back to bite you. If you're unsure about what if anything you need to disclose about your receiving therapy, then please contact your JAG for a confidential consultation. I'm telling you all of this because I care what happens to you and don't want you to be blindsided by anything. I myself will not disclose any information to your command, unless you tell me to or give me signed permission—or one of those other reasons we talked about earlier (e.g., danger to self, child or spouse abuse, etc.). So, what we're talking about is what, *if any*, obligation you might have to give folks at medical a heads-up. Like for example, if you got orders to deploy tomorrow, it probably would not help you to then tell your command that you shouldn't because of x, y, z … does that make sense?" If there is an accident or incident, and the customary investigation determines that the service member had a diagnosis that is incompatible with his or her assigned duties (e.g., piloting a jet), and the member had intentionally made false statements to conceal that fact—well, the reader can see where this is going.

Reviewing Limits of Confidentiality

This is why it's critical that therapists be aware of and dutifully inform their military clients of the full, potential limits of confidentiality that pertain not only to the psychotherapist-client privilege, but also to potential obligations that the client may have for disclosure to their commands regarding special qualifications or military readiness issues. Therapists, even those on active-duty, are not expected to know every requirement for every military job; therefore the burden of notification typically falls upon the military client. Bear in mind that most military positions do not have stringent qualification and notification requirements, and that many times medical and command personnel in those specialized jobs want to work with the individually so they can receive proper treatment that won't negatively impact their qualifications or careers. The military has invested a lot of resources in training service members for these specialized roles and most commands, and will, therefore, desperately try to avoid losing valuable personnel, and will go to great lengths to take actions to help their people and their military careers. However, if officials are not informed and issues are raised after the fact—then that ship has sailed.

The Therapist's Duty and Confidentiality

The therapist's duty is to properly advise clients that they need to consider if any information related to diagnosis may require them to notify medical or unit leaders. If they are uncertain about what, if any duty they have in terms of disclosure, they should be advised to contact the JAG for a confidential consultation. The main emphasis here is that it is always better to be as "above board" as possible, and avoid situations that can blindside or negatively impact the client's welfare. Therapists need to cover all bases of the limits of confidentiality with their clients at the outset of the initial session and to try doing so in a matter of fact manner that doesn't scare away clients. The more knowledgeable the therapist is, the better he or she will be at managing the client's natural anxiety around the confidentiality issue.

Disclosures on a "Need-to-Know Basis"

If the therapist does have a "need-to-know" obligation, then they should inform the client about what kinds of information would be communicated to the command either verbally and/or via written assessment or treatment summary, as well as to whom this information would be given. Many military units have their own medical detachment, and this typically is the liaison point for the therapist and the client's command and most, if not all issues. If unit medical is not available, the therapist should communicate to the client's Commanding Officer/Commander, Executive Officer, or the senior enlisted leader. The purpose is to limit the amount of disclosure to only those with a need to know. If after hours, that may be the Command Duty Officer or whomever is designated as the senior person at the command. Therapists should generally not be communicating to the military client's NCO or SNCO or Division Officer, in other words, the client's immediate work center supervisors, unless no other command leaders are available. In many cases, the therapist will collaborate with the client as to who to notify at their command, unless it's a command directed evaluation. Whenever possible, let the client read the draft of the written report and discuss the content or phrasing.

What information can be disclosed? If it's a safety issue, then the client's mental status in terms of dangerousness, gross incapacitation (e.g., psychotic reaction), recommendations, and, if applicable, their fitness for duty (e.g., should they be carrying a weapon, etc.). These determinations are almost always made by a military or civilian-DoD psychiatrist or psychologist, but if a non-DoD therapist has similar urgent concerns, then they should attempt to get the client to sign a release, or refer the client to the emergency room department (ERD) at the base clinic, or, in the case of an acute emergency, contact either the military ERD or 911. This is why it's critical for therapists to work out the "what if" scenarios should a client enter into an acute crises. The therapist should inform the client that details about his or her past history, or contents of any discussion in the therapy office, or any other such issues, will not be released.

Malingering

Malingering is the intentional deception of impairment for the sake of personal gain (e.g., disability pension) or escape from undesired duty (e.g., avoiding deployment). It is a complicated clinical issue, and, in the military, it is a crime punishable under the Uniformed Code of Military Justice (UCMJ): *Act 915. Art. 115. Malingering:* Any person subject to this chapter who for the purpose of avoiding work, duty, or service

1. Feigns illness, physical disablement, mental lapse, or derangement; or
2. Intentionally inflicts self-injury shall be punished as a court-martial may direct.

Most therapists want to believe that their clients are being truthful and do not suspect deceitful intension—and, most of the time, they are correct. However, some clients are not seeking the truth, they are actively avoiding it. With military populations in particular, the therapist may encounter a moral dilemma never before imagined. This is more true for active-duty and DoD-civilian therapists, who are usually the ones who make the judgment call over whether to challenge a military client suspected or known to be malingering or to look the other way, especially if, by confrontation, the client might face jail time or possibly worse—being maimed or killed in war. Military clinical psychologists and psychiatrists are routinely put into these gut-wrenching decisions. Some take the simple, personally convenient route, by either always siding for or against the military client. The M-16 wielding "therapists" view their client as the military mission, and if they can go to the sandpit and kick down doors, then everyone else should too. Yes, they exist. Conversely, therapists who routinely shirk from any culpability may think they are saving their clients, but they are too self-focused to think of the other service members who must go in place of their clients (or of the families of those who serve). Yes, they exist too. And yes, somebody always must go. Those choosing the middle ground must wrestle with their conscience and the larger picture on a case-by-case basis and are more susceptible to compassion stress and fatigue—the price for caring.

Special Ethical and Legal Considerations with EMDR Use in the Military

As of this date, using EMDR is not in violation of the UCMJ, nor is it a Courts-Martial offense. The jury is still yet out in regards to researching EMDR in institutional military medicine.

Ethics and EMDR

Readers are probably familiar with the caution of using EMDR with eye witnesses or victims before or during legal testimony (see Shapiro, 2001). The same would apply for witness testimony in a military Courts Martial. The concern being that reprocessed memories may interfere with the effectiveness of client's testimony. Therapists are advised to consult with the client and his or her attorney (if necessary).

Client Welfare and EMDR Treatment Planning

A much more common scenario is the clinical decision when or if to use EMDR and what protocol based upon the referral question, time and environmental constraints, client preference, and clinical judgment (see Chapter 5, this volume). Therapists' clinical decision-making should be informed by their knowledge of the ethical principles and standards of their profession—at a minimum—"Do no harm." This means that when the referral source and/or clients are requesting EMDR, and the therapist is concerned about the client's suitability for EMDR, that whatever decision is make has the client's best interest in mind. One hopes, of course, to collaborate with clients and to avoid an adversarial role, but, in the end, the therapist and client will be best served by doing what is right. Most ethical by-laws recommend consultation, and that would be most prudent to consider before making a final decision. It may be that the therapist may feel uneasy or not so confident about using EMDR with a certain client or set of problems, but otherwise the client would be considered stable and suitable. Therapists need to consider the treatment setting and timing issues seriously and will want to avoid reprocessing traumatic events from early in life within a few days of a major transition or event for the client. Conversely, therapists should not feel intimidated to not offer and use EMDR with military clients whenever appropriate. There might not be another opportunity to help this military client, so if no clear contra-indicators are present and the client is dutifully informed, "do no harm" can also be translated as "don't withhold."

Boundaries of Competence

Therapists need to practice within the scope of their competence and, again, be open to seeking professional consultation. Be sure to document when consultation occurs in the record. Some therapists might say to themselves that as they have never treated phantom-limb pain or medically unexplained conditions, they are not competent to do so with EMDR. As long as the therapist is clear in his mind and can articulate to the clients and others involved that EMDR is not a treatment *for* pain, (pseudo)seizures, TBI, major depression, substance abuse, etc., but is rather an evidence-based treatment for reprocessing experiential contributors that might be contributing to whatever symptoms are present, then the therapist should be on solid ground in justifying the use of EMDR beyond the PTSD diagnosis. Clients are less likely to bolt right away if their pain, fatigue, and associated problems are accepted (validated) as absolutely real, and all we can offer with EMDR is to help them with the frustrations and aggravations that have built up over the years and continue today, that we know (and they know) do contribute or make things worse. Where EMDR clinicians can run into turbulent waters is in not being precise in describing the AIP model and how it applies to these other conditions. Having familiarity with the literature will help assure there is some empirical support even in the form of published case studies in peer reviewed journals—something to counter an impression of loose cannons trying to cure leprosy with a wave of the hand.

16 Enhancing Resilience/ Performance and Preventing Compassion Stress Injury

In this chapter, we will examine how modified EMDR protocols may be effective in strengthening resilience and improving work performance of members in the military population, as well as vital self-care for warrior healers.

RESILIENCE AND POST-TRAUMATIC GROWTH IN THE MILITARY

The concept of resilience has been defined as the capacity to resist and bounce back from adversity. Since antiquity, military powers worldwide have had a vested interest in the physical and mental strengthening of its armies to avert the ravages of war stress, while at the same time devising new methods of delivering the potent effects of combat stress to break the resilience of its enemies. Historically, after every major conflict since the First Great War (1914–1918) to end all wars, military organizations and their supportive governments have gone to great lengths to prevent the scourge of escalating rates of war stress injury.

Contemporary Approach to Building the Resilient Warrior

In the January 2011 issue of the *American Psychologist*, Brigadier General Rhonda Cornum, Comprehensive Soldier Fitness, Headquarters, Department of the Army, indicated that psychology's "business as usual" reaction to war stress injuries has missed the mark by overemphasizing treatment of a problem that it should be preventing. The Army's "all-in" adoption of the relatively untested fruit of positive psychology has yet to prove capable of steeling human minds to resist and bounce back from the toxic adversity of war. History does not appear to be on the Army's side, but we pray to be wrong. Meanwhile an all-out effort is underway to develop new strategies for improving resilience and post-traumatic growth within the military population. According to Zoellner and Maercker (2006, cited in Tedeschi & McNally, 2011), posttraumatic growth may be nurtured via psychotherapy through cognitive processing, supporting attempts at mastery of new experiences, and enhancing relationships. Tedeschi and McNally (2011) delineated a strategy for the U.S. Army's massive Comprehensive Soldier Fitness program to promote posttraumatic growth by enhancing certain key elements such as emotional regulation, constructive self-disclosure, and organizing a war narrative that includes central domains of personal strength, enhanced relationships, spiritual change, appreciation of life, and openness to new possibilities. As Congress and the Department of Defense have invested $125 million into researching nascent interventions to avert war stress injuries, we thought it appropriate to add similarly unproven, yet highly promising approaches to strengthening resilience and enhancing performance of military personnel. In particular, two modified EMDR protocols have demonstrated considerable untapped potential to assist service members: Resource Development and Installation (RDI) and Brief Intervention Focusing Protocol (BIFP).

EMDR APPLICATIONS FOR IMPROVING RESILIENCE AND PERFORMANCE

In regards to the prevention of war stress injury, the *DVA/DoD Clinical Practice Guidelines for the Management of Post-Traumatic Stress* (2010) indicate that little is directly known about our capacity to prepare individuals or communities for trauma exposure, but it is possible to identify principles of preparation that are consistent with empirical research on risk and resilience factors and with current theories of PTSD development. Such pre-trauma preparation can include attention to both the ability to cope during the trauma itself and shaping the post-trauma environment so that it will foster post-trauma adaptation. Other theories suggest that individuals who develop negative trauma-related beliefs (e.g., about personal guilt) will be more likely to experience continuing trauma reactions because such beliefs will maintain a sense of threat and personal incompetence. Research on risk factors for PTSD indicates that post-trauma social support and life stress affect the likelihood of development of the disorder.

A few EMDR-related protocols have been developed with the purpose of increasing resilience and work performance, some with published case studies to support their replication. Interested readers are referred to Luber (2009). We selected RDI (Korn & Leeds, 2002) because it has been incorporated in standard EMDR trainings and shown to have clinical effectiveness in stabilizing chronically distressed clients by increasing access to their adaptive neural networks-which is the essence of resilience. Lendl and Foster's (2009) *Brief Intervention Focusing Protocol* has instant appeal by offering a quick, simple intervention to potentially reduce internal and external distractions such as performance anxiety, fear of failure that prevent military personnel from performing to the best of their ability in high-stress operational environments. Unfortunately, the body of research for either technique is waning. However, published case studies in peer-reviewed journals indicate that therapists and researchers are justified to replicate their use and expand the empirical literature on future innovation and human resilience.

Resource Development and Installation (RDI)

RDI is an effective, brief intervention, modeled after EMDR that was originally designed to prepare emotionally and behaviorally unstable clients for the intensity of trauma-focused therapy (Korn & Leeds, 2002). Adult clients who experienced years of childhood abuse, neglect, and other adverse childhood experiences may develop conditions known as "complex PTSD" "Borderline Personality Disorder," or "Disorders of Extreme Stress Not Otherwise Specified (DESNOS)" all characterized by poor affect tolerance, impulsivity, insecure attachment, suicidal ideation, inadequate self-regulation and coping, poor self-esteem and self-worth, and so on. It would be an understatement to label this a high-risk group for the emotionally potent and painful trauma-focused therapy. RDI has been shown clinically to significantly help stabilize this high at-risk group of adult clients to acquire sufficient levels of self-control, stress-coping, mastery, confidence, and self-esteem skills to undergo trauma-focused treatment like EMDR.

Would a brief, relatively simple, strength-based protocol, coupled with short-sets of eye movements or other bilateral stimulation have any application for building resilience and enhancing performance of military personnel—absolutely. What are resources? Leeds (2009) describes resources as natural experiences that develop out of three categories of experience: mastery memories, relational resources, and symbols. Recollections of past successes and achievement, assertiveness, and self-care are examples of mastery experiences. The supportive people in our life, those who have taken care of us, showed us kindness, mentored, nurtured, or coached us, helped celebrate our victories, and consoled us in our defeats, have become internal "resources" in our lives, their legacy resonating in the adaptive neural networks that we have been working throughout this text. Other types of relational resources are people we look up to and revere, or marvel at their strength, stamina, honesty, humility, integrity, or courage. These role models often inspire us to follow in their worthy footsteps. Role models may also be historical figures, superheroes, or an action-movie star. The third category of resource pertains to the symbols and metaphors that originate out of our cultural, religious, or spiritual worlds, including dreams and archetypes, as well as a future goal or sense of self that beckons (see Chapter 6, this volume, for the RDI protocol).

BRIEF INTERVENTION FOCUSING PROTOCOL

Jennifer Lendl and Sandra Foster (2009) have developed an EMDR variant, the Brief Intervention Focusing Protocol (BIFP). The BIFP is a rapid, time-sensitive, task-oriented protocol that utilizes bilateral stimulation (BLS) and the future template from EMDR but emphasizes only strengthening or enhancing future-oriented performance issues by decreasing performance-related anxiety, fear of failure, self-defeating beliefs, worries of past setbacks, and other behavioral inhibitions which can interfere with individuals performing at their full-potential. The BIFP was initially developed for creative artists and professional performers but has since been implemented successfully with Olympic athletes and business leaders. Case studies (e.g., Foster & Lendl, 1996) and controlled research on master swimmers (Linebarger, 2005, cited in Lendl & Foster, 2009) lend some empirical support. It was designed to enhance imminent performance—by reducing internal and external distractions and fostering self-confidence that lead to off-task behaviors. Anything outside of the present task is regarded as an intrusion. Internal distractions (e.g., self-defeating thoughts, worrying, performance anxiety, or fear of failure) and external distractions from environmental conditions (e.g., crowd noise) are set aside as expediently as possible so the client can fully focus on the mission task. Client strengths as well as areas where improvement is needed are identified through a series of questions: (a) What abilities are needed? (b) What deficits exist in education, training, or emotional management? (c) Do they have the ability to stay present? (d) What distractions impair focus? (e) What motivates them? And (f) Do they have a sense of life purpose?

Brief Intervention Focusing Protocol (see Lendl & Foster, 2009)

1. **Establish the hours available to do the intervention and explain the protocol to the client**. "We can work on past issues when we have more time. For now, we'll focus on what you can do for this event. We will set aside any distractions and concentrate on the specific elements of your upcoming performance and what you are already prepared to do for it."

2. **Quickly identify internal and external distractions. Have the client determine each distractions importance and immediacy in regards to the upcoming performance.** "What thoughts or distractions get in the way of your having confidence in your upcoming event?" For example: "I'm worried about letting people down," or "I'm not prepared." Next, the therapist says, "Can you put them in order of importance?"

3. **Help the client problem solve around each distraction and do short saccades while they visualize the solution**:
   - "What is the problem that is getting in the way of _____ (state what the goal is)?"
   - "What can you do to take care of ____ (state what the issue is) before the event?"
   - "Good; imagine ___ (state the solution)."—Do BLS (eye movement: 6–12 sets)
   - "What can you do during the event to make sure that __ (state the issue) is taken care of?"
   - "Good, imagine ____ (state the solution)."—Do BLS (6–12 sets)

4. **Assist the client in letting go of the distractions when they intrude.** "Think of your event. When an intrusion comes up, ask yourself, 'Is this thought useful right now?' Remember your solution ____ (state the solution), and then refocus on the task by saying, 'What is my job right now for this event?'"—Do BLS (6–12 sets)

"Remember how important it is to stay focused on the event. There is limited time. You need to stay present and let go of any concerns to get the best possible results. To this end it is useful to hold the intention, 'I will move through my performance, staying on task, no matter what comes up.'"

5. **Assist the client with installing an Expanded Future Template as follows:** "Please imagine the entire performance. When a distraction intrudes, ask yourself, 'Is this useful right now?' Build in a plan. Go back on task by saying, 'What is my job right now?' And continue until you can visualize the entire event. Imagine the event as fully as possible and notice your posture, muscle movements, voice quality, gestures, and so forth. Let me know when a distraction arises, and we'll use BLS to help move it to the background by putting a plan in place and returning to the task."

6. **Continue this until the client can move smoothly through the entire performance.**

7. **Using BLS, install the entire performance from start to finish with the client staying focused on the task throughout:** "Now that you have your distractions under control, please run your performance from start to finish, feeling your body fully." "We will use BLS let me know when you're finished." Do BLS (6–12 sets)

COMPASSION STRESS INJURY IN THE HEALERS OF WARRIORS AND EMDR

The occupational hazards in the military are regular exposure to chronic, inescapable, and potentially traumatic stress. Exposure to stressors such as war or combat does not predestine one to cultivate war stress injury. In fact, many who have gone to war report quite positive stress effects and even post-traumatic growth. A similar two-sided coin exists with other vocations. Helping professions, particularly psychotherapists and the healers of warriors, endure occupational hazards of exposure to chronic stress and traumatic events that may lead to compassion-stress injury such as compassion fatigue or burnout, as well as increased compassion satisfaction or traumatic growth (Figley, 2002). The variety of labels used to describe the phenomenon (e.g., secondary, vicarious, and fatigue) are accurate, but incomplete. They imply that the exposure to someone's trauma or PTSD symptoms was either somehow internalized or ingested by the witnessing person, or that the helper is temporarily in a tired or exhausted state, just needing rest—precisely the military's thinking when terms like "battle fatigue" and "combat exhaustion" were adopted in favor of shell shock and traumatic neurosis. Anyone with the capacity for experiencing compassion, empathy, concern and caring is vulnerable to compassion-stress injury. We try to stay within professional boundaries and adhere to training guidelines, but our greatest strength (empathy) is also our greatest vulnerability. Not a characteristic most in the helping professions want to give up.

The Healer Occupational Hazards

There is a dose-response relationship with the more intense the traumatic circumstances of the clients, the cumulative effects pose greater risk to the therapist. Other risks include: (a) repeated exposure to traumatic events, (b) exposure to intense emotional or physical pain, (c) carrying out difficult and exhausting tasks, (d) exposure to unusual demands to meet others' needs, (e) feelings of helplessness, (f) frequently facing moral/ethical dilemmas, (g) exposure to anger and/or lack of gratitude, (h) frustration with bureaucratic policies, (i) heightened sense of lack of control, and (j) being reminded of one's own traumatic experiences. In terms of symptoms, compassion stress and fatigue invoke the similar spectrum of physical, cognitive, social, emotional, spiritual, and behavioral effects of human adaptation to chronic, inescapable, and potentially traumatic stress (e.g., Figley, 2002).

Therapists' Potential Impairment Indicators (The Silencing Response)

In regards to their relationship with clients, therapists experiencing compassion fatigue sense a reduction in their baseline empathy for others, feel numb to patients' and families' pain, are cynical regarding clients' ability to change, and/or perceive them as being responsible for many of their problems. In addition, certain "silencing behaviors" may be evident: (a) avoiding certain topics, (b) providing pat answers, (c) minimizing client distress, (d) suggesting the client "get over it," (e) feeling boredom during sessions, (f) expressing anger or sarcasm towards clients, (g) using humor to change or minimize the subject, (h) feeling incompetent, (i) faking interest or pretending to listen, (j) fearing what the client may say, (k) blaming clients for their experiences, (l) difficulty paying attention, (m) being reminded of one's own traumatic experiences.

Prevalence of Compassion Fatigue

- Thirty-three percent of behavioral health personnel reported a "high level" of burnout (U.S. Army, 2008).
- Fifty percent of workers suffered from high or very high levels of trauma from helping others (Conrad & Kellar-Geunthar, 2006).

- Thirty-seven percent of child protective workers experienced clinical levels of emotional distress associated with secondary traumatic stress (Meyers & Cornille, 2002).

Prevention of Compassion Stress Injuries

As with other stress injuries, healers can be proactive and take steps to reduce risk factors and increase protective factors as a means to prevent cumulative effects of compassion stress. Those protective variables are: (a) be well rested, (b) utilize your positive supportive connections to process your feelings, (c) take negatives and turn them into positives, (d) know how to turn off thoughts about work to be more resilient during your career, (e) exercise, and (f) have good social support. Like war stress injuries, early identification and intervention is key to avoid chronic or long-term health effects.

USING EMDR TO PREVENT AND TREAT COMPASSION STRESS AND FATIGUE

Preventing Compassion Stress Injuries with EMDR

After the author's (Mark Russell) unceremonious introduction to the stark consequences of not practicing adequate self-care and taking compassion fatigue seriously, a search was made to ensure there would be no recurrence. Warning! If therapists allow a compassion-stress injury to progressively worsen to the point of collapse, there will usually be some modest to serious long-term health and professional repercussions. Transient, intermittent periods of compassion fatigue, like any stress-injury, are a common and often unavoidable hazard of the mental health occupation. However, unlike combat veterans and other survivors of traumatic stress injuries, compassion-stress injuries are entirely preventable.

Regular self-screening for compassion stress injury can be an effective way to monitor things, but we all need to have other means to assure the balance of protective factors far outweighs the inescapable risks. We all know that activities like regular physical exercise, recreation, social engagement, spirituality, relaxation, and moderation of diet are essential to keep us healthy, but they are absolutely critical to thwart the preventable type of chronic stress injury.

Case-Study: EMDR Compassion-Stress Prevention "Protocol"

Therefore, a compassion-stress EMDR "protocol" was researched, designed, and pilot tested by the author to avert the cumulative effects of exposure to chronic, inescapable, and potentially traumatic stress. After 3 years of implementing the self-care model, it is ready to be published in the public domain. The build-up is really overselling. In a nutshell, in addition to the traditional stress-management package, every day after work, or after a particularly stress-ful or demanding day, the author puts on the headphones from a Neurotek portable EMDR device and listens to the rapid bilateral tone, while recalling the daily events in mind. The images, thoughts, and visceral reactions are concentrated upon while listening to the BLS. On average, approximately 10 minutes a day will suffice, but if needed or on especially troublesome days, maybe a few minutes more. While still on active-duty, there was an old Neurotek in the work office, one of the first generations, but it still worked fine.

In 2008, a year before leaving, it was decided to incorporate EMDR into the compassion-stress management program in order to prevent the cumulative effects of ongoing stress and exposure to traumatic stress reactions from triggering a relapse. Therefore, every day at work, during the short breaks, in between seeing traumatized combat veterans, 10 minutes after the clinic closed (before returning home), and, upon arrival at the office, 10 minutes before the first client, time was devoted to the BLS—10 minutes of focusing on the BLS and sympathetic arousal, while thinking about the to-do list, specific clients, picturing answering the phone, or pager, and other stimuli that came to mind. Having implemented this "protocol," it has reduced the amount of total persistent war- and compassion-stress symptoms from a 9 to maybe a 3 on average. That may not sound impressive, but a steady 3 is well within the functional range. There have been no further seizures or the other debilitating compassion stress symptoms for the past 3 years despite maintaining a fairly high stress load. Whenever traumatic scenes either witnessed first-hand or internalized from patients arise, the headphones come on and the intrusions are put-down. It needs replication, clearly—and probably hundreds of providers have done the same for years. No false illusion of discovery here—it just needs to be researched. For the enterprising reader, review the earlier section on occupations and prevalence of compassion-stress injuries.

Case Study: EMDR Treatment of Compassion Stress Injury

A fourth issue in treating compassion fatigue is assessing and enhancing social support. Psychotherapists gradually view themselves as others view them: someone who is an expert at helping others cope with life's challenges. They seem to forget that they are human beings as well. A physician sometimes gets sick and needs another physician's services, for example. Often the therapist has a rather limited social support system composed of colleagues and only a few intimate relationships. It is vital to increase the therapist's support system in both numbers and variety of relationships so that she or he is viewed apart from the therapist persona. Moreover, some relationships may be a source of strain and stress. These toxic relationships are an additional demand and should be addressed (Figley, 1997).

Mitigating Mike's Compassion Fatigue

A man in his late thirties (Mike) sought treatment from the second author (Charles Figley). His presenting problem was his feelings of guilt about his mother's life-threatening condition and his inability to address his dysfunctional relationship with her.

Test results confirmed our assessment that he was suffering from compassion fatigue, a restricted social support network, and that he suffered from considerable traumatic stress. But rather than being the classic struggle between mother and son, it became obvious that there was some secret he had not disclosed yet. This secret was the fact that his mother was attacked by a dog and nearly killed and he felt somehow guilty about letting it happen, being the male.

During the next session, the treatment team shared the results with Mike, discussed the treatment options, and agreed upon a treatment plan. The plan was to increase his self-soothing and stress management skills (e.g., workbooks, video training), increase the number and variety of social supporters (e.g., through volunteer work and involvement in extracurricular activities), and utilize a cognitive-behavioral therapy approach that minimized exposure and clinical time that would result in desensitization (i.e., reduction or elimination of traumatic stress). He selected EMDR and the dog attack as the traumatic event. As an indicator of success, we would use the same case material he used in class (the young college student adjusting to being away and feeling guilty about leaving his anxious mother).

For the next five sessions, using EMDR, Mike worked through the dog attack, the first signs of his mother's chronic illness, his sacrifices, feelings of resentment toward his mother, and the embarrassments he felt—particularly during his teenage years—having to take care of her mother.

By the final session Mike's symptoms subsided (desensitization). He shifted from self-blame and self-hatred to a more realistic view of himself and his mother. The team discussed the clinical cases he found challenging were now interesting but rather routine. He recognized that he still has work to do; that he remains reactive around his mother. He is, however, patient with himself and confident that he knows that practice is necessary to be fully differentiated from his mother emotionally and, as a result, finds it easier to love and appreciate her.

Final Observations

It is vital that today's psychotherapists continue to work with empathy and compassion. Yet, there is a cost to this work that is obvious to any practitioner working with the suffering. As the evidence mounts proving the negative consequences of a lack of self-care and the presence of compassion stress injury, so will the ethical imperative for the suffering practitioner to do something or something will be done for him. We cannot afford to not attend to the mistakes, misjudgments, and blatant clinical errors of psychotherapists who suffer from compassion fatigue. It is, therefore, up to all of us to elevate these issues to a greater level of awareness in the helping professions. Otherwise we will lose clients and compassionate psychotherapists.

Resources for Compassion Fatigue Prevention and Treatment
When Helping Hurts: Sustaining Trauma Workers
Produced by Gift From Within
(207) 236-8858 www.giftfromwithin.org

Compassion Fatigue Self-Tests
Professional Quality of Life: Compassion Satisfaction and Fatigue Subscales-III (Hudnall Stamm 1995–2002)
Secondary Trauma Scale (Figley, 1995)

Appendix A
Military Mental Health Referral Resources

TRICARE
http://www.tricare.mil/mhshome.aspx
(877) 874-2273 North Region
(800) 403-3950 South Region
(888) 874-9378 West Region
(888) 363-2273 Main TRICARE Information Service number
TRICARE has three regional claims offices that can be contacted for information about healthcare benefits, including benefits for mental health and substance abuse services.

Deployment Health Clinical Center
http://www.pdhealth.mil/family.asp
The Deployment Health Clinical Center site offers a list of resources for service members and their families and a link to the Department of Defense Mental Health Self-Assessment Program (alcohol and mental health screening).

Center for the Study of Traumatic Stress
http://www.cstsonline.org

Defense and Veterans Brain Injury Center
http://www.dvbic.org

National Institute of Mental Health
http://www.nimh.nih.gov/health/topics/post-traumatic-stress-disorder-ptsd/index.shtml

Afterdeployment.org
http://www.afterdeployment.org

Walter Reed Army Institute of Research – Psychiatry & Neurosciences
http://wrair-www.army.mil/Psychiatry-and-Neuroscience

Military Treatment Facility Locator
http://www.tricare.mil/mtf

Center for Deployment Psychology
http://www.deploymentpsych.org/

Department of Veterans Affairs
http://www.va.gov
The official website for the Department of Veterans Affairs offers information about benefits for returning veterans, those who have lost a loved one, health insurance information, and a facility locator to help find the closest VA Medical Center and the services it offers.

Vet Centers
http://www1.va.gov/directory/guide/vetcenter_flsh.asp
Vet Centers provide readjustment counseling and outreach services to all veterans who served in any combat zone. Services are also available for their family members for military-related issues. Veterans have earned these benefits through their service, and all are provided at no cost to the veteran or family. The 207 community-based Vet Centers are located in all 50 states, District of Columbia, Guam, Puerto Rico, and the U.S. Virgin Islands

National Center for PTSD
http://www.ncptsd.va.gov

Military OneSource
http://www.militaryonesource.com
(800) 342-9647 (24-hour, toll-free number)
• ARMY—Army OneSource: 800-464-8107
• MARINES—Marines OneSource: 800-869-0278
• NAVY—Navy OneSource: 800-540-4123
• AIR FORCE—Air Force OneSource: 800-707-5784
A Military OneSource consultant can provide a brief assessment and referral to mental health professionals across the country for six free counseling sessions.

HOMECOMING

Dept. of Defense Helpline
(800) 796-9699
This is a deployment helpline at Walter Reed Medical Center.

Veterans and Families
http://www.veteransandfamilies.org
This organization provides information and resources to help homecoming veterans and their families in their transition from military to civilian life. Links to additional online support groups are at the site.

Army Reserve Family Programs
http://www.arfp.org
(800) 318-5298 (Army HR Command)
The Army Reserve Family Programs offers homecoming and reunion resources, including tips and links to resources.

National Guard Family Programs
http://www.guardfamily.org
(888) 777-7731
The National Guard Family Programs offer information about programs, benefits, and resources, including family, youth, and community outreach initiatives.

Iraq and Afghanistan Veterans of America
http://www.iava.org/index.php.
The Iraq and Afghanistan Veterans of America provides support through advocacy, education, and fundraising (fundraising mainly for VA hospitals).

National Veterans Foundation
http://www.nvf.org
(888) 777-4443 (hotline; 9 a.m.–9 p.m. PST)
The National Veterans Foundation is operated by veterans and helps veterans and families access the help they need, including suicide and crisis intervention and mental health/PTSD counseling.

WOUNDED SOLDIER SUPPORT

Military Severely Injured Joint Operations Center
http://www.militaryonesource.com
(888) 774-1361 (24-hour hotline)
The Center offers assistance for severely wounded service members and their families by connecting them with various military and government agencies. It offers help with medical care, rehabilitation, education, employment, mental health counseling, and financial assistance and accommodation issues. It also offers regional ombudsmen/advocates. The Center is staffed with registered nurses, master's level researchers, and counselors working as care managers who can answer questions and provide nationwide assistance.

National Amputation Foundation
http://www.nationalamputation.org
(516) 887-3600
This organization provides support for recent amputees, including in-person peer support and phone support. They also offer donated medical equipment and printed information.

LOSS OF A FAMILY MEMBER

American Gold Star Mothers
http://www.goldstarmoms.com
(202) 265-0991
This is a non-profit membership organization for mothers who have lost a son or daughter in the military. They provide support and sponsor memorial programs and events.

TAPS (Tragedy Assistance Program for Survivors)
http://www.taps.org
(202) 588-TAPS (8277)
TAPS offers support for survivors: peer support as well as 24-hour crisis intervention. TAPS also provides information about benefits and other services, survivor seminars, camps for children, and an online chat service.

VA/DoD Clinical Practice Guidelines
http://www.healthquality.va.gov
Post-Deployment Health Evaluation and Management (PDH-CPG)
Management of Major Depressive Disorder in Adults (MDD-CPG)
Management of Medically Unexplained Symptoms (MUS-CPG): Chronic Pain and Fatigue
Management of Post-Traumatic Stress Disorders (PTSD-CPG)
Rehabilitation of Lower Limb Amputation (AMP-CPG)
Management of Concussion/mild Traumatic Brain Injury (mTBI CPG)
Management of Substance Use Disorder (SUD)

EMDR-RELATED RESOURCES

EMDR Institute
http://www.emdr.com
General information about EMDR, contact information for EMDR therapists by area, summary of EMDR research, information on subscribing to general EMDR Internet discussion list, and order forms for EMDR books are available.

EMDR International Association
http://www.emdria.org
Available here are training standards for certification and approved consultant status, contact information for approved consultants by area, information on the annual conference, schedule of EMDRIA-approved workshops, and instructions for subscribing to military SIG Internet discussion list (members only).

EMDR Humanitarian Assistance Programs
http://www.emdrhap.org
This organization has information on pro-bono training programs as well as order forms for EMDR books, pamphlets, and treatment aids.

NEUROTEK Corporation
http://www.neurotekcorp.com
Information is available on ordering light-bars, lap-scans, and tactile and audio-scans.

Appendix B
EMDR Reprocessing Troubleshooting Guide

A group of clients appear to fall into the "under-responder" category; however, course of treatment may vary greatly. For instance, some clients may be on track with reprocessing using only the basic protocol, but for some reason the reprocessing becomes temporarily derailed or blocked. In most scenarios, the therapist can restart the reprocessing utilizing brief interventions summarized later. However, a sub-group of "under-responsive" clients does not seem to respond to reprocessing at the outset. There are a variety of possible, often inter-related reasons why clients may report no-reprocessing effects, including possible treatment-to-client mismatch, meaning EMDR is not effective for that particular client. However, before reaching that conclusion, there are a slew of other plausible explanations for client non-response, many of which the therapist and/or client have control over, that, if identified and resolved, can move reprocessing forward. We have summarized some of the main obstacles for reprocessing below and grouped many in what phases of EMDR treatment that these issues may arise, or be proactively identified if possible. Often the attempted solution is evident by the nature of the problem itself. Many times client's beliefs, fears, secondary gain, and the like may not be knowable until the reprocessing phase has started. Sometimes it is never known, even when the therapist has inquired. Therapists should pay particular attention to the potential variables that can derail reprocessing and seek consultation. Here is our summary of some reasons for not or under-responding to EMDR reprocessing:

Problems Related to EMDR Treatment and/or Client Match: (a) *EMDR is not a panacea and may not be effective for every client!* (b) Before arriving at a conclusion of treatment mismatch (e.g., that EMDR does not work for client X), multiple factors that the therapist and client do have some control over should be thoroughly investigated and addressed if possible. (c) No empirical data exists predicting which clients will or will not respond to EMDR, or any other psychotherapy or psychopharmacological intervention.

Problems Related to Therapeutic Alliance: (a) Insufficient trust, credibility, and rapport has been developed in the therapeutic alliance. (b) Absence of legitimate client consent because of coercion (e.g., command-directed referral, spousal threat, court-ordered). (c) Therapist's self-doubt, confusion, discomfort, anticipatory anxiety, and/or disbelief or mistrust of EMDR is communicated verbally and/or non-verbally to the client. (d) There is insufficient dual-focused attention (e.g., need greater therapist verbal reassurance). (e) The client has concerns that the therapist may feel shame toward them (e.g., especially higher ranking military enlisted and officer ranks, and healthcare professionals). (f) The client has concerns over limits of confidentiality (e.g., fear of disclosing unlawful acts witnessed or perpetrated, private information will be shared with command, etc.).

Problems Related to Client History, Preparation, and Readiness for Reprocessing: (a) The client is uncertain and confused, regarding EMDR treatment. (b) There is mismatch of type, speed, direction, and/or length of bilateral stimulation. (c) The therapist did not develop a treatment plan resulting in haphazard approach. (d) The client's preoccupation with compliance of the therapist's instructions to *retain* the image, negative cognition, emotions, and sensations during BLS (inform the client *to just know* they are thinking about the components and do not try to force themselves to hold onto all or any component). (e) The client is engaging in meta-cognition of analyzing EMDR process. (f) The therapist failed to screen for serious dissociative disorder.

Presence of a Blocking Belief: (a) The client has excessive guilt and the belief that he or she does not deserve better (e.g., survivor guilt). (b) There's absence of legitimate client consent because of coercion (e.g., command-directed, spousal threat). (c) Treatment of the war stress injury will negatively impact the client's "fitness for duty" status and will result in he or she being pulled from primary duties (e.g., down-chit for pilots, submariners, Special Forces, police/security personnel, etc.). (d) The client believes he or she deserves punishment for a mortal sin (e.g., killing). (e) The client does not believe the diagnosis and is suspicious of mental healthcare, or EMDR specifically. (f) The client has concern that the therapist may feel shame toward the client. (g) The client is concerned that the war stress injury will be viewed as personal weakness (e.g., "Just suck it up!"). (h) The client has concern over the mental health treatment due to stigma and negative career repercussions. (i) The client has top-secret or higher security clearance and is concerned about inadvertently revealing classified material. (j) The client already decided to commit suicide and/or homicide and views treatment as either futile or counter to implementing their destructive plan.

Fear of the Reprocessing: (a) A timing issue—the client has concerns over being unable to be functional at work or a special event. (b) The client has a fear of losing his or her competitive, fighting combat-edge. (c) The client has a fear of the unknown. (d) The client has a fear re-experiencing early traumatic experiences. (e) The client has a fear of forgetting fallen combat buddies (f) The client has a fear of losing control either temporarily or permanent. (g) The client has a fear of going crazy. (h) The client has a fear of forgetting positive and personal growth experiences. (i) The client has an ambivalence toward further deployment or retention on active-duty and treatment for their war stress injury. (j) The client has a fear of disclosing unlawful acts (witnessing/

perpetrating). (k) The client has a fear that he or she may *not* be able to deploy (e.g., once initiating treatment of a war stress injury, he or she will become debilitated and determined to be "unfit for duty").

Secondary gain: (a) The client does not want to remain on active-duty after successful treatment of a genuine war stress injury. (b) The client does not have a genuine stress injury and is faking to avoid deployment, return-to-duty, or military discharge and to receive disability compensation (aka "malingering"). (c) The client wants to remain in an illness-seeking role as a patient (aka "factitious disorder"). (d) The client is involved in pending legal or forensic testimony, civil settlement, or sentencing phase.

Problems Related to EMDR Assessment: (a) There is insufficient access and activation of the target memory and associated maladaptive neural network (e.g., incomplete assessment, low-disturbance targets selected), (b) There is presence of a "feeder memory" or blocking belief.

Problems Related to Reprocessing Itself: (a) There is a mismatch or habituation of type, speed, direction, and/or length of bilateral stimulation. (b) Acute intoxication or heavy sedation from prescribed or illicit substances is present. (c) There is insufficient dual-focused attention (e.g., need greater therapist verbal reassurance). (d) There is insufficient access and activation of the target memory and associated maladaptive neural network (e.g., incomplete assessment, low-disturbance targets selected, limited emotional charge from selected target memory components). (e) The client self-reports exclusively on a single specific-target memory component (e.g., after a BLS set the therapist repeatedly asks, "What happens now with the *picture?*"). (f) The therapist does not adhere to the treatment plan and establish baseline target memories to return to, instead is continually adding "new" target memories based upon the week to week presentation. (g) There is presence of a "feeder memory." (h) The client is engaging in meta-cognition of analyzing EMDR process.

Therapist-Related Factors That Interfere With Reprocessing: (a) The therapist is new and/or inexperienced with adhering to the standard EMDR protocol and avoids utilizing EMDR treatment worksheet that may confuse both therapist and client. (b) The therapist has a personal disbelief in EMDR theory or treatment. (c) The therapist is not developing or utilizing an EMDR treatment plan and/or becoming confused by continuously adding new target memories from either client weekly report or from reprocessing, thus preventing resolution of the original target memory. (d) The therapist is not adhering to the standard EMDR protocol *during* the reprocessing phase by over-responding with idiosyncratic or other theoretical methods (e.g., active-listening, exploration, interpretation, cognitive disputation, etc.) that severely limits availability of dual-focus and BLS. (e) The therapist has discomfort with client's intense emotional reprocessing (aka "abreaction"). (f) The therapist has fear of his or her own unprocessed trauma being activated by the client. (g) Silencing behaviors due to excessive compassion stress and/or fatigue are present (see Chapter 12 in this volume).

EMDR Interventions for Over- and Under-Responses to Reprocessing

A number of procedures have been identified to intervene with over- and under-responding clients. Francine Shapiro (2001) describes three general options that therapists might use to initiate or restart reprocessing when it seems to be derailed or blocked: (1) Change the BLS mechanics, (2) utilize the so-called TICES (Trigger, Image, Cognition, Emotion, and Sensation) strategies, and (3) perform a cognitive interweave. Determining which intervention to use depends on where the problem may reside. Generally speaking, starting with the simplest and least invasive is preferred. The first option every time for blocked processing is to change the BLS mechanics.

Changing BLS Mechanics (rank ordered by preference): (a) Solicit client input regarding the angle, speed, width, and distance; (b) Check distance and position of the chairs—side-by-side "ships passing" is preferred; (c) The therapist or (Neurotic) is either too far or too close to the client; (d) Change direction or speed of eye movements: (1) using the same direction and speed may foster stimulus habituation—mix it up. (2) If using horizontal eye movements, try diagonal from the client's lower right quadrant to the upper left. (3) Slower speed leads to quicker habituation and decreases dual focus—speed it up. (4) Lengthen or shorten the set—err on the side of longer versus shorter sets. (5) Widen or shorten width or range. (e) Focus on body sensations—especially very cognitive-oriented, meta-cognitive clients that report on the process EMDR versus their material. (f) Switch to sounds, vibration pads, or taps (obtain client assent before switching). (g) Combine BLS types—the author (Mark Russell) has on a dozen or more occasions combined visual and auditory BLS via the Neurotic device for clients where processing appeared to be blocked and under-responders. About 50% of the time the increased intensity restarted reprocessing. However, the author has no experience with combining three or different combinations; this is just anecdotal.

TICES Strategies

TICES strategies contain various ways that the therapist might intentionally alter the client's perception of the image, cognition, emotion, or sensation in order to heighten or reduce emotional arousal and change the perceptual set in a manner that allows reprocessing to occur (e.g., switch from color image to black and white/or a black and white image to color, view still shot instead of movie, visualize perpetrator without action, etc.). Therapists are advised to return to the target memory that was altered via TICES and reprocess without said distortions. In truth, the author has never needed or sought to use TICES strategies, but others may find them helpful. Regardless, therapists should tread very lightly when considering whether to deliberately distort the client's memory.

Cognitive Interweave

When clients appear "stuck" in their reprocessing—characterized as reaching a plateau where the SUDS is not coming down or they appear to be "looping" or recycling through negative associations without any end in sight—the therapist's initial course of action is to always change the BLS mechanics (see above). If that does not work, then therapists may utilize what Shapiro (2001) refers to as a "cognitive interweave." Simply put, a cognitive interweave is an attempt by the therapist to assist the client in accessing and strengthening associations in the client's adaptive neural network. A cognitive interweave is nothing more than a comment, statement, image, or question from the therapist containing adaptive information for the client to ponder, while bilateral stimulation is added. It is believed that dual-focus attention and BLS combined mimic or activate the brain's own adaptive information processing mechanism. Therapists who have used EMDR for a while become accustomed to an extraordinary effect from EMDR reprocessing. Namely, the spontaneous self-generated adaptive statements that clients produce as they move beyond desensitization of disturbance toward personal growth. However, some clients get close but don't quite pull the maladaptive and adaptive networks together. Used judiciously, the therapist's clinical judgment of the client's history and circumstance inform the selection of very concise adaptive stimuli for clients to chew on or spit out.

TYPES OF COGNITIVE INTERWEAVES

[Adapted from: *Eye Movement Desensitization and Reprocessing (EMDR) Training Manual*, by F. Shapiro (2005). Watsonville, CA: EMDR Institute; used with permission]

Education or New Information

Clients may have distorted or incomplete information that is interfering with their reprocessing. For example, military clients may feel deeply ashamed, and secretly label themselves as cowards if they had urinated or defecated during a firefight. Not knowing if it is true, of course, the therapist can provide the client with a copy of Menninger's (1948) classic study on the "normal" reactions to combat: (a) 50%—experience pounding heart, (b) 45%—experience sinking stomach, (c) 30%—experience cold sweats, (d) 25%—experience nausea, (e) 25%—experience shaking/tremors, (f) 25%—experience muscle stiffness, (g) 20%—experience vomiting, (h) 20%—experience general weakness, (i) 13%—experience involuntary bowel, and (j) 6%—experience involuntary urination. Clients may or may not react but can be asked by the therapist to "Just think of that" and add BLS; they ask, "What comes to mind?" The "interweave" is designed to enhance the connections between the target memory and the adaptive neural networks. If it did not relate to the client's situation, it's spit out.

Other Tactics to Use

"What if your child did it?"
Metaphor or analogy

"Let's pretend ..."
Socratic questioning

"I'm confused ..."
Atonement metaphor (Silver & Rogers, 2002)

For example, a very depressed, demoralized, and defeated appearing Marine Corporal was blocked in his processing because he could not forgive himself. He thought he should have heard his SNCO's verbal order to move to an adjacent covering during the middle of an intense fire-fight that resulted in one of his squad members being wounded.

C: If I only had listened to the Staff Sergeant's order to pull back.
Th: Wait a minute. I thought you said that you guys were getting slammed by RGS and small-arms fire from every direction it seemed.
C: Yeah, that's right.
Th: Did you talk to anyone in your squad during the fire fight?
C: Absolutely, hard as shit to hear anyone though with all that crap going on, you could scream in someone's ear and they might not hear you.
Th: Sounds chaotic ... you know the fog of war!
C: Yeah, but if I had done my job right Smitty would still be here.
Th: I'm confused here, Corporal ... help me understand this, you had to scream in the ears of your squad members next to you and they may not have heard everything you said given the chaos.... How far away was your SSGT?
C: Oh ... shit, he was on the other side of the road!
Th: Think of that. [Add BLS]
C: That's right ... he was actually about two squads over ... in fact I don't remember even seeing him until it was over.
Th: Stay with that.

Chaos of Combat—The Fog of War: The following are descriptions from service members of common contributing factors to the inherent confusion that may exist when under fire, often termed "the fog of war": (a) intense elation, fatigue, and fear; (b) noise, and blast effects; (c) tough-to-discriminate targets; (d) difficulty identifying leaders; (e) hard-to-maintain contact or control of movement; (f) disorder from many yelling commands simultaneously and screams of the injured; (g) concentration on the wounded and/or dead; (h) elusive enemy, rarely visible and poorly defined.

Themes and Cognitive Interweave: Three general themes have been identified that may negatively impact client reprocessing: Responsibility (e.g., an Airmen flight crewmember has survivor guilt because he was sick and the co-worker who took his slot was killed during landing mishap. Therapist: "Who made the call to ground you that day?" Client: "The flight surgeon." Therapist: "Think of that" (add BLS). Safety (e.g., a survivor of military sexual trauma-rape incident 2 years ago and consumed with fear over safety. Therapist: "What can you do now to make yourself feel safer?" Client: "Don't get drunk at night and stay with my roommate" Therapist: "Think of that" (add BLS). Choices (e.g., a client made a bad call; can they learn from this experience and make better choices in the future?—Notice that and add BLS).

Issues of Responsibility in Military Populations

All three themes (responsibility, safety, and choices) apply to military personnel, but issues related to excessive, unwarranted ownership of bad things happening that the Creator him/herself could not have foretold or prevented—are routinely present amongst military leaders in both enlisted and officer ranks—but especially the NCO/Petty Officer and SNCO/Chiefs. Intense self-blame, guilt, shame, and self-condemnation can block or impede reprocessing. What complicates matters is military culture and socialization instills and reinforces individual culpability—all the time.

In fact, leaders who fail to anticipate and accept appropriate responsibility for their subordinates' actions or inactions usually receive the mediocre annual performance evaluations for leadership traits that end their careers. That's why when a Private fails his or her barracks room inspection for the second time, the NCO might join in cleaning it up, after each received a good dressing down. The purpose, of course, is to teach young men and women to accept responsibility for looking out for each other, and to think proactively of contingencies, because, when people don't, people die. That's the hard truth, and military culture is about training people to survive and win wars. Even if that means an individual is guilt riddled and suicidal, he was in charge, he was responsible. For example, the author (Mark Russell) met with one of the naval leaders aboard a submarine that crashed into an undersea mountain. The particular leader was off duty, in the rack, when the tragedy struck. The fact that the leader was unconscious and not at the scene did not matter. In his mind, "It was my fault I should have trained them better!" Leadership training starts the day of accession, and every military member knows what the warrior cultural response will be whenever something isn't completed on time or up to standards or an accident happens. Someone(s) is *always* in line to receive the blame for not anticipating that it would rain on the Colonel's parade. So, it's no mystery why many military personnel returning from war are consumed with guilt and self-denigration.

Cognitive Interweave on Killing

Knowing that cognitive interweave can help, therapists should keep their radar out for detecting signs of excessive responsibility in the military client's narrative and be prepared to use cognitive interweave if necessary—sparingly, of course. For example, cognitive interweave may be useful for blocked processing around common issues related to lines-of-authority—who is responsible for issuing and implementing military orders? A female NCO is depressed and has excessive guilt and suicidal ideation. During reprocessing she keeps returning to the negative cognition that "I was responsible for killing civilians!" Referring to an incident whereby guard entries she was supervising fired upon a vehicle that did not stop at a sensitive military checkpoint—killing two and wounding two Iraqi non-combatants. The therapist asks, "What was the ROE (rules of engagement)?" The client cites line and verse. The therapist says, "And who actually issued the ROE, the orders that the sentries were following? Think of that"—and add BLS. The therapist does not always need to wait for the client to respond before initiating the BLS. Just the fact that she is thinking it over opens the channel for adaptive information to enter; the dual focus and BLS combined are intended to pry open that adaptive hatch even further, and, in many cases, that small opening may be sufficient for an associative link to be created with the adaptive neural networks. Once reprocessing resumes, the therapist does not utilize cognitive interweave and retreats to the "ground" (as in figure-ground), relying upon the client's own adaptive learning mechanism to take it from there.

Appendix C
References

Ahmadizadeh, M. J., Eskandari, H., Falsafinejad, M. R., & Borjali, A. (2010). Comparison of the effectiveness of "cognitive-behavioral" and "eye movement desensitization reprocessing" treatment models on patients with war posttraumatic stress disorder. *Iranian Journal of Military Medicine, 12*(3), 173–178.

Albright, D. L., & Thyer, B. (2009). Does EMDR reduce post-traumatic stress disorder symptomatology in combat veterans? *Behavioral Interventions.* doi:10.1002/bin.295

American Psychiatric Association. (2000). *Diagnostic and statistical manual of mental disorders–fourth edition text revision.* Washington, DC: Author.

American Psychiatric Association. (2004). *Practice guideline for the treatment of patients with acute stress disorder and posttraumatic stress disorder.* Arlington, VA: Author.

American Psychiatric Association. (2009). *Practice guideline for the treatment of patients with acute stress disorder and posttraumatic stress disorder.* Arlington, VA: Author.

Aurora, R. N., Zak, R. S., Auerbach, S. H., Casey, K. R., Chowdhuri, S., Karippot, A., … & Morgenthaler, T. I. (2010, August). Best practices guide for the treatment of nightmare disorders in adults. *Journal of Clinical Sleep Medicine, 6*(4), 389–401.

Beck, A. T., Rush, J., Shaw, B. F., & Emery, G. (1979). *Cognitive therapy for depression.* New York, NY: Guilford.

Beebe, G. W., & Appel, J. W. (1958). *Variation in psychological tolerance to ground combat in World War II.* Washington, DC: National Academy of Sciences.

Bisson, J., & Andrew, M. (2007). *Psychological treatment of post-traumatic stress disorder (PTSD).* Cochrane Database of Systematic Reviews, 3, Art. No.: CD003388. doi:10.1002/14651858.CD003388.pub3

Bisson, J. I., Ehlers, A., Matthew, R., Pilling, S., Richards, D. A., & Turner, S. W. (2007). Psychological treatments for chronic post-traumatic stress disorder: Systematic review and meta-analysis. *British Journal of Psychiatry, 190*(2), 97–104.

Bleich, A., Kotler, M., Kutz, I., & Shalev, A. (2002). A position paper of the (Israeli) National Council for Mental Health: *Guidelines for the assessment and professional intervention with terror victims in the hospital and in the community.* Jerusalem, Israel: National Council for Mental Health.

Boudewyns, P. A., & Hyer, L. A. (1996). Eye movement desensitization and reprocessing (EMDR) as treatment for post-traumatic stress disorder (PTSD). *Clinical Psychology and Psychotherapy, 3*, 185–195.

Boudewyns, P. A., Stwertka, S. A., Hyer, L.A, Albrecht, J. W., & Sperre, E. Y. (1993). Eye movement desensitization for PTSD of combat: A treatment outcome pilot study. *The Behavior Therapist, 16*, 30–33.

Bradley, R., Greene, J., Russ, E., Dutra, L., & Westen, D. (2005). A multidimensional meta-analysis of psychotherapy for PTSD. *American Journal of Psychiatry, 162*(2), 214–227.

Bremner, J. D. (2005). *Does stress damage the brain? Understanding trauma-related disorders from a mind-body perspective.* New York, NY: Norton.

Buss, A. H., & Perry, M. P. (1992). The aggression questionnaire. *Journal of Personality and Social Psychology, 63*, 452–459. Retrieved from http://www.psychology.iastate. edu/faculty/caa/Scales/BussPerry.pdf

Carlson, E., Palmieri, P., Smith, S., Kimerling, R., Ruzek, J., & Burling, T. (n.d.). A brief self-report measure of traumatic events: The trauma history screen. (Unpublished manuscript). Retrieved from http://www.ptsd.va.gov/professional/pages/assessments/ths.asp

Carlson, E. B., & Waelde, L. (2000, November). *Preliminary psychometric properties of the Trauma Related Dissociation Scale.* Paper presented at the Annual meeting of the International Society for Traumatic Stress Studies, San Antonio, TX.

Carlson, J. G., Chemtob, C. M., Rusnack, K., Hedlund, N. L., & Muraoka, M. Y. (1998). Eye movement desensitization and reprocessing for combat-related posttraumatic stress disorder. *Journal of Traumatic Stress, 11*, 3–24.

Casey, G. W. Jr. (2011). Comprehensive soldier fitness: A vision for psychological resilience in the U.S. army. *American Psychologist, 66*, 1–3.

Chambless, D. L., Baker, M. J., Baucom, D. H., Beutler, L. E., Calhoun, K. S., Crits-Christoph, … Woody, S. R. (1998). Update of empirically validated therapies, II. *The Clinical Psychologist, 51*, 3–16.

Chang, S. H. (2005, August). *Mechanism of EM in EMDR: Change strength of semantic associations.* Paper presented at the American Psychological Association Annual Convention, Washington, DC.

Conrad, D., & Kellar-Guenther, Y. (2006) Compassion fatigue, burnout, and compassion satisfaction among Colorado child protection workers. *Child Abuse and Neglect, 30*(10), 1071–1080.

Creamer, M., & Forbes, D. (2004). Treatment of posttraumatic stress disorder in military and veteran populations. *Psychotherapy: Theory, Research, Practice, Training, 41*, 388–398.

Clinical Resource Efficiency Support Team (CREST). (2003). *The management of post traumatic stress disorder in adults.* Belfast: Clinical Resource Efficiency Support Team of the Northern Ireland Department of Health, Social Services and Public Safety.

Da Costa, J. M. (1871). On irritable heart: A clinical study of a form of functional cardiac disorder and its consequences. Reprinted November, 1951, *American Journal of Medicine*, 559–567.

Department of the Army. (2006). Combat and operational stress control: Field Manual 4-02.51 (FM 8-51). Washington, DC: Author.

Department of the Army. (2009). *Combat and operational stress control manual for leaders and soldiers: Field Manual No. 6-22-5.* Washington, DC: Author.

Department of Veterans Affairs & Department of Defense. (2004). *VA/DoD clinical practice guideline for the management of post-traumatic stress.* Washington, DC: Veterans Health Administration, Department of Veterans Affairs and Health

Affairs, Department of Defense. Office of Quality and Performance publication 10Q-CPG/PTSD-04. Washington, DC. Author.

Department of Veteran's Affairs & Department of Defense. (2010). *VA/DoD clinical practice guideline for the management of post-traumatic stress.* Veterans Health Administration, Department of Veterans Affairs and Health Affairs, Department of Defense. Office of Quality and Performance publication 10Q-CPG/PTSD-10. Washington, DC. Author.

de Roos, C., & van Rood, Y. R. (2009). EMDR in the Treatment of Medically Unexplained Symptoms: A Systematic Review. *Journal of EMDR Practice and Research, 3,* 248–263.

Devilly, G. J., & Spence, S. H. (1999). The relative efficacy and treatment distress of EMDR and a cognitive-behavior trauma treatment protocol in the amelioration of posttraumatic stress disorder. *Journal of Anxiety Disorders, 13,* 131–157.

Dutch National Steering Committee Guidelines Mental Health Care. (2003). *Multidisciplinary Guideline Anxiety Disorders.* Utrecht, The Netherlands: Quality Institute Health Care CBO/Trimbos Institute.

Elofsson, U. O., von Scheele, B., Theorell, T., & Sondergard, H. P. (2008, May). Physiological correlates of eye movement desensitization and reprocessing. *Journal of Anxiety Disorders, 22*(4), 622–634.

Erbes, C. R., Curry, K. T., & Leskela, J. (2009). Treatment presentation and adherence of Iraq/Afghanistan era veterans in outpatient care for posttraumatic stress disorder. *Psychological Services, 6,* 175–183.

Figley, C. R. (Ed.). (1995). *Compassion fatigue: Coping with secondary traumatic stress disorder in those who treat the traumatized.* New York, NY: Brunner/Mazel.

Figley, C. R. (Ed.). (1997). *Burnout in families: The systemic costs of caring.* New York, NY: CRC Press.

Figley, C. R. (2002). *Treating compassion fatigue.* New York, NY: Brunner-Routledge.

Figley, C. R., & Nash, W. P. (2007). *Combat stress injury: Theory, research, and management.* New York, NY: Routledge.

Fischer, H. (2010, September 28). *U.S. military casualty statistics: Operation new dawn, operation Iraqi freedom, and operation enduring freedom.* Congressional Research Service RS22452. Retrieved from http://www.crs.gov

Fitzgerald, L. F., Magley, V. J., Drasgow, F., & Waldo, C. R. (1999). Measuring Sexual Harassment in the Military: The Sexual Experiences Questionnaire (SEQ-DoD). *Military Psychology, 11,* 243–263.

Foa, E. B., Keane, T. M., Friedman, M. J., & Cohen, J. A. (2009). *Effective treatments for PTSD: Practice guidelines of the International Society for Traumatic Stress Studies.* New York, NY: Guilford.

Foa, E. B., & Kozak, M. J. (1986). Emotional processing of fear: Exposure to corrective information. *Psychological Bulletin, 99,* 20–35.

Foster, S., & Lendl, J. (1996). Eye movement desensitization and reprocessing: Four case studies of a new tool for executive coaching and restoring employee performance after setbacks. *Consulting Psychology Journal, 48,* 155–161.

Frank, J. D., & Frank, J. B. (1991). *Persuasion and healing: A comparative study of psychotherapy* (3rd ed.). Baltimore, MD: Johns Hopkins University Press.

French, L., McCrea, M., & Baggett, M. (2008, Winter). The Military Acute Concussion Evaluation (MACE). *Journal of Special Operations Medicine, 8*(1), 68–77. Retrieved from http://jsomonline.org/Publications/2008168French.pdf

Garcia, H. A., Kelly, L. P., Rentz, T. O., & Lee, S. (2011). Pretreatment predictors of drop-out for cognitive behavioral therapy for PTSD in Iraq and Afghanistan war veterans. *Psychological Services, 8*(1), 1–11.

Government Accountability Office. (1997). *Military attrition: DOD could save millions by better screening enlisted personnel* (Chapter Report, 01/06/97, GAO/NSIAD-97-39). Washington, DC: Author.

Government Accountability Office. (2011). *Personnel and cost data associated with implementing DOD's homosexual conduct policy.* Jan 2011-GAO-11-170. Washington, DC: Author.

Grossman, D. (1996). *On killing: The psychological cost of learning to kill in war and society.* New York, NY: Little, Brown.

Grossman, D. (2007). On combat: *The psychology and physiology of deadly conflict in war and in peace–second edition.* Belleville, IL: PPCT Research Publications.

Hacker-Hughes, J., & Wesson, M. (2008, June). *Anecdotal reports, EMDR on the frontline: Early interventions during military operations.* Paper presented at the annual meeting of the EMDR Europe Association, London, England.

Hammond, W. A. (1883). *A treatise on insanity in its medical relations.* London, England: H. K. Lewis.

Harper, M. L., Rasolkhani-Kalhorn, T., & Drozd, J. F. (2009). On the neural basis of EMDR therapy: Insights from qEEG studies. *Traumatology, 15,* 81–95.

Howard, M. D., & Cox, R. P. (2006). Use of EMDR in the treatment of water phobia at navy boot camp: A case study. *Traumatology, 12,* 302–313.

INSERM. (2004). *Psychotherapy: An evaluation of three approaches.* Paris, France: French National Institute of Health and Medical Research.

Institute of Medicine. (2008). *Treatment of posttraumatic stress disorder: An assessment of the evidence.* Washington, DC: The National Academies Press.

Jarero, J., Artigas, L., & Luber, M. (2011). The EMDR protocol for recent critical incidents: application in a disaster mental health continuum of care context. *Journal of EMDR Practice and Research, 5*(3), 82–94.

Jayatunge, R. M. (2006). *The efficacy of EMDR–A study based on Sri Lankan combatants.* New Hope, PA: EMDR Humanitarian Assistance Program.

Jayatunge, R. M. (2011). *Healing combat trauma in Sri Lanka via EMDR.* Retrieved May 5, 2011, from http://www.lankaweb.com/news/items/2011/05/10/healing-combat-trauma-in-sri-lanka-via-emdr

Jones, E., & Wessely, S. (2005). *Shell shock to PTSD: Military psychiatry from 1900 to the Gulf War.* New York, NY: Psychology.

Kohnke, C., Lempa, W., Sack, M., Matzke, M., & Munte, T. (2004). Event-related potentials and EMDR treatment of post-traumatic stress disorder. *Neuroscience Research, 49,* 267–272.

Korn, D. L., & Leeds, A. M. (2002). Preliminary evidence of efficacy for EMDR resource development and installation in the stabilization phase of treatment of complex posttraumatic stress disorder. *Journal of Clinical Psychology, 58,* 1465–1487.

Korn, D. L., Weir, J., & Rozelle, D. (2004, September). *Looking beyond the data: Clinical lessons learned from an EMDR treatment outcome study,* Session 321. Paper presented at EMDR International Association Conference, Montreal, Quebec.

Koss, M. P., & Oros, C. J. (1982). Sexual experiences survey: A research instrument investigating sexual aggression and victimization. *Journal of Consulting and Clinical Psychology, 50*(3), 455–457. Retrieved from http://www.amptoons.com/blog/files/koss_SES.pdf

Kuiken, D., Chudleigh, M., & Racher, D. (2010, December). Bilateral eye movements, attentional flexibility and metaphor comprehension: The substrate of REM dreaming? *Dreaming, 20*(4), 227–247.

Kulka, R. A., Schlenger, W. E., Fairbank, J. A., Hough, R. L., Jordan, B., Marmar, C. R., & Weiss, D. S. (1990). *Trauma and the Vietnam War generation: Report of findings from the National Vietnam Veterans Readjustment Study.* New York, NY: Brunner/Mazel.

Kutz, I., Resnick, V., & Dekel, R. (2008). The effect of single-session modified EMDR on acute stress syndromes. *Journal of EMDR Practice and Research, 2*(3), 190–200.

Lamprecht, F., Kohnke, C., Lempa, W., Sack, M., Matzke, M., & Munte, T. (2004). Event-related potentials and EMDR treatment of post-traumatic stress disorder. *Neuroscience Research, 49,* 267–272.

Lande, R. G. (2003). *Madness, malingering & malfeasance.* Washington, DC: Potomac Books.

Lande, R. G., Marin, B. A., & Ruzek, J. I. (2004). Substance abuse in the deployment environment. In the Department of Veterans Affairs National Center of PTSD (Eds.), *Iraq War clinician guide: Second edition* (pp. 79–82). Washington, DC: Department of Veterans Affairs, National Center of PTSD. Retrieved from http://www.ptsd.va.gov

Lansing, K., Amen, D. G., Hanks, C., & Rudy, L. (2005). High-resolution brain SPECT imaging and eye movement and reprocessing in police officers with PTSD. *Journal of Neuropsychiatry Clinical Neuroscience, 17,* 526–532.

Lee, C. W., & Schubert, S. (2009). Omissions and errors in the Institute of Medicine's report on scientific evidence of treatment for posttraumatic stress disorder. *Journal of EMDR Practice and Research, 3,* 32–38.

Leeds, A. M. (2009). *A guide to the standard EMDR protocols for clinicians, supervisors, and consultants.* New York, NY: Springer.

Levin, P., Lazrove, S., & van der Kolk, B. A. (1999). What psychological testing and neuroimaging tell us about the treatment of posttraumatic stress disorder (PTSD). *Journal Anxiety Disorders, 13,* 159–172.

Lendl, J., & Foster, S. (2009). EMDR performance enhancement psychology protocol. In M. Luber (Ed.), *Eye movement desensitization and reprocessing (EMDR): Scripted protocols basics and special situations* (pp. 387–392). New York, NY: Springer.

Lipke, H. J. (1995). EMDR clinicians survey. In F. Shapiro (Ed.), *Eye movement desensitization and reprocessing: Basic principles, protocols and procedures* (pp. 376–386). New York, NY: Guilford.

Lipke, H. J., & Botkin, A. (1992). Case studies of eye movement desensitization and reprocessing (EMDR) with chronic post-traumatic stress disorder. *Psychotherapy, 29,* 591–595.

Luber, M. (2009). *Eye movement desensitization and reprocessing (EMDR): Scripted protocols basics and special situations.* New York, NY: Springer.

Marcus, S. V., Marquis, P., & Sakai, C. (1997). Controlled study of treatment of PTSD using EMDR in an HMO setting. *Psychotherapy, 34,* 307–315.

Marcus, S. V., Marquis, P., & Sakai, C. (2004). Three- and 6-month follow-up of EMDR treatment of PTSD in an HMO setting. *International Journal of Stress Management, 11,* 195–208.

Marshall, S. (2003). *Virtual tour, real cure 9/11 post-traumatic stress therapy breaks ground.* Retrieved from http://www.patss.com/about/12_01_03

Maxfield, L., & Hyer. L. (2002). The relationship between efficacy and methodology in studies investigating EMDR treatment of PTSD. *Journal of Clinical Psychology, 58*, 23–42.

Meichenbuam, D. (1994). *A clinical handbook Practical therapist manual: For assessing and treating adults with PTSD.* Ontario, Canada: Institute Press.

Menninger, W. C. (1948). *Psychiatry in a troubled world* (pp. 134–152). New York, NY: MacMillan.

Meyers, T. W., & Cornille, T. Z. (2002). The trauma of working with traumatized children. In C. R. Figley (Ed.), *Treating compassion fatigue* (pp. 39–55). New York, NY: Brunner-Routledge.

Miller, J. R. (1994, September–October). Eye movement desensitization reprocessing: Application on the battlefield. *Army Medical Department Journal* (PB-8-947/8): 33–36.

Nardo, D., Hogberg, G., Looi, J. C. L., Larsson, S., Hallstrom, T., & Pagani, M. (2010). Gray matter density in limbic and paralimbic cortices is associated with trauma load and EMDR outcome in PTSD patients. *Journal of Psychiatric Research, 44*, 477–485.

Narimani, M., Ahari, S. S., & Rajabi, S. (2010). Comparison of efficacy of eye movement, desensitization and reprocessing and cognitive behavioral therapy therapeutic methods for reducing anxiety and depression of Iranian combatant afflicted by post-traumatic stress disorder. Medical Sciences. *Journal of Islamic Azad University, Tehran Medical Branch, 19*, 236–245.

Nasby, W., & Russell, M. C. (1997). Posttraumatic stress disorder and the states-of-mind model: Evidence of specificity. *Cognitive Therapy and Research, 21*, 117–134.

National Institute for Clinical Excellence. (2005). *Post-traumatic stress disorder (PTSD): The management of adults and children in primary and secondary care.* London, England: NICE Guidelines.

National Research Council. (2006). Assessing fitness for military enlistment: Physical, medical, and mental health standards. Committee on the youth population and military recruitment: Physical, medical, and mental health standards. In P. R. Sackett & A. S. Mavor (Eds.), *Board on Behavioral, Cognitive, and Sensory Sciences, Division of Behavioral and Social Sciences and Education.* Washington, DC: The National Academies Press.

Nijenhuis, E. R. S., Spinhoven, P., Van Dyck, R., Van der Hart, O., & Vanderlinden, J. (1996). The development and the psychometric characteristics of the Somatoform Dissociation Questionnaire (SDQ-20). *Journal of Nervous and Mental Disease, 184*, 688–694.

Nijenhuis, E. R. S., Spinhoven, P., Van Dyck, R., Van der Hart, O., & Vanderlinden, J. (1997). The development of the Somatoform Dissociation Questionnaire (SDQ-5) as a screening instrument for dissociative disorders. *Acta Psychiatrica Scandinavica, 96*, 311–318.

Office of the Surgeon Multinational Force-Iraq & Office of the Surgeon General, United States Army Medical Command (2008, February 14). *Mental Health Advisory Team (MHAT)-V: Operation Iraqi Freedom 06-08 Operation Enduring Freedom 8: Afghanistan report.* Washington, DC: United States Army Medical Command.

Ohtani, T., Matsuoa, K., Kasai, K., Katob, T., & Katoa, N. (2005, May). Hemodynamic response to emotional memory recall with eye movement. *Neuroscience Letters, 380*(1–2), 75–79.

Ozakinci, G., Hallman, W. K., & Kipen, H. M. (2006). Persistence of symptoms in veterans of the first Gulf war: 5-year follow-up. *Environmental Health Perspectives, 114*(10), 1553–1557.

Ozer E. J., Best, S. R., Lipsey, T. L., & Daniel, S. (2003). Predictors of posttraumatic stress disorder and symptoms in adults: a meta-analysis. *Psychological Bulletin, 129*(1), 52–73.

Pitman, R. K., Orr, S. P., Altman, B., Longpre, R. E., Poire, R. E., & Lasko, N. B. (1993, May). *A controlled study of EMDR treatment for post traumatic stress disorder.* Paper presented at the 146th annual meeting of the American Psychiatric Association, Washington, DC.

Pivar, I. (2004). Traumatic Grief: Symptomatology and Treatment in the Iraq War Veteran. In the Department of Veterans Affairs National Center of PTSD (Eds.), *Iraq War clinician guide: Second edition* (pp. 75–78). Washington, DC: Department of Veterans Affairs, National Center of PTSD. Retrieved from http://www.ptsd.va.gov

Prigerson, H. (2005). Complicated grief home page. Yale University School of Medicine. Retrieved from http://info.med.yale.edu/psych/cgrief/Defined.htm

Quinn, G. (2009). Emergency response procedure. In M. Luber (Ed.), *Eye movement and desensitization and reprocessing: Scripted protocols basics and special situations* (pp. 271–278). New York, NY: Springer.

Raboni, M. R., Tufik, S., & Suchecki, D. (2006). Treatment of PTSD by eye movement desensitization reprocessing (EMDR) improves sleep quality, quality of life, and perception of stress. *Annals of New York Academy of Sciences, 1071*(1), 508–513.

Ross, R. J., Ball, W. A., Dinges, D. F., Kribbs, N. B., Morrison, A. R., Silver, S. M., & Mulvaney, F. D. (1994). Rapid eye movement sleep disturbance in posttraumatic stress disorder. *Biological Psychiatry, 35,* 195–202.

Rothbaum, B., Astin, M., & Marsteller, F. (2005). Prolonged exposure versus eye movement desensitization and reprocessing (EMDR) for PTSD rape victims. *Journal of Traumatic Stress, 18,* 607–616.

Roy, M. J., Koslowe, P. A., Kroenke, K., & Magruder, C. (1998). Signs, symptoms, and ill-defined conditions in Persian Gulf War veterans: Findings form the comprehensive clinical evaluation program. *Psychosomatic Medicine, 60,* 663–668.

Russell, M. C. (1992). Attentional focus and states-of-mind in post-traumatic stress disorder among Vietnam combat veterans. Dissertation Abstracts International (93183460).

Russell, M. C. (2006). Treating combat-related stress disorders: A multiple case study utilizing eye movement desensitization and reprocessing (EMDR) with battlefield casualties from the Iraqi war. *Military Psychology, 18,* 1–18.

Russell, M. C. (2008a). Scientific resistance to research, training, and utilization of EMDR therapy in treating post-war disorders. *Social Science and Medicine, 67*(11), 1737–1746.

Russell, M. C. (2008b). Treating traumatic amputation-related phantom limb pain: A case study utilizing eye movement desensitization and reprocessing (EMDR) within the armed services. *Clinical Case Studies, 7,* 136–153.

Russell, M. C. (2008c). War-related medically unexplained symptoms, prevalence and treatment: Utilizing EMDR within the armed services. *Journal of EMDR Practice and Research, 2*(2), 212–225.

Russell, M. C., & Friedberg, F. (2009). Training, treatment access and research on trauma intervention in the armed services. *Journal of EMDR Practice and Research, 3,* 24–31.

Russell, M. C., Lipke, H. E., & Figley, C. R. (2011). EMDR Therapy. In B. A. Moore & W. A. Penk (Eds.), *Handbook for the treatment of PTSD in Military Personnel* (pp. 74–89). New York, NY: Guilford.

Russell, M., & Silver, S. M. (2007). Training needs for the treatment of combat-related post-traumatic stress disorder: A survey of Department of Defense clinicians. *Traumatology, 13*(3), 4–10.

Russell, M. C., Silver, S. M., & Rogers, S. (2007). Responding to an identified need: A joint DoD-DVA training program in EMDR for clinicians providing trauma services. *International Journal of Stress Management, 14*(1), 61–71.

Russell, M., Shoquist, D., & Chambers C. (2005). Effectively managing the psychological wounds of war. *Navy Medicine,* (April–March), 23–26.

Schneider, J., Hofmann, A., Rost, C., & Shapiro, F. (2007). EMDR and phantom limb pain: Theoretical implications, case study, and treatment guidelines. *Journal of EMDR Practice and Research, 1,* 31–45.

Seidler, G. H., & Wagner, F. E. (2006). Comparing the efficacy of EMDR and trauma-focused cognitive-behavioral therapy in the treatment of PTSD: A meta-analytic study. *Psychological Medicine, 36*(11), 1515–1522.

Seifert, A. E., Polusny, M. A., & Murdoch, M. (2011).The association between childhood physical and sexual abuse and functioning and psychiatric symptoms in a sample of U.S. Army soldiers. *Military Medicine, 176*(2), 176–181.

Shapiro, E. (2009). EMDR treatment of recent trauma. *Journal of EMDR Practice and Research, 3*(3), 141–151.

Shapiro, F. (1989). Efficacy of the eye movement desensitization procedure in the treatment of traumatic memories. *Journal of Traumatic Stress, 2,* 199–223.

Shapiro, F. (2001). *Eye movement desensitization and reprocessing: Basic principles, protocols, and procedures (2nd edition).* New York, NY: Guilford.

Shapiro, F. (2005). *Eye movement desensitization and reprocessing (EMDR) training manual.* Watsonville, CA: EMDR Institute.

Shapiro, F. (2008). *Eye movement desensitization and reprocessing (EMDR) Part 2 training manual bound with military field manual.* Watsonville, CA: EMDR Institute.

Shapiro, R. (2005). *EMDR solutions: Pathways to healing.* New York, NY: Norton.

Shepard, B. (2001). *A war of nerves: Soldiers and psychiatrists in the twentieth century.* Harvard University Press: Cambridge, MA.

Silver, S. M., Brooks, A., & Obenchain, J. (1995). Treatment of Vietnam War veterans with PTSD: A comparison of eye movement desensitization and reprocessing, biofeedback, and relaxation training. *Journal of Traumatic Stress, 8,* 337–342.

Silver, S., & Rogers, S. (2002). *Light in the heart of darkness: EMDR and the treatment of war and terrorism survivors.* New York, NY: Norton.

Silver, S. M., Rogers, S., Knipe, J., & Colelli, G. (2005, February). EMDR therapy following the 9/11 terrorist attacks: A community-based intervention project in New York City. *International Journal of Stress Management, 12*(1), 29–42.

Silver, S. M., Rogers, S., & Russell, M. (2008). Eye movement desensitization and reprocessing (EMDR) in the treatment of war veterans. *Journal of Clinical Psychology: In Session, 64*(8), 947–957.

Stockholm: Medical Program Committee/Stockholm City Council. Sjöblom, P. O., Andréewitch, S., Bejerot, S., Mörtberg, E., Brinck, U., Ruck, C., & Körlin, D. (2003). *Regional treatment recommendation for anxiety disorders.* Stockholm: Medical Program Committee/Stockholm City Council.

Smith, L. (2010, January 19). *Virtual reality exposure therapy to combat PTSD.* Retrieved from http://www.army.mil/article/33128

Street, A., & Stafford J. (2004). Military sexual trauma: Issues in caring for veterans. In the Department of Veterans Affairs National Center of PTSD (Eds.), *Iraq War clinician guide: Second edition* (pp. 66–69). Department of Veterans Affairs: National Center of PTSD. Retrieved from http://www.ptsd.va.gov

Substance Abuse and Mental Health Services Administration (SAMHSA). (2010, October). *Eye movement desensitization and reprocessing.* Washington, DC: National Registry of Evidence-Based Programs and Practices, U.S. Department of Health and Human Services (HHS).

Sugawara, M., & Suzuki, K. (2004, July). *Methodological and conceptual issues and tests—EMDR (eye movement desensitization and reprocessing) and REM sleep.* Poster presented at the Annual Meeting of the Australian Society for the Study of Brain Impairment (ASSBI) and the International Neuropsychological Society (INS), Brisbane, Australia.

Tedeschi, R. G., & McNally, R. J. (2011). Can we facilitate posttraumatic growth in combat veterans? *American Psychologist, 66,* 19–24.

Therapy Advisor (2004–2007). National Institute of Mental Health–sponsored website listing empirically supported methods. Retrieved from http://www.therapyadvisor.com

United Kingdom Department of Health. (2001). *Treatment choice in psychological therapies and counseling evidence based clinical practice guideline.* London, England: Author.

U.S. Department of the Navy. (1996). *Manual of the medical department* (NAVMED P-117). Washington, DC: Author.

van der Kolk, B., Spinazzola, J. Blaustein, M., Hopper, J. Hopper, E., Korn, D., & Simpson, W. (2007). A randomized clinical trial of EMDR, fluoxetine and pill placebo in the treatment of PTSD: Treatment effects and long-term maintenance. *Journal of Clinical Psychiatry, 68,* 37–46.

van Minnen, A., Hendriks, L., & Olff, M. (2010). When do trauma experts choose exposure therapy for PTSD patients? A controlled study of therapist and patient factors. *Behavioral Research and Therapy, 48,* 312–320.

VHA/DoD. (2001). *Clinical practice guideline for the management of medically unexplained symptoms: Chronic pain and fatigue.* Office of Performance and Quality Management Directorate, United States Army MEDCOM: Washington, DC: Author.

Wain, H. J., Cozza, S. J., Grammer, G. G., Oleshansky, M. A., Cotter, D. M., Owens, M. F., … Kogan, R. M. (2004). Treating the traumatized amputee. In the Department of Veterans Affairs National Center of PTSD (Eds.), *Iraq War clinician guide: Second edition* (pp. 50–57). Department of Veterans Affairs: National Center of PTSD. Retrieved from http://www.ptsd.va.gov

Weathers, F., Litz, B., Herman, D., Huska, J., & Keane, T. (1993, October). *The PTSD Checklist (PCL): Reliability, validity, and diagnostic utility.* Paper presented at the Annual Convention of the International Society for Traumatic Stress Studies, San Antonio, TX.

Weathers, F. W., Ruscio, A. M., & Keane, T. M. (1999). Psychometric properties of the nine scoring rules for the clinician-administered post-traumatic stress disorder scale. *Psychological Assessment, 11*(2), 124–133.

Weiss, D. S., & Marmar, C. R. (1996). The Impact of Event Scale — Revised. In J. Wilson & T. M. Keane (Eds.), *Assessing psychological trauma and PTSD* (pp. 399–411). New York, NY: Guilford.

Wesson, M., & Gould, M. (2009). Intervening early with EMDR on military operations. *Journal of EMDR Practice and Research, 3*(2), 91–97.

Wilson, S. A., Becker, L. A., & Tinker, R. H. (1995). Eye movement desensitization and reprocessing (EMDR) treatment for psychologically traumatized individuals. *Journal of Consulting and Clinical Psychology, 63,* 928–937.

Wolpe, J., & Abrams, J. (1991). Post-traumatic stress disorder overcome by eye movement desensitization: A case report. *Journal of Behavior Therapy and Experimental Psychiatry, 22,* 39–43.

Zimmerman, P., Biesold, K. H., Barre, K., & Lanczik, M. (2007). Long-term course of post-traumatic stress disorder (PTSD) in German soldiers: Effects of inpatient eye movement desensitization and reprocessing therapy and specific trauma characteristics in patients with non-combat-related PTSD. *Military Medicine, 172*(5), 456–460.

Zayfert, C., DeViva, J. C., Becker, C., Pike, J. L., Gillock, K. L., & Hayes, S. A. (2005). Exposure utilization and completion of cognitive behavioral therapy for PTSD in a "real world" clinical practice. *Faculty Publications, Department of Psychology.* Paper 333. Retrieved from http://digitalcommons.unl.edu/psychfacoub/333

Index

A

Acute combat-related PTSD,
  reprocessing, case study, 155–156
Acute Stress Disorder
  early treatment, 95–96
  Eye Movement Desensitization, 170
    case study, 171–176
Acute stress injuries, EMDR
  research, 176–177
  treatment considerations, 176–177
Acute Stress Reactions, 94–101
  defined, 8
Acute war stress injury
  client preparation, case study, 101–105
  EMDR assessment, case study, 142–143
Adaptive associations, neural networks, 14
Adaptive outcomes, 10
Adaptive resources
  military-related, 79
  post-military, 79
Adaptive Stress Reactions, defined, 10
Adverse childhood experiences, EMDR, 27
Affirmation
  interpersonal violence, 199
  traumatic grief, 199
Agency, 150
Aggression, 221–224
  reprocessing, 222–224
AIP model, 15, 54
  client education, 111
  EMDR assessment, 132–133
  history taking, 61
  hypothesized mechanism of action, 12–14
  Military Sexual Trauma, 216
  psychopathology, 12
  reprocessing, 152–153
  target memories, 131–133

  treatment planning, 61
American Psychiatric Association,
  EMDR evidence-based treatment
  research results, 39–41
Amputation, 190–197
  Body Scan, 196
  client history, 192–193
  desensitization, 193–195
  EMDR treatment, traumatic leg
    amputation case study, 192–196
  medical discharge, 192
  prevalence, 191, *191*
  reprocessing, 193, 196
  treatment issues, 191–192
Anger, 221–224
  reprocessing, 222–224
Assessment, 261
  assessing suitability, 79–82
  example script, 17
  goal, 16
  intake assessment, 61–62
  medically unexplained symptoms, 184–185
  objectives, 16–17
  traumatic grief, 207–208
Association, 18
Associative memory process, 14
Atonement, 202, 204
Attrition
  childhood trauma, 28–29
  EMDR, 48
Auditory sounds, bilateral stimulation, 112

B

Baseline measures, ecological validity, 158–159
Battlemind resiliency training program, 26

Behavioral model, 15
Bilateral stimulation, 12, 13, 152
    auditory sounds, 112
    combining, 113
    eye movements, 112
    kinesthetic vibrations, 112–113
    stimulation, 13
    taps, 112–113
    therapist response after stopping, 154
Blocked processing, reprocessing, 149
Blocking belief, 260
Body Scan
    amputation, 196
    case study, 166–167
    example script, 19
    goal, 19
    objectives, 19
    protocol, 166
Brain, information processing systems, 11
Brake and gas pedal metaphor, 115
Brief Intervention Focusing Protocol
    post-traumatic growth, 247–249
    resilience, 247–249

C
Childhood trauma, 27–28
    attrition, 28–29
    EMDR, 46
    pre-military history, 46
Chronic pain, EMDR research, 196–197
Chronic war stress injury, client
        preparation, case study, 105–110
Client demographics, 72
Client expectation, reprocessing, 149
Client history
    goal, 16
    objectives, 16
Client preparation, 171–172, 260
    acute war stress injury, case study,
        101–105
    ambivalent military client, 122–130
    chronic war stress injury, case study,
        105–110
    coerced client, 122–123
    fear of absolution, 129
    fear of forgetting fallen heroes, 127
    fear of losing control, 127–128
    fear of losing edge, 126–127
    fear of losing it, 127
    fear of revealing embarrassing,
        shameful, or unlawful material,
        128–129
    goal, 16

    interfering with deployment,
        promotion, and career, 125–126
    medically unexplained symptoms, 184
    military client treatment concerns,
        121–130
    objectives, 16
    secondary gain, 123–124, *124*
Client stabilization, 86–88, 96, 97–99
    case studies, 101–110
    Emergency Response Procedure, 96, 97
        case studies, 101–110
    Eye Movement Desensitization,
        96.97–99
        case studies, 101–110
    Resource Development and
        Installation, 99–101
        case studies, 101–110
    stability checklist, 84
Client-therapist introduction, 55
Clinical intake, 55–71
Clinical Practice Guideline for the
        Management of Post-Traumatic
        Stress, DOD, 38–39
Closure, 175, 227–230
    example script, 19–20
    goal, 19
    objectives, 19
    time management, 227
Cluster memories
    chronological ordering of combat
        experiences, 68
    earliest-worst-recent reprocessing
        sequence, 64–65
    participant cluster, 65
    starting with current *vs.* past, 66
    starting with least *vs.* most disturbing,
        66
    starting with worst memory first,
        65–66
Cognitive Behavioral model, 15
Cognitive model, 15
Cognitive Processing Therapy, 108
    drop-out rates, 42
Combat Operational Stress Reaction
    defined, 8
    symptoms, 9, *9*
Combat Operation Stress Control,
        94–101
    early treatment, 95–96
    recommended interventions, 95–101
Combat/Tactical Breathing, 118–119
Co-morbidity, 32
    EMDR, 45

Co-morbid substance use disorder,
   219–221
   informed consent, 219
   treatment planning, 219–220
Compassion stress injury, 160, 249–254
   EMDR
   case study prevention protocol,
      251–252
   treatment, 252–253
   healer occupational hazards, 250
   impairment indicators, 250
   prevalence, 250–251
   prevention, 92–93, 251
   resources, 254
   silencing response, 250
   treatment, 92–93
Comprehensive reprocessing, 90–91
Comprehensive Soldier Fitness (CSF)
   program, 26
Confidentiality, 237–241
   breaching privilege, 238
   civilian therapists, 239–240
   disclosures on need-to-know basis,
      241
   limits, 56, 240
   mandatory reporting, 238
   military personnel issues, 238–239
   military population importance, 57–58
   multiple relationships, 238
   therapist considerations of managing
      in military populations, 59
   therapist's duty to advise, 240–241
Control, 150
   interviewing, 60
Cost-effectiveness
   EMDR, 43, 48
   Virtual Reality Therapy, 43

D
Dangerousness to self or others,
   assessment, 84–85
Department of Defense
   *Clinical Practice Guideline for the
   Management of Post-Traumatic
   Stress*, 38–39
   EMDR funded research, 25
   war stress injury funded research,
      25–26
Department of Veterans Affairs
   1993-1999: EMDR research, 21–23
   clinical trials, 21–23
   combat PTSD with treatment fidelity,
      23–24

reasons for lack of EMDR reserarch,
   24–25
Deployment history
   cycle, 74–78
   identifying EMDR specific
      deployment-related past
      contributors, 76
   non-war-related, 75
Desensitization, 148–149, 173–175
   goal, 17–18
   medically unexplained symptoms,
      185–186
   reprocessing, compared, 148–149
   target memory, 18
De-Tur Protocol, 220–221
Diet history, 73–74
Disability compensation, EMDR, 48
Dissociation
   reprocessing, 119–121
      grounding activities, 120–121
   screening, 82
Domestic violence survivor, EMDR
   treatment, case study, 212–215
Drop-out rates
   Cognitive Processing Therapy, 42
   EMDR, 48
   Prolonged Exposure, 42
Dual-focused attention, 12–13, 151
Dualism, 7

E
EMDR, 11
   access, 15
   acute stress and trauma military
      treatment results, 32–34
   Acute Stress Disorder, 170
      case study, 171–176
   acute stress injuries
      research, 176–177
      treatment considerations, 176–177
   advantages, 41
   adverse childhood experiences, 27
   AIP model, 11
      psychopathology, 12
   assessment (*see* Assessment)
   attrition, 48
   benefit to military clients and armed
      services, 47
   childhood trauma, 46
   chronic pain research, 196–197
   chronic war and traumatic stress injury
      treatment in military settings
      reports, 34–37

EMDR (*continued*)
    client role expectations, 111–112
    metaphor, 114–115
    co-morbidity, 45
    comparative theoretical approaches, 15
    compassion stress injury
        case study prevention protocol,
            251–252
        treatment, 252–253
    consecutive sessions, 47
    contraindications, 79–82
    cost-effectiveness, 43, 45–46, 48
    cost savings, 48
    credibility among practitioners, 49
    credibility with military culture, 50
    demonstrating, 112–113
    disability compensation, 48
    drop-out rates, 42, 48
    early intervention, 94–101
        research summary, 34
    efficacy, 39
        non-war-related trauma, 27–28
    ethical issues, 242–244
        therapist competence, 243–244
        treatment planning, 243
    flexibility for military populations, 44
        amount of exposure and self-
            disclosure, 44
        decreased compassion stress and
            fatigue, 44
        treatment option flexibility, 44–45
    follow-up session, 234
    functional brain imaging studies, 13
    holistic framework, 16
    hypothesized mechanism of action,
        12–14
    initial timing, 56–59
    integration into primary care, 48
    medically unexplained symptoms
        research, 183
    move, 15
    neuropsychological therapeutic frame
        credibility, 49
    neuro-scientific research, 29–31
    phantom-limb pain research, 196–197
    potentially rapid treatment course,
        46–47
    practicality for military populations,
        41–43
    prepping for, 96
    primary substance use or other
        addictive disorder, 220–221
    PTSD, Vietnam veterans, 21, 23–24
    rationale for military use, 38–50

    readiness for reprocessing, 79–82
    re-assess, 15
    reduced demand characteristics, 42–43
    reduced time demands on military
        clients, 41–42
    REM sleep, recent research, 224–225
    reprocessing, causes of, 156–157
    research meta-analysis, 22
    research studies, 21–37
    Resource Development and
        Installation, compared, 118
    sexual trauma, 27–28
    single treatment protocol efficiency,
        45–46
    stabilization interventions, 96–101
    standard protocol, 16–17
        goals, 16–17
        objectives, 16–17
        phases, 16–17
    stimulate, 15
    terminating therapy, 234
    terrorism
        acute trauma, 29
        chronic trauma, 29
    theory, 11
        importance, 14–15
    therapist role expectations, 111–112
    three-pronged protocol, 144–145
        treatment summary, 144–145
    traumatic brain injury, 197
    underlying experiences, 12
    unfunded research on military
        effectiveness, 31–32
Emergency Response Procedure, client
    stabilization, 96, 97
    case studies, 101–110
Emotions, target memories, 138
Ethical issues, 237–244
    EMDR, 242–244
        therapist competence, 243–244
        treatment planning, 243
Eye movement
    bilateral stimulation, 112
    role, 13–14

F
Family of origin history, 73
Feeder memories, 68–69
    affect scan, 69
    asking, 69
    float back, 69
First meeting, 55–71
Flashback experience, 222
Functional assessment, 83

G
Gestalt model, 15
Guilt
    interpersonal violence, 200–201,
        202–204
        cognitive interweaves, 202
        useful metaphors and approaches,
           202
    Kubany's guilt typology, 202–204
    sources, 202–204
    traumatic grief, 200–201
Gulf War, medically unexplained
    symptoms, 7
Gulf War Illness, 7

H
History taking, 72–74, 171, 260
    AIP model, 61
    elements, 60–61
    identifying current contributors, 69
    identifying future contributors, 69–70
    identifying past contributors, 63–68
    medically unexplained symptoms,
        184
    traumatic grief, 205–206
Hobbies, 73
Homicidal ideation, 85–86
Humanistic model, 15
Hypervigilance, 13

I
Image, target memories, 133–134
Information processing systems, brain, 11
Informed consent, 56, 106–111
    co-morbid substance use disorder, 219
    specific to EMDR treatment, 110–111
    treatment options, 107–110
Installation, 162–163
    example script, 18–19
    goal, 18
    medically unexplained symptoms,
        188–190
    objectives, 18
    protocol, 162–163
Intake assessment, 61–62
Interpersonal violence
    affirmation, 199
    clinical considerations, 200
    cognitive interweave on killing, 266
    EMDR treatment, case study, 212–215
    guilt, 200–201, 202–204
        cognitive interweaves, 202
        useful metaphors and approaches,
           202

psychological impact of killing, 201–204
    reevaluation, 214–215
    reprocessing, 213–214
    shame, 200–201
    support, 199
    timing of presentation, 198–199
    understanding, 199
Interviewing
    control, 60
    strategies, 59–63

K
Kinesthetic vibrations, bilateral
    stimulation, 112–113

L
Labeling issues, 4–5, 6
Lateralization, 13
Legal history, 74
Lifestyle history, 73–74
Looping, 18

M
Malingering, 241–242
Marital history, 72–73
Medical discharge, amputation, 192
Medical history, 77
Medically unexplained symptoms, 4, 5
    assessment, 143–144, 184–185
        case study, 143–144
    causality, 5–6
    desensitization, 185–186
    EMDR treatment research, 183
    Gulf War, 7
    history of, 6–7
    history taking, 184
    installation, 188–190
    overview, 5–6
    preparation, 184
    reevaluation, 187–188
    symptoms, 6
    treatment, 182–183, 184
        case study, 184–190
    war stress injury, 5–6
Medications, 108–109
Medico-legal issues, 237–244
Memory clusters, *see* Cluster memories
Mental health care
    barriers to seeking, 58–59
    military career ramifications, 58–59
    stigma, 58–59
Military career, 72, 125–126
Military mental health, referral resources,
    255–258

Military Sexual Trauma, 216–218
    AIP model, 216
Military stress injury, 3–4
Military unit risk factors, assessing, 85
Mind-body unitary theory, 7
Misconduct stress behaviors, 10, 128–129
Modern industrialized warfare,
    accumulative toxic psychosomatic
    effects, 5–6
Modified EMDR, 170
Moral symptoms, 9
Myoclonic jerks, 35

N
Negative cognition, target memories,
    135–136
Neural networks
    adaptive associations, 14
    maladaptive, 151–152
Neurobiological model, 15
Neurobiological studies, 29–31
Neuroimaging studies, 29–31
Neuropsychiatric conditions, 5
    causality, 5
    diagnoses, 5
Neuropsychiatric symptoms, 4
    contemporary diagnoses, 6
    symptoms, 6
    World War II, prevalence, 6–7, *7*

P
Participating-witnessing atrocity, 204
Perceptual disturbance, target memories,
    139
Performance enhancement, 91–92
Phantom-limb pain, 34, 190–197
    EMDR research, 196–197
    reprocessing, 163–166
Popky's De-Tur Protocol, 220–221
Positive cognition, target memories,
    136–138
Positive war stress reactions, 78–79
Post-deployment history, 76–78
Post-traumatic growth, 78–79, 245–254
    Brief Intervention Focusing Protocol,
        247–249
    contemporary approach, 245
    defined, 10
    EMDR applications, 246–249
    Resource Development and
        Installation, 247
Post-Traumatic Stress
    defined, 8
    vs. PTSD, 8

Pre-deployment history, 74–75
Pre-military adaptive resources, 78
Pre-military traumatic stress injuries,
    EMDR treatment, 181–182
    case study, 181–182
    recruit training setting, 181–182
Presenting complaint, 63–64
Primary symptom reduction, 88–90,
    170–171
Prolonged Exposure, 107–108
    drop-out rates, 42
Psychological testing, traumatic grief, 206
Psychosomatic complaints, incidence, *7*
PTSD
    EMDR, Vietnam veterans, 21, 23–24
    EMDR assessment, case study, 143–
        144
    reprocessing, 155–156
    reprocessing, case study, 163–166

R
Recent Events protocol, 170–171
Recreational activities, 73
Reevaluation, 175–176, 230–234
    between-session changes, 231–232
    conducting, 231–232
    goal, 20
    interpersonal violence, 214–215
    medically unexplained symptoms,
        187–188
    objective, 20
    target memories, 232–234
        complete session, 233
        incomplete session, 233
    transitioning from welcoming to, 231
    transitioning to reprocessing, 232–234
    traumatic grief, 211–212
Referral question, 56–59
Relaxation activities, 73
Religious history, 73
Reprocessing
    acute combat-related PTSD, case study,
        155–156
    aggression, 222–224
    AIP model, 152–153
    amputation, 193, 196
    anger, 222–224
    blocked processing, 149
    blocked reprocessing, 157, 161
        returning to target memory, 157
    causes, 156–157
    client expectation, 149
    client-therapist role expectation,
        149–150

closing complete session, 228
closing incomplete session, 228–230
cognitive interweave, 263–266
  types, 263–266
coping strategies, 116–117
debriefing, 230
desensitization, compared, 148–149
dissociation, 119–121
  grounding activities, 120–121
instilling client sense of agency and
    control, 150
interpersonal violence, 213–214
interventions for over- and under-
    responses to, 262
language of change, 154
maladaptive neural network, 151–152
managing intense emotional
    reprocessing, 159–160
metaphor, 115
over-responding, 161
phantom-limb pain, cse study, 163–166
phases, 116–117
PTSD, case study, 163–166
reaffirming therapist presence, 150–
    151, 152
safety checklist, 148–149
standard protocol, 148–155, 162–168
SUDS rating, 157–158
target assessment, 62
therapeutic alliance, 150–151
therapist-related factors that interfere
    with, 261
therapist response after soliciting client
    self-report, 154
traumatic grief, 208–211
troubleshooting guide, 259–266
under-responding, 161
when therapist should stop, 227–228
Resilience, 10, 245–254
  Brief Intervention Focusing Protocol,
      247–249
  building, 91–92
  contemporary approach, 245
  EMDR applications, 246–249
  Resource Development and
      Installation, 247
Resource Development and Installation,
    117–118
  client stabilization, 99–101
    case studies, 101–110
  EMDR, compared, 118
  post-traumatic growth, 247
  resilience, 247
Responsibility, 265

S
Safety checklist, reprocessing, 148–149
Secondary gain, 77–78
  client preparation, 123–124, *124*
Self-absorption, 13
Sensory memories, target memories, 134
Sexual trauma, *see* Military Sexual
    Trauma
Shame
  interpersonal violence, 200–201
  traumatic grief, 200–201
Sleep dysfunction, EMDR treatment,
    224–226
Social history, 73
Spiritual history, 73
Spiritual symptoms, 9
Stop signal, 115
Stress injury, 1
Substance use disorder co-morbidity,
    219–221
Substance use disorders, 219
  EMDR De-Tur Protocol, 220–221
Substance use history, 77
SUDS rating
  ecological validity, 158–159
  reprocessing, 157–158
  target memories, 139
Suicidal ideation, 85–86, 203
Support
  interpersonal violence, 199
  traumatic grief, 199
Survivor guilt, 203
Symptom history, 63–64
  dimensionalizing, 64
Symptoms, Signs, and Ill-Defined
    Conditions (SSID), 4

T
Taps, bilateral stimulation, 112–113
Target memories
  AIP model, 131–133
  chronological ordering of combat
      experiences, 68
  cluster memories
    participant cluster, 65
    starting with worst memory first,
        65–66
  considered desensitized, 158
  desensitization, 18
  emotions, 138
  identifying core components, 131–141
  image, 133–134
  military client censorship, 134
  negative cognition, 135–136

Target memories (*continued*)
  optimal number, 70–71
  perceptual disturbance, 139
  physical sensation, 139–141
  positive cognition, 136–138
  reevaluation, 232–234
    complete session, 233
    incomplete session, 233
  returning, 18
  sensory memories, 134
  starting with current *vs.* past, 66
  starting with least *vs.* most disturbing,
    66
  starting with worst memory first,
    65–66
  SUDS, 139
  Validity of Cognition, 138
Terrorism, EMDR
  acute trauma, 29
  chronic trauma, 29
Therapeutic alliance, 56–57, 259
  clinical skills enhancing, 55
  enhancing, 94
  establishing client-centered military
    culture, 55–56
  reprocessing, 150–151
Therapeutic frame establishment, 113–114
Three-pronged protocol, 17, 20
TICES log, 230230
TICES strategies, 262
Time management, closure, 227
Touchstone event, 12
Traumatic brain injury
  EMDR, 197
  phantom-limb pain, 197
Traumatic grief
  affirmation, 199
  assessment, 207–208
  clinical considerations, 200
  guilt, 200–201
  history taking, 205–206
  psychological testing, 206
  reevaluation, 211–212
  reprocessing, 208–211
  reversing the flow, 212
  shame, 200–201
  support, 199
  timing of presentation, 198–199
  treatment plan, 204–205
    acute traumatic grief reaction, 204
    case study, 205–212
    chronic traumatic grief reaction,
      204–205

  understanding, 199
Traumatic stress injuries,
    psychoeducation, 105–106
Treatment, *see also* Treatment planning
  acute war stress injury, case study,
    142–143
  AIP model, 132–133
  altering script or sequence, 141–142
  amputation, 192–196
  domestic violence survivor, case study,
    212–215
  first meeting, 55–71
  interpersonal violence
    case study, 212–215
  medically unexplained symptoms,
    184
    case study, 143–144, 184–190
  potentially rapid treatment course,
    46–47
  primary diagnosis not targeting
    substance use disorder, 219–221
  PTSD, case study, 143–144
  single treatment protocol efficiency
    and cost-effectiveness, 45–46
  sleep dysfunction, 224–226
  summary statement, 141
  traumatic leg amputation case study,
    192–196
  treatment options, informed consent,
    107–110
  treatment session flow considerations,
    146
  treatment session length, 115–116
  treatment session pace, 115–116
Treatment planning
  AIP model, 61
  elements, 60–61
  goals, 86–93
  identifying current contributors, 69
  identifying future contributors, 69–70
  identifying past contributors, 63–68
  intervention choice, 86–93
  key factors, 86
  practical considerations, 71–86
  primer, 62–63
  three-pronged protocol, 63
  traumatic grief, 204–205
    acute traumatic grief reaction, 204
    case study, 205–212
    chronic traumatic grief reaction,
      204–205
Trust, 59
  therapist's earning, 56–57

U
Understanding
  interpersonal violence, 199
  traumatic grief, 199
Unlawful behaviors, 128–129

V
Validity of Cognition, target memories,
  138

Virtual Reality Therapy, 108
  cost-effectiveness, 43

W
War, history of, 3
Warrior class, 3–10
  society's pact with, 3
War stress injury
  incidence, 7.7
  medically unexplained symptoms, 5–6